Jesus – One Hundred Years Before Christ

Jesus – One Hundred Years Before Christ

A Study In Creative Mythology

Professor Alvar Ellegård

Century · London

First published by Century in 1999

Copyright © Alvar Ellegård 1999

Alvar Ellegård has asserted his right under the Copyright,
Designs and Patents Act, 1988, to be identified as the author of this work

First published in the United Kingdom in 1999 by
Century, 20 Vauxhall Bridge Road, London SW1V 2SA

Random House Australia (Pty) Limited
20 Alfred Street, Milsons Point, Sydney,
New South Wales 2061, Australia

Random House New Zealand Limited
18 Poland Road, Glenfield
Auckland 10, New Zealand

Random House South Africa (Pty) Limited
Endulini, 5a Jubilee Road,
Parktown 2193, South Africa

Random House UK Limited Reg. No. 954009
A CIP catalogue record for this book
is available from the British Library

Papers used by Random House UK Limited are natural, recyclable
products made from wood grown in sustainable forests.
The manufacturing processes conform to the environmental
regulations of the country of origin.

ISBN 0 7126 7956 1
Typeset by Deltatype Ltd, Birkenhead, Merseyside
Printed by Mackays of Chatham plc, Chatham, Kent

Acknowledgements

On the completion of this book, which has taken me far into territiory previously rather unfamiliar to me, I wish to express my gratitude to all those who have helped me find my way in it.

First of all, theological and historical scholars, who have provided material – editions of texts, translations, and comments – which has furnished me with a starting point, has allowed me to push further, and helped me sharpen my argument. Most of these people are named in my bibliography.

Secondly, I thank all the many scholars, from different disciplines, with whom I have been able to talk about the ideas presented here. They form two groups. One is in the University of Göteborg, my home base. Another is in the Royal Academy of Letters, History and Antiquities, whose monthly meetings in Stockholm have offered excellent opportunities for broaching ideas in a convival and congenial atmosphere.

Special thanks go to Professor Bertil Albrektson, Uppsala, for answering many questions about the Old Testament, and for joining me in discussions about wider aspects of theology, religion, and history of ideas.

Professor Geza Vermes, Oxford, generously allowed me to use parts of his translation of the Qumran Scrolls in my book.

I also thank my editor, Mark Booth, London, for advice not only on matters of style and presentation, but also on matters of substance.

Penguin Books granted me permission to include quotations from *The Dead Sea Scrolls* translated by Geza Vermes.

Alvar Ellegård
University of Göteborg, Sweden
October 1998

Contents

Part II: Deconstructing the Gospels and Acts

Introduction

I shall argue in this book for an entirely new perspective on the earliest history of Christianity. In Part I, where I deal with texts dating to the first century AD, I argue that the earliest Christians, among them Paul, regarded Jesus as a great Jewish prophet and teacher of their movement – but one who had lived in the distant past. To them, accordingly, he was not a contemporary, crucified before their eyes, but a historical figure, on a par with Old Testament prophets. His teaching, however, or rather what they believed to be his teaching, was very much in their thoughts. When Paul and his companions experienced ecstatic visions of Jesus as a heavenly figure, they inferred that Jesus had been 'raised from the dead' by God. They also thought that Jesus' appearance to them at this particular time, in the thirties of the first century AD, was a sign from heaven that the Last Day, God's Final Judgment, was now at long last approaching. From now on, they started to regard Jesus not only as the founder of their movement, their prophet and teacher, but as their Saviour, the Messiah.

In the Gospels, however, written in the second century AD (as I shall argue in Part II), and thus long after Paul's visionary sights, the Gospel writers took those visions to have been experiences of real events. The Gospel writers located these presumed events in Palestine, and dated them to the time of the notorious Roman prefect of Palestine, Pontius Pilate. In other words, they placed *their* Jesus about as far back from their own time as Paul had placed *his* Jesus from his time. It was now that Jesus was presented as an itinerant preacher and wonder-worker in Palestine. That almost wholly fictional story was gradually elaborated and extended in various ways, by means of legendary and doctrinal material from many different sources, and the creative imagination of the gospel writers.

Previous scholars – as well as innumerable laymen and amateurs –

1

have almost without exception taken the story of the Gospels and Acts as their foundation – for the simple reason that they are the only sources that tell us anything substantial about Jesus' life on earth, and present it in a vivid and colourful narrative. In Part II I shall show how and why this fiction was built up, to form the groundwork for a moving and magnificent myth.

The Gospels offer a dramatic story of the earthly Jesus. Yet they are obviously unreliable as historical sources, both because they are often inconsistent with each other, and because they rely so heavily on the miraculous element. Many theological scholars admit that large parts of the Gospels are indeed legendary fiction. But practically all of these scholars maintain that the basic story is to be trusted: Jesus was a Palestinian itinerant teacher from Galilee, whose most active period was around AD 30, ending with his crucifixion in Jerusalem under Pontius Pilate.

As my own research background is in the humanities, I approach my subject as a historian, not as a theologian. Therefore the question of sources is paramount. In our case, the sources are mainly texts written by people who were either participants in the Christian movement, or observers of it. The Bible is a primary source, the Old Testament for both Jews and Christians, and the New Testament for Christians only. But the Bible is problematic as a source, first, because it is composite – there are disagreements about what books really belong to it, and about when they were written, second, because it was (and is) interpreted differently by different readers.

In view of the fact that only a few per cent of all the literature of Antiquity has survived to the present time, the incompleteness of the record is obvious. The historian's task is not only to collect the available literature (though that is of course a prerequisite), but above all to reconstruct the historical development that has led to the production of the source material.

In all historical research, a necessary preliminary task is to establish the dates of origin for the source material – texts, in our case. In the present instance, that problem is especially difficult, since texts which do not get copied by scribes tend to be forgotten. Left to themselves in cellars and storerooms, they just disintegrate or disappear with the passing of the centuries. Not only, therefore, are our sources very far from being a complete record of what has been said or written. The picture they give is also biased, since we know that much material has been deliberately destroyed. We have many instances of book burning and book destruction through the ages.

I started out by trying to get an overview of the relevant primary sources, and the views that scholars have taken of them. There appeared to be a fair consensus that Paul's principal letters should be dated to the fifties of the first century AD. The originals of the Gospels were generally placed in the period AD 70–100, and the remaining literature in the New Testament in the period 70–130 or later.

My own impression after this first reading was that the arguments for placing the Gospels as early as the end of the first century were rather weak. I found that the respected theological scholar Helmut Koester, editor of the *Harvard Theological Review*, made a good case for a later date, early second century, for most of the Gospels.

As I delved more deeply, I found more and more arguments for dating the Gospels after AD 100. At the same time, I found good reasons for dating another group of source texts (the ones treated in Chapter 2) significantly *earlier* than most other scholars have done hitherto. Accordingly, I had now got two clearly distinct groups of Christian texts, which differed both as regards date of composition, and as regards theological content.

The clear distinction, on more than one level, between first-century and second-century Christian texts, yielded further support to my basic hypothesis of the origin of Christianity from within a group of pious Jews called the Essenes. Concurrently, the support thus obtained focused my attention on evidence for Essenes in the Diaspora, which had previously been largely neglected by scholars, probably because they did not possess the other pieces of information that formed part of the puzzle which I could by now discern, for instance the evidence from 1 Clement on the early Roman Christians.

Historical research is most of the time concerned with minute details. But the researcher must never tire of comparing the various details with each other, in order to see whether hitherto unnoticed patterns will stand out. When they do, the researcher gets his reward.

I do not claim that the picture which I have drawn of the development of earliest Christianity is the only possible one. Indeed, I am quite sure that those scholars who have for a long time placed the data in a different context, and put the emphasis differently, will also draw different conclusions. The real issue, now, is to what extent the different conclusions are able to generate new questions, more fruitful research, and thus ultimately increase our insight into a fascinating period of the history of civilisation.

My analysis in this book has led me to conclude that *all* the earliest Christian documents, first and foremost among them Paul's Letters, present Jesus as somebody who had lived and died a long time ago. Hence neither Paul nor any of his contemporaries could have had any experience of the earthly Jesus, nor of his death. To them the crucifixion and resurrection were spiritual events, most likely in the form of overwhelming revelations or ecstatic visions. It was this heavenly Jesus that was important to these earliest Christians, just as the heavenly, spiritual world was vastly superior to the material one.

Many scholars have considered Paul's obvious lack of interest in Jesus' earthly life as surprising and hard to explain. After all, according to the Gospels, the chief disciples, Peter, James and John, had accompanied Jesus on his preaching tour from Galilee to Jerusalem. Moreover, from the Acts of the Apostles we learn that those men had met Paul several times, something which is confirmed in Paul's own letters. Remarkably, however, Paul never talks of them as Jesus' *companions*, and never says, nor implies, that they had told him anything about their master. That Paul himself, though clearly their contemporary, had never seen Jesus in the flesh, appears both from his Letters and from Acts, and has always been taken for granted by the Church from early on. I now find that *none* of Paul's contemporaries had, either.

I shall show that not only Paul, but *all* Christian writers who can be plausibly dated to the first century AD looked upon Jesus in the same light. They certainly believed that Jesus had once lived as a leader, teacher and prophet in their Church, which they mostly called the Church of God. But by the time they wrote about him, roughly from the forties to the seventies of the first century, they saw him as a heavenly figure, sitting on a throne beside God, the Father.

On the other hand, the Gospels' picture of Jesus as a Palestinian wonderworker and preacher is, as I shall show, a creation of the second century AD, when their Church had to meet challenges caused by competing movements inside and outside their church. An important way to meet the new situation was to create a history for that church, a myth of its origin. The central ideas in that myth were that Jesus was a man who had lived and preached his Gospel in Palestine at the beginning of the previous century, and that he had been crucified and raised to heaven around AD 30.

4

None of this mythical history is supported by *any* first-century writings, whether Christian or not. Judging by Paul and his contemporaries, earliest Christianity was predominantly to be found outside Palestine: all the writers of the earliest Christian texts were themselves, by all indications, non-Palestinian Jews in the Diaspora: Paul himself (Tarsus), Clemens Romanus (Rome), Hermas (Rome), John, the author of Revelation (the island of Patmos, south-west of Ephesus). And their addressees were almost all to be found in Asia Minor, Syria, Greece and Rome itself – all places where the Greek-speaking Jewish Diaspora was strongly represented. It is true that their Church of God included an important community in Jerusalem, which was visited several times by Paul. But in the main the Christian missionary work had its origin in the Diaspora, and was directed towards the Diaspora. This is important because, although Christianity obviously has deep Jewish roots, its Jewishness was from the start strongly influenced by its Hellenistic environment.

Once we realise that the Christian mission was not only much more successful in the Diaspora than in Palestine, but actually originated there, some long-standing problems simply disappear. For instance, if, as the Gospel story goes, Jesus was born in a simple carpenter's family in Galilee, where the common language was Aramaic, it is hard to see why all early Christian writings are in Greek – even those purporting to be written by Jesus' companions. To solve this problem many scholars in the past have supposed that the original versions of the Gospels were indeed in Aramaic. As many scholars think that at least the Sermon on the Mount goes back directly to Jesus, they have spent much ingenuity on finding traces of an Aramaic original in the Greek text of that part of the Gospel. Nothing very substantial has come out of these efforts.

Another problem for the myth of origin that was largely created in the second century AD, is the notable similarity between Christianity and Diaspora Judaism, as exemplified primarily by Philo Judaeus, the Jewish philosopher–theologian of Alexandria in Egypt. Why should Jesus, as a Jew from Galilee, who according to the myth had never set foot outside Palestine, exhibit so many points of agreement with the learned hellenised Egyptian Jew? Again, the problem disappears if the Gospel story is rejected as history, and the Diaspora matrix of Christianity is admitted.

The position of the Jews in the Greco–Roman world is accordingly an important subject for the historian of Christianity. The number of

Jews in the Greek-speaking Diaspora around the beginning of our era has been estimated at around 4 million, while the Palestinian Jewry counted perhaps 1.5 million. The historical importance of Palestine and, in particular, Jerusalem, is of course not in question. But even in those days there were apparently considerably more Jews outside than inside the Holy Land.

Whatever we think of the reliability of such figures, we may at least conclude that the Diaspora Jews were an important group in the Roman Empire, especially in its Greek-speaking parts. Moreover, they lived especially in the cities and, as the cities were in all respects, culturally and economically, dominant over the surrounding country, the Jews could certainly carry considerable clout. They did not attain the position of the Greeks in such big cities as Alexandria and Antioch: they did not as a rule possess full citizen rights. Nor were they automatically admitted to Roman citizenship, though some could be given such rights on personal merits. It is clear, however, that they possessed more privileges than the indigenous population in Egypt, Syria and Asia Minor.

The position of the Diaspora Jews in the Roman Empire shows remarkable analogies with that in the modern world. Alexandria two thousand years ago compares well with present-day New York, for instance. When considering the importance of the Jews in Roman times, we should also take into account the strong social cohesion of the Jewish communities, their religious duty to help the poor and needy of the community, and generally the moral seriousness of their religious commitment. All of this impressed many of their Gentile contemporaries. In addition, the strict monotheism of their religion was rated highly, at least among the educated Gentiles. Further, the venerable age of their religious tradition was in itself a cause of admiration and awe.

Taken together, all this tended to raise the status of the Jews in the Roman Empire. The raised status certainly also raised the self-esteem of the Jews. But it also led to envy, which partly explains the occurrence of anti-Jewish pogroms, which were especially severe in Alexandria, documented by Philo. It also seems reasonable to infer that increasing tension between Jews and Gentiles partly explains the rise of Jewish Messianism, and the several Jewish revolts in Palestine in 66–73, in Cyrenaica in 113–15, and again in Palestine in 133–5. All of them were crushed, inexorably and completely, by the Roman military forces.

The establishment of the Roman Empire by Augustus, and his remarkably long reign (42 BC–AD 14) started a period of more than two centuries of peace and prosperity around the Mediterranean – the famous *Pax Romana*. Political changes naturally also led to changes in the cultural sphere. Above all, many self-governing states lost their independence. Many local loyalties disappeared. Increased communications across the Mediterranean, which the Roman navy kept reasonably free from pirates, led to an increased mixture of peoples. The total population of the Empire increased, new techniques in industry and warfare spread rapidly. New ideas could be disseminated over wide areas, and could compete or mix with each other, giving rise to new ways of thinking. The Roman Empire became one large melting-pot of ideas – and of religions. Above all, Roman expansion eastwards offered free entrance to Oriental religious ideas.

This was the world in which Christianity took shape.

The general Roman policy as regards religion in the Empire was one of toleration within a polytheistic framework. That is hardly surprising, since polytheism, worship of many gods, had been the rule not only in Rome, but in practically all the states conquered by the Romans. There was one exception: the Jews.

The increasing international exchange of customs and ideas inevitably led to a weakening of the old, traditional beliefs. At the same time, people had to find new ways of satisfying their religious needs and cravings. The old systems of beliefs, with their firm local foundation, were becoming inadequate in the new Empire-wide context. The new political authorities, the Emperor and his administration, might support and encourage worship of the traditional gods. But the masses wanted stronger stuff. They found it in the often ecstatic and sometimes orgiastic mystery cults. These had enjoyed a long local history. Now some of them spread throughout the Empire, for instance, the Egyptian cults connected with the goddess Isis, her husband Osiris and her child Horus.

People with a more reflective temperament were looking for 'wisdom' rather than emotional experience. They turned to the philosophers. In Augustus' times Plato and Aristotle were still the leading lights, towering above the rest. The philosophical schools which they had founded in Athens were still flourishing, though they had naturally changed with the times. Plato's followers were moving towards Neo-Platonism, which had an increasingly metaphysical and indeed religious flavour. New philosophical schools came into being, among which was Stoicism, which had two famous Roman writers, Cicero and Seneca, as its adherents.

These philosophical schools had strong religious connotations. Ancient philosophers, in fact, were looked upon as teachers of wisdom rather than just as inquirers into the ways people think. It is therefore not surprising that Josephus, the Jewish historian, uses the term 'philosophies' for what he considers the three main Jewish religious sects: Sadducees, Pharisees and Essenes. (He never mentions Christianity among them.)

Practically all the philosophical schools, except the outspokenly atheistic Epicureans, had a vaguely monotheistic outlook. God was seen as a remote, personified principle of order, governing from afar the universe and the affairs of men. It is no wonder, therefore, that the ancients, at least before the Jewish revolts, looked upon Jewish monotheism as a markedly philosophical religion. Some Jews returned the compliment: Philo Judaeus called Plato 'the divine Plato'.

Yet in spite of the Roman and Greek high regard for the Jewish religion as a philosophical one, the Jews did not mix easily with the Gentiles. For, while the polytheistic cultures of other nations conquered by the Romans usually raised no objections to accepting new gods in their pantheon, and could worship them in the local temples, the single God of the Jews was a jealous God, who tolerated no other gods beside him. This prohibition was spelled out explicitly in the Torah, the Law of Moses, the founding document of the Jewish community. Hence no righteous Jew could worship the local gods, nor participate in the religious ceremonies and feasts of the cities in which they lived. They had to keep themselves apart. Their neighbours, the Gentiles, naturally regarded such behaviour as antisocial. And it certainly built up tensions which put pressure on the Diaspora Jews to accommodate to their new surroundings.

One important result was the spread of a less literal, less 'fundamentalist' reading of the Law of Moses in the Diaspora. Philo was one important, and probably not untypical, Diaspora Jew who came to interpret the Torah 'allegorically', as he said. Paul is another example, whose acceptance of an allegorical interpretation of the Mosaic Law was certainly a weighty factor behind his success in the Diaspora. Paul's Christianity was in effect a kind of Judaism strongly modified to meet the demands of both Jews and Gentiles in the Roman Empire.

Philosophical arguments and speculations were of course no

concern of the large majority of the population of the Empire. The masses, in general, were extremely credulous and superstitious. In fact, superstition formed a general background for all activities and beliefs in the ancient world, even among the educated: in Antiquity superstition was not yet balanced by the methodological scepticism of the modern scientist or scholar. Plato was convinced that the stars of heaven were living souls. Philo was a strong believer in the symbolic meaning of numerology. Ptolemy, the famous astronomer, was at the same time an astrologer. 'Such was the spirit of the age', as Gibbon said in *Decline and Fall of the Roman Empire.*

Part I
Recovering First-Century Christianity

Chapter 1

Paul, the Apostle of Jesus Christ

Paul's life and his revelations

We start our investigation of earliest Christianity with Paul, whose letters are admitted by all scholars to be the earliest unquestionably Christian writings. There is also fair agreement about their dating: around the fifties of the first century AD. They therefore provide a kind of benchmark for our study of other early texts, such as the ones dealt with in Chapter 2, about whose dating there has been far less agreement.

Paul has a unique position in early Christianity. His Letters (we shall include here only the ones generally accepted as genuinely by Paul: Romans, 1 and 2 Corinthians, Galatians, 1 Thessalonians, Philippians) are substantial enough for us to draw some interesting conclusions about his theology and his view of Jesus. Also, his letters afford us precious glimpses of some of the early Christian communities.

Luke's portrait of Paul in Acts, written probably some seventy years after Paul's death, will be kept completely out of our discussion here.[1] This of course does not mean that whatever Paul says about himself is true. But when Luke contradicts Paul we shall follow Paul.

Luke says Paul was born in Tarsus, and was taught under Gamaliel in Jerusalem. Luke may well be right about Tarsus, but we have no evidence from Paul himself about this. In Galatians Paul indicates Damascus as a kind of home base, to which he returns after a sojourn in Arabia, which probably here refers to the regions east of the river Jordan. Luke also has Paul say that he was a Roman citizen, about which Paul says nothing. Apparently only a tiny proportion of the Jews, even of the wealthier classes, were Roman citizens before Caracalla's edict of 212, which made every free man in the Empire a

Roman. Moreover, as a Roman citizen Paul would hardly have been exposed to the degrading punishments that he writes about in his letters. Therefore many modern scholars think it is very unlikely that Paul was a Roman citizen.[2] Luke's assertion may be due to his obvious desire to present Christianity in a favourable light to a Roman audience.[3]

Luke's story of Paul's meeting the risen Christ outside Damascus is much more elaborate than anything we can gather from Paul himself. Paul does indeed claim to have 'seen Jesus', apparently in a vision (1 Cor 9:1). He also refers to a vision he had when transported, apparently in a trance, to the 'third heaven' (2 Cor 12:2). From 1 Corinthians 15:3–8 quoted below, p. 16 (see also Chapter 12) we gather that Paul's vision was of the risen Christ. Moreover, he takes it for granted that the other apostles had received similar revelations of Christ in heaven. From Paul's frequent references (e.g. 2 Cor 12:7) to revelations direct from 'the Lord', he probably experienced several revelations about the interpretation of Old Testament passages. As we shall see in Chapter 2, many of his colleagues among the early Christian writers seem to have looked upon such interpretations as allegorical readings, whereby they illustrated the career of Jesus.

According to Luke, Paul went to Jerusalem directly after his experience at Damascus. Paul himself declares (Gal 1:18–19) that he did not go to Jerusalem until three years later, after a sojourn in Arabia. His intention was to confer with Peter (Cephas). He also says he saw James. After that meeting, he says, he only went to Jerusalem fourteen years later, and saw James, Cephas and John, who were, he says, the 'pillars' of the Jerusalem community. If we place the Damascus incident in AD 35, the first Jerusalem visit would be in 38, and the second in AD 52.

In this connection it is very important to keep in mind that, when Paul writes about James, Cephas and John, he never indicates that they had been Jesus' companions and disciples. The reader of the New Testament gets that impression because the Gospels and Acts are always placed first in the New Testament. Hence he takes it for granted that the James, Cephas and John whom Paul refers to are the disciples and companions of Jesus so vividly presented in the Gospels. On other occasions Paul talks about Peter as an apostle (a word which, in Paul's usage, means 'missionary', not, as in the Gospels, 'disciple'). James is also called an apostle. On one occasion he is called 'the Lord's brother', which theologians have all too rashly interpreted as 'brother in the flesh', something which I discuss at some length in Chapter 11. It is noticeable that Paul seems to look upon Peter, the apostle, as a different person from Cephas, the 'pillar', a point which is also dealt with in Chapter 11.

In the Gospels, Paul is not mentioned at all. In Acts 7:58 he first appears as a young and zealous persecutor of Christians, before his meeting with the risen Jesus outside Damascus. This meeting is generally equated with the visionary experience which Paul tells us about in Galatians, and may therefore be dated to about AD 35.[4] Paul, accordingly, must have been roughly of the same age as the Jesus of the Gospels. This renders his silence about Jesus' life and works even more remarkable.

Moreover, as Paul, by his own account, had seen Peter in Jerusalem three years after his vision of the risen Christ, it would be natural to suppose that he had received plenty of information about Jesus' teaching, if, as the Gospels have it, Peter had been one of the twelve chief companions of Jesus only a few years before. But Paul nowhere indicates that Peter told him anything about Jesus or, indeed, that he himself inquired about him. On the contrary, Paul insists several times that his knowledge about Jesus and his teaching is not from men, but from 'the Lord' himself[5]. Since we may assume that he had never met Jesus in the flesh, it seems that he must have got it all through a process of revelation, perhaps, as we indicated above, in the form of insight into the hidden meaning of some Scriptural passage. This is also what he repeatedly claims in his letters. The significance of visions and revelations is treated more fully in Chapter 12.

In fact, everything that Paul says about Jesus is theologically oriented. It centres on Jesus' crucifixion and resurrection. We hear nothing about Jesus' family, his deeds, his preaching and how his audience reacted to it. In Chapter 2 I shall show that Paul's contemporaries show a similar lack of interest in Jesus' earthly life.

In view of the extremely strong symbolic importance assigned to the cross in Paul's thinking, it is surely remarkable that neither the crucifixion nor the resurrection are described by him as actual events. He gives no indication about when and where they took place. What is important to Paul seems to be his conviction, supported by his visions, that Jesus is now in heaven. The fact that Jesus has recently appeared in visions seems to be interpreted by Paul as a sign that Jesus, as the Messiah, is now preparing to descend to earth for the last Judgment.

Interestingly, Paul never refers to Jesus' forthcoming descent as a *return*. I shall discuss this at several points.

In two places Paul goes into some detail about what happened to Jesus while he was living on earth. On close examination, both of them turn out to be revelations of some sort, not reports of real events. One is a passage in 1 Corinthians 11:23: 'For I have received of the Lord that which I also delivered unto you, That the Lord Jesus the same night in which he was betrayed took bread: And when he had given thanks, he brake it, and said, Take, eat: this is my body which is broken for you: this do in remembrance of me. After the same manner also he took the cup . . .'. Paul says explicitly that he has received this 'of the Lord'. Accordingly, he does not derive this account from an oral tradition, current among the members of the Church of God, about what in the 'synoptic'[6] Gospels is represented as the Last Supper. As I suggest below, however, Paul's revelation may have had an empirical foundation in a ritual practice observed in the Church of God.

The other instance, by contrast, does explicitly refer to what Paul has received from others. It is found in the beginning of 1 Corinthians 15:3–8, where the subject-matter is the crucifixion and the resurrection. 'For I delivered unto you first of all that which I also received, how that Christ died for our sins according to the scriptures; And that he was buried, and that he rose again the third day according to the scriptures: And that he was seen of Cephas, then of the twelve. After that, he was seen of above five hundred brethren at once; of whom the greater part remain unto this present, but some are fallen asleep. After that, he was seen of James, then of all the apostles. And last of all he was seen of me also, as of one born out of due time.'

This passage, to which I return in Chapter 2, has generally been taken as a confirmation of the sequence of events at Jesus' death as set forth in the Gospels.[7] But on close inspection we find that this is not so. It is true that Paul's words here imply that Jesus' death, burial and resurrection took place within a time-span of a few days. But we are not told *when* all this occurred. More important, we are not told how many days, weeks, months, years or even centuries had elapsed between Jesus' resurrection and the time when the apostles and the brethren had 'seen' the resurrected Jesus. (Paul says nothing about Jesus' ascension to Heaven.)

This may appear as quibbling. But we must keep in mind that Paul never represents the men he calls the 'apostles' as Jesus' companions and disciples. To him they were, like himself, apostles, *missionaries*,

16

of the faith that Jesus had given rise to. And, for all we know from Paul, Jesus might have been a prophet who had lived and died long ago. Moreover, he had no reason to think that the other apostles viewed Jesus differently. In fact, the eminent German liberal theologian Adolf Harnack, writing in 1922, thought just that: the experiences of Peter, James and the rest were not visions of the *man* Jesus, or of the crucified one, but of Jesus as the Son of Man in glory. For that, says Harnack, 'is how the promises were expressed, and that is where they directed their expectations'.[8] Those 'promises' were of course the Biblical passages that were taken as prophecies about the Messiah.

A highly significant detail is that Paul stresses that both Jesus' death and his resurrection after three days are 'according to the scriptures'. A modern reader may interpret this as just a way of underlining the religious significance of the events. In the next chapter I shall show that the early Christians, and other Jews too, instead regarded the scriptural references as *in themselves* evidence for the events. Thus we have no reason to suppose that the 'tradition' Paul refers to contained any real and independent evidence at all.[9]

What 'scriptures' might Paul have had in mind? In view of the freedom of interpretation practised by many Christians and Jews at the time (see Chapters 2–4), that question can have no definite answer. But there is a possibility that Paul refers to Biblical (or, for that matter, apocryphal) passages where God's 'Wisdom' is presented as a hypostatised, personified, figure.[10] One such passage is Proverbs 8:23 ff., where Wisdom says: 'The Lord possessed me in the beginning of his way, before his works of old. I was set up from everlasting, from the beginning, or ever the earth was.... When he prepared the heavens, I was there ... I was by him, as one brought up with him: and I was daily his delight, rejoicing always before him ... for whoso findeth me findeth life ...'

That Paul associated Wisdom with Jesus is obvious from 1 Corinthians 1:24: 'Christ the power of God and the wisdom of God', and 1 Corinthians 2:7: 'We speak the Wisdom of God in a mystery.' In the apocryphal book 1 Enoch, which Paul certainly knew well (see Chapter 5), we read in 42:1–2: 'Wisdom found no place where she might dwell', where the personification is quite concrete. Wells (1996), who discusses the association of Wisdom and Jesus, draws attention (p. 178) to a passage in Luke 11:49: 'Therefore also said the Wisdom of God, I will send unto them prophets and apostles, and some of them they shall kill and persecute.' In the corresponding passage in Matthew these word are laid in Jesus' mouth: 'I send unto you prophets, and wise men, and scribes: and some of them ye shall kill and crucify, and some of them shall ye scourge in your synagogues, and persecute them from city to city. . . . Verily I say unto you, All these things shall come upon this generation.' Thus Luke's Wisdom is Matthew's Jesus.[11]

We find the association on a more abstract level in the opening words of John's Gospel: 'In the beginning was the Word, and the Word was with God, and the Word was God', where Wisdom, which in Hebrew (*Hokmah*) is masculine is translated by the Greek masculine *Logos* (literally 'word', but also 'order'), not the usual *Sophia*. Obviously the parallelism between Wisdom and Jesus was widely known among the Christians of the time. See also Chapters 2–3.

If the 'Scriptures' in 1 Corinthians 15:3–4 are references to Wisdom passages, we have here an important support for the view that Paul took Jesus' earthly career to have occurred some time in the indefinite past. We should also remember that Paul, like his contemporaries (see Chapter 2), never refers to Jesus' appearance at the end of times as a 'second coming', a 'return'. Instead, the usual word is *parousia*, 'appearance'. With Jesus equated with the Wisdom figure, he naturally belonged to the eternal, heavenly world. His sojourn on earth was just an episode, although certainly of supreme importance to mankind. When Jesus was to appear as Christ at the Day of Wrath, he would be quite a different kind of figure.

The order in which the witnesses of Jesus' death appear in the above quotation from 1 Corinthians 15:3–8, does not agree with the accounts in the Gospels. In none of them, in fact, is Cephas singled out as the *first* witness of the risen Christ – moreover, the synoptic Gospels never use *Cephas* for Peter. It is true that Luke 24:34 describes how some (unspecified) followers meet the risen Jesus outside Jerusalem, and that, when they return to their companions, they are told, 'The Lord is risen indeed, and hath appeared to Peter.' But Luke never says explicitly that Peter was the *first* to see Jesus.[12]

The discrepancies between Paul and the Gospels on this point make it hard to believe that either of the accounts go back to reports of real events. Doubts about the authenticity of 1 Corinthians 15 are strengthened by a remark by Irenaeus (c. AD 180). Trying to controvert the followers of Marcion and others 'who allege that Paul alone knew the truth and to him alone the mystery [of the resurrection] was manifested by revelation', Irenaeus goes on to make the rather lame remark that Paul himself maintained 'that the same God worked in himself and Peter' (*Against the Heresies* 3:13). It is remarkable that Irenaeus here does not instead refer to the above-quoted passage in 1 Corinthians 15:3–8, which would have given him far stronger support, since Paul himself there says explicitly that Peter and all the other apostles saw the resurrected Jesus *before* him. A plausible conclusion is that this passage was not present in the version of Corinthians seen by Irenaeus.[13] This kind of argument is of course far from conclusive. Unfortunately it is rather typical of the situation we have to deal with in discussions about the interpretation of texts which have been copied by many scribes, each with his own ideas about what the text is supposed to say. On these problems, see Chapter 9.

The fact that practically all of the little that Paul says about the earthly Jesus is also to be found, in one form or another, in the Gospels, may lead the unwary reader to the conclusion that Paul built on the Gospels. The more so, as the Gospels and Acts always precede Paul in the Christian Bible. Modern Biblical scholars, who of course know that the Gospels were written much later than Paul's letters, present a variant of the argument: Paul did not, indeed, build on the Gospels as we have them, but on the *oral tradition* that 'must' have preceded them.

This argument may seem plausible enough. If the Gospels were written long after Jesus' death, how could the authors have got the information about Jesus, except by relying on traditions? So, if there were no written traditions, there must have been oral ones. The flaw in this argument is that we cannot assume that the Gospel writers – any more than, say, Homer, or the authors of the Arthurian romances – had to build on any *traditions* about their heroes at all. Their aim was to launch a story which brought out the conceptions about Jesus that they and their churches had formed, from whatever material they found suitable: historical sources, fictional stories, imagination.[14] Presumably both the Homeric and the Arthurian heroes had some sort of historical foundation, though we cannot know anything about it for certain. As I shall show, Jesus may also be identified with a historical figure, one living in the second century BC, not, as the Gospels have it, in the first century AD.

Paul's communities

While the figure of the earthly Jesus is very elusive in Paul, his letters have more to offer as regards the Christian communities. Paul usually addresses them according to the formula, 'to the church of God in X', or 'To the saints in X' or 'To the saints in Christ which are in X'[15]. Further, he used the designation 'Church of God' not only for individual communities, but also for the totality of those communities, as if they formed a single body.[16] There are also several indications that, even before Paul arrived upon the stage, they had achieved some sort of organisational unity. They seem all to have been prepared to welcome apostles from the sister communities. These apostles were apparently entitled to financial support in return for their services, something which Paul often refers to in his letters.[17] And, though we cannot discern any hierarchical structure in the organisation as a whole, there seems to have been some kind of authorisation for the apostles, possibly arranged by the Jerusalem community. The central position of the Jerusalem community, not surprising in a Jewish context, is indicated by the importance Paul assigns to it, both by visiting Peter and James three years after he joined the Church of God, and by arranging a collection of money among his own communities in the Diaspora for the support of the 'poor saints' in Jerusalem, and by going himself to Jerusalem, apparently to deliver the money. At the same time, Paul vehemently defends his absolute independence of Jerusalem.[18] He was happy that they received him at their last meeting, but refused to conform to their recommendations as to Law observance. Paul himself does not say anything explicitly on the overall organisation – perhaps because it created difficulties for him, among other things, in the matter of financial support, to which he returns again and again.

As for the organisation of the individual churches, we do not gather much either. Paul mentions members with special functions: 'God hath set some in the church, first apostles, secondarily prophets, thirdly teachers, after that miracles, then gifts of healings, helps, governments, diversities of tongues' (1 Cor 12:28). But the people enumerated here certainly do not appear to be elected or appointed office-holders, but rather people with particular God-given talents. That Paul looked upon himself in this light is obvious: he considered himself as called by the Lord, not by men, to be an apostle.

Luke, in Acts, has it that the conference between Paul and the

Jerusalem community was initiated by James, and that it ended in complete harmony. As regards the converts from the Gentiles, James in Acts spelled out a compromise solution whereby, in particular, meat from sacrificed animals should not be touched. Paul says nothing about this, and makes it quite clear that he does not consider himself subordinate to James.

It is remarkable also that Luke by no means stresses the contrast that Paul makes between himself and Peter, one preaching to the Jews, the other to the Gentiles. As Paul says about the Jerusalem people in Galatians 2:7–8: 'When they saw that the gospel of the uncircumcision was committed unto me, as the gospel of the circumcision was unto Peter . . . [then] James, Cephas, and John, who seemed to be pillars . . . gave to me and Barnabas the right hands of fellowship'. In Luke (Acts 15) both Peter and Paul preach successfully to both Jews and Gentiles.

In fact Paul certainly had both Jews and Gentiles in his audiences.[19] It is true that there are some passages in his letters which convey the impression that his audience consisted wholly, or almost wholly, of Gentiles. For instance, 1 Corinthians 12:2: 'ye know that ye were Gentiles' (though a little later, 1 Cor 12:13, he says 'whether we be Jews or Gentiles'), 1 Thessalonians 1:9: 'how ye turned to God from idols to serve the living and true God', paralleled by Galatians 4:8: 'when ye knew not God, ye did service unto them which by nature are no gods'. We should not exclude the possibility, however, that he also included lapsed Jews among the Gentiles.[20] And, when in Romans 16:4 he says: 'not only I, but also all the churches of the Gentiles', it seems we might infer that he meant churches having only, or chiefly, Gentiles as members. But he probably simply means 'all the churches in the countries of the Gentiles', a usage which is also found elsewhere.[21]

At other places Paul is quite evidently addressing communities which include Jews, or more likely, were mainly Jewish. In 1 Corinthians 9:20–1 we read: 'unto the Jews I became as a Jew, that I might gain the Jews . . . to them that are without, as without law . . . that I might gain them that are without law.' To the Corinthian community itself he says (1 Cor 10:1–2) 'all our fathers were under the cloud, and all passed through the sea; and were all baptised unto Moses', thus taking for granted that his audience would identify themselves with the Jews. In Romans 7:1 he says, 'I speak to them that know the law', which indeed does not exclude non-Jews, but certainly excludes non-Jews who were not quite well informed about the Jewish Bible.

Though Paul made a point of reaching the Gentiles, his interest in the salvation of the Jews is also strong. In Romans 1:16 he says that the gospel of God is for everybody: 'to the Jew first, and also to the Greek', echoed in Romans 2:10 'to the Jew first, and also to the Gentile'. In Romans 11 he develops the idea that Israel was to be saved by becoming jealous of the salvation of the Gentiles. Israel, he says, has a special place in God's plan for the world, but the Jews were temporarily blinded. The blindness would not end until 'the fulness of the Gentiles be come in' (Rom 11:25). Thus the fate of the Jews was bound up with that of the Gentiles – though the exact meaning of Paul's phrase is obscure.

In the Churches of God approached by Paul, Jesus was clearly a well-known and revered figure. Also, since Paul evidently believes that what he calls the 'gospel of Christ', or 'gospel of God', conveys *new* information about Jesus (he makes a point of not preaching his gospel where others had been before him), it is important to try to figure out what might be new to his audience in that gospel. Judging from Paul's insistence on the crucifixion and the resurrection, it seems reasonable to infer that for him the most important message was that Jesus, *whom they must have known already*, presumably as a prophet, was the Messiah, the Christ, that his crucifixion was a sacrifice, that his blood would wash away men's sins and that his resurrection proved the reality of life after death.

A corollary of this hypothesis is that Jesus, as a well-established figure in the Church of God, must have been known and revered among the members for a long time. A second corollary is that the 'Church of God', before Paul appeared on the scene, indeed looked upon Jesus as a great leader, perhaps a prophet, but that Paul represented him to them as a truly divine figure – God's son – primarily on the strength of revelations that he had received.

We have direct evidence in Paul's letters that the early Christians were not a homogeneous group. This diversity is quite natural if, as I argue throughout this book, the Christian church of God developed within an already flourishing Essene or para-Essene matrix. It is not to be expected that *all* members in an old community like that of Corinth, for instance, should immediately accept Paul's 'gospel of Christ'. In 1 Corinthians 1:11 Paul writes that he has heard 'there are contentions among you', and goes on, 'every one of you saith, I am of

Paul; and I of Apollos; and I of Cephas, and I of Christ', and asks, rhetorically, 'Is Christ divided?'

The 'Christ faction' hinted at here has puzzled scholars. Naturally enough, since they have always assumed that a Christian community must self-evidently have looked upon Jesus Christ as its very foundation. But, if my argument about a pre-Christian, para-Essene Church of God is accepted, there must have been a time when some members continued to look upon Jesus as their founder and teacher, but did not yet follow Paul's idea that he was the Christ, the Messiah. I shall return to this subject in Chapter 2.

In Galatians 1:8 Paul vehemently criticises, and even goes as far as cursing, apostles who 'preach another gospel'. He does not specify the 'perversions' he accuses them of. But one important point is apparently that they demand strict obedience to the Mosaic law. This also seems to have been a major difference between Paul and the Jerusalem community. Paul discusses it at some length in Galatians 3, where he also makes it clear what it is that has 'ended the Law': the advent of Jesus as the Messiah. This is a point, incidentally, that connects Paul with similar ideas expressed in the Dead Sea Scrolls, where we read that the law regulations in the Community Rule (1QS) are to be followed 'until there shall come the Prophet and the Messiahs of Aaron and Israel' (fol. 9).[22]

The fact that Paul attached such great importance to the question of the observance or non-observance of the Mosaic Law should not mislead us into thinking that this was, in his day, a major distinction between 'Jews' and 'Christians'. As will appear from our discussion of other early texts, the issue of circumcision, for instance, does not seem to have roused very strong feelings among Diaspora Jews, who were after all the ones Paul chiefly addressed. A self-confessed Jew like Philo of Alexandria (see Chapter 3) said that it was the symbolic, 'inner' meaning of the law that was important. On the other hand, he also insists that the literal observance should not for that reason be abandoned. At the same time, many self-confessed Christians, especially in Palestine, but certainly also in the Diaspora, continued to observe the law literally. On *both* sides there were both literalists and non-literalists.

The communities which Paul visited and addressed in his letters were clearly in existence before Paul started his evangelisation. They also seem to have achieved some kind of organisational unity, since Paul often refers to, or sends greetings from, the 'Churches of God' in general.[23] It has often been thought, probably largely on the authority of Acts, that Paul used the synagogues in the Diaspora as a channel for reaching an audience. However, Paul himself never mentions synagogues (or its Philonian synonym, *proseuchē*) in his letters.[24] But clearly he did not have to start from scratch: the Churches of God, the communities of Saints, were prepared to receive itinerant apostles, to give them a hearing and, if need be, to provide them with food and shelter.

There is no evidence that Paul had to create this organisation. In Rome the Church of God was in existence when he first approached them by letter. The same seems to have applied in Corinth, to judge from Paul's statement (1 Cor 1:14) that he had baptised only a few. As for the Galatians and Thessalonians, Paul regards them as his own children. But there as well we seem to have to do with organised communities, ready to receive apostles from sister churches. Paul naturally wishes to believe that they had been particularly impressed by his particular gospel, his particular interpretation of the Biblical prophecies. Hence his dismay when he finds that 'other apostles' could also achieve some success.

The Church of God in Paul's time had an unmistakably Jewish character. The members were a close-knit brotherhood (and sisterhood) who kept somewhat aloof both from pagans and from other Jews, and they were careful to live a quiet and orderly life which would not offend anybody. Paul encouraged this way of life: 'Give none offence, neither to the Jews, nor to the Gentiles' (1 Cor 10:32), and further: 'walk honestly toward them that are without' (1 Thess 4:12). His frequent warnings against disorderly living, especially in sexual matters (e.g. 1 Cor 6:9), may have a similar background, though it may also be seen as a consequence of the efforts to achieve religious 'perfection' and the 'holiness' implicit in their self-designation, the Saints.[25] It is also in this light that we should interpret occasional admonitions not to mingle with outsiders: 'What concord hath Christ with Belial? . . . Come out from among them, and be ye separate' (2 Cor 6:15–17).[26]

Though I stress the predominantly Jewish membership of the Church of God, Gentiles were obviously not excluded.[27] This must have been the case even before Paul appeared on the scene, since Paul never explicitly directs his appeal to two different groups, one Jewish, the other Gentile. They seem to be well integrated, which indicates that they had been working harmoniously together for quite some time. The Gentiles in the Church of God certainly do not appear to be newcomers recruited by Paul. In other words, even before Paul, the Church of God was a Jewish religious association with a universalistic orientation, though Paul's work presumably led to an increase of the Gentile element. But as we have seen, it also led to conflicts with more conservative Jewish members of the communities.[28]

The members of the Church of God had a deeply religious outlook, which probably made them receptive to Paul's visionary and mystery-laden type of theology – the kind of ideas which connected him with the Gnostics (see the last section of this chapter, and Chapters 7, 10 and 12). The chief link between Paul, the newcomer, and the common members of the Church of God, however, was the person of Jesus. The common members seem to have regarded Jesus as self-evidently a great religious authority, which was obviously also Paul's view. Paul, however, raised the authority of Jesus to new heights by claiming that he had seen Jesus in heaven. Jesus could now be regarded not only as a great religious teacher and prophet, but as a divine figure, the promised Messiah. His crucifixion, heavily stressed by Paul, could be seen as a human sacrifice for the salvation of all his followers. His resurrection, which was implied by the fact that he had been raised to heaven, and sat 'at the right hand of God' (Rom 8:34), guaranteed life after death, as Paul himself says.[29]

All of this acquired further significance from Paul's insistence on the imminence of the Last Judgment, where Jesus, as the Messiah, would assist God in rewarding the faithful and punishing the wicked.[30] The brevity of the time that remained for humanity increased the urgency for the members to confirm their allegiance to the Church of God, and for prospective proselytes to join. Paul does not say why he was so sure that the time was short, that the Day of Wrath was approaching fast. It must be admitted, however, that he was not alone in his views. The Book of Daniel, especially, also contains prophecies of the end of times. The popularity of the Enoch literature, which Paul and other Christians certainly knew[31], points in the same direction. It also shows that the repeated failures of the prophecies about the end of the world did not much affect people's belief in them. Paul could therefore well have argued that since he now knew that Jesus was the Messiah, his appearance in a vision to the apostles was a sign from God that Doomsday was at hand.[32] We must also keep in mind that the frequent division of human history into well-defined epochs – four, or seven, or ten, probably largely on the basis of number magic, combined with equally popular astrology – made it easier to explain away failed prophecies. The forecast meant the final epoch, which might well last a thousand years.

However that may be, it is quite clear that both Paul and his audiences were convinced that the Last Judgment would come within the lifetime of at least most of them. Paul expresses this most clearly in 1 Thessalonians 4:14–17: 'them also which sleep in Jesus will God bring with him . . . this we say unto you by the word of the Lord, that . . . the dead in Christ shall rise first. Then we which are alive and remain shall be caught up together with him in the clouds, to meet the Lord in the air.' We note Paul's very concrete picture of the heavenly world, which often echoes the words in Daniel, or in the Enoch literature.[33] As is said above, it is also interesting that Paul, when writing about Jesus' coming for the last Judgment, never describes this as a *return*: he makes no obvious connection between the earthly Jesus and the heavenly one.[34] This seems to me a further indication that Paul did not look upon Jesus' life on earth as an event that his contemporaries could have witnessed. Also, when Paul says that Jesus was the 'firstfruits of them that slept' (1 Cor 15:20), while at the same time declaring that those believers who had died before the coming of Jesus would be resurrected first, it is obvious that he did not regard the time that the dead – among them, Jesus – had spent in their graves as in any way important. Further, if my argument, above, about Paul's use of the Wisdom literature for details about Jesus' life are acceptable, they provide additional support for supposing that Paul placed the life of the earthly Jesus far back in time: a time associating Jesus with the Old Testament prophets.

Most of Paul's communities are to be found in Syria, Asia Minor and Greece. The absence of any mention of Egypt is conspicuous, and rather mysterious, since Alexandria probably had the greatest Diaspora community of all, and several early Christian texts are probably Egyptian, among them the Letter to the Hebrews. We shall discuss this enigma in Chapter 3.

Paul's letters are in all probability the oldest unquestionably Christian texts in the New Testament; most authorities agree that they were probably written in the late forties and in the fifties of the first century AD. But his position should not be misunderstood. He was indeed a great apostle, and Marcion, in many ways Paul's chief supporter, maintained that Paul alone had 'seen the Lord'.[35] But Paul was by no means the only apostle. As he himself says, there had been apostles before him. And it is obvious that there were differences of opinion between them.

Paul's gospel, his version of Christianity (a word never used by him) was not the only one, as he makes quite clear in his letters both to the Corinthians and to the Galatians, and as appears also from his obvious difficulties with the Jerusalem community of Saints, led by James, Cephas and John. Such diversity in first-century Christianity is not surprising in the light of the hypothesis about its origin in an already diverse and wide-ranging, at least century-old Jewish religious movement, about which more will be said in Chapters 3 and 4.

Paul and the Gnostics

Paul's form of early Christianity was certainly a very important branch within the Church of God. First of all, Jesus held a central position. He was the Son of God, the Messiah and as 'the firstfruits of the dead' he had shown that resurrection was a reality. His suffering on the cross had immense redemptive power, guaranteeing for his followers the forgiveness of their sins and entry into heaven at the impending Last Judgment. In other words: immortality.

Paul, and presumably the majority of his followers, had a rather concrete picture of heaven, conforming roughly to widespread views of the shape of the universe, to some extent influenced by widely spread Greek astronomical (or astrological – the two were not kept apart in antiquity) ideas. Heaven, to Paul, consisted of three layers above the earth, with God placed in the highest heaven, Paradise. God was surrounded by innumerable angelic messengers, led by the archangels. The angels traversed the space between God's heaven and the earth, carrying messages from God to men, and from men to God. Paul is never very explicit on these matters – perhaps because he took it for granted that everybody else had more or less the same picture. But he declares that he had once been raised to the third heaven (he says he cannot specify whether it was bodily or spiritually), and that he there heard and saw things which he said must be kept secret.

At other places Paul makes it clear that in the space between the highest heaven and the earth, and also, apparently, in the underworld, below the surface of the earth, there were also evil spirits, bent on luring man away from the straight path of obedience to God – also called 'The Way'. The chief of these evil spirits is Satan (Paul once calls him Belial). But we often hear about intermediate evil spirits,

27

called principalities, *archai*, and powers, *dunameis* (e.g. Rom 8:38). On the whole, this world view is rather similar to the one outlined in other Jewish writings of the time. Nor does it differ much from that propagated by popularised and highly syncretistic versions of the common Greek philosophies of the period, and also by Gnosticism (see Chapter 3).

As for man's place in this universe, Paul attempts to explain how he envisages the form of man after his resurrection. He neither asserts, nor denies, that we shall be raised in bodily form. But he emphasises that, on being raised, 'we shall all be changed' (1 Cor 15:51). Man, he says, 'is sown a natural [*psuchikon*] body, but is raised a spiritual [*pneumatikon*] body' (1 Cor 15:44). And, when he declares that 'flesh and blood cannot inherit the kingdom of God', it seems fairly clear that the 'spiritual body', which is the one that does inherit the kingdom of God, is non-material. But as it is still a 'body' it seems to be in some sense material. Apparently Paul took it to be constituted by a superior kind of matter – a not uncommon view through the ages.

Understandably, Paul does not seem to have fully worked out these questions. For instance, the word *pneuma*, used about the human soul, is also used about the Holy Ghost, God's Spirit. The believer is in some mysterious sense included in it, since 'he that is joined into the Lord is one spirit'. The converse also holds, for 'your body is the temple of the Holy Spirit which is in you'. In Galatians 4:6 Paul says: 'God hath sent forth the Spirit of his Son into your hearts.'

Paul's letters contain rather little about the worship practised in his churches. We know that the members came together for communal meals, a practice described in the 'Community Rule' among the Dead Sea Scrolls, and which we also find documented in Pliny' s letter to Trajan about the Bithynian Christians, probably from AD 112. Paul exhorts the Corinthians to conduct themselves worthily at these communal meals, which indicates that he had heard about disorderly behaviour in connection with them.

In two instances Paul goes into some detail about ritual practices. In 1 Corinthians 10:16 we read, 'the cup of blessing which we bless, is it not the communion of the blood of Christ? . . . The bread which we break, is it not the communion of the body of Christ?' Clearly, therefore, the blessing of the cup and of the bread is performed in memory of Jesus' death. We have a confirmation in 1 Corinthians 11:23–5, where practically the same scene is presented by Paul as a revelation about Jesus 'in the same night in which he was betrayed'. In

Paul's revelation, Jesus first blesses the bread, then breaks it, and says, 'Take, eat, this is my body, which is broken for you: this do in remembrance of me'. Then the same procedure is repeated with the cup.

This ritual may well go back at least as far as the early Essenes, who, as I shall argue more fully in Chapters 2 and 4, were likely to form the matrix in which Christianity came into being. We now know from the Dead Sea Scrolls that the founder of the Essene community, the Teacher of Righteousness, was indeed declared to be betrayed by a community member and taken prisoner by the priestly establishment that had long planned to have him killed. The Diaspora communities, who had no access to the Scrolls, presumably knew the outline of this story from traditions within the church, including this ritual. The ritual was a way of honouring their revered Teacher after his death. Paul's revelation reinterprets the ritual as a prophecy by Jesus himself about his own death, and at the same time as a kind of testament for the church he (Jesus) had founded. In the second-century Synoptic Gospels the ritual was developed, in accordance with Paul's revelation, into the dramatic central scene of the Last Supper.

Paul's theology has clear indications of links with that of Gnosticism, a religious movement gaining ground both among Gentiles and Jews of the intellectual middle class in the first century AD. The Gnostics had a dualistic view of the material world as primarily evil, and the spiritual world as primarily good. The favourite metaphor, also employed by Paul, was that the material world was darkness, while the spiritual world was pure light. For the Gnostics, God could be seen as the essence of the world of light, and his good angels were the sparks of light that God sent to his elect among the humans.

Though there is nothing exclusively Gnostic about Paul's theology, it cannot be denied that his world-view was wide open to Gnostic ideas. We know about Gnosticism chiefly from later documents, but Gnostic ideas were certainly developing already in the first century, or even earlier. Gnostic traits in Paul are, for instance, the plethora of spirits in Paul's writings, his 'spiritual' view of the resurrection, the union of the spirit of the believer with the Spirit of God, combined with God's sending of 'the Spirit of his Son' into the heart of the believer, and finally, the Pauline – and for that matter, also Essene – deterministic insistence that the salvation of the soul, or even the belief in Jesus, was entirely in God's hands. It was the grace of God; it was not something that the believer earned by his own efforts. I shall have more to say about these matters in chapters 3, 4 and 12.

The main difference between Paul and the Gnostics was that Paul regarded Jesus as the *sole* purveyor of salvation from God to man, though even this was not necessarily a fundamental difference, since the Gnostics could well imagine a hierarchy of divine messengers, with Jesus as the supreme one, and alone capable of providing enough force to establish the communion with God. When Paul talks about God sending forth 'the spirit of his Son into the hearts of men', or about 'the spiritual body' that inherits the kingdom of God, and that 'he that is joined unto the Lord is one spirit', he and the Gnostics seem to be living in the same universe.

Chapter 2

The Church of God in the Jewish Diaspora

In this chapter I shall examine six texts which I will show to be roughly contemporary with Paul: the *Pastor* of Hermas, *Didachē* (the Teaching of the Apostles), The First Letter of Clemens Romanus (1 Clement), the Letter of Barnabas, The Letter to the Hebrews and The Revelation of John.

Naturally, as always, we shall have to reckon with the probability that the texts have been tampered with by later scribes, sometimes for purposes of harmonisation with the views of the Church, as its theology developed (see Chapter 9). As such changes, however, are difficult to ascertain, the texts will on the whole have to be accepted as they stand. Doubts and difficulties will be taken up as we go along. Of the six texts, two are probably in the main as old as any of the Pauline letters, or even older: Hermas' *Pastor*, and the Didachē. Of the others, Barnabas is probably somewhat later than the fall of Jerusalem in AD 70, while the rest can be placed in or around the sixties of the first century AD. Earlier scholars have mostly placed all these in the second century AD and, above all, considered them as on the whole later than the Gospels. Most modern scholars have placed them after AD 90. Whatever the date of their originals, however, the texts have probably been exposed to later Christian deletions, additions and modifications – something which inevitably makes them somewhat problematic as historical sources.

It is obvious that the general problems of dating texts associated with early Christianity are formidable.[1] But it is also clear that a historian cannot shirk the responsibility of dating the texts which, together with archaeological material, are the sources of our knowledge about 'what really happened', to use the terse phrase of the famous nineteenth-century German historian Ranke.

It is in the nature of things that in most cases we cannot hope to

31

arrive at exact, absolute dates for individual texts. However, failing that, we can sometimes at least achieve a relative dating. In the present case, I think I can say with some confidence that the six texts to be treated here must be dated before the canonical Gospels, a question which I deal with at some length in Chapter 9. Most modern scholars have accepted that the letters of Paul are older than the Gospels. But an age-old tradition is still alive, to the effect that non-canonical texts should be seen as younger than and dependent on the Gospels, and therefore as generally less reliable as sources. This has led to a tendency to exaggerate the age of the canonical Gospels, and to assign unjustifiably late dates to the non-canonical texts, and indeed to most New Testament texts other than the Gospels and Acts. In this connection we should keep in mind that at least some Church Fathers definitely accepted Hermas, Barnabas, Didachē and 1 Clement as part and parcel of the canon.[2]

I shall cite evidence for my dating in my presentation of the individual texts in this chapter. Some general problems of dating will be discussed in Chapter 9. At this point I shall point merely to two particular indications of date that I have come across at a rather late stage in my investigation, long after the individual texts had been dated on other grounds.

One such indication concerns the word *sunagōgē*, synagogue. That word is quite common in the Gospels and Acts – altogether some sixty instances. But in Paul's letters it does not occur at all.[3] As the Pauline letters are universally admitted to be older than the Gospels, this looks like a systematic difference of usage between an earlier group of texts as against later ones. And, indeed, that suspicion gets support when we find that the six texts, which I have classified, on independent grounds, as roughly contemporary with Paul, also consistently avoid the word *sunagōgē*.[4] Not only that, all the non-Pauline letters in the New Testament, which are often taken to be quite early, exhibit the same usage. Non-use of the word *sunagōgē*, therefore, can be tentatively employed as at least a rough dating criterion for Christian texts. It distinguishes with surprising efficiency between first-century texts (where the word is rare or absent) and second-century ones, where it is frequent. By this criterion the Gospels can be classed as second-century, which is also the dating I argue for in Chapter 9.

There is a lively ongoing debate on the origin of the synagogue as an institution (irrespective of whether the word used is *sunagōgē* or something else, e.g. *proseuchē*, the word preferred by Philo). The prevailing view among modern scholars is that the synagogue originated in the Diaspora.[5] But for a long time the word *sunagōgē* referred to the community, not to a building. MacKay 1994 says (p. 250) 'There is no archaeological or epigraphic evidence that points unequivocally to the existence of synagogue buildings in first-century Palestine.' Philo, however, uses the word *sunagōgē* once in his treatise on Dreams (II:127), referring to places where the Jews of Egypt gathered to discuss their 'ancestral philosophy', and once in his treatment of the Essenes, referring to 'sacred spots' in Palestine. In both instances the meaning may, however, be 'gathering', rather than 'building'.

In view of this it is interesting to note that Paul, and the six texts treated in the present chapter, do not use the word *sunagōgē* at all. By contrast, all the Gospels have it, and commonly with reference to a building, though the 'community' meaning is often not excluded. The exact figures are: Matthew 9 times, Mark 12, Luke 17, John 5, Acts 22. I present this argument for a second-century date for all the Gospels and Acts, not because it is a decisive one, but because it is, as far as I know, both new and quite straightforward.[6]

A second general indication of dating is the use of the word saints (*hagioi*) for the members of the Christian communities. Paul uses it quite consistently for the members of the Church of God. The same holds for each of the six texts treated in this chapter. This can again be looked upon as an indication that they are largely contemporary with Paul. The same holds for the non-Pauline letters in the New Testament. In the canonical Gospels, on the other hand, we find only a single instance: Matthew 27:52 'And the graves were opened, and many of the bodies of the saints which slept arose.' In Acts the word saints is used about Christians in four instances, all of them in connection with Paul's activities at or before his conversion. Luke therefore probably took his cue from Paul in these instances. Accordingly, using saints for the Christians seems to be a terminology largely abandoned in the second century AD. By this criterion, too, our six texts are placed in an earlier period than the Gospels.[7]

Before going on to a discussion of the individual texts, a general remark on the dating may be in order. As will appear, I date 1 Clement around AD 65. Some remarks in the letter about the venerable age of both the Corinthian and the Roman Church of God lead to the conclusion that both were probably in existence in the first few decades of the first century AD.[8] But on the traditional assumption that all Christian communities were based, ultimately, on Jesus' work in Palestine, and the apostles' spreading of the Word to the world outside, such an early date for Rome or Corinth would be impossible.

However, if we abandon that traditional assumption, and adopt instead the hypothesis I am exploring in this book, it is perfectly possible for the Roman (and Corinthian) Churches to go back even to the first pre-Christian century. Moreover, they might have started out as Essene communities, which were also, as we now know, called Churches of God, with members called Saints. That designation was also used by the Essenes about themselves. It probably derives from Isaiah 62:11–12: 'Say ye to the daughter of Zion [Jerusalem], Behold, thy salvation cometh; behold, his reward is with him, and his work before him. And they shall call them, The holy people, The redeemed of the Lord: and thou shalt be called, Sought out, A city not forsaken.'

The very existence of Essenes in the Diaspora has often been flatly denied. I shall have more to say about this in Chapter 4. At this point I wish to draw attention only to a debated passage in Horace's Satires – a work probably written in the last third of the first century BC. In a poem where Horace speaks about Roman Jews, he employs the expression *tricesima Sabbata*, 'the thirtieth Sabbath'. Commentators have been puzzled by this expression. But we now know, thanks to the Qumran discoveries, that the Essenes used a calendar where the sabbaths were numbered consecutively through the year. The thirtieth Sabbath would be some time in October.[9]

Thus Horace's expression indicates that he had heard about Jews in Rome who followed an Essene-type calendar. In other words, we here have a direct reference to Essene-type practices in Rome. In fact, if Horace took this kind of expression to be the normal one among the Jews of Rome, we might even argue that the Essenes made up a noticeable portion of the Jewish population there. This would admittedly be building on a rather slight foundation: we cannot be certain that the Essenes were the only Jews to follow an Essene-type calendar. But my argument illustrates the danger of shutting our eyes to possibilities which are simply excluded by our preconceived ideas.

Besides questions of dating, I shall deal in this chapter above all with two topics: the nature of the communities to which the writings were directed, and the Jesus figure presented in them. In a final section the main theological ideas of the six texts will be considered. There I also give numerous examples of Old Testament passages used in the New Testament to describe Jesus' sayings and doings.

None of our six documents ever employ the term *Christian* for the members of the communities addressed. All of them instead use, like Paul, one or more of the terms the *Elect*, the *Saints*, the *Church of God*.[10]

Also like Paul, the six documents have almost nothing to say about Jesus' life on earth, and provide practically no information about Jesus' preaching, or his theological ideas, except insofar as this can be inferred from the numerous Old Testament quotations laid in Jesus' mouth. What the writers focus on, again like Paul, is his death and especially his resurrection, and the theological implications of these two events. But we are not told when or where they occurred. None of the authors ever claim to have seen or heard Jesus in the flesh, nor to have known anybody who had done so. The main sources of information seem to be revelations, as in Paul, and above all – a feature hardly found at all in Paul – interpretations of Old Testament Scripture passages, especially the Psalms and the prophets, including apocryphal texts, and particularly the Enoch literature. No doubt such interpretations were often connected with revelations.

One remarkable feature of the six documents is that they were apparently all addressed to a predominantly Jewish audience, chiefly in the Diaspora. It is not only that they all consistently base their arguments on the Hebrew Scriptures in their Greek dress, the Septuagint, thus obviously presupposing that their audiences were thoroughly familiar with that text. But there are also more specific indications in most of the texts that the addressees are at least predominantly Jews. Revelation repeatedly criticises people who, the author says, 'call themselves Jews, but are of the synagogue[11] of Satan'. And Hermas' *Pastor* refers to outsiders as 'gentiles and sinners', scolding those who 'acquire too high a renown among the gentiles'. Didachē is based on a document which scholars agree is of purely Jewish, pre-Christian origin. That document, *Duae Viae*, is also incorporated in the Letter of Barnabas, and is quoted in Hermas.[12]

In spite of their Jewish appearance, our six texts have always, in the main, been regarded as Christian. The Letter to the Hebrews and The Revelation of John have even been included in the canon, though not without persistent opposition. The others are known to have circulated in Christian communities at least since the second century AD, and some authorities have regarded them as 'inspired', though in the end they were kept out of the canon, both in the Western church and in the

Eastern one. It is therefore important to find out what kind of Christianity our documents exhibit.

The earliest Christians of Rome: 1 Clement

1 Clement is a letter of about forty ordinary pages addressed to the Corinthian Church of God. It appears to have been occasioned by reports to Rome about dissensions within its sister community. The spokesman of the Roman Church, Clement, referring to Paul's Letter to the Corinthians, impresses upon his addressees the importance of unity and orderly behaviour. In particular, he criticises them for deposing, without proper cause, elders *(presbuteroi)* of long standing. Rome, however, does not explicitly claim superiority or hierarchical precedence over Corinth. Rather, the tone of the letter is that of an elder, more experienced sister community. We should perhaps keep in mind that Corinth had been established as a Roman colony by Julius Caesar in 46 BC, after the old Greek city had been razed to the ground by the Romans. By now, more than a hundred years later, Corinth had become a thriving international commercial and maritime centre. The letter is particularly interesting for the glimpses it provides about traditions and practices in the early Church. As I shall show, it also provides intriguing pieces of information about the previous history of both the Roman and the Corinthian branches of the Church of God.

The letter has been attributed to one Clement, who, according to the Church father Irenaeus, writing *c.* AD 180, was bishop of Rome in *c.* AD 95. Other Christian writers from the second half of the second century AD also refer to, or quote, the letter, thus proving that it was widely used in the early Church. In the letter itself, however, the author does not give his name. Nor does he claim to be bishop of Rome.

Referring to Irenaeus and the fourth-century church historian Eusebius, most modern scholars date the Clement letter to *c.* AD 95. Internal evidence, however, points to an earlier date, which might be at the time of the emperor Nero, in the sixties of the first century. If so, 1 Clement would be only slightly later than the Letters of Paul, whose letter to the Corinthians is directly referred to in Clement's letter.

1 Clement confirms on many points the picture of the earliest Christians that we can derive from Paul. The word Christian is not used: the communities are called the Church of God, and the members the Saints, or the Elect. Further, the term Church of God is applied

both to the individual communities, that of Rome and that of Corinth, and to the totality of such communities, suggesting the existence of an Empire-wide organisation. The communities keep in touch both by means of itinerant 'apostles' (missionaries) and by means of letters and messengers.

As to the organisation of the individual Churches, Clement compares it with the hierarchy of an army. However, we get no clear view of the organisation of either the individual churches or the totality of the Christian communities. He does stress the importance of obeying the elders. He seems to imply that the elders are appointed by the individual communities, possibly in a process involving the approval of the Church as a whole. He also insists that once appointed, the elders could not be dismissed without proper cause, something which had apparently happened in Corinth. But we are given no hints about just how the elders were selected and appointed.

The word bishop (*episkopos,* 'overseer') is used only once, in a passage (42:4) where it is said that the apostles appointed bishops and assistants (*diakonoi*). At another place, where the episcopate (*episkopē*) is discussed (44:1–4), Clement apparently uses the term 'elders' as a near-synonym of 'bishops'. Like Paul, he nowhere implies that a community should have just one bishop. The bishops, just like the elders, are always presented as a group. The apostolic succession, clearly set forth in 42:1–4 and 44:1–5, and supported by a reference, typical of Clement, to the Old Testament (Isa 60:17), applies to the elders as a group. The individual members of this group in each church are apparently appointed for life, or at least for as long as they can perform their duties satisfactorily. Accordingly, the Corinthians had acted wrongly by deposing elders who, according to Clement, had served 'piously and conscientiously'.

Just how the vacancies in the group of elders should be filled does not appear. Clearly Clement presupposes that the whole community should have their say. But we are not told in what way the Church of God as a whole was to be involved. Thus 1 Clement does not contain any direct information about the origin of the Roman papacy.

The main reason for most scholars to date the letter to the last decade of the first century AD is derived from Eusebius' *Historia Ecclesiastica* (HE), written in the first half of the fourth century. In HE 4–23–11 Eusebius refers to a letter written, he says, by one Dionysius, bishop of Corinth around AD 170. He reports Dionysius as saying that the Corinthians are still in the habit of reading the letter sent from the

Roman church to the Corinthian one through Clement (*dia Klemen-tos*).

At two other places (HE 3–16, 4–22–1) Eusebius writes about the Clement letter, referring to a treatise by Hegesippus, now largely lost. Hegesippus had apparently made a journey to Rome around 160. Further, in HE 5–6–1,2, Irenaeus, who wrote *c.* AD 180, is quoted as follows: 'when the blessed apostles had founded and built the church, they gave the ministry of the episcopate to Linus. Paulus mentioned this Linus in his epistle to Timothy [2 Tim 4:21].[13] Anencletus succeeded him, and after him Clement obtained the episcopate in the third place from the apostles. He had seen the blessed apostles.' Irenaeus continues: 'in the time of Clement . . . the church in Rome sent a most powerful letter to the Corinthians urging them to peace'. Judging from HE 3–15 and 3–34, Clement was bishop in Rome between AD 92 and 101.

All this seems clear enough. However, we should keep in mind that Eusebius writes his history with a definite purpose in mind: to show the unity and continuity of the Church from the earliest apostles, the disciples of Christ, onwards and, in particular, that the bishops of the Church succeeded each other in a straight line from the first apostles.[14] Thus Eusebius gives us bishop lists for the great sees of Rome, Corinth, Jerusalem, Antioch and Alexandria. But, as he provides no contemporary evidence, the lists are suspect, and it may well be that they are purposely arranged (not to say invented) in order to support his own preconceived ideas. The general reliability of Eusebius concerning the early history of the church must be characterised as low: he is far too prone to resort to hearsay and downright fabrications, if it suits his purpose. Grant (1980) illustrates Eusebius' way of subordinating his narrative to his theological concerns. Speaking about Eusebius' treatment of Tertullian (p. 66), he writes: 'Where the evidence did not go far enough, Eusebius amplified it. Where it went too far, he suppressed it.' Grant finds that Eusebius does not refer to any sources (outside the NT) older than the middle of the second century AD. I would add that Eusebius' assertion that Mark was the first bishop of Alexandria lacks all probability.[15]

Let us therefore for the moment leave Eusebius aside, and consider the internal evidence of the letter itself. In chapter 41 there is an interesting reference to the Jerusalem temple: 'Not in every place, brethren, are the daily sacrifices offered, or peace offerings, but in Jerusalem only. And even there one does not offer in just any place, but before the sanctuary, at the altar, after a careful examination of the victim by the high priest and his attendants.' It is surely remarkable to find the Temple cult referred to in the present tense, if the letter was written some twenty years after Temple's destruction in AD 70. Some scholars refer to Josephus, *Antiquities*, Bk III, chapters 7–11, where the present tense is also used for ancient practices in the Temple. However, Josephus introduces his account by passages in the past tense, so that the reader is left in no doubt that what he describes is the situation as described in the Pentateuch. Other scholars speculate that some sort of temple service was perhaps continued in Jerusalem even after the destruction of the Temple.[16]

Both explanations imply, it seems to me, a very forced reading of the text. After all, Clement brings forward the example of the Temple to impress upon the Corinthians the need to conform to established, age-old regulations which ought to be scrupulously followed (chapter 44:1). If analogous regulations could no longer be adhered to in Jerusalem, or only in a highly modified form, the example lost its force. Surely the natural interpretation of the passage is strong evidence that Clement in fact knew nothing about the destruction of the Temple, and accordingly, that he wrote before AD 70. The alternatives suggested must be seen as attempts to reconcile the text with the assumption, based chiefly or wholly on Eusebius, to the effect that the letter was written after the Roman conquest of Jerusalem. A contributory factor may be the general reluctance to date a non-canonical text earlier than the Gospels.

Once our suspicions on the accuracy of Eusebius' dating have been roused, we have no difficulty in finding additional internal evidence for placing the letter before the year 70. In 1 Clement 5 we read, in a section devoted to the dire effects of 'jealousy' (*dia zēlon*): 'Let us take the noble examples of our own generation (*tēs geneas hēmōn*)'. The examples given are first of all Peter and Paul, whose deaths as martyrs are referred to in surprisingly veiled language. Since both Peter and Paul must be assumed to have been active apostles as early as the thirties, we may take it that they were born at the very beginning of the first century, or even before. 'Their generation' would be nonagenarians in the nineties. There is little likelihood that Clement himself, or the Corinthians he addressed, were of such an advanced age. In general, the active church leaders were probably under 60.[17] It may of course be argued that Clement uses 'generation' in a wide sense: 'our own times' as against 'the time of our ancestors'.

But even with the more literal interpretation everything falls very neatly into place if we take 1 Clement to have been written in the sixties, instead of the nineties.

The opening phrase of the letter reads: 'The disasters and calamities that have suddenly and repeatedly [*aiphnidious kai epallēlous*] struck us, have delayed us [*bradiōn*] in turning to your affairs.' The writer obviously here refers to very recent happenings: apologising for the delay in writing a letter is hardly relevant several years after the occasion. Further, in 1 Clement 6, after the mentions of Peter and Paul, there is again a reference to 'our own generation', declaring that 'an immense crowd of the elect ones' have suffered 'terrible and monstrous outrages'. In both cases, the description fits excellently the Neronian persecution of Christians in connection with the great fire of Rome in 64. Most scholars, following the Eusebian dating, have instead focused on the persecutions under Domitian which, to judge from the meagre evidence that we have, do not seem to have struck with such great force.[18] Moreover, the indications are that they aimed at Jewish proselytising, not at the Jews, or Christians, as such. Also, it is highly doubtful that our sources, Suetonius and Tacitus, when using words such as Christian or Christ, had what we nowadays call Christians in mind. Christ after all, means 'messiah', and Christianity was not the only Messianic movement of the time.[19]

Outside 1 Clement itself, support for an early dating can be found in the *Pastor* by Hermas. That work has often been placed in the mid-second century by scholars, chiefly on the basis of a notice in the Muratori fragment, where it is said that the book was written 'quite recently [*nuperrime*] by Hermas, when his brother Pius was bishop of Rome'. I shall return to Muratori and the dating of the *Pastor* in the next sub-section. For the moment, I will only say that I find very strong grounds for dating the *Pastor* much earlier, probably around the middle of the first century. In the present connection I only wish to say that in Vision 2–4–3 an angel tells Hermas: 'make two copies [of what I say to you], one for Clement, and one for Grapte. And Clement will send it to the other cities – *that is his job*' (my italics).

The idea that the Clement mentioned here is Clemens Romanus has been discussed widely, but has generally been rejected, chiefly, it seems, on the ground that it is contradicted by the Muratori dating of Hermas. But if, as I shall soon argue, the Muratori evidence should be rejected, we discover that the Clement mentioned in Hermas forms a perfect fit for the author of 1 Clement. Not only do they have the same name, they also seem to play the same role in their community. As A. Jaubert explains in her edition of 1 Clement, the letter was sent as a communication from the Roman church to the Corinthian one. Clement acts as a spokesman for the Roman church, not in a personal capacity. This is exactly what Hermas implies about him. We should keep in mind that it is Eusebius, writing in the fourth century, and referring to late second-century witnesses, who says Clement was bishop of Rome.

A further, admittedly somewhat weaker support for an earlier dating of 1 Clement is the fact that Paul mentions both a Hermas and a Clement as contemporaries in his letters. In Romans 16:14 – the whole of chapter 16, however, may be a late addition – he says 'Salute Asyncritus, Phlegon, Hermas, Patrobas, Hermes, and the brethren which are with them' – clearly one of several communities of 'saints' or 'elect ones' in Rome. We note that all the names are Greek, which is to be expected in a Jewish Diaspora community at the time. And in Philippians 4:3 we read: 'Help those women which laboured with me in the gospel, with Clement also, and with other my fellow-workers.' Whether this Clement is a Roman is not made clear, but several scholars have concluded, from mentions of Caesar's household (4:22) and the palace (1:13), that Paul wrote Philippians from Rome, probably in the early sixties. These mentions naturally do not prove anything. Still, they contribute their share to the probability that 1 Clement belongs to the sixties, rather than to the nineties of the first century AD.

Yet another indication of date must be mentioned. In 47:6 the Corinthian church is characterised as 'very firm and ancient' (*archaia*). And in 63:3 the messengers carrying the letter from Rome are said to be 'trusted and wise people, who have lived among us from their youth [*apo neotētos*] until their old age [*gerous*]'. As our editor, Annie Jaubert points out, these expressions make good sense if the Roman community had been in existence for some fifty years. This, she continues, argues for a dating of the letter in the nineties.

But, if my dating of the letter is correct, the same argument carries us back to the *first few decades* of the first century AD. This is of course impossible according to the received view that Christianity was launched by a Palestinian Jesus crucified around 30, whereas it is quite consistent with my hypothesis of its origin in already existing Essene communities. Interestingly, the Roman Church of God is at least equally old, since the messengers appointed to bring the letter are said to have been members 'from their youth into old age', again a time span of 30–50 years (63:3).

Another interesting chronological indication is that Paul's activity is referred to as 'the beginning of the evangelisation' (47:2), thus explicitly confirming that the Christian mission did not significantly predate Paul. Now, as Paul apparently started his missionary work in Greece in the forties, i.e. some twenty years before Clement's letter, we have here a confirmation of indications in Paul's own letters, that he spread his gospel (i.e. his message, his good news about Jesus) in communities that were already well established before the forties. As I have argued,[20] there is independent evidence indicating that the Roman church may well have been in existence even before the end of the first century BC. Before Paul, the community had considered Jesus, long since dead, as their founder and main teacher and interpreter of the Scriptures.[21] Now, according to the hypothesis that I am developing here, Paul and other apostles convinced them that Jesus was the Messiah, who would soon come down from Heaven to introduce the Kingdom of God. It is significant that the writer does not speak about 'Jesus' death', or 'the time of Jesus', or something to that effect, but of *the start of the mission of the apostles*. On my hypothesis, that is entirely natural: what happened around AD 30–40 was that the news, the *euaggelion*, about Jesus being the Messiah, not the news of his crucifixion and death, spread among the Churches of God.

The Jewishness of Clement's communities is beyond doubt. In the address, they are described as 'living as strangers' (*paroikousa*) in Rome and Corinth, respectively. That is the expression normally used by and for Diaspora Jews. Throughout the letter Clement refers to Old Testament examples, consistently using the pronoun *we* about the Jews, *they* about non-Jews.

However, beyond insisting on the imminent establishment of the Kingdom of God, for which the communities were preparing themselves by pursuing their ideal of a saintly life, there is little in the letter to inform us about their religious concepts. Jesus is almost always named as Jesus Christ, except in two places, where the bare name Jesus occurs. Jesus as Christ is the guarantee of salvation and of life after death. His passion and his death are indeed brought out. Thus in 16:2 ff. they are described in terms of the suffering servant of Isaiah 53 and of Psalm 22, introduced by the words 'The Lord Jesus Christ says', after which follow direct quotations from Isaiah

42

53:1–12 and Psalm 22:7–9: '. . . to whom is the arm of the Lord revealed? . . . Surely he hath borne our griefs . . . yet we did esteem him stricken, smitten of God, and afflicted . . .'. (See below, section on Jesus' sayings.)

Crucifixion is never mentioned, which is surely remarkable, in view of Paul's intense involvement in the mystique of the cross, a mystique that he quite likely originated. Clement never goes beyond bare mentions of the 'blood' of Christ, without any concrete elaboration whatever.

Clement tells us nothing about Jesus' life, his disciples, his baptism by John, his betrayal by Judas, his trial and the manner of his death. His resurrection is represented as a fact, not as an event (see below). There is no hint as to when and where it occurred. Precisely as in Paul and, as we shall see, in all the other texts examined in this chapter, Jesus is thus presented as a figure who might well have lived a long time ago, like the Old Testament prophets. Indeed, many passages in 1 Clement are hard to reconcile with the idea that Jesus had lived only a few decades ago. For instance, in 32:2 God is praised because 'from him come all the priests and levites, from him the Lord Jesus according to the flesh, from him come kings, and princes and leaders within Judah': Jesus here appears in an entirely historical, Old Testament context. Similarly, taking Old Testament sayings as said by the Holy Ghost, inspired by Jesus, points in the same direction. Further, Clement sometimes calls Jesus 'High Priest', thus emphasising the connection with ancient Jewish history, and also, it should be noted, with the Qumran Essenes. Finally, when Clement in 5:1, turns from 'ancient examples from the OT' of the consequences of 'jealousy', and talks of 'our own generation', he mentions Peter and Paul – whose deaths he refers to as recent events – but does not mention Jesus, who *according to the Gospels* must have been exactly contemporary with them.

1 Clement 13:1ff quotes 'words of Jesus', which are roughly, but not literally, paralleled in the Sermon of the Mount. 1 Clement 46:8 similarly parallels Matthew 18:6, about 'whoso shall offend one of these little ones'. Jaubert's suggestion that these passages are taken from *florilegia*, collections of *logia* ('sayings', chiefly from the Old Testament), is very plausible; we should note that several such sayings are also found in the *Didachē*. But there they are not attributed to Jesus, but are said to occur in 'the gospel', which in the *Didachē*

seems to mean just such a collection. Fragments of florilegia have been found among the Dead Sea Scrolls.[22]

At other places Clement incorporates sayings from the Bible (notably the Prophets, the Psalms and Job) which he ascribes without hesitation to Jesus, using some such formula as 'This is what Jesus says through the Holy Spirit' (e.g. 1 Clem 16:2). In other words, he does not presume to quote Jesus' own words, but takes the Scriptural version as valid evidence of them. Such use of Biblical passages as direct proof of what Jesus said or did on earth is found not only in Clement, but also in the Letter to the Hebrews and above all in Barnabas. As the personification of God's Wisdom, existing from the beginning of the world, he was in possession of God's Word, and could instruct the prophets, and speak through them. (See the final section of this chapter.) In Chapter 4 we shall see that exactly the same technique – which of course also contributed to placing Jesus far back in history – was used in some Qumran Scrolls about the Teacher of Righteousness.

One topic is conspicuously absent in 1 Clement: the problem of Law observance, which figures so prominently in Paul's letters. As Clement obviously knew at least 1 Corinthians (and presumably much more about Paul and by Paul), his silence about circumcision and table printing must have been deliberate. The most probable explanation is that he did not agree with Paul's views on these matters; he probably did not perceive the conflict between Law observance and non-observance as acute, at least not in the churches he was here concerned with, Rome and Corinth. It seems in fact as if Paul's position on this issue was rather extreme. Of the six texts studied in this section, only Barnabas discusses the problem at all, arguing that a literal interpretation of the law is not only not obligatory, but downright wrong. He argues strongly for a non-literal, 'symbolic' interpretation of the Mosaic Law. On the other hand, Barnabas does not even mention Paul and his theological argument, to the effect that Jesus, as the Messiah, has superseded the Law.

The realisation that the first-century Church exhibited a wide diversity of opinions on various theological issues has been slow in coming, naturally enough, since the overwhelming majority of theological scholars – who have been practically alone in studying these matters in depth – have assumed that Christianity began with the preaching of a Jesus living in Palestine in the first three decades of the century.[23] I have insisted on the extremely weak foundation of that assumption and, conversely, on the plausibility of the hypothesis I am propounding here, namely, that Christianity started in those early decades as the result of ideas spread within a branch of the para-Essene Church of God in the Jewish Diaspora. The development of Christianity was not from unity to diversity, but on the contrary, from a diversity which existed all along within the Essene movement, and naturally also between the individual apostles, to the very deliberate attempts to establish a Christian orthodoxy towards the end of the second century AD.

The *Pastor* of Hermas: an allegory of the Church of God

The *Pastor* of Hermas,[24] though probably originating in Rome, is written in Greek, like all early Christian literature. It is not a theological treatise, but a kind of allegorical religious novel, dealing with the importance of repentance (*metanoia*) and of complete devotion to the Church, i.e. the community of the elect and holy ones. The book, of approximately 150 ordinary pages, is subdivided into three sections. In the first 5 chapters, *Visiones* (abbreviated: Vis), Hermas receives revelations which are explained to him by angelic beings, one of whom is the Pastor, who declares himself to be the Angel of Repentance. In some visions, the Church is represented as an old woman; in others as a stone tower under construction. The following 12 rather brief chapters, *Mandata* (Mand), contain sermons in which rules of moral conduct are expounded, partly through visions. Finally, the last 10 chapters, *Similitudines* (Sim), covering the whole of the second half of the book, contain parables which convey moral lessons, explained by angelic figures. The great number of these beings, often presented as hypostases of abstract powers or qualities, is typical of Gnostic writings (see Chapter 3).[25]

   I have already said that scholars' dating of Hermas[26] has been strongly influenced by the notice in the Muratori fragment (a list of early 'canonical' Christian writings), which says that Hermas was written quite recently by the brother of Pius, the bishop of Rome. We must bear in mind, however, first, that the commonly accepted date for the Greek original of the late Latin translation called the Muratori fragment, late second century, is by no means firmly established. In the last few years several scholars have advanced good grounds for placing it as late as the fourth century, which of course means that its notes about Hermas and Clement become even more suspect.[27]

Secondly, we do not know who wrote the note, and thus cannot examine his credentials. Accordingly, just as with 1 Clement, we had better try to find out what the text itself may tell us about its date. That Hermas was read widely in Christian circles is clear both from the references to it in Clemens Alexandrinus and Origen, and from the numerous papyrus fragments found. Its nearly canonical status is also indicated by its presence in the famous fourth-century Biblical MS Sinaiticus.[28] It is quoted as an authoritative Christian text by such influential Christian writers as Irenaeus, Tertullian, Clemens Alexandrinus and Origen. It is generally taken to have originated in Rome, because of its contents.

Let us begin with Hermas' mention of Clement, discussed above. Since we have found many other *independent* grounds for dating 1 Clement to the sixties of the first century, we now have a right to argue, without circularity, that the mention of Clement in Hermas yields support for placing the *Pastor* in the same period. Further support, although admittedly marginal, is provided by Paul's mention of Hermas as a member of one of the Roman communities which Paul was in touch with. We may add that one of our earliest witnesses, Origen, was convinced that the author of the *Pastor* was the Hermas mentioned by Paul in Romans 16:14. But of course none of this is conclusive.

The first four Visions of Hermas seem to imply that the community he belonged to had recently been subjected to persecutions (2–27, 3–1–9, 3–2–1; see also Sim 9–28–35). This might be a reference to the persecutions under Nero after AD 64, or to the troubles which the Jews were exposed to a few decades earlier under Caligula and under Claudius.[29]

Earlier scholars, and also our editor, Joly, have sometimes justified a mid-second-century dating of Hermas by maintaining that he has used the Gospels. However, the parallels suggested are not verbally exact, and we may either have to do with a common source or common sources, or, indeed, Hermas might be the source, or one of the sources used by the Gospel writers. If Hermas was written in the sixties, as I suggest, that would be the most likely explanation of the similarities.

Several passages in Hermas which have parallels in the Gospels, concern points of doctrine, morality and behaviour, but never Jesus as a person. In general, the christology of Hermas is extremely rarefied – one might almost say, nonexistent. In the first place, neither the name

Jesus, nor the designation Christ, occur anywhere in the text. The term Son of God (*ho huios tou theou*) occurs frequently, but it is explained in a very abstract manner. For instance, we read that the Son of God is the Law (Sim 8–3–2). Sometimes he is the Holy Ghost (Sim 9–1–1, 5–5–2), and he is said to have been born before the creation, and to have served as God's adviser (Sim 9–12–2, apparently referring to Prov 8:27). Such hypostases of God's 'potencies' were a common feature in Gnosticism and contemporary Hellenistic Judaism, e.g. Philo.[30]

In the early visions, the Church is represented as a woman. Later, she appears as a stone tower, built on a rock which is called the Son of God.[31] The tower is built of carefully selected stones which represent the members of the Church. Rather confusingly, the porch of the tower is also called the Son of God. Somewhat similar ideas are expressed by Paul, when he describes the church and the members of the church as parts of the body of Jesus Christ.[32] We also find similar ideas in the Gnosticising letters to the Colossians and Ephesians, whose Pauline status is, however, very doubtful. See Chapter 7.

Very little is said about the Son's possible human incarnation. In Sim 9–12–3, where the Son of God is symbolised as a gate in the tower representing the Church, the Son, though 'born before the Creation', is said to have 'become manifest in the last days of the dispensation [*ep' eschatōn tōn hēmeron tēs synteleias phanēros egeneto*)'. Here the word dispensation, which translates *synteleia*, suggests that the course of history is preordained by God, a widespread idea in antiquity, characteristic of both Christianity and Stoicism. In the Hermas context, this 'manifestation' might well be the establishment of the Church of God. Moreover, 'the last days' very often was a phrase used about the final epoch of the number which made up the predestined history of the universe (see Chapter 4).

The most elaborate reference to what might be an incarnation is found in Similitude 5:6, which contains the parable of the master who left a vineyard in the care of his servants. A similar parable is found in all the Synoptics (Mt 21:33; 25:14, Mk 12:1, Lk 19:12; 20:9). Ultimately, the parable might go back to Isaiah 5, where the deterioration of the vineyard is explained as God's punishment because the workers, Israel, have not obeyed his law. In Hermas' version the focus is shifted to the Son (not mentioned explicitly in Isa 5, where it is presumably Israel as a whole that is the 'Son of God'), who by hard and painful labour restores the vineyard, that is, 'redeems the sins of the people' (Sim 5–6–2). 'Nobody can cultivate a vineyard without pain and fatigue.' That is the nearest we get to a possible allusion to the passion of Christ. To my mind, such an interpretation of the text appears very far-fetched. We can hardly take Hermas' parable of the vineyard as a development of the versions in the Synoptics. As, moreover, the Hermas version is nearer to its probable origin in Isaiah 5, it is natural to infer that the Hermas story is either older than the Synoptics, or at least independent of them. Here again, therefore, we have an indication that Hermas should be dated early, earlier than the Gospels.[33]

We also read (5–6–5) that God has caused the Holy Ghost, 'which has created everything', to 'inhabit the flesh which he had chosen [*eis sarka hēn ebouleto*]'. It is of course possible to regard this passage as a reference to Jesus, and it is natural that later Christian readers of Hermas did so. But the passage can also be interpreted as aiming at *any* individual member of the community of 'elect ones', or indeed the community as a whole. The more so as such an idea is expressed quite clearly at other places (e.g. Mand 5–1–2: 'the holy Ghost who inhabits you'; Sim 5–6–7: 'All flesh ... where the holy Ghost has found its dwelling place.' Again, this way of looking at the working of the Spirit is similar to that of Paul, and also of the Gnostics (see Chapters 3 and 12).

Though the Church occupies a central place in the *Pastor*, we do not discover any elaborate ecclesiastical hierarchy. Precisely as in 1 Clement, no distinction seems to be made between bishops and other church functionaries. See Vis 3–5–1: 'apostles, bishops, teachers and deacons', and Sim 9–27–2 'bishops and people who welcome guests in their houses'. Note, as in 1 Clement, the plural: we are still far from the monarchical bishop that we find, for instance, in Ignatius.

Hermas never names Paul or any other apostle: in Sim 9–15–4 the number of apostles is stated to be forty. Hermas' very rudimentary theology does not suggest any Pauline influences. On the other hand, he refers to his community in the same way as Paul does (and, for that matter, Clemens Romanus also): the church of God (*ekklēsia tou theou*), the elect of God. All this fits in well with an early dating, while the absence of any mention of Jesus, or even Christ, is, to say the least, highly surprising if the text was produced in the second century.[34]

Several scholars have remarked on the strong Jewish flavour of the *Pastor*. Our editor, Joly, mentions[35] that the nineteenth-century German theologian Spitta maintained that the book was originally a

Jewish work, which had later been 'violently christianised'. Joly calls this a 'dangerous and useless hypothesis'.

I do not agree. We may admit that the several centuries during which Hermas' book was in Christian hands may have left traces. But surprisingly few such traces can be pin-pointed. Even as it stands today, the text can best be read as directed to a wholly, or almost wholly, Jewish community with an eschatologically flavoured Messianic orientation. For instance, the *Parousia* (appearance)[36] is not the arrival of Christ, but of God (*despotēs*, Sim 5–5–3). That is of course the traditional Jewish view of the Last Judgment. And, though Joly often takes the word *kurios* to refer to the Son of God, it is in most cases equally, or more, natural to interpret it as God, as a Jew would. Further, like the *Didachē*, and also like several Qumran documents, and also the Gospels, Hermas uses the term hypocrite to refer to Jewish opponents who are apparently Pharisees.

Characterising the Holy Ghost as the Son of God, and as God's assistant at the Creation, and as intimately linked with the Law (Sim 8–3–2) is also far more compatible with contemporary Jewish ideas than with mainstream Christian ones of the second century and later. Philo and the rich Enoch literature, loved by the Essenes, provide examples. I return to this question in Chapter 5.

There are also direct indications in the text that the Roman community of Hermas was almost wholly Jewish.[37] Outsiders are called 'gentiles and sinners'[38] (Sim 4–4), and neighbours are criticised for having 'acquired too high a renown among the gentiles' (Sim 8–9–1). Such expressions are quite natural in an all-Jewish community. But they would be inappropriate if the community included even a small minority of non-Jews. However, it must be stressed that Hermas is a universalist in the sense that he wishes to include the gentiles in the Church. Thus in Sim 9–17–1 an angel explains to him a vision of twelve multicoloured mountains. These mountains, says the angel, represent the twelve tribes 'which divide the world among them, and form twelve nations [*ethnē*]'. The Son of God, the angel continues, was 'preached to them by the apostles ... all the nations have accepted the name of the Son of God'. The Son of God should here presumably be taken to be the Law, or God's word – an interpretation which goes well with the verb 'preach' (*ekēruchthē*). The underlying idea seems to be a world completely obedient to the Law, led by the elect – members of the Church of God – who are self-evidently taken to belong to the 'twelve tribes' of Israel.[39]

It seems clear to me that previous writers have been very much misled by their assumption that Hermas is late (second century AD or even later), and have tried to make sense of it against the background of second-century Christianity. If we accept it as much earlier, and the people it addresses as members of a basically Essene, predominantly Diaspora Jewish Church of God, everything falls neatly into place.[40]

Instructions for the Gentiles: *Didachē*

The full Greek text of *Didachē tōn apostolōn*, the Teaching of the Apostles, a brief treatise setting forth precepts of morality and conduct, as well as liturgical rules, was discovered in 1873 in Constantinople. In spite of its modest size (some ten ordinary pages), the Didachē is not a unified whole. The first six chapters form a moral treatise, usually designated *Duae Viae*, major portions of which are also found in *Doctrina apostolorum* and in the Letter of Barnabas.[41] A few short passages from it are also incorporated in Hermas' *Pastor*. Most scholars nowadays regard the *Duae Viae* as a pre-Christian, purely Jewish work, apparently used as a kind of manual of instruction in synagogal schools. The two Ways are the Good one and the Evil one, or the way of Light and the way of Darkness. The dualism has clear affinities with the doctrines of the Qumran community.[42]

But while the Qumran community was exclusive and indeed xenophobic, Didachē is, like Hermas, universalistic and proselytising. It may be that the *Duae Viae* that we have here was designed as a sort of preliminary instruction for proselytes in the Diaspora. The subtitle of the text in the H manuscript says precisely that: 'The teaching of the Lord for the Gentiles' (*Didachē kuriou tois ethnesin*).[43]

The manuscript, written in 1056, is now in Jerusalem, and therefore bears the siglum H (for *Hierosolymitanus*). It contained, besides Didachē, also the Letter of Barnabas, the Letters of Clement, and the Letters of Ignatius. It seems probable that H was copied from a much older MS, perhaps of the fourth or fifth century.

Besides H, however, we possess fragments and more or less free translations of the text, some of which are older than H: the *Doctrina apostolorum* in Latin, as well as Coptic and Ethiopian versions. These translations, as well as mentions or allusions by early Church fathers, such as Justin Martyr, in the mid-second century, Clement of Alexandria in the late second, and Eusebius in the fourth, indicate that Didachē was well known in the early Church, particularly in the East.

Though many modern scholars place Didachē in the second century, my own preferred dating of the core parts of it is the middle of the first century AD. The first modern commentators, among them Adolf Harnack (1851–1930), the leading German theologian of his time, assigned a mid-second-century date to the text. Later editors, including J. P. Audet (1958) and W. Rordorf and A. Tuilier (1978), have found grounds for placing it in the first century, in Audet's case roughly between 50 and 70 for the original.[44] If that is correct, the Didachē would be one of the earliest Christian texts, and contemporary with Paul.[45]

The original title, which Audet, on the strength of various early mentions, believes was 'Teachings of the Apostles' (*Didachai tōn apostolōn*), was modified by various later writers into 'The teaching of the twelve apostles', a title which naturally suggests that we have to do with the twelve disciples of Christ, famous from the Gospels and Acts. One late version of the text even went so far as to assign different parts of it to each of those disciples (Judas excluded). In the actual text no apostle is ever named, not even Paul.

After the *Duae Viae*, mentioned above, follow five chapters containing instructions for community services and prayers, and finally practical advice on the treatment of itinerant apostles and missionaries.

In a few places the process by which the text was Christianised can be discerned when different versions of the text are compared. Thus while the H manuscript has, in 10:6, *Hosanna tōi theōi David* (Hosanna to the God of David) which is of course decidedly Jewish, other manuscripts, for *theōi* (God), offer *oikōi* (house) and, more significantly, *huiōi* (son). The latter, which is certainly Christian, changing the reference from God to Jesus, is the phrase found in Matthew 21:9,15.

In 14:1 the H manuscript has the tautological *kata kuriakēn de kuriou*, which literally translated is 'on the Lords' Lord's day'. Audet, emends the phrase to *kat' hēmeran de kuriou*, 'on the Lord's day', where 'the Lord' can, and I think should, be taken as God himself.[46] Another manuscript offers *tēn anastasimon tou kuriou hēmeran*, 'the day of our Lord's resurrection', where the Lord is equally clearly Christ. Again, therefore, the reference has changed from God to Jesus, indicating a Christian emendation.

It is not always the H manuscript that contains what seems to be the oldest reading. Thus in 12:4, H has 'do not allow a Christian [*christianos*] to live in idleness among you'. Here the Ethiopian version omits 'Christian', saying simply 'do not let him'. As no text which is reliably dated before 100 ever uses the word *Christian*, we may take it that the H version here has a Christian interpolation.

In several cases, of course, we may suspect a Christian interpolation without being able to adduce variant readings as support. In 9:5, we read: 'do not let anybody eat or drink at the eucharist, if he is not baptised in the name of the Lord [*eis onoma kuriou*]'. Especially without the definite article, *kurios* normally refers to God. In two other places, however, we find the trinitarian formula 'in the name of the Father, the Son and the Holy Ghost' (7:1, 3). It is possible that this is a later Christian interpolation, though we should keep in mind that Hellenistic philosophers in general were fond of postulating under-lying substances, *hypostases*, for whatever conceptual qualities they found important. Thus to many Hellenistic Jews and early Christians, the Trinity concept must have seemed quite natural. It is also important to keep in mind that the rite of baptism was at the time also an important, even decisive rite of initiation into Judaism.[47]

Even with the undoubted Christianisation that the text has undergone, Didachē remains, in most respects, a very Jewish text. The only place where the word Christ (Jesus Christ) occurs (9:4) is one where several manuscripts omit it. Hence we have reason to regard it as a Christian interpolation.

Otherwise Jesus is mentioned four times, all of them in chapters 9 and 10. Remarkably, he is called neither Christ, nor the Son of God, but the Child, or boy, or servant (*pais*) of God, i.e. the designation normally used for the Old Testament prophets, and also Moses, in the Septuagint. And Jesus does not appear as a Saviour, nor as a Judge, but as the one through whom God has revealed truths – including faith in immortality. In other words, Jesus in Didachē appears as a prophet and teacher, not as the Messiah. Such a view of Jesus would be entirely compatible with a purely Jewish, pre-Christian outlook – and with the Teacher of Righteousness of the Essenes. As we have seen, there are also indications in Paul and 1 Clement that the Church of God members may have regarded Jesus precisely as a prophet and teacher, before Paul and his colleagues came along to raise him to the position of the Messiah. Didachē gives some support to this conclusion.

It is therefore interesting to note that, in spite of this, the text contains many passages which have parallels in the Gospels, although the wording makes it clear that they do not depend directly on the Gospels. The largest number of these parallels occur in 1:3–2:2, where we discover half a dozen parallels with the Sermon on the Mount.[48] In the Didachē text, however, they are presented as ordinary moral precepts, without being attributed to Jesus.

In Did 8 we also find the whole of the Lord's Prayer. That should not be taken as implying that it is taken from the Gospels (Mt 6:9–13, Lk 11:2–14), where the prayer is laid in Jesus' mouth. As scholars have noted, the prayer has close parallels in older Jewish writings.[49] Thus, for example, the Lord's Prayer begins (quoted from Matthew 6.9 ff): 'Our Father which art in heaven, hallowed be thy name . . . Thy kingdom come'. In the Qaddish, a well-known Jewish prayer (see *Encyclopaedia Judaica* under Kaddish) we read: 'Glorified and sanctified be God's great name throughout the world . . . May he establish his kingdom'. In Didachē the prayer is introduced by the words: 'Do not pray as do the hypocrites, but as the Lord has demanded in his gospel'. 'The Lord' here, as in many other places, presumably means God rather than Jesus. In the same way, 'his gospel' should be interpreted as the Gospel of God, as I argue below.

The term *hypocrite*, used also by Hermas and in Qumran, apparently about Pharisees,[50] is found also in 8:1: 'do not fast at the same time as do the hypocrites: they fast the second and fifth day of the week. You should fast on the fourth day and on the day of the preparation of the Sabbath.' This passage suggests that the Didachē, at least in this respect, uses the calendar favoured by the Essenes.[51] The Essene fasting days were taken over by the Christians: Wednesday and Friday.

The term gospel (*euaggelion*) might seem to indicate one of the Synoptics, where of course the Lord's Prayer occurs. But in Didachē the word *gospel* is clearly used in another meaning than the one applying to the Canonical Gospels.[52] There are three other occurrences of the word: 'As to apostles and prophets, do according to the precepts [*dogma*] in the gospel' (11:7). 'Reprove each other, but not in anger, but in peace, as you have it in the gospel' (15:3). 'As for your prayers, your alms, and all your acts, do as you have it in the gospel of our Lord' (15:4). In all these instances the word 'gospel' seems to refer to a written text, available to the communities which Didachē addresses. That text is evidently concerned with advice on religious practice and behaviour. Accordingly we seem to have to do with a kind of handbook of precepts, not with a text of the kind that the canonical

Gospels exemplify. In fact, we may take 'gospel' in Didachē to refer to the class of *florilegia*, anthologies of Biblical passages, which were evidently popular reading among the Saints, whether Essene or Christian. See the sections on Barnabas and Hebrews in this chapter, and Chapter 4.

We should observe also that when Didachē speaks of 'the gospel of our Lord', the word Lord (*kurios*) can, and in the earliest versions of course should, be interpreted as God, rather than as Christ – the more so, as the gospel in effect consisted of the Church's interpretation of appropriate passages in the Old Testament, God's Word. The expression the Gospel of God, as we have seen, is also to be found in Paul (e.g. Rom 1:1). It is worth pointing out that Paul also uses the term *gospel* in a similar sense, different from that prevalent in the second-century Church.

According to the subtitle of the H manuscript, Didachē was 'God's teaching to the gentiles' (*tois ethnesin*). But the addressees were called 'saints', which is the term that practically all first-century writers – but as we have seen, not the canonical Gospels – use about their communities, which are certainly in the main Jewish. Given the strong Jewish character of Didachē, we may assume the same for at least most of its addressees. They were, we may infer, Jewish Diaspora communities, who lived among the gentiles and had to accommodate to that situation. One possibility is that *tois ethnesin* should be taken in a geographical, rather than in a religious sense, including both Jews and Gentiles in the Diaspora. We have found what seems to be a related usage in Hermas, when he speaks about the 'twelve tribes' – clearly the tribes of Israel – forming 'nations' (*ethnē*) in the world at large. Paul also may have a similar usage, for instance, in Romans 1:6, where the Jews whom he addressed seem to be included among the Gentiles.[53]

Barnabas: a Hellenistic–Jewish theological treatise

The Letter of Barnabas is not a proper letter, but rather a theological treatise, which concentrates on two principal themes. The first, mainly developed in chapters 5–7, is concerned with explaining the incarnation and passion of Jesus as a fulfilment, in detail, of sayings in the Scriptures which are taken to be divinely inspired prophecies about him. This is a practice we have drawn attention to in the section about 1 Clement, above. Barnabas uses it much more extensively, and may be said to carry to an extreme what occurs as a minor theme in the canonical Gospels, especially Matthew and John, who often claim that an episode in Jesus' history took place in order to fulfil a prophecy in the Old Testament.[54] But whereas the Gospel writers place Jesus' words and deeds in a continuous story of his life on earth, Barnabas just quotes Scripture passages, asserting, without adducing any evidence, that they are meant to apply to Jesus. Clement and, as we shall see, the Letter to the Hebrews do the same, though on a smaller scale.[55]

The Letter of Barnabas is placed by most scholars in the first half of the second century, although with much hesitation.[56] A reference (16:3) which almost certainly refers to the Roman occupation of Jerusalem indicates that it was written after 70. The fact that the letter contains a version of the Jewish moral treatise *Duae Viae*, parts of which are also found in the Didachē, is of little help for the dating. The same may be said about a parallel with Jewish apocalypse in 4 Ezra, fairly securely dated to the end of the first century AD. As Barnabas does not at any point quote or refer to the Gospel story, it seems to me natural to infer that his treatise was composed before the Gospels had come into being, i.e. before the second century AD. The most probable date, I would say, would be fairly soon after AD 70.[57]

The second main theme, developed mainly in chapters 2–3, 9–10 and 15–16, is to argue for a non-literal, allegorical or symbolic interpretation of the Mosaic Law, and indeed, for a complete rejection of the literal interpretation, which is declared to be wholly false (2:10; 3:6). On this point Barnabas goes much farther than Paul – whose name, by the way, never occurs in the text. There is no reason to believe that the author of the letter is to be identified with the Barnabas that Paul mentions at several places in his correspondence. He certainly does not give any prominence to the idea which Paul insists on so strenuously, namely, the contrast between 'the works of the law' and 'faith'.[58]

Barnabas takes the incarnation, crucifixion and resurrection of Christ for granted. But he has extremely little to say about Jesus' earthly life, though he asserts that Jesus 'taught Israel and performed miracles and signs' (5:8). Somewhat surprisingly, Jesus is also said to have chosen as apostles 'the worst of sinners', in order to make it clear that 'he had not come in order to call the righteous, but the sinners'. The latter idea is also found in Matthew 9:13 and Mark 2:17. These authors put the words in Jesus' mouth, but certainly do not represent the disciples or apostles as great sinners. Barnabas' statement is the most extreme, however, and may perhaps be due to his Diaspora perspective: the Diaspora Jews, who often interpreted the Mosaic law allegorically, may have felt that many other Jews did regard them as sinners because of their slackness in Law observance, though of course they themselves would not agree.

In fact, Barnabas, like the other writers in our group of six, never refers to any eyewitnesses of Jesus' earthly life. No disciples are ever referred to individually: we must keep in mind that *apostle*, in first-century texts, means 'missionary', not 'disciple'. Nor does he ever claim to quote any actual saying by Jesus, at least not explicitly.

Under the circumstances it is natural that we find nothing about Mary and Joseph, nor about Pilate, nor about the trial of Jesus. Perhaps more surprisingly, Barnabas argues explicitly against Jesus' Davidic origin (12:9–11).[59] In support he quotes Psalm 110: 'The Lord said unto my Lord, Sit thou at my right hand.' Barnabas comments (12:11) 'So David calls him Lord, and not son!' The argument, which presupposes that 'my Lord' here refers to Christ, may appear somewhat lame, and very formalistic. But we should remember that the Psalms were generally ascribed to David himself. On this point, as on several others, Barnabas is in line with the Gnostics: Jesus, as God's son, is essentially a divine hypostasis. Therefore he cannot have a human father. (Barnabas does not even consider the mother.)

Another point where Barnabas takes a different line both from Paul and from the Gospels is the resurrection. He explains the communities' celebration of the Sunday, 'the eighth day', by saying (15:9) that it was 'also the day when Jesus was resurrected from the dead, and after having appeared, rose to the heavens' (*en hēi kai Iēsous anestē ek nekrōn kai phanērōtheis anebē eis ouranous*).[60] The resurrection and the ascension thus took place on the same day. As Barnabas advances his views on all these matters without making any attempt to argue against other ideas, it is natural to surmise that he did not know about those. This, again, is fairly strong evidence that his text originated before the second century. His quite explicit reference to the destruction of the Temple (16:3) implies that it was written after AD 70.

Scholars are generally agreed that Barnabas, like many other Jewish writers of the time, often relied on collections of Scriptural sayings, *florilegia*, rather than resorting to the Bible itself.[61] It is a fact, in any case, that Barnabas' references to the Scriptures are very often composite ones, combining material from several different Biblical books, including non-canonical ones. In many cases the references cannot be located at all. This is not surprising, since it is obvious that much of the non-canonical literature – taken to be authoritative and Biblical, and often worked into the *florilegia* material – that circulated at the time has been lost without trace. We discuss this further in Chapter 5.

Barnabas' second main topic, as we said, is the allegorical interpretation of the Mosaic Law. The most important regulation, in many respects, was that on circumcision. Barnabas explains: 'Abraham, who was the first to practise circumcision, did so because the Spirit directed his eyes prophetically, by giving him instructions about three letters' (9:7). The three letters are explained as denoting the number of men said to be circumcised by Abraham, 318, which in Greek is written T (300), I (10) and H (8). Barnabas interprets IH as IH (SOUS), Jesus,[62] while T is taken to be a symbol of the cross. This kind of fanciful play with figures and symbols was not at all uncommon in antiquity. The Pythagoreans, with their highly developed number mysticism, conferred a kind of philosophical respectability to it, and Philo Judaeus practises it at several places, though of course not in the present case, as he knows nothing about Jesus.

Barnabas' metaphorical interpretations of the Law must appear to the modern reader as wild fantasies. For instance, he takes up the prohibition against eating pork, saying 'This is the meaning . . . Do not seek the company of those people who are like swine, forgetting God while they live in abundance, but remember him when they are in need' (10:3). Further, we read about the prohibition against eating the hare: 'This means: do not practise pederasty . . . for the hare adds each year to the number of his anal orifices' (10:6). Again, this kind of popular fantasy about animals was widespread in antiquity (and beyond). The elder Pliny's *Natural History* provides plenty of examples.

About Moses' exhortation to eat ruminant animals with a cloven hoof, Barnabas says: 'Seek the company of those who fear God . . . and who meditate on the Lord's word . . . cloven hoof . . . means that the righteous [*dikaios*] walks in this world in expectation of the holy era [*ton hagion aiōna*]' (10:11).

Finally, Barnabas also finds Scriptural support for not observing the Sabbath, and to celebrate Sunday instead. Interpreting Psalm 90:4 in an eschatological sense, he concludes (15:9) that the rules for keeping the sabbath are really meant for the time after the Day of Judgment, when God will start a new era 'on the eighth day', i.e. Sunday. This also seems to be the reason why he locates the resurrection of Jesus, which of course marks the beginning of a new era, on a Sunday.[63]

Barnabas' placing of Christ's resurrection on a Sunday should therefore not be taken to have come from some 'tradition' about this event: no first-century writer, as we have seen, says anything about when the resurrection occurred. Barnabas is the first, and it is significant that he adduces a theological reason for his assertion – which, moreover, does not implicate a date, but a day of the week. We should note that he places the theological reason first ('the eighth day' marking the beginning of the new era), and then adds, 'this is also [*kai*] the day when Jesus was resurrected'.[64] There are indications that the celebration of Sunday as a holiday originated in the Essene calendar, which, starting from Pentecost (itself fifty days after Easter Sunday) introduced a further two feast days falling on a Sunday, at fifty-day intervals.[65] Hence they had four consecutive feast days all falling on a Sunday: Easter, Pentecost, Wine and Oil.

Just as we do not know who Barnabas was, we do not know who his addressees were, except what we can infer from the text itself. Unfortunately the information we can collect is somewhat contradictory. In 16:7 we read: 'Before we believed in God, our hearts ... vomited idolatry, and were nothing but the habitations of demons.' This seems to indicate quite unambiguously that the receivers, and for that matter Barnabas himself, had been pagans, gentiles.

But things are not quite so straightforward. First of all, the central theme of the letter, namely, adducing Scriptural support for Jesus' incarnation and passion, as well as for his teaching, presupposes that the addressees were thoroughly acquainted with the Jewish Scriptures, and with Jewish ways of interpreting them.

Secondly, the last four chapters contain a fairly complete version of the purely Jewish treatise *Duae Viae*. As Prigent and Kraft say, the ideas expounded there fit in very well with the earlier portions of the Barnabas text.

Thirdly, in 3:6 Barnabas writes that 'we must not, *in the manner of proselytes* [my italics] hit our heads against their law'. He seems here to use proselyte to refer to Gentile converts to mainstream Judaism, whereas he looks upon the members of the Church of God – his own church – as a homogeneous group, whether of Jewish or Gentile descent. Thus Barnabas distances himself clearly from the Jews outside the Church of God. For instance, when he says in 16:4 'because of *their* [my italics] war, the temple was destroyed', the word 'their' presumably indicates the Jewish insurgents in Palestine. And of course his firm rejection of a literal interpretation of the law implies a clean break with those Jews who adhered to them faithfully.

At the same time, however, we probably have to recognise that the question of the interpretation of the Mosaic law was not generally such a contentious issue among the Jews of the first century, at least in the Diaspora, as Paul and the Gospels may have led us to believe. For instance, 1 Clement does not refer to the subject at all, nor does Hermas, nor Didachē, all of them, in my view, roughly contemporary with Paul.

Moreover, we may point to the attitude of Philo (*c.* 20 BC–AD 40), whose interpretation of the Bible is in general of the allegorical type. Philo agrees that the law about the Sabbath and the circumcision should indeed be interpreted allegorically. But this does not mean, he says, that we should disregard the literal meaning (see Chapter 3). We have no reason to think that Philo's position on this matter was unique among the Jews of the time.

Thus Barnabas' treatment of the Mosaic law does not necessarily mean that his addressees were not Jews. Later Christian readers of the text have of course taken them to be Christians. To be sure, they were Christians in the sense that they took Jesus to be Christ. But Barnabas' christology is very thin, though not quite so thin as that of Hermas. We should also note how he describes his community: they are the elect, the saints, the righteous ones, the perfect – all of them words used by Paul and other early writers about the members of their community – but also, we should remember, by the Essenes.

The Letter to the Hebrews: a sermon on Psalm 110

All the texts we have dealt with so far were eventually eliminated from the canon, though they continued to be read and copied in some parts of the Christian world. We shall turn now to two texts which were eventually included in the canon, though only after considerable resistance: the Letter to the Hebrews, and the Revelation of John.[66]

The Letter to the Hebrews, like the Letter of Barnabas, is a theological treatise rather than an ordinary letter. Its main thrust is to emphasise the importance of complete fidelity to the Church of God, and the dire consequences of apostasy.

As in many other cases, the best indicator of the date of Hebrews is provided by its references to the Temple of Jerusalem, whose destruction was obviously, among Jews, the most momentous event of the first century AD. One of the prominent theological tenets of Hebrews is that the arrival of Christ had not only superseded the traditional service of the Temple priests, but had also established a new Temple, a spiritual one, which is founded in the hearts of the members of the community of 'saints'. When contrasting the new with the old order of things, the author of Hebrews emphasises that Christ offered himself as a sacrifice only once, while 'the high priest entereth into the holy place *every year* [my italics] with blood of others' (9:25). A little further on we read: 'in those sacrifices there is a remembrance made every year' (10:3).

A similar picture is implied by 10:11: 'Every priest standeth daily ministering and offering oftentimes the same sacrifices.' Nobody, I think, whether Jew or not, could express himself in this way without any comment at all after the fall of Jerusalem and the destruction of the Temple in AD 70.[67] As moreover these passages are part of a central theological argument in the text, we must conclude that Hebrews was written before AD 70. I find nothing in the text itself which would contradict this conclusion. It is also the conclusion of many modern commentators.[68] My own dating of the letter is *c.* AD 60.

The theology of Hebrews, and the way in which the author argues for it, is very similar to that of Barnabas. In both cases the authors present and defend what they consider to be the essential theology of the 'New Covenant', based on Jesus Christ, who has sacrificed himself for the salvation of those who put their faith in him. C. Spicq 1972–5, pp. 451–4 calls it, very properly, 'a *midrash* [commentary] on Psalm 110'.

The main feature of the argument, in both Barnabas and Hebrews, is to take up Old Testament passages, which are then interpreted as either aiming at Jesus, or as uttered by him. In this way we get a fairly full account of the essential characteristics of Jesus. But no historical evidence is ever adduced. No contemporary witnesses of Jesus' life on earth are ever appealed to. There is no indication when 'the days of his flesh' (1:2) had been, except for vague statements: 'in the last days'

60

(1:2), and 'now once in the end of the world hath he appeared to put away sin by the sacrifice of himself' (9:26). In the historical philosophy of those days, with its subdivision of universal history into a limited number of eras, the 'last days' generally meant the last of the eras – a period of usually several thousand years. No exact date was ever intended. Hence the numerous prophecies could never be proved wrong.

No apostles are named, except Jesus himself, who is called 'apostle and High Priest' (3:1). We read that 'Unto us was the gospel preached, as well as unto them' (i.e. the non-believers) (4:2). But we are not told when, and by whom. On these points Hebrews is a little less forthcoming than Barnabas, who after all does at least say that Jesus chose apostles, and refers to 'the twelve' – though not by name. And while Barnabas at least mentions that Jesus 'performed miracles and signs', Hebrews says nothing about this, though 2:4 conveys a somewhat similar idea: 'God also bearing them witness, both with signs and wonders, and with divers miracles, and gifts of the Holy Ghost'. Also, Hebrews has nothing specific at all to say about the resurrection.

It is interesting to note that Hebrews differs from Paul (who is not mentioned) in omitting any obvious references to *visions* of the heavenly Christ. In the main, Old Testament references are enough for the author of Hebrews, just as for Barnabas.[69]

Though Barnabas and Hebrews are very similar both in outlook and method of argumentation, they differ markedly in one respect. While Barnabas argues vigorously against a literal and for an allegorical interpretation of the Law, Hebrews does not enter into that kind of discussion at all. On this point Hebrews resembles 1 Clement.

Hebrews does not dwell on the eschatological (End-time) expectation of the Last Judgment, but its author clearly expected it in the near future. In this he agrees with all the other documents in our group of six, and of course with Paul. In 10:37 he quotes Habakkuk 2:3: 'yet a little while, and he that shall come will come, and will not tarry'. But the Last Judgment is not a topic that occupies a front position in his mind. The author of Hebrews is a man of learning and a thoughtful theologian. But he was apparently not, like Paul, an enthusiastic seer.

On one point Hebrews advances arguments which are hardly found at all among his contemporaries. This is when the author combines the idea of Jesus as a High Priest with the general assumption that he should belong to the tribe of Judah, 'of which tribe Moses spake nothing concerning priesthood' (7:14). Hebrews solves the problem by referring (by means of Ps. 110:4) to Melchizedek, who was made 'an high priest forever' (6:20) although he was 'without father, without mother, without descent' (7:3). No such information about Melchizedek is found in the canonical books which mention him (Gen 14:18, and Ps. 110:4). Fragments of a text (11 Q Melch) concerning Melchizedek, however, have been discovered among the Dead Sea Scrolls. The fragment is not very informative but in 2 Enoch Melchizedek appears as a Messianic figure (see Chapter 6). The writer of Hebrews, like other New Testament writers, was probably acquainted with the Enoch literature, much of which we know has been destroyed. Barnabas, we may recall, took the line that Jesus, as son of God, could not be 'son of David', which was otherwise the predominant view among the Jews at the time. Clement, for his part, solved the problem by assuming that the earthly Jesus, Jesus 'in the flesh', descended from Jacob, thus avoiding a choice between Levi, who started the priestly line, and Judah, who started the royal line.[70]

Hebrews returns repeatedly (6:6, 10:26, 12:25) to the question of apostasy, that is, how community members who abandoned the Church should be treated – a subject which also troubled Hermas, as we have seen. Hebrews takes a hard line: 'It is impossible, for those who were once enlightened . . . if they fall away, to renew them again unto repentance, seeing they crucify to themselves the Son of God afresh' (6:4–6). 'For if we sin wilfully after that we have received the knowledge of the truth, there remaineth no more sacrifice for sins' (10:26). 'For if they escaped not [the judgment] who refused him that spake on earth, much more shall not we escape, if we turn away from him that speaketh from heaven' (12:25). It is of interest that Philo also viewed apostasy as unforgivable.[71]

As Hebrews is not really a letter, but a theological treatise, we should not expect any receivers to be addressed directly. But the use of expressions like the saints, the elect, the righteous, and exhortations to seek fellowship within the community and to practise hospitality, indicate the same sort of audience as the other texts treated here.[72] A firm organisation of the community is implied by 13:17: 'Obey them that have the rule over you, and submit yourselves, for they watch for your souls.' This attitude resembles that of Clemens Romanus in his letter to the sister church at Corinth.

The Revelation of John: Messianic hopes

The first three chapters of the Revelation of John consist chiefly of letters to seven individual churches, all of them in the western part of Asia Minor.[73] The letters are partly based on visions – hence the name Apocalypse (the Greek *apokaluptō* means literally uncover, more particularly, uncover the secrets of God about the future). Chapters 4–22 set out one continuous vision, which purports to be a prophecy about things to come. The prophecy spells doom and disaster for the rulers of the present world, i. e. the Romans, and forecasts the eventual victory of God.

I date John's Revelation to AD 70, in agreement with a substantial number of modern scholars. It is regularly placed at the end of the New Testament. Many Churchmen, among them Martin Luther, have been hesitant about including it at all, and it must be admitted that it is rather different both in style and content from the other New Testament books. It has been the subject of innumerable commentaries and interpretations, by scholars, and perhaps above all by amateurs, who have been fascinated by, and have often extended, the fantastic number and symbol magic of the book. In spite of the allegory, the document has value for the historian.

No definite events or names are mentioned whereby we might date the text. There are, however, veiled hints which may provide some help. The most promising is a passage which can be interpreted as a reference to the Roman siege of Jerusalem: 'Measure the temple of God. . . . But the court which is without the temple leave out . . . for it is given to the Gentiles, and the holy city shall they tread under foot forty and two months' (11:1–2). As we know that Jerusalem fell in AD 70, and continued to be kept by the Romans for hundreds of years afterwards, it seems reasonable to infer that the passage was written during the siege, but before the fall of the city.[74]

The figure 42 months, incidentally, returns at several places in Revelation, expressed in various ways: 42 months (11:2, 13:5); 1260 days (12:5); 'A time, times, and half a time' (presumably $1+2+\frac{1}{2}$, three and a half years, 12:14). In 11:11 we read about three and a half days. Thus in all these instances the figure three and a half is involved in some ways, and it may be worth considering that it is exactly half of seven, a holy figure for most Jews, and emphatically so for the Essenes. This kind of number juggling is a common feature in the esoteric, 'hermetic', literature of the time, and also elsewhere, for instance, in Philo. Revelation probably had the figure 42 from Daniel 7:25 and 12:7.

Some support for our dating may be found also in 17:10, where the reference is fairly unambiguously to Roman emperors: 'There are seven kings: five are fallen, and one is, and the other is not, and when he cometh, he must continue a short space.' The five that are fallen can be interpreted as Julius Caesar, Augustus, Tiberius, Caligula, Claudius. The sixth then would be Nero. We would then, perhaps, arrive at a date close to Nero's death, in AD 69.[75]

This dating also agrees well with the author's violently expressed hatred towards the Romans in general, and towards one particular Roman ruler, who is represented as a beast, who demands that all his subjects worship his image, and persecutes to death those who refuse. All this fits very well with Nero.

The Jewish background of both the author and his audience comes out very strongly. In the letter to the church at Ephesus the angel is made to say 'I know the blasphemy of them which say they are Jews, but are the synagogue of Satan' (2:9, and similarly in the letter to Sardis, 3:9). This kind of expression, also found, for instance, in the Sibylline Oracles, the bulk of which is unmistakably Hellenistic–Jewish,[76] obviously implies that the author regards 'Jew' as an honorific, and assumes that his audience does the same. In other words: they, or at least a substantial majority of them, are Jews. This in itself provides an excellent explanation for the author's strong anti-Roman feelings, and further reinforces our conclusion about dating the text at the culmination of the great Jewish rebellion against the Romans in 66–74.

There are also other indications of the Jewishness of Revelation. In chapter 7 we read about angels putting the 'seal of the living God' (7:2) on the foreheads of the assembled cohorts of the twelve tribes of Israel, 144,000 altogether (i.e. 12x12,000), 'which came out of the great tribulation' (7:14). Further, when describing the New Jerusalem, the writer says that the twelve gates of the city wall bear the names of the 'twelve tribes of the children of Israel' (21:12). Further, on the foundation of the gates were written 'the names of the apostles of the Lamb' (21:14). Much of this is quite similar to the War Scroll (1QM) from Qumran.[77]

At the same time there is certainly no doubt that the author is a Christian. Jesus Christ, so named, is introduced as 'the faithful witness, and the first begotten of the dead . . . that loved us, and washed our sins in his own blood' (1:5). We also read about 'the Lion of Juda, the Root of David' (5:5), and Jesus himself is made to say: 'I am the root and offspring of David, and the bright morning Star' (22:16), no doubt referring to the oft-quoted Messianic prophecy in Numbers 24:17, about the Star out of Jacob.

But beside the bare references to Jesus' Davidic descent, to his sacrificial death, and to his resurrection, we find absolutely nothing about Jesus' earthly life. An intriguing statement is found in 11:8, which talks about 'the great city, which spiritually is called Sodom and Egypt, where also our Lord [*ho Kurios*, ''the Lord''] was crucified'. This is the only mention of the crucifixion in Revelation. What is meant by 'the great city' is obscure.[78] As it stands, the reference might well be to Rome, the object of the author's glowing hatred. In any case we must not jump to the conclusion that Jerusalem is intended here. We had better keep in mind that neither Paul, nor any of the other first-century texts discussed here, have anything at all to say about either the time or the place of Jesus' crucifixion – which is quite natural, if, as I argue, it took place in the distant past. It is not at all improbable that John assumed Jesus' crucifixion had taken place in Rome. After all, the Romans were his main target, whereas Luke, who shaped all later Christians' picture of their early history, obviously aimed at exonerating the Romans, and blaming the Jews.

The Last Judgment occupies a prominent place in the theology of Revelation, as is natural in a work in which the sufferings of the Church (perhaps rather, of the Jews in general) at the hands of the Roman oppressors is a constant theme. The Day of the Lord, the Day of Wrath, is expected in the near future: 'He which testifieth these things saith, Surely, I come quickly. Amen' (22:20). The visionary says: 'Even so, Come, Lord Jesus', which seems to echo the *maranatha*, 'Come, Lord', of Didachē and of Paul (1 Cor 16:22). The author's impatience is evident: 'How long, O Lord, holy and true, dost thou not judge and avenge our blood?' (6:10).[79]

In the concluding chapters, where the triumphant victory of the followers of Christ is outlined, the author describes how the Jesus of his vision, here called the Lamb, prepares his marriage, the wife obviously being the Church, adorned as a bride: 'her fine linen is the righteousness of the saints' (19:8). We have found a somewhat similar symbolism in Hermas' *Pastor*. The saints are of course the Christians, the members of the Church of God.

Although I have stressed the Jewishness of Revelation, it is important to note that non-Jews are explicitly included among the saved: 'a great multitude ... of all nations, and kindreds, and peoples, and tongues, stood before the throne and the Lamb, clothed with white robes' (7:9). A similar thought is expressed in 21:24, where the heavenly Jerusalem is described: 'the nations of them which are saved shall walk in the light of it [i.e. the Lamb], and the kings of the earth do bring their glory and honour unto it'.[80]

Overview: Central ideas in the six documents

Jesus' death

As regards the historical Jesus, Jesus 'in the flesh', the six documents studied here yield about as meagre a harvest as Paul. Hermas, if read on its own terms, and not in the light of later Christian presuppositions, does not even mention Jesus or Christ. This agrees with my own dating of Hermas at around AD 50. Didachē, which may be equally early in its original version, presents Jesus as a teacher and interpreter of the Old Testament. He is not called the Messiah, and there is nothing at all on his suffering and death, or its redemptive power, and likewise nothing on his resurrection.[81]

Both Hermas and Didachē, however, speak about the imminence of the Last Judgment, though they say nothing about Jesus' possible function there. They do imply, however, that their people, the Saints, will be saved thanks to their faithful adherence to the Church of God. All this seems to be pre-Pauline.

In the remaining four texts, Jesus the Christ, the Messiah, is the central figure, just as in Paul. But, again as in Paul, it is not Jesus in the flesh, but Jesus as raised to heaven, Jesus the Messiah, Jesus the Saviour. And the most important occurrence is his resurrection.

About the resurrection, 1 Clement says: 'The Lord continually reveals to us our future resurrection, of which he has given us a foretaste in our Lord Jesus Christ, by resuscitating him from among the dead' (24:1). Clement also refers to the witness of the apostles who, he says, were 'filled with certitude through the resurrection of our Lord Jesus Christ' (42:3). But there is nothing in Clement about the resurrection as an actual event.

It is interesting to compare Clement's statements with Paul's in 1 Corinthians 15:3–8, quoted Chapter 1. Traditionally, Paul's account is regarded as a general (by no means complete) confirmation of Luke's story, according to which both the resurrection, the three days in the grave, Jesus' presence among the disciples, and (in Acts) his ascension, were witnessed by several people. In other words, we seem to have witnesses at every point, and the events all take place within a few days. But a closer comparison with Clement's statements yields a different result. Both Paul and Clement talk about God resuscitating Jesus 'from the dead', without saying anything about when his death and his resurrection took place. They never refer to the resurrection as an *event*. From Clement we only learn that the *fact* of the resurrection filled the apostles with certitude. The natural interpretation is that the apostles *inferred* the resurrection from having *seen* Jesus, as Paul says. At no place does any of them assert or imply that he had seen Jesus in the flesh, or that their visions occurred in connection with the death and the resurrection.

Both Clement's and Paul's accounts make excellent sense, if we interpret their references to Jesus' resurrection as inferences from *visions* of Jesus.[82] These visions were, naturally, of the heavenly Jesus, Jesus as raised to heaven.[83] Paul's description of his own transportation to the 'third heaven' in 2 Corinthians 12 provides a model. We may add that belief in angels and demons, and in the existence of a quite palpable multi-tiered heaven, was almost universal in antiquity. Paul was by no means exceptional in this respect. There is reason to think that Paul believed that the other apostles had received experiences similar to his own, i.e. that they had experienced visions of the risen Christ. As I said in Chapter 1, this was also the opinion of Harnack as early as 1922.[84] Clement's wording, in which he does not even mention Paul, supports this interpretation. Further indirect support is the lack of congruence in details between the different Gospel accounts, whose legendary character, moreover, is quite evident. (More about this in Chapter 11.)

Since neither Clement nor Paul represent the burial and the resurrection as events witnessed by anybody, the question of *when* Jesus had been raised did not arise.[85] Paul, instead, refers to 'scriptures',[86] and we have seen many examples in our documents – particularly in Barnabas – that 'scriptures' were assumed to refer to Jesus directly, without any need for witnesses. Thus Paul's reference to the scriptures can be seen as an indication that both the burial and the resurrection were events recorded, or interpreted as recorded, in the Scriptures (canonical or not). Both events thus could have occurred long before the apostles were granted their revelations. It is not until the Gospels and Acts that the contents of the revelations and visions are represented as real events taking place before the eyes of the disciples. If we study our six texts on their own terms, without assuming that they have the Gospels and Acts as their background, the most natural interpretation of what they say, and do not say, about the earthly Jesus, is that it was not a contemporary that now appeared to them as raised to heaven, but rather, as seems definitely to be the case in Paul and in 1 Clement, a figure of the distant past – though, to be sure, this is never said explicitly. We therefore now have an explanation of the remarkable lack of information about the historical, earthly Jesus, not only in Paul, but in *all* the earliest Christian texts, outside the Gospels and Acts. Jesus' death, burial, and rising are 'according to the scriptures', and there is no indication that they were looked upon as recent events at the time when the apostles (note: itinerant missionaries, *not* 'disciples'!) had seen Jesus in heaven. Those visions, which were by no means all simultaneous, as may be seen from 1 Corinthians 15:3–8, may be said to be the only real *experiences* involving Jesus which the apostles could refer to. Anyhow, it was those experiences which started off the evangelisation in the thirties of the first century AD.

As I said above, neither Hermas, nor Didachē, ever mention Jesus' death, or his suffering.[87] 1 Clement speaks more than once about the blood of Christ, and its redeeming power (10:1, 10:5, 10:26). But death by crucifixion is never spelled out explicitly in 1 Clement. In Hebrews the most specific mentions are in 12:2, where it is said that Jesus 'endured the cross, despising the shame, and is set down at the right hand of the throne of God', and in 6:6: 'they crucify the Son of God afresh'. Revelation often mentions blood in connection with the Lamb. But crucifixion is mentioned only once, in the bewildering passage about the great city 'spiritually called Sodom and Egypt' (Rev 11:8).[88]

Of our six authors, the one who dwells most on the crucifixion is Barnabas. He does not, however, provide any details regarding time, place and circumstances, except for extensive quotations of Old Testament passages. At one point Barnabas, like 1 Clement, and of course Paul, stresses the importance of Jesus' resurrection for belief in immortality. He declares that 'the prophets, to whom Jesus had shown his grace, have prophesied about him . . . and . . . he had to manifest himself in the flesh in order to abolish death and to prove the resurrection of the dead' (5:6). Note that Barnabas himself does not claim to have seen or experienced Jesus 'in. the flesh'. However, he takes it for granted that Jesus, as a heavenly figure, existed before the world, and could therefore communicate directly with the Old Testament prophets.

Why did Jesus have to die by crucifixion? Barnabas answers (5:13): 'He had to suffer on the cross, for *the prophet says in regard to him* [my italics]: ''Deliver my soul from the sword, and pierce my flesh, for an assembly of the wicked have inclosed me'' ' and goes on (5:14): 'I presented my back to the whips, and my cheeks to the slaps in the face'. These are fairly accurate quotations from Psalm 22:20, 26, and from Isaiah 50:6. We have, in other words, a typical example of Barnabas' technique of extracting information about Jesus from the Old Testament. Much of this was later incorporated in the Gospel stories of the crucifixion, e.g. Matthew 27.

Redemption

1 Clement, Hebrews and Barnabas exhibit quite clearly the doctrine of the redeeming effect of Jesus' passion. 1 Clement 7:4 says 'Let us fix our eyes on the blood of Christ . . . spent for our salvation' (see also 12:7, 21:6). Hebrews 9:12 is even more detailed and explicit: 'Neither by the blood of goats and calves, but by his own blood he entered in once into the holy place, having obtained eternal redemption for us' (see also 13:12). So is Barnabas: 'If our Lord has offered up his flesh to corruption, it is in order that we should be purified by having our sins forgiven by the sprinkling of his blood' (5:1. See also 7:5).

In Revelation, passion and redemption are referred to in 1:5: 'Jesus Christ, who is the faithful witness, and the first begotten of the dead . . . that loved us, and washed us from our sins in his own blood.' Redemption is also obliquely hinted at in the passages mentioning the blood of the Lamb. The redeeming power of Jesus' suffering seems also to be implied in 14:3: 'And they sung as it were a new song before the throne . . . and no man could learn that song but the hundred and forty and four thousand, which were redeemed from the earth.' But we find nothing specific on what Jesus' sufferings consisted of.

All our six texts, without exception, insist on the imminence of the Day of Judgment, something which supports my inference that the apostles regarded their visions or their allegorical interpretations of Biblical passages as signs that the End of the World was approaching. On the other hand, the participation of Jesus in the Judgment is not always made clear.[89] In Revelation, however, God and Jesus (more precisely, God and the Lamb) both sit on heavenly thrones. And in the visions set forth in the final chapter Jesus indeed seems to take an active part in the Judgment.

In several documents Jesus is not specifically mentioned in connection with the Last Judgment. It is true that the word *Kurios* is somewhat ambiguous in the texts, since it can be used both about God and about Jesus. But the most likely interpretation for the Jews in our early congregations was certainly God. That the Last Judgment should be God's is of course what we should expect in documents with predominantly Jewish characteristics.

Not one of our six documents contains anything that might help us infer, for instance, the time and place of Jesus' earthly existence. Hermas does not even name Jesus, and his Son of God figure is a hypostasis primarily identified with the community of Saints as a whole. Didachē's Jesus, called the Servant of God, like the Old Testament prophets, is simply the originator of doctrinal interpretations. In Revelation, Jesus only appears in John's visions, often disguised behind the figure of the Lamb. His sacrificial death is obscurely hinted at, but no details are provided.

Jesus' sayings and doings

Clement, Hebrews and Barnabas do offer material that is clearly intended to throw light on what Jesus did and said on earth. In the main, what we find in the documents are chiefly quotations – often only paraphrases – from the Old Testament, by which Jesus' life and work are illustrated. For instance 1 Clement 22:1, 'Come, ye children, hearken to me' is from Psalm 34:11, and 1 Clement 16 incorporates a long passage from Isaiah 53, on the 'suffering servant' of Yahweh: 'For he shall grow up before him as a tender plant.' But we never get a definite comparison between the Old Testament passage and a purely historical account, which we find in later documents, e.g. the Gospels and Justin Martyr.[90] Instead, the biblical text itself, often modified to suit the present context, provides all the details. The technique, which was also used extensively by the Jewish rabbis,[91] is employed above all by Barnabas, while Hebrews uses it more sparingly. 1 Clement provides a great many Scripture quotations, but few of them are explicitly applied by Clement to Jesus. Some of these, e.g. 1 Clement 16:2–3, are introduced by some such formula as 'This is what Jesus says through the Holy Spirit', after which follows a full quotation of Isaiah 53:2–12. For most such instances, however, the application to Jesus is left implicit. In this respect Clement resembles Paul.[92]

When our authors apply an Old Testament saying or event to Jesus, they most often give no reasons for doing so. They take it as self-evident. Since the Old Testament was considered as God's own words, the truth of the statements made there naturally could not be put in doubt. The allegorical mode of interpretation, explicitly recommended by Barnabas, hardly put any restrictions on them. This is amply exemplified also by Philo and by such Qumran texts as the Habakkuk commentaries applied to the Teacher of Righteousness (see Chapter 4).

Barnabas writes (5:1): 'That which in the Scriptures concerns Jesus, has a bearing on both Israel and us. This is what is written: "he was wounded because of our iniquities, he was maltreated because of our sins . . . like a lamb which is dumb before its shearers" '. The text is from the well-known chapter on the suffering servant in Isaiah 53:5, 7: 'He was wounded for our transgressions, he was bruised for our iniquities . . . he is brought as a lamb to the slaughter, and as a sheep before her shearers is dumb, so he openeth not his mouth.' In Isaiah, needless to say, there is no mention of Jesus.

Some further examples. Quoting Genesis 1:26 'Let us make man in our image', Barnabas says (5:5) that this was what God said to Jesus at the creation of the world. This may sound surprising to people who regard Jesus as a man who came to the world long after its creation by God. But at the time when our texts were written, this way of looking at matters was not unnatural. Many early writers, among them both Philo and Paul (Rom 16:25),[93] considered the Son of God, or the Holy Spirit, to have been created before the world. As Moses and the prophets were the spokesmen of the Holy Spirit, any statement in the Old Testament could be, and indeed was, interpreted as something said by God. It should also be remembered that Hermas repeatedly refers to the Holy Spirit as the Son of God.

A similar example is Barnabas 5:13, where the words 'The prophet says about him' (Jesus) are followed by a composite quotation – and therefore very likely taken from a *florilegium* – from Psalm 22: 'The assembly of the wicked have enclosed me: they pierced my hands and my feet', and from Isaiah 50:6–7: 'I gave my back to the smiters, and my cheeks to them that plucked off the hair. I hid not my face from shame and spitting. For the Lord God will help me.' Much of this is incorporated in the Gospel account of Jesus' passion, e.g. Matthew 26:67: 'Then did they spit in his face, and buffeted him, and others smote him with the palms of their hands.'

1 Clement 16:3 quotes the passage from Isaiah 53:1–12 in its entirety. Clement introduces it by the words: 'The Holy Spirit said this about Jesus.' It is hardly surprising that the Gospel writers followed these learned early Fathers when they composed their own stories about the Passion of Christ.

The author of Hebrews uses the same technique. When he tries to explain how Jesus, as a non-Levite, could become a priest, he declares that he was 'called of God an high priest after the order of Melchisedek'. The obvious reference is to Psalm 110:4: 'The Lord hath sworn, and will not repent, Thou art a priest for ever after the order of Melchisedek.' In the Psalm, needless to say, there is no reference to the Christ.

In 7:3, Barnabas says that Jesus, on the cross, was given vinegar and gall. Barnabas does not explicitly quote this as Scripture, though he says a few lines before (7:1): 'You will understand that the good Lord has revealed everything in advance.' Hence we may take it that he here implicitly refers to Psalm 69:21: 'They gave me also gall for my meat, and in my thirst they gave me vinegar to drink.' Matthew applies this directly to Jesus (27:34): 'They gave him vinegar to drink mingled with gall.' The learned writers of these first-century texts apparently took it for granted that their audience would be able to identify such quotations, or near quotations, without explicit guidance.

It also happens that a Scripture passage is quoted without being explicitly attributed to Jesus, though it may be later applied to him in the Gospels. Didachē, for instance, which does not use the technique which Barnabas employs so consistently, writes in 16:7: 'The signs of the truth will appear. . . . It has been said: "The Lord will come and all his saints with him." . . . Then the world will see the Lord come on the clouds of heaven', which can be seen as a paraphrase of Zechariah 14:5 and Daniel 7:13. Note that in Zechariah and Daniel, and originally also in Didachē, 'the Lord' of course means God. But in Matthew 24:30 the gist of the passage is laid in Jesus' own mouth: 'And then shall appear the sign of the Son of man in heaven: and then shall all the tribes of the earth mourn, and they shall see the Son of man coming in the clouds of heaven with power and great glory.'

An interesting variant of this technique of extracting information about the present from the Old Testament is found in the references in Hebrews to Jesus' temptation.[94] Hebrews says: (2:18) 'He himself hath suffered being tempted'; (4:15) 'He was in all points tempted like as we are, yet without sin.' The author clearly assumes that Jesus was tempted, in order to be like other men. But no details are given, and the most pregnant part of the passage, (3:8) 'As the Holy Ghost saith . . . Harden not your hearts as in the day of provocation, in the day of temptation in the wilderness' harks back to Psalm 95:8: 'Today if ye will hear his voice, Harden not your heart, as in the provocation, and as in the day of temptation in the wilderness, when your fathers tempted me, proved me, and saw my work. Forty years long was I grieved with this generation.' Accordingly, the words of God, directed to the ancient Jews in the desert, are here applied to the earthly Jesus. It is the last part of this passage that apparently forms the basis of the elaboration in Mark 1:12–13: 'And he was there in the wilderness forty days, tempted of Satan, and was with the wild beasts', with 'forty days' substituted for 'forty years'.[95]

In Barnabas 7 there is a long explanation of the significance of the story of the scapegoat in Leviticus 16. At the end of it Barnabas writes 'That is the prefiguration of Jesus who was to suffer'. Then he concludes: 'Thus those who want to see me and reach my kingdom must seize me through trials and sufferings'. This looks like a quotation, but it is not to be found in the Bible as we know it. Some commentators (e.g. one editor, Prigent) actually take it to be a saying by Jesus. It is certainly more natural to regard it as an attempt by Barnabas to summarise what to him seems to be the gist of the Old Testament texts he has quoted, a technique he uses repeatedly.

We have a different case in Barnabas 12:1: 'When does the consummation of all this arrive? The Lord says, ''when a tree has been felled and then raised again, and when blood trickles from the wood''.' Here there is no doubt that Barnabas himself regards the quotation as Scripture (note 'the Lord says'). Probably the quotation was taken from some apocryphal text unknown to us, but considered as 'authoritative' by Barnabas.[96] We may compare Barnabas' words with a passage about the end times in 4 Ezra 5:5: 'the sun shall suddenly shine forth at night/ and the moon during the day./ Blood shall drip from wood/ and the stone shall utter its voice.' Somewhat surprisingly, this dramatic and pithy saying has not been picked up anywhere in the New Testament canonical texts.

But there are also sayings of this kind which have indeed been incorporated in the New Testament. One is Barnabas 4:14: 'Let us take care that at the Last Judgment we are found, as it is written, ''many called, but few chosen''.' No such saying occurs in the OT as known to us. But we meet it again as a saying by Jesus in Matthew

20:16: 'Many be called, but few chosen', and also in Matthew 22:14: 'For many are called, but few are chosen.' Some scholars have regarded this as one of the few instances where a New Testament passage has been quoted as Scripture in early Christian literature.[97] In view of the well-documented habits of Barnabas in this letter, that seems rather far-fetched. It is far more likely that the New Testament writers took the phrase from some non-canonical text, e.g. Enoch, which is often quoted as Scripture in the earliest Christian (and Essene) texts. The same thing may be said about Barnabas 6:13: 'The Lord says: I make the last things as the first', which corresponds to the Jesus *logion* in Matthew 20:16: 'So the last shall be first, and the first last.' It is important to bear in mind that many other versions of Enoch than the ones we now have access to were circulated in the period of time we are concerned with. In 1 Clement there are indeed some instances where it is explicitly said that Jesus himself uttered the words. Thus 1 Clement 13:2: 'Be ye merciful, that ye may obtain mercy . . .' or 1 Clement 46:8: 'Woe to that man . . . it would have been better that he had not been born . . .'. Both of these have fairly complete correspondences in the Gospels (Lk 6:37 and Mt 18:6, respectively). Our editor, Jaubert, thinks these are genuine sayings of Jesus, passed on in the oral tradition. I think, however, that it is far more likely that they are taken by the author as Scriptures. After all, we have many examples of such 'scriptures', said to be taken from Enoch, but which are not found in the Enoch texts known to us. See Chapter 5.

In Didachē we find several sayings which are similar to pronouncements laid in Jesus' mouth in the Gospels. Thus Didachē 1:4 reads: 'if somebody slaps you on your right cheek, then offer him also the left one, and you will be perfect'. This corresponds to Matthew 5:39: 'whosoever shall smite thee on thy right cheek, turn to him the other also'. We note that Matthew does not include the phrase 'and you will be perfect'. In our early Christian documents, on the other hand, the idea of perfection – which presumably goes back, ultimately, to God's words to Abraham in Genesis 17:1 – was often insisted on.[98] And in the central Essene texts from Qumran, the members of the Essene community sometimes referred to themselves as the perfect ones, implying that they sought to comply perfectly with God's Law. Here again, therefore, we have an indication that our documents should be dated earlier than the Gospels. And Didachē 3:7 says: 'Be meek, for the meek will receive the world as their portion.' The corresponding passage, where the underlying idea reminds us of Isaiah 61:1, is found in the Sermon on the Mount. Matthew 5:5 runs: 'Blessed are the meek, for they shall inherit the earth.' Further, in Didachē 16:1 the author says: 'Be prepared, for you do not know at what hour the Lord will come', which Matthew, in 24:42, quotes as the words of Jesus: 'Watch therefore: for ye know not what hour your Lord doth come.' A few lines further on (24:44) the same idea is expressed: 'Therefore be ye also ready: for in such an hour as ye think not the Son of man cometh.' We note here the subtle change from 'the Lord' to 'the Son of man'. In the original, Jewish Didachē we do not have 'your Lord', but 'the Lord', i.e. God himself.

Jesus' pre-existence

I have said above that our texts often refer to Christ as being created before the world, and as being addressed by God in the Old Testament. The idea is first found in Proverbs 8:22–31, a text which scholars usually date to the second century BC.[99] Similar ideas are also found in Philo, the Jewish Platonist. But while Plato regarded the world of ideas as superior to the world perceived by the senses, Philo looked upon the superiority as a chronological one, in keeping with the historical outlook of Judaism, as expressed in the Bible. For Philo, who often calls God 'the Uncreated', implying eternal existence, history begins when God himself creates his Potencies, and then gives rise to the visible world, working through these potencies, such as his Word, and his Wisdom. Very possibly both Philo and our documents were inspired by Proverbs 8:22–3, where the hypostatised figure of Wisdom is made to say 'The Lord possessed me in the beginning of his way, before his works of old. I was set up from everlasting, from the beginning, or ever the earth was.' As I said above, Paul also identified Christ with Wisdom in 1 Corinthians 1:24. 'Christ the power of God, and the wisdom of God', and less explicitly in 1 Corinthians 15:3–4, where Jesus' career on earth is said to be 'according to the Scriptures'.

In Vis 2.4.1 Hermas sees the Church as an old woman about whom an angel says that she is old because she 'was created before everything . . . it is for her sake that the world was created'. In Sim 9.12.1–2 we have a different metaphor: a rock is represented as the Son of God. On the rock is a tower, symbolising the church, with a gate in it, symbolising, again, the Son of God. The rock is old, because 'the Son of God was born before everything, so that he was God's assistant at the creation'. Further, the angel explains that 'the gate is new because it is in the last days of the dispensation that he [i.e. the Son of God] has manifested himself ... the gate has been made recently so that those who shall be saved can enter by it to the kingdom of God'. It must be admitted that the luxuriant symbolism is not crystal clear. But the close connection between the Church of God and the Son of God is brought out.

Barnabas explains, in 5:5, how God speaks with Jesus at the creation. In 6:12 he expands this idea, declaring that God, through Scripture, 'speaks about us when he speaks with his Son'. Thus the idea of a pre-existing Christ was a means of explaining how God's Word, the Bible, could be read as exact prophecies. God had foreseen everything from the beginning, and his Son, the Word, formed the blueprint for the history of the universe.

The idea of pre-existence is also expressed in Hebrews (1:2): 'God ... hath in these last days[100] spoken unto us by his Son, whom he hath appointed heir of all things, by whom also he made the worlds.' Among the parallels we can also include Revelation 1:7, in which Jesus, seen in a vision, says: 'I am the first and the last, I am he that liveth, and was dead, I am alive for evermore.' Revelation also expresses the idea of pre-existence, and thus of prophecy, in mystical language in 3:14: 'These things saith the Amen, the faithful and true witness, the beginning of the creation of God.'

Resurrection

As none of our authors had seen or heard Jesus in the flesh, and do not mention anybody who has done so, it is not surprising that the same holds for his death. Jesus was obviously a well-established and revered figure among the Saints, who were mostly living in the Diaspora, far from Jerusalem, where Jesus, according to the Gospels, was supposed to have been active. They could therefore hardly have had any direct experience of him. And indeed none of our writers say anything of substance about him: if Jesus had lived centuries ago, he must of course be dead by the time they were writing. His death was a historical fact that the communities had learned to live with. But it was not of current, immediate interest, except as a proof that resurrection was possible.

The words used about Jesus' resurrection are also significant. Revelation calls Jesus 'the first begotten of the dead' (1:2), and Hebrews 13:20 says that 'God brought from the dead our Lord Jesus'.

Barnabas 15:9 talks about Jesus being 'resuscitated from the dead' and 1 Clement 24:1 says 'The Lord ... reveals to us our future resurrection, of which he has given us a foretaste in our Lord Jesus Christ, by resuscitating him from among the dead.' In no case is the time that Jesus has spent among the dead specified.[101] Jesus, as one of the countless people who had died in the past and now dwelt in the realm of the dead, had been singled out by God in order to show men that resurrection was possible. For most Jews – and most early Christians were indeed Jews – this resurrection would come in connection with the Last Judgment. That Jesus was 'the first-begotten of the dead' was therefore to be taken quite literally: all other dead people were still resting in their graves, waiting for the Day of the Lord. Only Jesus had so far been resurrected by God, as a sign of what would be done later to the believers.[102]

It is also remarkable that (as we have noted above) when our writers refer to Jesus in connection with the Day of Judgment, they do not talk about his *return*, his *coming back* to the earth, but about his *coming* or *arriving,* or *being seen* (the Greek word is usually *parousia*, 'arrival', 'presence'). In other words, Jesus' previous life on earth is not connected with the immediately impending future event.[103] This would surely be surprising, if Jesus had been living quite recently, and if the moment of his death – as distinct from his appearance, in visions, as a resurrected heavenly figure – had been actually witnessed by many of those who now expected him back. In subsequent centuries, Jesus' presence at the Last Judgment is routinely referred to as his 'second coming'. The early texts did not present it in such a light.

Let us summarise. The Jesus of the six early documents treated in this chapter was primarily a teacher and prophet, and an adviser on points of liturgy and worship. He was closely attached to the communities which in the first century, and earlier, were commonly referred to as the Saints, or the Church of God. They regarded him as a pre-existent interpreter of God's words, and as a revealer of religious truths and mysteries, e.g. the promise of immortality. He and his followers, the Saints, had been harassed by the established authorities among the Jews. The communities had no personal memories of him. He spoke to them through the voice of the Holy Ghost. In this respect he was like all other Old Testament prophets and teachers. As appears from our first-century texts, the Saints came to look upon Jesus as having impersonated the Suffering Servant of Isaiah 53, and his suffering and

77

death came to be interpreted as a sacrificial act. Finally, the Saints' eager expectation of the Last Judgment created a climate of religious fervour among them, where several apostles claimed that they had experienced visions of their long-since dead prophet and founder. They took this as proof that Jesus had been resuscitated from the dead, which in turn they took as a sign that God was now preparing for the Last Judgment, in which the Saints would be saved, while all sinners would perish.

Chapter 3

Egypt, Philo and the Gnostics

In the two preceding chapters we have been considering first-century texts which have always been regarded by scholars as Christian. Several of them were included in the New Testament, whose canon, however, only began to take shape in the late second century. We now turn, in Chapters 3–5, to other Jewish texts of roughly the same period. They are not Christian, but form an essential part of the milieu in which, and out of which, Christianity developed. The Essenes of the Dead Sea Scrolls, on my hypothesis, may well be the matrix of early Christianity, while the Gnostics are an important movement which both competed with Christianity in the early centuries, and partly coalesced with it.

Philo

In Paul's Letters Egypt is never mentioned, and the name is found only very rarely in the other books of the New Testament too. Beyond the instances where it occurs in connection with Old Testament traditions about Moses, Egypt is referred to only in Matthew's story about Joseph's and Mary's flight to Egypt; in Acts 2:10, where Egypt is found in a list of places where the apostles preach the gospel,[1] and in Revelation 11:8, in the mysterious reference to 'the city spiritually called Sodom and Egypt'. Nor do we hear about any Egyptian 'Church of God' in any of the six early texts discussed in the previous chapter.

In view of the fact that almost all first-century references to Christian communities are to the Diaspora, the virtual silence about Egypt is highly remarkable and surprising.[2] After all, Alexandria in the first century almost certainly held the biggest Jewish population of any city in the Empire.[3] In Egypt as a whole, the Jewish population amounted to a million, according to Philo Judaeus of Alexandria, who

79

lived *c.* 20 BC–AD 45, and who was a widely known Jewish theological philosopher, and a very prolific writer. He is a prime example of a liberal Jewish intellectual, who gives us direct insight into the thought-world of the upper social stratum of Diaspora Jews in Antiquity. Much Jewish literature was produced in Egypt. The translation of the Jewish Bible, the Septuagint, had been completed in Egypt by around 200 BC. In addition, many very early Christian documents have been preserved in Egypt, among them the earliest known fragment of the Gospel of John. Above all, a whole collection of Christian Gnostic texts from the fourth century AD and earlier were discovered near the village of Nag Hammadi in 1945.

It is true that the abundance of early manuscript finds in Egypt is largely due to the dry climate, in which papyrus is not so liable to rotting as in more humid regions. Still, even if the texts found were not actually produced in Egypt, it is indisputable that Christian documents were circulated there, probably from the earliest times onwards. So the problem is real: why do we hear so little of Egyptian Christians in the Christian writings from the first century and the larger part of the second?

One reason might be the disasters that repeatedly struck the Alexandrian Jews in that period. Philo describes extensive pogroms in AD 38. Even more serious were the calamities that hit the Jews of Egypt in AD 113–15. They began as an uprising of the Jews in Cyrenaica and Cyprus, apparently fomented by Messianic hopes among the Jewish populace.[4] The Cyrenaican insurgence spread into Northern Egypt. The Alexandrian mob reacted with frightful pogroms. That they were on a massive scale can be inferred from the drastic reduction in the number of Jewish inscriptions in Alexandria during the second century.[5] There is no doubt that the Jewish population of the city was substantially reduced.

But they were not wiped out completely. Towards the end of the second century the Jews of Alexandria had recovered much of their strength, and the Christians also, to judge from such people as the church fathers Clement of Alexandria and Origen. A few decades earlier, another Christian writer, Valentinus, had arrived in Rome from Alexandria and started propagating Gnostic Christianity there.

Thus it would seem that Christianity had, from the middle of the second century onwards, at least as strong a position in Alexandria as in the rest of the Greek-speaking parts of the Roman Empire. But we have very little hard evidence about it from before *c.* AD 150. Information has to be sought out by indirect means.[6]

An especially important informant is Philo, who is a self-confessed Jew, and proud of his Jewish heritage. Indeed, he looks forward to a time when the whole world will recognise the superiority of the Jewish religion, and the Bible as the key to understanding the governance of the world. In his numerous writings Philo mentions neither Jesus, nor Christ, nor Christians, though he was exactly contemporary with the Christian evangelisation.

Philo is obviously a universalist: he regards the Bible[7] as valid for all men, not only for Jews.[8] The God of the Bible, says Philo, is righteous and fair. He has laid down his law for the good of mankind, not merely for the good of Israel. Whoever lives righteously, whether Jew, or Greek, or Ethiopian, will receive God's protection.

Philo belonged to a very rich and influential Jewish family in Alexandria. A nephew of his held leading posts in the Roman administration in Egypt. Philo himself was a trusted member of the Jewish community in Alexandria. He was one of the spokesmen in an embassy of the Alexandrian Jews to the emperor Caligula after the pogrom in 38. Philo's report about that embassy has been preserved.[9] The embassy did not, however, move Caligula. But the emperor died shortly afterwards. His sacrilegious plans for the Jews were therefore never realised.

Philo was a deeply religious man, well versed in the Bible, and in Jewish theology. But he was also a philosopher.[10] He may have received his education in a Greek gymnasium in Alexandria. In any case he was thoroughly acquainted with Greek classical literature, religion and mythology. He attended the theatre, an important vehicle of Greek cultural values, and he appreciated athletic competitions, including boxing matches – things which were certainly frowned upon by many religious Jews. However, the Jews of Alexandria probably took a more liberal attitude than the Palestinian Jews. Philo certainly did.

Philo was well read in classical Greek philosophy. Plato was unquestionably, to him, the greatest philosopher of all: as we have seen, at one place he even calls him 'the divine Plato'. But Philo had also assimilated much of Aristotle and the leading philosophical schools of his own time, above all the Stoics.[11] Further, he was evidently impressed by the Pythagoreans, including their number symbolism and number mysticism.[12]

For it is quite clear that Philo had strong leanings towards mysticism, both in philosophy and in religion – two fields which were hardly distinguishable in those days. Plato's philosophy, as set forth especially in Timaeus and Theaetetus, is in important respects both philosophy and religion, setting forth an overall view of the nature of the universe, in which both material and spiritual aspects are taken into account. For instance, Plato regarded the stars as spirits, embodied in immaterial light. Thus the world of ideas could be apprehended as another aspect of the spiritual world, discernible not through the senses, but through a higher faculty, namely, the intellect.[13]

This crudely schematic sketch of course does not do justice to the depth and richness of Plato's thought. But it is probably not far from the way Plato was apprehended in Philo's time, and by Philo himself. It is also, I think, a useful way of approaching the ideas of the Neo-Platonists, and especially Plotinus, who may be said to have developed further the religious and mystical aspects of Plato. Philo, inspired by the 'divine Plato', apparently stood nearer to the Neo-Platonists than to Plato himself. It may not be a coincidence that Plotinus was born and educated in Egypt, where Philo had been active almost two centuries before, probably exerting, directly or indirectly, an influence on Christian writers like Clement of Alexandria and Origen, who in turn may have influenced Plotinus.[14] According to his biographer, Porphyrius, Plotinus 'tried all philosophies' while in Egypt.[15]

The extremely close affinity of philosophy and religion in the centuries around the beginning of our era – an affinity which has weakened gradually with the rise of natural science – appears also from the Palestinian Jewish historian Josephus, writing in the last quarter of the first century AD, directly after the Roman victory in the Jewish War of 66–74. Josephus' books contain, among other things, an account of the chief religious sects among the Jews. He calls them 'philosophies': that of the Sadducees, that of the Pharisees and that of the Essenes, to which he adds 'a fourth philosophy', that of the Zealots.

Josephus identifies himself as a Pharisee. But in his exposition of the Jewish 'philosophies' he devotes by far the most space to the Essenes. For instance, he says that 'all who have once tasted their philosophy are attracted by it'.[16] Indeed, it appears that Josephus had at one time lived among them for a period of at least a year.[17] He estimates their number in Palestine at 4000 (as against 6000 Pharisees), and says that 'they occupy no one city, but settle in large numbers in every town'.[18] They seem to be firmly organised, for they are said to do nothing without orders from their superiors. Further, they 'take an extraordinary interest in the writings of the ancients ... After God, they hold most in awe the name of their lawgiver, any blasphemer of whom is punished by death'.[19] As for their theology, Josephus draws attention above all to their belief in the immortality of the soul.

It is interesting that Philo, Josephus' senior by some sixty years, also looks very favourably on the Essenes. The larger part of the book entitled *Quod omnis probus liber sit* ('That every good man is free') deals with the Essenes, a name Philo translates as the Pious or Holy Ones (*hosioi*).[20] And his treatise *De vita contemplativa* ('Of the Contemplative Life') is a kind of companion volume to that on the Essenes, since the exponents of the contemplative life, called by Philo Therapeutae, are paralleled with the ideal of the active life which Philo here says the Essenes stand for. The Therapeutae can clearly be regarded as a special branch of the Essenes.[21]

Whereas the Essenes are mentioned by at least three first-century authors, Philo, Josephus and Pliny, only Philo ever mentions the Therapeutae. Yet Philo maintains about them that 'this kind exists in many places in the inhabited world ... but abounds in Egypt, and especially round Alexandria'.[22] It is interesting to note that Philo says about the Therapeutae that they come together to read and allegorically interpret the Holy Scriptures, and the 'writings of men of old, the founders of their way of thinking, who left many memorials of the form used in allegorical interpretation' (*Vita contemplativa* 29). This is obviously consistent with what we have found about the Saints and their teacher, Jesus, in our six documents, above. The parallel is further underlined by the fact that the Essenes and the Therapeutae, according to Philo, were also called the holy or pious ones, very much like the communities addressed in our six texts, the Saints. It is interesting also to note that Philo mentions Pentecost as the chief festival of the Therapeutae, again a point where they agree with the Essenes[23] – and of course with the early Christians.

There are several points of theology and philosophy where Philo is seen to be in agreement both with the Essenes and with the early Christians, as evidenced by the texts we have analysed in Chapter 2, above. His praise of poverty is one important point of agreement – note that Philo belonged to one of the richest families in Alexandria. Further, Philo argues for an allegorical interpretation of the Bible. For instance, he agrees that the law about the Sabbath and about circumcision should indeed be interpreted allegorically. However, this does not mean, he says, that we should disregard the literal meaning: 'It is true that receiving circumcision does indeed portray the excision of pleasure and all passions . . . but let us not on this account repeal the law . . . Why, we shall be ignoring the sanctity of the Temple . . . if we are going to pay heed to nothing except what is shown us by the inner meaning of things. Nay, we shall look on all these outward observances as resembling the body, and their inner meanings as resembling the soul. . . . If we keep and observe these, we shall gain a clearer conception of those things of which they are symbols' (*De Migr. Abr.* 92).

The fact that Philo argues against an *exclusively* allegorical interpretation indicates that he was aware that some Jews did adopt that position. Barnabas, as we have seen, clearly did. Considering the social and cultural pressures that Diaspora Jews must have been exposed to, such a development appears entirely natural.

Another point where Philo is in agreement with the early Christians, concerns the view that Wisdom, Greek *sophia*,[24] as a hypostasis of God, existed before the creation of the world. Such a scenario makes intelligible the assertions about Christ 'existing before the world' which we have found in several of the texts analysed in Chapter 2. Very possibly both they and Philo were inspired by Proverbs 8:22–3, where Wisdom is made to say 'The Lord possessed me in the beginning of his way, before his works of old. I was set up from everlasting, from the beginning, or ever the earth was.'

We shall return to the possible connections between the Christians and the Essenes in Chapter 4. For the present I shall concentrate on the sub-group Philo calls the Therapeutae, a word meaning, roughly, servants – in this case, presumably, meaning servants of God. Their affinities with the Christians are evident not only from what Philo says about them (see below), but also from the remarkable fact that the foremost and extremely influential Church historian of antiquity, Eusebius of Caesarea, in the fourth century, actually took them to be Christians, without qualification.

Eusebius' judgment about Philo's Therapeutae cannot, of course, be taken at face value: he was, as we have seen, far from being an objective historian. He was writing three hundred years after the event, and was moved by an obvious desire to confirm his own view that Jesus, through the disciples/apostles, continuing in an unbroken line through the bishops and priests of the Church, was the unique origin of Christianity. It was therefore natural for him to bring the Therapeutae into his story by positing Mark as the founder of the Alexandrian Christian community of Therapeutae. His source about the Therapeutae, Philo, has of course nothing about Mark: Eusebius' history is pure fabrication at this point. Further, in accordance with Eusebius' general policy of giving bishop lists beginning with some apostle, for all the major cities in the Empire, he declares Mark to be the first of the line in Alexandria.

What Eusebius does show is that an influential churchman of the fourth century found enough correspondences between Christians and Philo's Therapeutae for him to present them as the founders of the Christian church in Egypt. Thus Eusebius believed that the Egyptian church was established at the same time and in the same manner as all the other churches in the Roman Empire. Unfortunately Eusebius' story about Mark, the Therapeutae and Alexandria only confirms his general unreliability, and emphasises that his account of the early Church is more a piece of pious propaganda than history.

Philo describes himself as an old man when he participated in the embassy to Caligula in AD 39 or 40. It is reasonable to assume that he was born *c.* 20 BC, and that he died *c.* AD 45. We have no means of knowing when he wrote his piece about the Therapeutae, though we may guess that it was more probably in the twenties or thirties than in the forties. If so, the Therapeutae were in existence in Egypt and elsewhere in the Empire in the first third of the first century AD. In fact, they had probably been established long before that, since Philo says explicitly that they ('their kind') were at that time already to be found 'in many parts of the inhabited world'. Presumably, given the purely Jewish background of the Essenes, and the strong Jewish flavour of the Therapeutae, we should expect to find them above all in places where the Jewish Diaspora was strong. And the spread of their ideas could hardly have taken place overnight. Accordingly their origin must be sought no later than the very beginning of the first century AD. Philo's Therapeutae would thus predate Christianity, as it is presented in the Gospels, in which the 'evangelisation' starts soon after the crucifixion of Jesus – or, as I would put it, after the apostles had experienced their visions and revelations of the crucifixion. But it is in good agreement with the conclusions we have arrived at in our discussion of Roman and Corinthian Christianity referred to in 1 Clement, chapter 2.

This chronology seems reasonable enough if, instead of regarding the Therapeutae as Christians, as Eusebius does, we take them to be forerunners of the Christians. Briefly, Essenes of the universalistic kind we should expect in the Diaspora. Or, if we prefer, representatives of a preliminary stage of Christianity. As we have seen, such a conclusion squares well with what emerges from Paul and from the six early Christian texts of Chapter 2. In the Didachē, for instance, Jesus is primarily a wisdom teacher and an interpreter of the Bible, whereas in Paul and the Gospels it is the Messiah, the Redeemer and the Saviour, that occupies the scene. It is only at this stage that we can regard them as fully formed Christians.

Philo, for his part, says nothing at all about Jesus. But his high appreciation of Jewish Wisdom need hardly be emphasised. And he does write about the Therapeutae that they 'study the writings of the founders of their way of thinking', which fits excellently with what we know from the Qumran library about the Teacher of Righteousness of the Essenes, and also with the Jesus of Didachē. Indeed, it agrees with all the texts analysed in Chapters 1 and 2. The Christian features that we discover in the Therapeutae therefore connect them with these early texts, rather than with the Gospels and Acts, where salvation at the Last Judgment looms so large. In fact, Philo's silence about Jesus is quite in order, if his piece about the Therapeutae was written before AD 30. That was before the evangelisation was started by Paul and other apostles. It was only *then* that Jesus was given Messiah status among the Essenes.

The Gnostic movement

Philo himself, and the Therapeutae in particular, can be taken as evidence that some Egyptian Jews held opinions and attitudes which would at least make them receptive to the kind of Christianity that Didachē represents. But another philosophical movement of the times, which we may somewhat loosely call Gnosticism, offers perhaps an even better fit. Unfortunately we have very little hard evidence for the Gnostic movement before the second century AD. Moreover, that evidence was until recently highly biased and unreliable. Most of it was derived from an early church father, Irenaeus (fl. *c.* AD 180), who wrote a large volume, *Against the Heresies*, which is primarily aimed against the Gnostics, and in particular against such representatives as Cerinthus, Valentinus, Basilides and Marcion. Of these, Valentinus and Basilides came from Egypt, whereas Marcion hailed from Pontus in Asia Minor. Cerinthus' origin is unknown. All this is at least an indication that Gnostic ideas were still current in Egypt more than a century after Philo.[25]

But there is more. In 1945 some Egyptian villagers from the little township of Nag Hammadi found by chance an earthenware jar of ancient origin, which proved to contain a whole library of ancient manuscripts. None of them was younger than the fourth century AD, and the oldest were judged to be from the first and second centuries AD. Most of the texts were Coptic (Egyptian) translations of Gnostic texts originally written in Greek. Many of them were known from mentions and commentaries by hostile church fathers, such as Irenaeus and Justin Martyr, whereas others were completely unknown to modern scholars.

When the Nag Hammadi texts were eventually translated and published in the 1960s[26], we could at last read what the Gnostics themselves had to say about their views. We did not any longer have to rely on the biased accounts of their adversaries. We also got a better grip on the chronology of the Gnostic movement.

The general picture that now emerges is the following. The Gnostic movement – we might even say, the Gnostic religion[27] – arose around the beginning of our era as a religious movement chiefly among Jews and Judaisers in the Greek-speaking Diaspora, in which Alexandria was a leading intellectual centre. The word *gnostic* is derived from the Greek noun *gnōsis*, knowledge: the members thought of themselves as those who know the secrets of the world. Gnostic was not their self-designation. It seems mainly to have been used by opponents as a term of derision. Their self-designations varied: the Saints (or the Holy ones), the Children of Light, the Perfect Ones – terms used also by the Essenes and, as we have seen, also by the early Christians, something which may be taken as an indication of the links between the three categories.

The main idea among the Gnostics was that the universe was under the influence of two opposed forces or principles, Light and Darkness. The human soul is a spark coming from the Light, which is more or less synonymous with God, the eternal divine principle of the universe. Hence the Gnostics often called themselves the Children of Light, an idea which can be seen as a universalistic version of the Jewish view that God is the Father of all Israel. The expression is also found in the Letter to the Ephesians (Eph 5:8), one of the most gnostically coloured of the letters ascribed to Paul in the New Testament canon. (On Ephesians, see Chapter 7.)

While the human soul is essentially Divine Light, the human body is constituted by matter. And matter is, in the Gnostic metaphysics, essentially without light. It is an emanation of Darkness. The soul is imprisoned in the body, and its light is constantly in danger of being snuffed out altogether. Still, it retains vague memories of its divine origin. Further, God, the source of Light, sends out messengers, angels, who have the power to lead responsive souls back to their real home, which is the region of Light, Paradise, God. If the human soul does not succeed in establishing such contact with the angels of Light, it is doomed to remain for ever in its material prison, and die there, in the heart of Darkness.[28]

Thus the world view of the Gnostics is strongly dualistic. There are two ultimate powers in the universe: Good struggling with Evil, Light with Darkness. Good men are those who constantly strive upwards, towards the Light, and they receive essential help from the angels of Light. On the other hand, the Powers of Darkness, devils and evil spirits, are equally anxious to retain the souls in their prisons of matter.

The dualism of Gnosticism has been seen by many scholars as the result of Persian influences, since the Persian religion of Zoroastrianism is also strongly dualistic. On the other hand, it must be recognised that dualism is fairly widespread in the world. Plato's view of the world of ideas as the ultimate reality, with the perceptible world, the world of the senses, seen as an imperfect copy or shadow of the higher world of ideas, is of course also dualistic, though certainly of a different kind. Related lines of thought can also be found in Buddhism, where the sensory world is considered fundamentally evil. To the Buddhist, the highest state is that which implies complete liberation from dependence on the material world of the senses: nirvana.

We can be fairly sure that neither Persian nor Indian ideas were wholly unknown in the Hellenistic world, where Plato, also a dualist of a kind, was one of the intellectual pillars. Thus from all directions dualistic trends of thought exerted their influence, and especially so in a dominant intellectual centre and melting-pot like Alexandria. We have also found it in the *Duae Viae* treatise, incorporated, as we have seen, in Didachē and Barnabas, and quoted in Hermas. In general, I think historians of religion have been too prone to regard each religious concept as originating in a certain community and spreading gradually from there. They have not attached enough importance to the natural free commerce of ideas, wherever people of different cultures meet. In most cases, certainly, the ideas themselves are neither clear nor consistent, and they are often misunderstood at the receiving end. Still, something is communicated, however vague, and may continue to develop in different directions in many individual minds. This kind of situation certainly existed in the Greek-speaking world ever since the eighth century BC, when Greek colonies were formed round the coasts of the Mediterranean: we have reason to think that both Pythagoras and Plato could have picked up ideas that were current, for instance, in Persia, and even India. Alexandria in the centuries around the beginning of our era offered excellent opportunities for such exchanges. The Gnostic and Hermetic literature has evidently received (and developed) impulses from many quarters.

Hence it is not at all surprising that Philo himself also shows some Gnostic characteristics.[29] But he is too much of a traditional Jew to accept the fundamental dualism of the typical Gnostics. For a traditional Jew of that time it was impossible to question the omnipotence of God. Philo of course recognises that there are evil men and evil spirits. But there are not for Philo, as in the Persian religion and for many Gnostics, two opposing forces or principles in Heaven.[30] The perennial metaphysical question as to how there could be evil in the world, if everything was created and designed by God, was answered by Philo in the traditional Jewish manner: evil was the result of men's failure to obey God. Most modern philosophers would find such an answer unsatisfactory.

On the other hand, Philo's scorn of wealth and material goods, and his admiration of the world of the spirit, has strong links with the world-view of the Gnostics. The same holds for his mysticism, and his conviction that angelic spirits are able to establish contact with humans, if these are receptive enough, and if they nurture that receptivity by meditation and contemplation.

However, Philo was far too well integrated in the society in which he lived, and too strongly attached to mainstream Judaism, to follow the Gnostics in their wide-ranging metaphysical speculations. It is true that, like many Jews, and in particular, it seems, Diaspora Jews, he preferred what he called an allegorical interpretation of the Bible. But he still considered himself basically bound by the Bible as the revealed Wisdom of God, which he considered far superior to the merely human wisdom of the Greeks.

The Gnostics went much further than allegorising the Bible. They constructed a metaphysical universe of their own, where the names and characteristics of the good and evil spirits were indeed mainly taken from the Bible, either directly, or reconstructed out of Biblical material.

The predominance of Jewish names in the Gnostic world of Spirits indicates that the Gnostic movement had a strong Jewish component. But the metaphysical inventiveness of the Gnostics soon led them into conflict with basic Jewish religious convictions. The Gnostics had taken from the Bible the notion that God, the Jewish God Yahweh, had created the world. But, as the world was full of evil, how could Yahweh be good? Some Gnostics drew the conclusion that Yahweh could not in fact be the highest God, the Principle of Goodness and Light, but must have an even higher God above him, a God who was entirely Goodness and Light. This supreme God had no human features, and men could only reach him thanks to the divine spark which flickered in their hearts. For these Gnostics, Yahweh was himself a creation of the Highest God. But he had turned awry, they said, and he thought, mistakenly, that he was indeed the highest God. The Gnostics, adopting the term used by Plato in *Timaeus*, called him, somewhat contemptuously, the Demiurge, 'the Builder', who had created the material, sensory world. He thought he was in full control of it, including the men and women living there. He was unaware of his own creator, the Highest God, and did not know that the souls of men were really emanations of the divine principle, and that they were able to free themselves from their material bodies, and thus from the bondage under Yahweh.

Therefore, in the view of these Gnostics, the main duty of man was to free himself from the domination of Yahweh and his hierarchy of evil powers. Humans ought to establish contact with the powers of Light. But, as the supreme God was unreachable by human efforts, he sent out angels of light, who could instruct the faithful, the Children of Light, in such a way that they could penetrate to the highest region, avoiding the evil designs of the Powers of Darkness. The ways to reach the angels of Light, and to avoid the powers of evil, were closely guarded secrets, *mysteries*, conveyed by angels to the select few, those who had Knowledge, *Gnōsis*. Hence the name that other men gave them, the Gnostics.

The metaphysics of the Gnostics is bound up with astronomical/ astrological conceptions. Educated people in the Hellenistic world considered the earth as a huge ball surrounded by layer upon layer of concentric moveable spheres, each containing one of the 'wandering stars', namely, the moon, the sun and the five known and named star-like planets. Outside these seven spheres was the sphere of the fixed stars, and outside that, in turn, was the ultimate Light, the Supreme God. Each sphere was 'ruled' by its own guardian or *archōn*, whose power was shown by the regularity with which the heavenly bodies moved. In the Gnostic view, the Archons were under the rule of the Demiurge, and were therefore forces of Darkness.[31] Accordingly humanity was enclosed in a prison, with the Archons serving as prison guards. The movement of the stars went on unperturbed, illustrating the relentlessness of Fate, which was called *heimarmenē*. The human soul, striving to negotiate its way past the mighty Archons in order to reach the highest region, was in dire need of guidance from the angels of Light.

The world view of the Gnostics may seem fantastic. But in many ways it was beautiful and grandiose, and in antiquity it was in good agreement with the astronomy of the times (later to be codified in the *Mēgistē Suntaxis* of Ptolemy).[32] And the existence of unseen spirits, such as the Archons, was taken for granted by almost everybody. Plato's picture of the world in his dialogue *Timaeus* is not very different from the Gnostic one, nor the Neo-Platonic one of Plotinus. It is true that Plotinus wrote a treatise against the Gnostics. But what he objected to was rather the 'unphilosophical' way in which at least some Gnostics justified their beliefs. In fact, Gnosticism may be regarded as a kind of popularised Platonism – the ancient version of popular science, using philosophy, religion and faith, rather than natural science, as its point of departure.[33]

Gnostics and Christians

Gnostics and Christians have their Jewish roots in common. For both, the Jewish Bible, the Old Testament, is a rich source of mystical inspiration and metaphysical speculation, the Gnostics turning mainly to the book of Genesis, while the Christians looked especially to the Prophets and the Psalms. But both groups also shared the world-view of the ancient world, where the earth was placed in the centre of a system of revolving shells, the outside ones enveloping the inner ones.

The concept of a single, supreme God was a Jewish heritage, though the idea had also gained ground in many philosophical schools of antiquity. Among many Gnostics and Christians, as well as among many Jews, especially in the Diaspora (with Philo as paragon) the Jewish God had also assumed many universalised features.

The main difference between the Gnostics and the Christians lies in their metaphysics. The Gnostics held that God cannot be apprehended or described in human terms. The Godhead is a metaphysical abstraction, attainable only by the pure intellect, which is to be found only in the elect, the Knowers. Christians in general retained much more of the concretely human features of the ancient Jewish God, God the Father of Israel. This difference on the abstract–concrete dimension is important for the way the two groups apprehended the Jesus figure. On this point, however, our evidence is not only insufficient, but also strongly biased, since we know that very much of the early literature of both the earliest Christians and the earliest Gnostics was systematically destroyed by the Church, as part of its efforts to strengthen the kind of orthodoxy that it developed in the course of the second century and later, and where opposition to Gnostic ideas was an important element. Moreover, there were differences among Christians on these points. As we have noted, Paul, in particular, exhibits many Gnostic characteristics. We discuss this in Chapters 10 and 12.

Accordingly much of our reconstruction of the relations between early Christianity and Gnosticism has to be rather speculative. But thanks to the Nag Hammadi and Qumran discoveries in the 1940s, our knowledge of the philosophical and religious trends in the South-Eastern Mediterranean area during the centuries around the beginning of our era has increased considerably during the last few decades. A steady trickle of archaeological finds has also contributed, as can be seen in the thirteen large volumes of Goodenough's *Jewish Symbols in the Greco–Roman World*.[34]

Irenaeus' *Against the Heresies*, (c. AD 180) deals almost exclusively with the Gnostics, whom he clearly regarded as the chief enemies of the orthodox Church in his time. His aim is polemical: he treats them entirely from the point of view of the Christianity of the Church. According to Irenaeus, the fount and origin of the Gnostic heresies is Simon Magus, who is referred to rather in passing in Acts 9, where he appears as a sorcerer, who is given short shrift by Peter. Simon Magus is also said by Justin Martyr (who died in AD 167) to have appeared before the Emperor Claudius (41–54) in Rome. As Irenaeus says very little about Simon's actual teaching, his characterisation of him as the 'founder' of Gnosticism is of little use to us. Further, in view of the fact that we have no mentions of Simon (outside the Acts) from before 160, even his historicity must be put in doubt.[35]

We have in fact no genuine Gnostic texts predating the earliest ones from Nag Hammadi, which are probably from around AD 100. By then Christianity had been around for a century, and had certainly exerted an influence on the Gnostics. Moreover, many of the people responsible for collecting and hiding away the Nag Hammadi library seem to have looked upon themselves as Christians. Hence it is likely that they had selected such documents from the Gnostic literature as were at least acceptable to Christians.

In many Nag Hammadi texts Jesus is given some prominence. Primarily he appears as a religious teacher and preacher. Very little, however, is said about Jesus' life on earth. When it is referred to, it is often underlined that Jesus was not really a human being, but a divine person, who only 'seemingly' was a man. This was called the 'docetic' heresy, a word derived from the Greek verb *dokein* 'to seem'. Jesus' passion and death are referred to rather perfunctorily. Many Gnostic texts present Jesus as he appears to his disciples after his crucifixion, sometimes for a prolonged period of time. The reader's overall impression is that the authors of the Nag Hammadi texts have nothing of their own to contribute on Jesus' earthly biography, and that it does not really interest them very much. Another remarkable circumstance is that Doomsday, the Last Judgment, hardly figures at all in the Gnostic texts, in contrast to its central importance in Paul and many of his contemporaries.

All this receives an explanation if we suppose that the Jesus figure was a late importation into the Gnostic texts.

We should by no means regard this as a sly calculation on the part of the Gnostics. We should not forget that neither Gnosticism nor Christianity in the first century AD were monolithic schools of thought. Both of them contained people with divergent opinions on important religious and theological issues. On the other hand, there was certainly sufficient overlap between the two movements for individual members to feel at home in both, and to believe that a merger would bring benefits. After all, both had important common roots in Judaism, and both tried in effect to achieve a reform of Judaism that would adapt it to the surrounding Hellenistic culture. Both were strongly influenced by Platonism, both exhibited mystical trends, and both were looking to Heaven for salvation. We should also keep in mind that, to judge from the texts analysed in the preceding chapter, Christianity and Gnosticism were nearer to each other in the first century AD than in the second, something we discuss at more length in Chapters 10–12, below. It was only in the second century AD that the Church placed more and more emphasis on Jesus as a historical figure of the past, and on Salvation at the Last Judgment as the dominant event expected in the future. In the first century, and particularly before Paul's 'evangelisation', Jesus, for the early members of the Church of God, had been above all an ancient teacher and an interpreter of God's message to men, just like the Gnostic apostles.

The close connection between Christians and Gnostics in the first century AD can also be seen as a confirmation of our analysis of the Christology of the texts discussed in Chapters 1 and 2. The Christians of the first century thought of Jesus mainly as a heavenly being. His life on earth, in their view, lay in the distant past. His current power was exerted from heaven, and experienced through visions and other kinds of revelation. Such a picture of Jesus was not radically different from the Gnostic one. Under such circumstances it is understandable that the first-century Christians did not object strongly to the views of the Gnostics. Rather the contrary.

The strong position of Gnosticism among the Christians in Egypt in the second century AD is evidenced not only by the preserved Gnostic library of Nag Hammadi, but also by such names as Valentinus, Basilides, Clement of Alexandria and Origen. On the other hand, we can say hardly anything at all on *first-century* Egyptian Christians or Gnostics, due to the almost total absence of data. But it is indeed hard to believe that Christian ideas did not reach Egypt at an early stage, both in view of the leading role that Alexandria played in the intellectual and religious world of the time, and in view of the character of the Jewish community there, exemplified by the Therapeutae and by Philo himself. Moreover, with the strong position of Neo-Platonism in Alexandria it would not be surprising if Christianity there took on a Neo-Platonic, and thereby also a Gnostic hue. Certainly the Therapeutae exhibit, though somewhat vaguely through Philo's text, both Gnostic and Christian traits.

All this is necessarily somewhat speculative. But if it contains some truth, it would offer an explanation why Gnosticism, in the second century, had such a strong position in Egypt, and also why practically no first-century Christian texts, or even mentions of Christians, have survived there. The texts may have disappeared (very likely destroyed by the victorious Church) because the first Egyptian Christians were predominantly Gnostic.[36] In a later chapter we shall see that one Nag Hammadi text, the so-called gospel of Thomas, may possibly date from the first century. It is undeniably both Christian and (mildly) Gnostic. If the gospel of Thomas originated in Egypt, which is not unlikely, it would give support to the speculations above. See also Chapter 12.

Chapter 4

The Essene Church of God

In this and the following chapter I shall turn to the rich storehouse of Jewish religious literature that has in general not been accepted either in the Jewish or the Christian Biblical canon. Traditionally these texts have been called Apocrypha (Greek for 'hidden') and Pseudepigrapha ('falsely named').[1] Most of them have been dated between 200 BC and AD 100. Further, the majority of them have been preserved by being copied and recopied by Christian scribes, and preserved in Christian libraries, often in monasteries, especially in Ethiopia, Arabia and the regions around the Black Sea. This history leads to problems of textual criticism, since we have reason to suspect that the Christian scribes introduced changes and additions, though they are hard to pinpoint.

All this, however, was changed radically by the discovery of the Dead Sea Scrolls in the late 1940s.[2] The 'Qumran library' has been found to contain some of the most important Pseudepigrapha (especially Enoch and Jubilees – see Chapter 5) and, in addition, many other writings not at all known before. Not only can we now see that several (by no means all) of the passages previously suspected of being Christian additions in those Jewish texts were found in the pre-Christian Qumran manuscripts, and thus belonged to the Jewish originals;[3] we have also a much better overview of the wide range of religious opinions among the Jews in Palestine and in the Diaspora at the time when Christianity arose.

I shall treat the Dead Sea Scrolls first, since they provide us with essential information about the Essenes, who may, according to my hypothesis, be the direct forebears of the first-century Christians. When discussing the relationship between Essenes and Christians, however, we must keep constantly in mind that most of the Qumran evidence consists of texts which are considerably earlier than most of the Christian ones.

At least since 1950 the general consensus among scholars has been that the Dead Sea Scrolls were the library of a monastic community of Essenes living at Qumran. Of late, however, more and more researchers have come to the conclusion that the central buildings at Qumran may not have been a 'monastery' at all, but at least partly a military establishment, and that the Scrolls discovered in the many caves around the place were taken there from libraries in Jerusalem, among them, that of the Temple, for safe-keeping during the height of the Jewish war against the Romans in 66–74. After the military fort was taken by the Romans, probably in AD 68, nobody remained to remember the hiding-places, and they were completely forgotten for almost two thousand years. The main propounder of this hypothesis has long been Norman Golb, who argues vigorously for it in his book *Who Wrote the Dead Sea Scrolls?* (1995).[4]

If Golb is right on this point, the Qumran library could in principle mirror a much wider spectrum of Jewish religious thought, than we could expect from a small and isolated sectarian community.[5] The manuscripts can be dated, both on palaeographical grounds and by Carbon 14 methods, from *c.* 200 BC to *c.* AD 70. The number of different manuscripts, including such as consist of only small fragments, is about eight hundred. They belong to three main categories: Biblical manuscripts, works related to the Essene movement, and works unrelated to that movement.[6] In theory the Scrolls might be quite representative of Palestine Judaism as a whole from that period. At least, we should not necessarily expect an exclusive emphasis on sectarian writings.

However, whether the manuscripts derive exclusively from Qumran, or in addition come from Jerusalem, it is obvious that a considerable proportion of the writings do exhibit a remarkably consistent kind of theology which agrees on many points with what we know about the Essenes. But especially the militancy and the strict legalism of many of the Scrolls were surprising, in view of Philo's, Josephus' and Pliny's pictures of the pious and peaceful Essenes. Against this, we must bear in mind that Philo, Josephus and Pliny may have had their own reasons for presenting the Essenes in the way they did. They may have exaggerated some features, playing down others. Josephus, who was eager not to offend the Romans, and who obviously wished to present a favourable picture of the Essenes to his Roman and Greek readers, cannot have been happy to report of their dreams of the Last Judgment, with complete victory and sweet revenge for the Jews on their oppressors. Likewise, and for the same reasons, Josephus disliked Messianism, which he tried to associate mainly with bandits and fanatics. So, even if he knew that at least some Essene groups held views of this kind, he would prefer to keep quiet about it. As for Philo, Josephus' senior by some 60 years, his interests were chiefly theological and philosophical. He accordingly dwelt mainly on those aspects of Essenism. As a very level-headed and liberal-minded man, he naturally kept aloof from fanatics and rebels. That may account for his silence on Jewish Messianism.

Moreover, we should also keep in mind that a large part of the Qumran evidence in general predates Philo, Josephus and Pliny by a century, on average. Therefore the contrast that we observe may partly be due to a development over time, and also, in Philo's case, to a changed perspective caused by the spread of the Essene movement in the Diaspora.

Anyway, it would be wrong to assume that the traditional picture of the Essenes, shaped for us by Philo, Josephus and Pliny, must be objectively correct. The Dead Sea Scrolls may well give a truer picture of the Essenes. Because of the extremely meagre documentation of Jewish writings from the period 200 BC–AD 100, except for documents which the Christians thought were useful, and therefore copied (and modified) in their monasteries throughout the Middle Ages, the Dead Sea Scrolls are now one of the main sources for that literature. As will appear from the discussion in the present chapter, the religious ideas found in the Scrolls give evidence of a high degree of internal consistency – though by no means amounting to uniformity – and agree in the main with what we know and can infer about the Essenes from other evidence.

Therefore I think we should now take the Scrolls, rather than Philo and Josephus, as our chief source for that obviously important branch of Judaism. We should not look upon them as a small, esoteric sect – though branches may have been just that – but as a broad movement of Judaism.[7] From this chapter on, therefore, I shall call the people responsible for producing or collecting the major part of the Qumran library by the name of Essenes, meaning by this a movement in Jewry which included, *among others*, the writers of the central documents in the Qumran library, and also, for instance, Philo's Therapeutae.

The word Essenes (*essēnoi, essaioi*) is somewhat problematic. Most scholars think it is a Greek loanword from Aramaic *hasēn*, said to be an Aramaic form of Hebrew *hasidim*, pious.[8] This is also in fair agreement with Philo, who says in *Quod omnis probus* 75: 'Their name is, I think, a variation, though the form of the Greek is inexact, of *hosiotēs* [holiness].' At another place he writes 'this congregation of Essenes or holy ones [*tōn Essaiōn ē hosiōn*]'. He apparently took the word to be related to the Greek translation, which is hardly acceptable to a modern linguist. Anyway he confirms that the meaning is 'holy, pious'. As we know that the Essenes (like the Christians) also called themselves the holy ones, *hasēn* would then simply be this designation in Aramaic. We shall discuss (in Chapter 11, section about Nazareth) the possibility that they also used about themselves another Hebrew word with a similar meaning, namely, in its Greek dress, *nazeiraios* (nazirite).

Among the central Essene texts are two documents of a constitutional nature, the Community Rule (1QS) and the Damascus Document (CD). The former is a fairly complete and well-preserved text, found only among the Dead Sea Scrolls. The latter is found in Qumran in a number of rather small fragments, whereas two more complete, but much later manuscripts of it, were found in a Cairo synagogue *geniza* (store-room for religious books) in 1896 and 1897. They set out the foundation rules about the organisation and leadership of the community, about the duties of the members, about the acceptance and expulsion of members, about ritual practices, etc.

In CD, we are also told something of the history of the communities. The two documents, CD and 1QS, exhibit many similarities, indicating that they were written for different branches of the same movement.[9] But there are also important differences. The Qumran Community Rule is on the whole stricter, for instance, in the matter of admitting new members, and excluding backsliders. Its community makes a monastic impression, and might in this respect fit in well with Pliny's account of the Essenes in the Judaean desert. The Damascus Document, especially in its historical part, also seems to indicate a monastic community, while some of the rules, e.g. about women and children, would fit in with Josephus' notes about a branch of Essenes living in 'all the towns' of Judaea, among people who were not Essenes.

The number of different manuscripts found in the Qumran caves is, as I said, estimated at about eight hundred. The large majority of these consist of only small fragments, while some are complete scrolls which cover twenty pages or more in a modern edition. Most of the large texts have been published, which means that most of the text material from Qumran is available in print. What remains are the small, but much more numerous fragments, of which many are hardly decipherable.

Of the 800 different manuscripts that have been identified, some 200 contain canonical Biblical texts. No fewer than 36 different manuscripts, mostly consisting of small fragments, contain the Psalms. The second most common canonical text is Deuteronomy (29), the third Isaiah (21). Then follow Genesis, Exodus and Leviticus with about 15 each. Daniel has 8 manuscripts, which is more than Jeremiah and Ezekiel. The other books of the Hebrew Bible contribute at most 4 manuscripts each. Completely absent is Esther.[10]

Three of the Pseudepigrapha are well covered. 1 Enoch has 11 manuscripts, Jubilees 15, early versions of the so-called Testaments of the Twelve Patriarchs 3. Other texts representing hitherto unknown Pseudepigrapha are distributed over a couple of dozen manuscripts.

The popularity of the Psalms, Isaiah and Daniel in the Qumran library indicates that the people responsible for collecting the texts were interested in prophecy, something which the Essenes were especially known for, according to Josephus.[11] The keen interest in Daniel, which contains the earliest reference in the Bible to the immortality of the human soul, also goes well with an Essene orientation. The same may be said, even more emphatically, about the strong representation of Jubilees and 1 Enoch.

End-time and Messianism

In the Qumran Community rule, the word Messiah is often used, as in the Jewish Bible, in a neutral sense, meaning just 'anointed'. It can apparently be applied not only to High Priests and kings, but also, for example, to prophets. Even when the Messiah is clearly a figure of the future, and associated with the End of Time, his function is only vaguely indicated. In the Community Rule we read about 'the Messiahs of Aaron and Israel', i.e. not one Messiah, but two, one being a priest (Aaron belonging to the priestly tribe of Levi), the other a worldly ruler, a king. Since the community for which the constitution is written is clearly dominated by priests, it is not surprising that the priest-Messiah is given priority over the king-Messiah. But, though these end-time Messiahs are no doubt conceived as leading figures, they are not called High Priest or King. Nor is there any indication at all that they are looked upon as superhuman figures. In the Damascus Document, at least in the rather late versions available to us, we hear instead of the Messiah (in the singular) of Aaron and Israel, implying that in some unspecified way he belongs to both tribes.[12] Somewhat surprisingly, David, who of course belonged to the tribe of Judah, is not mentioned in this connection.[13]

In the Qumran War Scroll, also a central text, dated to the period around the beginning of our era, the supreme commander in the final battle against Israel's enemies (here the Romans) is God himself, together with his angels. The same holds in most of the Qumran texts, for the Judge at the Last Judgment. In some texts the Messiah does, however, appear as an advocate for the members of the community, who are called the Elect, the Saints or Holy Ones, the Sons of Light and the like.

One rather fragmentary Qumran text is about Melchizedek (his name means 'Righteous King'). In the Old Testament he appears, briefly, as King of Salem, and is said to be 'the priest of the most high God'. He is a friend of Abraham.[14] In the Qumran fragment, however, he is given superhuman, angelic features. He is not called Messiah in the fragment of text that we have. But he does figure as a judge at the Last Judgment, and accordingly conforms at least partly to the picture of the End-time Messiah of Melchizedek in 2 Enoch, see Chapter 5.

The End-time is referred to as 'the day of revenge' in the Community Rule.[15] Rather naturally, we find a similar picture in the War Scroll: 'the God of Israel has called out the sword against all the nations, and he will do mighty deeds by the Saints of his people'[16] and, further, 'Their [the Gentiles'] kings shall serve you and all your oppressors shall bow down before you.'[17]

The Damascus Document, describing the origin and organisation of an Essene community, probably in the second century BC,[18] shows great interest in the End-time, and in the Messiah's role there, speaking about following the Laws and regulations 'until the coming of the Messiah of Aaron and Israel',[19] and 'until God shall visit the earth',[20] and 'until the coming of the Messiah of Aaron and Israel who will pardon their sins'.[21]

Further, the role of the Teacher of Righteousness (see below) is stressed: 'all those . . . who have listened to the voice of the Teacher of Righteousness . . . shall rejoice. . . . God will forgive them, and they shall see his Salvation.'[22]

Determinism and the calendar

The idea that God has preordained everything, including the life of each individual, even from the beginning of time, is something that we have encountered both in Philo and in early Christian texts. This concept is given prominence in many Qumran documents, which insist again and again that it is only thanks to the grace of God that man can avoid sin, and thus be saved. It is God's decision, before the Creation, which places a person either among the Sons of Light or the Sons of Darkness. In the Damascus Document we read about the sinners: 'from the beginning God chose them not. He knew their deeds before ever they were created. . . . He made known His Holy Spirit to them by the hand of His anointed ones. . . . But those whom he hated he led astray.'[23] Regarding the Bible as God's own words, a kind of emanation of the Holy Ghost, or Wisdom, the Essenes interpreted it allegorically as prophesying about the future. In other words, the history of mankind was preordained by God at the Creation – or even before, as a kind of blueprint (see Chapter 2 about Jesus' pre-existence).

In the Gospels, ideas of predestination are generally not expressed so starkly. But Paul offers parallels. In Romans 8:30 he says about God: 'whom he did predestinate, them he also called, them he also justified'. Further, in Romans 9:18: 'Therefore hath he [God] mercy on whom he will have mercy, and whom he will he hardeneth.' He also applies the idea to himself (Galatians 1:15): 'God . . . separated me from my mother's womb, and called me by his grace.' Naturally the epithets which the Essenes and early Christians applied to themselves, the elect, the chosen, also implied predestination. The philosophical problems that the idea of predestination creates about the origin of Evil in the world are not discussed in the Scrolls, but are a pervasive theme, in the Hymns (1QH). Why did God create evil men? Why did he allow Satan to lead men astray? Why create a being like Satan, in the first place? Apparently the Essenes, like many other deeply religious people before and after, looked upon this problem as one of the mysteries of God.

The deterministic world-view of antiquity, not only among the Jews, has connections with the study of the stars. As people discovered the regular periodicity of the moon, sun, planets and stars, they tended to take the heavenly cosmos as a model for terrestrial matters as well. Astronomy and astrology were not kept apart in primitive cultures and in antiquity, even by an astronomer like Ptolemy. It was considered self-evident that the movements of the heavenly bodies were divinely ordained.

The divinely ordained regularity of the heavenly world was mirrored in the calendar by which the religious festivals and rituals were determined throughout the year. A considerable number of Qumran documents contain a very special calendar, distinct from that of mainstream Judaism, and in some respects from any other known calendar, whether past or present. Before the Qumran discoveries, scholars might have inferred its existence from such texts as Enoch and Jubilees. But only the mass of evidence contained in the Dead Sea Scrolls made it possible to establish in detail how it was constructed.

Its main feature is the importance it attaches to the seven-day week. Like the year and the month, the week can be called a natural measure of time, since the intervals between new moon, first half-moon, full moon, second half-moon and new moon again are, to a first approximation, seven days. But when the seventh day, the Sabbath, was incorporated as an essential element in the Jewish religion, the seven-day period became not simply a practical time measure, but acquired the position of an essential constituent of the order of the universe. Uncivilised tribes might measure by the moon and its phases, which indeed led to the week having *generally* seven days, but sometimes six or eight. God's people, however, obeyed His orders, and scrupulously and consistently counted *exactly* seven days, no more, no less.

The seven-day week spread throughout the Roman empire around the beginning of our era. And there is little doubt that the Romans took it over from Alexandria, where Julius Caesar had found the experts that devised for him a new calendar for the Empire, which is, with small modifications, the one still in use all over the world.[24] Unfortunately the seven days of the week are difficult to coordinate with the 29 or 30 days of the lunar month, and also with the 365.24 days of the solar year. The Essenes, according to several Dead Sea Scrolls, solved the problem by, so to speak, cutting the Gordian knot. They decided to build the whole of their calendar on the week and the year, rather than on the month and the year.[25] In order to accommodate the week within the year, they declared that the year should contain exactly 52 weeks, that is, exactly 52x7=364 days. More than that: the 52 weeks could be easily divided into 4 equal quarters or 13 weeks, or 91 days. That number, in its turn, could be subdivided into 3 months of

30 days each, with an extra day, called 'addition' placed at the end of each quarter.[26]

Interestingly, the Essene theologians managed to take not only the regularity of the heavenly movements, but also their observed deviations from that regularity, as indications of the omnipotence of God. For if those movements were observed to be regular, God had evidently devised this regularity from the start. On the other hand, observed irregularities in the heavenly order could also be given a religious interpretation, as explained below.

Though the decision to have a calendar of their own must have led to a separation of the Essenes from other Jews,[27] the neat rationality of this calendar is obvious. An extra boon was that the quarters of the year were exactly like each other, with the days of the week always falling on the same day of the month from one quarter of the year to the other. Thus if the first day of the first month of a quarter was a Sunday, it was a Sunday in the other quarters too, year after year.

Unfortunately there is one serious hitch. The 1.24 days that the Essene 364 days' year falls short of the astronomical one causes the Essene year-reckoning to fail to keep up with the progress of the seasons. After thirty years, spring will appear more than a month too early. We have no information about how the Essenes solved that problem. The simplest way to do it would be to introduce 'leap days' whenever necessary, just as Julius Caesar introduced a leap day every fourth year in his calendar. Yet that simple and high-handed patching up of the system was unacceptable to the religious Essenes. Exactly every seventh day had to be Sabbath: one simply could not pretend that the leap day did not count as a day of the week. (Incorporating the leap day in the week, as our own Julian–Gregorian calendar does, would upset the beautiful symmetry of the Essene calendar.)

The Essenes found another way out of the dilemma. They continued to maintain that God had indeed instituted a year of exactly 364 days. The fact that the real year proved to be longer than that, so that the seasons kept arriving too early, was explained as God's punishment for men's sins.[28] The implication was that if men ceased sinning, the years and the seasons would again fall into line. Perhaps the Essenes eventually conformed to reality (the unceasing sinfulness of humanity) by introducing instead an extra 'leap week' when needed. In this way the integrity of the week would be preserved. But we find nothing about such a solution in our documents.

Though the Essene calendar, with such a leap week, must be

recognised as quite elegant and rational, it must have created numerous problems for the Essenes living among other Jews, who followed another time-reckoning, and whose festivals occurred on other days (the weekly Sabbaths were presumably the same – except in the case of the Essenes).[29] We have in fact indications of such a difficulty in several Qumran documents, where we are told that an early leader of the community, the Teacher of Righteousness, was taken from them by force, since they, but not their opponents, reckoned the day as a 'Sabbath of Rest', which prevented them from opposing their enemies.[30]

The very distinctive Essene calendar is one of the distinctive features connecting the Qumran texts with each other. We find essential parts of it in the Community Rule and the Damascus Document,[31] and it figures prominently in the Temple Scroll (probably pre-Essene, like Jubilees and most of Enoch) and in many different fragments. Its central feature, the 364-day year, is set forth in two non-canonical texts represented in several manuscripts, Jubilees and Enoch, both of which were accorded authoritative status in the Dead Sea Scrolls.

International Essenism

For the priestly leadership of the core Essene communities, the special character of their calendar was presumably important for keeping them apart from the established Jerusalem priesthood, and also from the mass of ordinary Jews who naturally continued to follow the leaders of the Jerusalem Temple. In fact, keeping apart, separated from the unbelievers, was an important part of Essene ideology – and also, apparently, of Pauline Christianity.[32] Yet, in spite of their élitist exclusiveness, there are indications that the Essenes were eager to win proselytes, and to win supporters. Somewhat surprisingly – in view of the fanatic Jewish nationalism of many Essene texts, and especially the War Scroll – the Essenes seem to have directed much of their attention to the Gentile world, or more exactly, to the large Jewish Diaspora there. This has not been sufficiently recognised in the scholarly discussion so far.[33]

We also have indications that the Essenes met with success in the Diaspora. In previous chapters we have seen how a leading Jewish figure in the Diaspora, Philo, expressed his own high appreciation of the Essene way of thinking. Philo, moreover, writes about the empire-wide spread of a contemplative Essene branch which he calls the Therapeutae. Further, in connection with our discussion in Chapter 2 on the dating of 1 Clement, we have found some support for supposing that at least some features of the Essene calendar had spread among the Jews of Rome as early as the latter half of the first century BC.

There is more. In chapter 14 of the Essene Damascus Document we read that 'the Guardian of all the camps' should be able to 'master all the sects of men and the languages of their clans'. This presumably implies people outside Palestine. To this we may add fragments of invocations in a fragmentary Qumran book of prayers: 'Remember Thy marvels which Thou didst to the Poor of the nations . . . to plant Thy Law into our hearts. . . . Thou wert gracious towards Thy people Israel in all the lands to which Thou didst banish them . . . deliver Thy people Israel from all the lands, near and far . . . every man who is inscribed in the Book of the living.'[34] Such prayers were obviously written for Diaspora Jews.

The inference from all this is inevitable: the Essenes were active throughout Jewry, not only in Palestine. Philo[35] says about the Essenes in Syria–Palestine, that on Saturdays they gather in 'sacred spots which they call synagogues [*kalountai synagōgai*]'. It is very likely that this Greek word was first used in the Diaspora, and by Essenes.[36]

It must also be said that the Diaspora must have been seen as a more promising field for proselytising than, especially, Judaea. Judaea was holy ground, and certainly many thought that non-Jews should not be allowed there. That was clearly the case with at least parts of the Temple, whereas such rules naturally could not be imposed and enforced in the Diaspora.[37]

Bible interpretation

Interpretation of Biblical texts seems to have been a constant preoccupation with the writers of the Qumran documents. Dozens of manuscripts contain such interpretations. The importance of Bible interpretation, and especially an allegorical one, is also what Philo emphasises about the Essenes and the Therapeutae.[38]

Typically each interpretation refers to just a short Biblical passage, as in the examples below. The passage is said to convey a meaning which, to the modern reader, does not seem to have any plausible connection with the words in their Biblical context. In fact, to a modern reader, the connection that the commentator makes often appears completely arbitrary and far-fetched. On the other hand, such interpretations provide a rich mine of information on what occupied the minds of the people who wrote them, and on the community members who obviously attached great importance to them.

The conviction that the community, or more exactly, its priestly leaders, were in possession of a unique ability to interpret the Bible, comes out very strongly in the foundation texts. All novices are to study the 'correct' interpretations provided by the leaders. Moreover, those interpretations are considered so precious that they are ordered to be kept secret: the members were not allowed to divulge them to outsiders. And outsiders included Jews who were not members of the Church of God.

In the Community Rule, where it should be remembered that 'the Law' means the first five books of the Bible, and that 'those of the Way' (as later among the Christians) are the members of the Community, we read: 'The master . . . shall conceal the teaching of the Law from the men of falsehood, but shall implant true knowledge and righteous judgment to those who have chosen the Way'.[39] The teachings are 'mysteries of marvellous truth', which other Jews, 'Israel', have no access to: 'The Interpreter shall not conceal from [the members] any of those things hidden from Israel which have been discovered by him'.[40] This recalls Paul's 2 Corinthians 6:14ff: 'Be ye not unequally yoked with unbelievers . . . what communion hath light with darkness? And what concord hath Christ with Belial? . . . Wherefore come out from among them, And be ye separate, saith the Lord.' Mixing with outsiders was evidently frowned upon.

In the Damascus Document similar ideas are expressed: 'all who enter . . . shall do according to the interpretation of the Law in which they were first instructed'.[41] More specifically, among other things: 'They shall keep the Sabbath day according to its exact interpretation, and the feasts and the Day of Fasting according to the finding of the members of the New Covenant in the land of Damascus.'[42] There is less stress in the Damascus document on the secrecy of the interpretation, and the necessity of not disclosing it to outsiders. However, the exclusiveness of the Community is emphasised: members 'shall separate from the sons of the Pit'.[43]

Interpretation among these Essenes, accordingly, was by no means up to the individual members. On the contrary, to read a text in one's own way was 'to walk in the stubbornness of one's heart' (CD 8, Vermes, p. 89). Against this background it is easy to understand the

107

tremendous authority of the Teacher of Righteousness within the community, a subject which we shall treat in the next section.

I shall give several examples of what kind of interpretations our writers 'discovered', as they put it themselves. However, the community also had other ways of giving expression to their views. Instead of providing an interpretation of the established Biblical text, they could rewrite it, or expand the Bible by producing new books, where their ideas were brought forward. An instance in point is contained in a fragment where, apparently on the basis of various passages of Deuteronomy, Moses is quoted as saying (presumably interpreting God's orders): 'When I have [established] the Covenant and commanded the [Way] in which you shall walk, [appoint wise men whose work] it shall be to expound [to you and your children] all the words of the Law.'[44] This conforms exactly with the regulations expressed in the foundation documents, and is a good example of the internal consistency of the Qumran texts. However, the community's way of interpreting led, somewhat paradoxically, to an uncontrollable expansion of the Biblical corpus of texts. It is hardly surprising that efforts to establish an agreed-upon canon of the Bible gained momentum in the following centuries, both among Jews and Christians. In this process two books which could almost be looked upon as foundation texts among the Essenes, namely, 1 Enoch and Jubilees, were excluded from the Christian canon,[45] and were eventually stigmatised as Pseudepigrapha, 'with false attribution'.[46]

The Teacher of Righteousness

The *moreh zedekh*, 'Teacher of Righteousness', of the Essene movement is, in Alphonse Dupont-Sommer's words, 'one of the most surprising revelations of the Qumran texts'.[47] Gert Jeremias, in 1963, agrees: 'the greatest personality of later Judaism known to us'.[48] In the historical part of the Damascus Document we read that 'God observed their [the community's] deeds, and he raised for them a Teacher of Righteousness to guide them in the way of His heart' (CD 1, Vermes, p. 83). Nothing much is said about just what the Teacher said or did, nor about when he lived. But his death is referred to in another context: 'From the gathering in of the Teacher of the Community until the end of all men of war who deserted to the Lion, shall pass about forty years' (CD B2, Vermes, p. 90). That statement is not very useful for dating purposes. Nor do we get much help from another notice,

108

where the writer praises the members 'who have listened to the voice of the Teacher and have not despised the precepts of righteousness when they heard them' (CD B2, Vermes, p. 91).

But though the Damascus Document had been known to modern scholars since the end of the nineteenth century, the outstanding place of the Teacher among the Essenes did not become clear until fragments of Biblical interpretation were found among the literally hundreds of scraps of manuscripts preserved at Qumran, especially in Cave 4. We have no texts dealing explicitly and directly with the Teacher, besides the Cairo manuscripts of the Damascus Document. But there are more than a dozen instances where a Biblical text is interpreted as a reference to the Teacher. Most of them are from a series of Habakkuk interpretations, dated by most modern scholars to the second half of the first century BC.

As will be obvious from the many examples quoted below, the Biblical text in itself contains no hint at all of the Teacher or his time. The interpretation is entirely a product of the commentator's imagination. As a matter of fact, the Bible interpretations are much more like interpreting dreams, than scholarly attempts to ascertain what the Biblical text 'really' meant, arrived at through an examination of the textual and historical background of the source text. It is indeed significant that the Hebrew word used, *pesher* (plural: *pesharim*) was also, perhaps originally, used specifically about the interpretation of dreams.[49]

That dreams were seen as giving access to the spiritual world and contained forecasts of the future was universally believed in antiquity, and is of course still a popular superstition all over the world. Joseph's interpretations of Pharaoh's dreams is just one example out of thousands. What the Essenes did, in effect, was to apply the same methods to Biblical interpretation. They tried to avoid complete subjectivity by accepting only specially 'elect' persons as interpreters, with the Teacher of Righteousness as the supreme example (see the third quotation, below).

There is a certain family likeness between the Qumran Bible commentaries, and Barnabas' and other early Christian writers' use of Biblical passages as statements referring to Jesus, exemplified earlier in Chapter 2. There is, however, also a fundamental difference. The Qumran Habakkuk commentaries about the Teacher of Righteousness make sense in terms of what we know about the historical situation of the Jews at the time. There is no indication that they contain legendary material. Moreover, they do not form part of a connected story, which might have imposed a certain pattern on them. Their main weakness is their vagueness: they give no dates, and hardly any names. The use of the Old Testament in Barnabas and Gospels is quite different. In them it is the Old Testament text itself, not the interpretation, that provides the information, and is simply asserted to apply to Jesus, and thus serves to build up their connected narrative about him.

Though we may therefore presume that the Habakkuk commentaries provide trustworthy information about the Teacher of Righteousness, it is of course still possible that what we have reflects a tradition that has been formed within the Qumran community about the Teacher. Needless to say, such a tradition may contain fictional material.

Consider the notice in the Damascus Document, quoted above: 'God . . . raised for them a Teacher of Righteousness to guide them in the way of His Heart.' Those words mirror a passage in Deuteronomy 18:15, where God speaks to Moses: 'I will raise them up a Prophet from among their brethren, like unto thee, and will put my words in his mouth: and he shall speak unto them all that I shall command him.' The quotation was obviously considered important at Qumran, since it is included also in another Qumran fragment, which Vermes calls 'A Messianic Anthology'. It is God speaking to Moses: 'I will raise up for them a Prophet like you . . . I will put my words into his mouth, and he shall tell them all that I command him. And I will require a reckoning of whoever will not listen to the words which the Prophet shall speak in my name.' [50] If, as seems likely, the founder applied this saying to himself, it may have laid the foundation for a subsequent elaboration, ending up in the impressive figure of the Teacher of Righteousness as interpreter of God's words. Such a development would be quite natural within the thought-world of the early Essene sect, where Messianism was an important element.

The following seven interpretations, most of them from Habakkuk, are quite typical. I have brought them together here because they all concern the Teacher of Righteousness, and thus indicate to what an extraordinary extent he occupied the thoughts of the Essenes at the time they were written down. Judging largely from palaeography, that seems to have been at the end of the first century BC, which would mean roughly a century after the presumed death of the Teacher.[51]

Neither the Teacher, nor his chief enemies, are ever identified by name in the Qumran texts. Among the persons mentioned are the Wicked Priest, the Spouter of Lies and the Liar. These, it is fairly generally surmised, probably refer to the same person[52] and, judging by the role he plays in the story, many scholars think Jonathan Maccabaeus is intended, High Priest and King 152–143 BC.[53] If so, the Teacher of Righteousness may have been one of the leading priests in Jerusalem, before he assumed leadership among the Essenes in the second half of the second century BC. But this is very uncertain: the fact that we do not know the name of the Teacher is after all hardly more remarkable than that we do not know the name of the author of Deutero-Isaiah, or, for that matter, of the book of Enoch.

On the other hand, we should also reckon with the possibility (see above) that the Teacher is largely a *construction* to give substance to their conception of the founder of their movement. If so, we would have among the early Essenes a near parallel to the reconstruction of the Jesus figure of the canonical Gospels. However, it seems on the whole more likely that the interpretations offered below refer to real, historical persons and events.

Habakkuk, the prophet, is supposed by most modern scholars to have lived in the seventh century BC, his pronouncements or prophecies referring apparently to Assyrians and Babylonians oppressing the Jews. Our interpreter, convinced that the prophet's words were meant as forecasts of the future, and, writing probably around the beginning of our era, transposes this to the history of his community as he understood it, or to conflicts of his own times, both those within his own community and those involving outsiders.[54]

1 Hab 1:4: Therefore the law is slacked, and judgment doth never go forth: for the wicked doth compass about the righteous; therefore wrong judgment proceedeth.
   1QpHab 1, Vermes, p. 283: */Interpreted. . . . The wicked is the Wicked Priest, and the righteous/ is the Teacher of Righteousness.*
2 Hab 1:13: Thou art of purer eyes than to behold evil, and canst not look on iniquity: wherefore lookest thou upon them that deal treacherously, and holdest thy tongue when the wicked devoureth the man that is more righteous than he?
   1QpHab 4, Vermes, p. 285: *Interpreted, this concerns the House of Absalom and the members of its council who were silent at the time of the chastisement of the Teacher of Righteousness and gave him no help against the Liar who flouted the Law in the midst of their whole [congregation].*
3 Hab 2:1–2: I will stand upon my watch, and set me upon the tower and will

watch to see what he will say unto me, and what I shall answer when I am reproved. And the Lord answered me, and said, write the vision, and make it plain upon tables, that he may run that readeth it.

1QpHab 7, Vermes, p. 287: *And God told Habakkuk to write down that which would happen to the final generation. But He did not make known to him when time would come to an end. And as for that which He said,* That he may run that readeth it: *interpreted, this concerns the Teacher of Righteousness, to whom God made known all the mysteries of the words of His servants the Prophets.*

4 Hab 2:8: Because thou hast spoiled many nations, all the remnant of the people shall spoil thee: because of men's blood, and for the violence of the land, of the city, and of all that dwelt therein.

1QpHab 9, Vermes, p. 288: *Interpreted, this concerns the Wicked Priest whom God delivered into the hands of his enemies because of the iniquity committed against the Teacher of Righteousness and the men of his Council, that he might be humbled by means of a destroying scourge, in bitterness of soul, because he had done wickedly to His elect.*

5 Hab 2:15: Woe unto him that giveth his neighbour drink, that puttest thy bottle to him, and makest him drunken also, that thou mayest look on their nakedness!

1QpHab 11, p. 289: *Interpreted, this concerns the Wicked Priest who pursued the Teacher of Righteousness to the house of his exile that he might confuse him with his venomous fury. And at the time appointed for rest, for the Day of Atonement, he appeared before them to confuse them, and to cause them to stumble on the Day of Fasting, their Sabbath of repose.*

6 Micah 1:5: For the transgression of Jacob is all this, and for the sins of the house of Israel. What is the transgression of Jacob? Is it not Samaria? and what are the high places of Judah? are they not Jerusalem?

1Q 14, Vermes, p. 278: *Interpreted, this concerns the Spouter of Lies [who led the] Simple [astray] ... [and] the Teacher of Righteousness [who expounded the law to] his [Council] and to all who freely pledged themselves to join the elect of [God to keep the Law] in the council of the Community: who shall be saved on the Day [of Judgment].*

7 Ps 37:32–3: The wicked watcheth the righteous, and seeketh to slay him/ The Lord will not leave him in his hand, nor condemn him when he is judged.

4Q 171.4, Vermes, p. 292: *Interpreted, this concerns the Wicked [Priest] who [watched the Teacher of Righteousness] that he might put him to death [because of the ordinance] and the law which he sent to him. But God will not aban[don him and will not let him be condemned when he is] tried. And [God] will pay him his reward by delivering him into the hand of the violent of the nations, that they may execute upon him [judgment].*

The above quotations, together with the brief notices in the Damascus Document, contain about all the *explicit* information about

the Teacher of Righteousness that we can gather from the Dead Sea
Scrolls. Tentatively and hypothetically, we may summarise it as
follows. The Teacher was (or was thought to be) a high-ranking Priest
who became the leader and reorganiser of the Essene community in
'Damascus'.[55] This was at a time, probably in the second half of the
second century BC, when the Jews of Palestine were trying, with
considerable success, to assert their independence of the Seleucid
kings of Syria. Jewish nationalism prospered. In the Essene community, led by a priestly élite, the Teacher's authority was supreme. His
interpretations of Scripture were unchallenged, and considered authoritative among the Essenes even a century after his death, to judge from
the third quotation above: God had made known to him 'all the
mysteries of the words of His servants the Prophets'.

However, the Essenes, and especially the Teacher, were apparently
harassed, or even persecuted, by the established Jewish élite, from
whom they had deliberately separated themselves. The Jerusalem
authorities tried to weaken the Essenes by taking the Teacher prisoner.
Eventually they succeeded, by taking advantage of a Day of Fasting
(see the fifth quotation above), something which the Essenes, with
their very special calendar (see above), considered as treason: the
Jerusalem priests, presumably former colleagues of the Teacher, 'gave
him no help' (second quotation). The Teacher's chief enemy,
presumably the High Priest, apparently schemed to capture him in
order to put him to death (seventh quotation). And though the
Teacher's death is not referred to directly in any of the fragments of
text available to us, there are good power-political reasons to suppose
that the High Priest could realise such a plan.[56] In any case it was
natural for the readers of these commentaries to assume that the
persecution eventually led to a martyr's death.

In addition to the direct evidence provided by the Damascus
Document and the Biblical commentaries, another possible source of
information about the Teacher of Righteousness is the Qumran Scroll
of Hymns, *Hodayot* (1QH). Many of those hymns seem to express the
feelings and experiences of a man who sees himself as the leader of
his community. As those experiences agree in general with what we
can infer about the Teacher, many scholars have thought it likely that
the hymns in question were indeed written by the Teacher.[57] But the
inference is uncertain: after all, many of the canonical Psalms of the
Bible also seemingly express the personal experience and feelings of
their authors. This may well have been a style that had come to be

regarded as appropriate for the genre of Psalms. Below I present a number of relevant extracts, as translated by Vermes. Even if they do not flow from the Teacher's pen,[58] they provide unique direct insights into the way of thinking that prevailed in the community he led.

I have numbered the quoted passages, for convenience of reference.

1 1QH 1 (Vermes, p. 167): Thou hast unstopped my ears/to marvellous mysteries.

2 1QH 2 (Vermes, p. 169): To traitors thou hast made of me/ a mockery and scorn/ but a counsel of truth and understanding/ to the upright of way.

3 the assembly of the wicked has raged against me ... but to the elect of righteousness/ thou hast made me a banner/ and a discerning interpreter of wonderful mysteries

4 To all those who seek smooth things/I have been a spirit of zeal

5 1QH 2 (p. 170): Thou made me an object of shame and derision/ in the mouth of all the seekers of falsehood

6 thou hast redeemed my soul/ from the hand of the mighty

7 1QH 3 (p. 173): Thou hast cleaned a perverse spirit of great sin/ that it may stand with the host of the Holy Ones/ and that it may enter into community/ with the congregation of the Sons of Heaven

8 (p. 174): The war of the heavenly warriors shall scourge the earth/ and it shall not end before the appointed destruction/ which shall be for ever and without compare

9 1QH 4 (Vermes, p. 175): They have banished me from my land/ like a bird from its nest

10 they withhold from the thirsty the drink of Knowledge/ and assuage the thirst with vinegar/ that they may gaze ... on their folly concerning feast days

11 (p. 176): All those who are gathered in Thy Covenant/ inquire of me/ and they hearken to me who walk in the way of Thy heart/ who array themselves for Thee/in the Council of the holy

12 Thou hast done wonders before the Congregation/ for the sake of Thy glory

13 (p. 177): When the wicked rose against Thy Covenant/ and the damned against Thy word/ I said in my sinfulness/ I am forsaken by thy Covenant

14 For Thou hast created the just and the wicked

15 1QH 5 (Vermes, p. 178): Thou hast caused me to dwell with the many fishers/who spread a net upon the face of the waters

16 For Thou hast not forsaken me/ in my soul's distress/ and Thou hast heard my cry/ in the bitterness of my soul

17 1QH 5 (Vermes, p. 179): [All who have eaten] my bread/ have lifted their heel against me/ and all those joined to my Council/ have mocked me with wicked lips./ The members of my [Covenant] have rebelled/ and have murmured round about me;/ they have gone as talebearers/ before the children of mischief/ concerning the mystery which Thou hast hidden in me.

18 1QH 6 (Vermes, p. 181): And I know there is hope/ for those who turn from transgression/ and for those who abandon sin

19 (p. 182): All the nations shall acknowledge Thy truth/ and all the people Thy glory

20 They shall cause a shoot to grow/ into the boughs of an everlasting Plant/ It shall cover the whole [earth] with its shadow [and its crown] (shall reach) to the [clouds]

21 (p. 183): For Thou wilt set the foundation on rock . . . and the tried stones [Thou wilt lay] by the plumb-line [of truth]

22 And then at the time of Judgment/ the Sword of God shall hasten/ and all the sons of His truth shall awake/ to [overthrow] wickedness

23 1QH 7 (Vermes, p. 184): Thou hast shed Thy Holy Spirit upon me/ that I may not stumble . . . Thou hast made me like a strong tower, a high wall,/ and hast established my edifice upon rock

24 (p. 185): But I lean on the [abundance of thy mercies]/ and hope [for the greatness] of Thy grace/ that Thou wilt bring [salvation] to flower

25 1QH 9 (Vermes, p. 190): I delight in my scourges/ for I hope for Thy loving kindness

26 (p. 191): Thou wilt conceal the truth until [its] time/ and [righteousness] until its appointed moment/ Thy rebuke shall become my joy and gladness/ and my scourges shall turn to [eternal] healing/ and everlasting [peace]

27 (p. 192): For Thou art a father/ to all [the sons] of Thy truth

28 1QH 10 (Vermes, p. 192): Clay and dust that I am/ what can I devise unless Thou wish it . . . nothing is done without Thee/ and nothing is known without Thy will

29 (p. 194): [for the soul] of Thy servant has loathed [riches] and gain/ and he has not desired exquisite delights/ My heart rejoices in Thy Covenant/ and Thy truth delights my soul

30 1QH 11 (Vermes, p. 195): I will sing Thy mercies/ and on Thy might I will meditate all day long/ I will bless Thy Name evermore/ I will declare Thy glory in the midst of the sons of men

31 Thou hast purified man of sin/ that he may be made holy for Thee . . . and partake of the lot of Thy Holy Ones

32 (p. 196): Thy truth shall be revealed in eternal glory/ and everlasting peace

33 1QH 12 (Vermes, p. 199): How shall I seek Thee unless Thou uncover my heart/ and how follow the way that is straight/ unless [Thou guide me]?

34 1QH 13 (p. 199): the host of Thy spirits/and the Congregation [of Thy Holy Ones/ the heavens and all] their hosts . . . for Thou hast established them from before eternity (p. 200) And Thou hast [appointed] all these things/ in the mysteries of Thy wisdom

35 (p. 200): By Thy goodness alone is man righteous

36 1QH 14 (Vermes, p. 201): Thou wilt blot out all wickedness [and sin] for ever/ and Thy righteousness shall be revealed/ before the eyes of all Thy creatures

37 But according as [Thou drawest a man near to Thee, so will I love] him/ and according as Thou removest him far from Thee/ so will I hate him/ and

none of those who have turned [from] Thy [Covenant]/ will I bring into the Council

38 1QH 15 (Vermes, p. 202): I have clung to the Congregation/ that I might not be separated from any of Thy laws

39 Thou alone didst [create] the just/ and establish him from the womb . . . (p. 203) but the wicked Thou didst create/ for [the time] of Thy [wrath]

40 [For according to the mysteries] of Thy [wisdom]/ Thou hast ordained them for great chastisements/ before the eyes of all Thy creatures/ that [for all] eternity/ they may serve as a sign [and a wonder]/ that [all men] may know Thy glory/ and Thy tremendous power

41 1QH 16 (Vermes, p. 204): And I know that man is not righteous/ except through Thee

42 1QH 18 (p. 206): [that he might be] according to Thy truth/ a messenger [in the season] of Thy goodness/ that to the humble he might bring/ glad tidings of Thy great mercy/ [proclaiming salvation]/ from out of the fountain [of holiness/ to the contrite] of spirit.

I do not think anybody can deny that the Hymns are great religious poetry, in which intensity and depth of feeling are beautifully united with complete devotion to God, and submission to his will. The style, and the ideas expressed in the above extracts also illustrate the very great similarity between the ideas expressed in the Hymns, and those found in the Community Rule, which many scholars think was written by the Teacher. All this fits in perfectly with the hypothesis that the Teacher of Righteousness is indeed the author of at least many of these Hymns.

That hypothesis receives further support from the fact that the Community Rule itself has a final, poetic part, whose style and contents are very close to the Hymns:

43 1QS 10 (Vermes, p. 76): I will sing with knowledge and all my music/ shall be for the glory of God

44 (p. 77): I will meditate on His power/ and will lean on His mercies all day long/ I know that judgment of all the living is in His hand

45 I will praise Him when distress is unleashed/ and will magnify Him also because of His salvation/ I will pay to no man the reward of evil;/ I will pursue him with goodness/ for the judgment of all the living is with God/ and it is He who will render to man his reward/ . . . / I will not grapple with the men of perdition/ until the Day of Revenge . . . my tongue shall always proclaim/ the goodness of God and the sins of men

46 1QS 11 (Vermes, p. 78): My justification is with God./ in His hand are the perfection of my way/ and the uprightness of my heart / He will wipe out my transgressions/ through his righteousness

47 and from His marvellous mysteries/ is the light of my heart

48 (p. 79): For mankind has no way/ . . . /since justification is with God/ and perfection of way is out of His hand

50 (p. 80): For without Thee no one is perfect/ and without Thy will nothing is done

52 There is none beside Thee to dispute Thy counsel/ or to understand all Thy holy design,/ or to contemplate the depth of Thy mysteries/ and the power of Thy might.

Whether the hymns from which the above quotations were taken were written by the Teacher of Righteousness or not – indeed, whether or not the Teacher was a figure partly imagined or created by the Essenes[59] – they are important, since they were part and parcel of the jealously guarded foundation documents at Qumran. Hence we can be sure that they express at least the community's ideal picture of their prophet.

He is an impressive figure, sure in his conviction that he has been selected by God for the position he fills: 'All those who are gathered in Thy Covenant/ inquire of me/ and they hearken to me who walk in the way of Thy heart/ who array themselves for Thee/ in the Council of the holy' (11). But he has also met with opposition within the community:' [All who have eaten] my bread/ have lifted their heel against me/ and all those joined to my Council/ have mocked me with wicked lips./ The members of my [Covenant] have rebelled/ and have murmured round about me;/ they have gone as talebearers/ before the children of mischief/ concerning the mystery which Thou hast hidden in me' (17; see also 5, 13).

Once he was even reduced to despair: 'When the wicked rose against Thy Covenant/ and the damned against Thy word/ I said in my sinfulness/ I am forsaken by thy Covenant' (13), a passage that points to Jesus' words on the cross 'My God, why hast thou forsaken me?' (Mt 26, Mk 15:34, echoing Psalm 22:1). But he recovers his faith: 'For Thou hast not forsaken me/ in my soul's distress/ and Thou hast heard my cry/ in the bitterness of my soul' (16).

He remains strong in his faith: 'Thou hast shed Thy Holy Spirit upon me/ that I may not stumble. . . . Thou hast made me like a strong tower, a high wall,/ and hast established my edifice upon rock' (27). But he emphasises that his faith is wholly due to God: 'How shall I seek Thee unless Thou uncover my heart/ and how follow the way that is straight/ unless [Thou guide me]?'(33); 'Clay and dust that I am/ what can I devise unless Thou wish it . . . nothing is done without Thee/ and nothing is known without Thy will' (28); 'And I know that man is not righteous/ except through Thee' (41). The determinism of the Essenes is obvious: 'By thy goodness alone is man righteous' (35); 'Thou alone didst [create] the just/ and establish him from the womb . . . [p. 203] but the wicked Thou didst create/ for [the time] of Thy [wrath]' (39).

Unlike Jesus in the Gospel, he explicitly pledges to hate the wicked: 'But according as [Thou drawest a man near to Thee, so will I love] him/ and according as Thou removest him far from Thee/ so will I hate him/ and none of those who have turned [from] Thy [Covenant]/ will I bring into the Council' (37). However, the harshness of this saying is somewhat softened at another place: 'I will pay to no man the reward of evil;/ I will pursue him with goodness/ for the judgment of all the living is with God/ and it is He who will render to man his reward/ . . . / I will not grapple with the men of perdition/ until the Day of Revenge . . . my tongue shall always proclaim/ the goodness of God and the sins of men' (45). He realises that his own righteousness is not something he has deserved by his own deeds: 'I know that man is not righteous/ except through Thee' (41, see also 35). This is more in conformity with Paul's attitude towards predestination (see p. 29).

He predicts the Final Judgment: 'The war of the heavenly warriors shall scourge the earth/ and it shall not end before the appointed destruction/ which shall be for ever and without compare.' But he also foresees the eventual conversion of the whole world to faith in God: 'All the nations shall acknowledge Thy truth/ and all the people Thy glory' (19), a saying which would have appealed to Philo, a universalist Jew who admired the Essenes.

His several references to 'mysteries', meaning 'revelations of secret knowledge' (1, 3), indicates affinities with Paul and the Gnostics, and his references to the necessity of repentance points to both Hermas and to the Gospels.

There are also turns of phrase in the hymns which may indicate a connection with the Gospels. For instance, 'They have banished me from my land, like a bird from its nest' (9), which we may compare with Matthew 8:20 and Luke 9:58: 'The foxes have holes, and the birds of the air have nests; but the Son of Man hath not where to lay his head.' Another verbal correspondence, though perhaps less remarkable, is the reference to 'foundation on rock' in (21), recalling Matthew 16:18 saying to Peter: 'upon this rock I will build my church', and also, the allegory of the *Pastor* of Hermas. And certainly the similarity of 'Thou has caused me to dwell with the many fishers/

who spread a net upon the face of the waters'(15) is intriguing, in view of the Gospel story of Jesus recruiting his first disciples among fishers at the Sea of Tiberias.

Although the hymns certainly stress the 'élitist' features of the Essene community – implicit also in the name they often employed, the Elect – there are also instances where a more universalist attitude appears: 'All the nations shall acknowledge Thy truth/ and all the people Thy glory' (19; see also 18, 20), views which could particularly appeal to people in the Diaspora.

Summarising, it is clear that the Qumran religious poetry contains a number of remarkable parallels with Christian writings, though naturally much more with first-century Christian texts than with the Gospels. This is what we should expect, if the dating which I argue for in Chapters 2 and 9 is accepted. Further, it is not surprising that the hymns, probably dating to the time before Paul's 'evangelisation', have little to say about such a subject as resurrection. Also, though suffering and persecution are often mentioned, their redemptive power is not clearly brought out. Altogether, the evidence presented here contributes its share of support to the hypothesis I am exploring and testing throughout this book, namely, that Christianity developed within an Essene matrix.

The Qumran texts quoted here put it beyond doubt that the memory of the Teacher of Righteousness was still treasured among the Essenes a century or more after his presumed death, and his stature as an interpreter of the Prophets had, if anything, increased. As they believed that God had 'made known to him all the mysteries of the words of His servants the Prophets', he was placed above the Old Testament Prophets, since his interpretation of them was the final word. Hence we are not surprised to find that the term *Unique Prophet* seems to be applied to him.[60]

Considering the great and positive interest that two such important Jewish figures as Philo and Josephus took in the Essenes, and Philo's assertion that the Therapeutae (as I have said, commonly considered to be a branch of the Essenes) were to be found 'in many parts of the inhabited world', it seems safe to conclude that the Essenes commanded a wide and important following, with branches of the movement throughout the Roman Empire. Therefore it is all the more surprising that we have hardly any mention of the Teacher outside the Qumran texts. My own solution to this riddle would run as follows.

Before the discovery of the Qumran manuscripts, our direct

evidence about Jewish religious literature from the centuries around the beginning of our era was very scanty. Most of what we do have, moreover, are writings that have been preserved, and certainly often modified, in a Christian milieu. And the traditional history of Christianity, largely based on Eusebius and Luke–Acts, has emphasised the antagonism of Jews and Christians. In this book I argue that Eusebius and Luke–Acts are not to be trusted: they present a highly biased picture of history, designed to strengthen their own view of the development of a Christianity entirely created by Jesus around AD 30. In particular, I have tried to bring out the *Jewishness* of the earliest Christians. Not only were the earliest apostles Jews, and regarded themselves as Jews, but the communities, most of them in the Diaspora, also seem to have consisted chiefly of Jews (see especially Chapter 2).

In Chapters 1–3 I have produced considerable evidence that the earliest Christian communities, the Churches of God, developed out of pre-existent Essene (or para-Essene) communities. Thanks to the 'evangelisation' carried out by the earliest apostles, Paul and his contemporaries, the communities were made to realise that the great teacher and prophet whom they took to be the founder of their Church, and who they believed had been dead for over a hundred years, had now been seen in Heaven, and should be regarded as the Messiah, their Saviour. In the Qumran texts – largely unknown to the Diaspora communities – he was never named, but referred to by the title Teacher of Righteousness. But after the apostles had been overwhelmed by the experience of seeing him in Heaven, they began to use instead, exclusively, the name Jesus, a name meaning, roughly, Salvation, and therefore very appropriate for somebody they had now come to look upon primarily as their Saviour. The designation Teacher of Righteousness disappears completely.

Whether Jesus was the real name that the Teacher (assuming he was real) had borne when he led the Essene sect in the late second century BC is impossible for us to say, since even the highly secret Qumran documents consistently avoid disclosing that name. Moreover, we have no reason to think that the early apostles were in a better position than we are. After all, nobody knew the real names of the several authors of the various texts known under the names of Isaiah and Enoch. Assigning, arbitrarily, an author's name to an important text, irrespective of its historicity, was a common practice among the

Christians as well. The names of the Gospel writers are instances in point.

All this is of course speculative. However, the complete disappearance of the designation Teacher of Righteousness is intriguing. One possible explanation may be that the term was in fact used in the first Christian communities (see Chapter 2), but was suppressed by the Church after it had come to accept the view that Jesus had lived in the early first century AD. Those community members who continued to regard the Teacher of Righteousness as a prophet of the second century BC would naturally be confused if the Jesus who was crucified under Pilate was identified with the Teacher who had lived some hundred and fifty years earlier.[61]

The Teacher and Jesus

In a book published in Paris in 1959 A. Dupont-Sommer discussed the possibility that the Teacher of Righteousness might be the prototype of the Jesus of the Christians. In the end he rejected the identification, pointing especially to the obvious differences between the Teacher of the Scrolls, and the Jesus of the New Testament:

Teacher	**Jesus**
priest of the Levi tribe	layman of the Judah tribe
active in Judaea	active in Galilee
book learning	popular wisdom
ascetic monk	living among the common people
Gnostic and esoteric	popular preacher

Essenism	**Christianity**
strictly hierarchical	'the first will be the last'
strongly disciplinarian	'do not judge'
secrets known only to the few	'things hidden from the wise'
members striving for perfection	the poor and simple
strict adherence to the law	laxity, e.g. about Sabbath rules

Christian theologians in general have naturally been glad to follow Dupont-Sommer on this score. They have been eager to defend the uniqueness of Jesus, which also safeguards the divine origin of Christianity. However, research on the Qumran literature and on the Judaism of the time has brought out the diversity of the religious situation of the Jews during the centuries around the beginning of our era. Throughout this book I have stressed that such diversity also characterised the Christian movement during the first century AD. For instance, though the question of circumcision loomed large in Paul's writings, it was clearly not such a burning issue for other Christians (and Jews, such as Philo) as Paul may have led us to think. And the strictness of the Community Rule of Qumran should be contrasted with the liberal philosophy of the Therapeutae, to show the range of diversity within the Essene movement also. Thus, while the contrasts listed by Dupont-Sommer are indeed real, their importance should not be exaggerated. There were other Essenisms and other Christianities.

For instance, we must constantly keep in mind that the Qumran documents are, for the most part, a century or more older than the Christian writings which are available to us. Thus some of the differences between the two categories may be due to developments over time.

Dupont-Sommer contrasts the Qumran literature with the New Testament as a whole. But throughout this book I argue that the Christianity of Paul, and in fact that of the whole genuinely first century, is radically different from that of the Gospels. As I shall show in Part II, the second-century Christian Church deliberately and systematically distanced itself from some of its roots, rewriting its history, suppressing the memory of its Essene precursors, and playing down its Gnostic elements.

Thus, instead of comparing the Essenes and their Teacher with the Christianity of the Gospels, we should compare them with what we can infer from the first-century Christian literature. For instance, my redating of 1 Clement, together with Paul's own account of his missions, allows us to infer that the 'Church of God' (a name used both by Essenes and first-century Christians) was an established organisation as early as the very beginning of the first century AD, and perhaps even earlier. It was apparently organised efficiently, though we cannot discern exactly how. Though that Church had an important community in Jerusalem, its main strength certainly lay among the Jews of the Diaspora. And I have shown above that the Essene movement, around the beginning of our era, made special efforts to reach the Diaspora, where it developed in a liberal, universalistic direction. This development naturally appealed to the Diaspora audiences, as shown by Philo's example, and also by such writings as the Enoch literature and the Testament of the XII Patriarchs, which were much read by both Essenes and Christians.

It is indeed now generally admitted among scholars that there was considerable overlap between Essenism and early Christianity, which I have exemplified above. Christians took over Essene ideas and read Essene books, and Essenes are widely believed to have joined the Christian Church. But the same scholars have unanimously refused to accept the Essene Teacher as the prototype of Jesus. No doubt the Jesus of the Gospels has little in common with the great Essene prophet. But, if we compare him instead with the Jesus figure of the first-century Christians, our difficulties vanish. It is true that Paul and his contemporaries have little of substance to say about the earthly Jesus, beyond that he was persecuted and died. But this agrees with what we can plausibly infer about the Teacher of Righteousness.

It is in fact *not* the positive correspondences between Jesus and the Teacher of Righteousness that are the main support for my contention that the figure that Paul and his contemporaries referred to under the name of Jesus was the Essene Teacher of Righteousness. Rather, it is the *position* of the Teacher among the Essenes, and the *position* of Jesus among the earliest Christians, that forms the foundation of the identification. In his Essene community he had established a supreme authority thanks to the power of his (assumed or real) personality. As their interpreter of the Bible he filled the function of a prophet. Indeed, he was placed above the Old Testament prophets, since it was he who interpreted their sayings. There is no evidence that he was regarded or regarded himself as a divine figure or a Messiah. The designation once found in the Scrolls, the Unique Prophet, fits him well.

After the Teacher's death (which, as I said above, we – and perhaps the apostles also – might infer took place around 100 BC), he remained a central figure in the thoughts and religious practice of the Essenes. He apparently continued to figure in their ritual meals, where his death as a martyr was commemorated. As time passed, and Messianic, apocalyptic speculations became rife among the Jews, and emphatically so among many Essene groups, it was inevitable that the figure of the Teacher, the Unique Prophet, should be drawn into that sphere of ideas. This is where Paul entered the scene. After joining a movement that he had originally at least stood aloof from, Paul was eventually convinced by a revelation that the movement's one-time founder and leader, the Teacher of Righteousness, was more than a Teacher: he was the promised Messiah.

123

This laid the foundation for the subsequent development of Christianity as a new religion, separate from Judaism.

Chapter 5

More Essene Writings

I shall treat here some other Jewish writings which have a bearing on early Christianity and on Essenism. Most of them are problematic, since, except for Qumran, they have been preserved only, or almost only, in Christian milieus. It is therefore difficult to decide to what extent the texts have been emended by Christian scribes. For an overview of this literature, see especially Charlesworth (ed.), *The Old Testament Pseudepigrapha* i-ii, 1983, 1985 and Nickelsburg, *Jewish Literature between the Bible and the Mishnah*, 1981.

In this chapter I shall first make a general survey of Enoch, Jubilees and the Testaments of the Twelve Patriarchs, and then specifically analyse Messiah concepts in a somewhat wider choice of texts.

Enoch and Jubilees

The Enoch (or Henoch) literature derives its name from the descendant of Seth and father of Methuselah, who is mentioned briefly in Genesis 5:24: 'And Enoch walked with God: and he was not, for God took him.' This passage was interpreted (not very plausibly) to mean that Enoch had been taken up to Heaven by God. Therefore, it was held, he had received revelations about heavenly secrets. This naturally attracted the Essenes to the Enoch figure.

1 Enoch consists of five parts, the earliest probably from the second century BC, the latest some time during the first century AD. Much of it is apocalyptic: it deals with revelations. Like the Essenes, the early Christians also evidently appreciated Enoch. The Letter of Jude quotes him, and Paul's letters contain many somewhat veiled references to him. In the Ethiopian Church 1 Enoch was considered canonical.

Jubilees is essentially a rewriting of canonical Old Testament Genesis and Exodus, where particular attention is given to explaining the calendar, which here is the Essene one. Numerous fragments of both Enoch and Jubilees were found in the Qumran caves. They are connected with each other in the sense that Jubilees 21:10 refers to 'the words of Enoch', as well as 'the Words of Noah', as if they were authoritative prophetic books, while Enoch, for its part, makes use of the same chronological and calendrical concepts as Jubilees.[1]

Jubilees and 1 Enoch are among the Biblical writings found most frequently in the Dead Sea Scrolls. They have not been finally accepted in either the Jewish or the Christian Biblical canon. In several of the Scrolls, however, Jubilees is used as an authoritative text, prescribed reading for the members of the community.

The contents and style of Jubilees and Enoch are such that it is natural to look upon them as belonging to the same branch of Jewish religious thought as the central Qumran texts.[2] We have here the same emphasis on the chosen 'remnant' of Israel, on the elect and righteous, those who followed perfectly the Way. Accordingly these people were convinced that they had renewed the covenant with God, so that he would save them into a life of everlasting bliss at the End of time, while the men of the Pit, those who followed the way of Darkness, would be punished with torture and death.[3] On all these points, of course, the Essenes and the Christians had similar ideas.

An important parallel in Enoch and Jubilees with the Essene writings is the unique 364-day calendar, subdivided into four identical quarters.[4] The festivals are also the same as in the Qumran texts, and great importance is attached to the Festival of Weeks, or Pentecost, which is also in memory of the 'renewal of the Covenant': the Covenant concluded by Moses with God on Sinai is traditionally connected with Pentecost.[5] It occurs, according to the Essene calendar, on a Sunday, fifty days after the Sabbath of Passover.

It is important to remember that, except for the fragments found at Qumran, the available manuscripts of Enoch and Jubilees have been preserved in a Christian milieu – a fact, by the way, which underscores the close contacts between Christians and Essenes in the early centuries of our era. Hence we must also expect Christian additions and changes in the texts, sometimes motivated theologically, and sometimes due to sheer inability on the part of the scribes to grasp the meaning of the text. For instance, the presentation of the calendar is in many cases so muddled in some versions of the Enoch books that the readers must have been hard put to make sense of the text.

Even when the fairly clear Christian emendations are discounted, we have to keep in mind that 1 Enoch, especially, is a composite text in the form we possess it: the most complete text was until recently an Ethiopian one, in a manuscript that is no older than the fifteenth century.[6] Scholars have identified at least five different parts, one of which, the Parables (also called Similitudes) covers chapters 37–71 and most of 91–4 in the standard Ethiopic text. Moreover, the discovery of fragments of an Aramaic version in Qumran[7] indicates that the Ethiopic text is an abbreviated one, something which might have been inferred from the many quotations from Enoch in other early writings, for instance, Barnabas (see Chapter 2), passages which have not survived in the Ethiopic text.

Some of this material may be recoverable from 2 Enoch, a text which is preserved only in a medieval Slavonic manuscript, certainly translated from the Greek. Several parts of it are probably old, and pre-Christian. One passage, for instance, has God saying about the Creation: 'The first-created day I named for myself[8] . . . and I blessed the seventh day, in which I rested from all my doings[9] . . . On the eighth day I likewise appointed, so that the eighth day might be the first, the first-created of my week.'[10]

The first and the eighth day here indicate Sunday, the Lord's day, as implied by the text. If these passages go back to a pre-Christian origin, we have here an important background to the Christian celebration of Sunday as a holiday, and the subsequent abandonment of the Jewish Sabbath. See also the passage about the Lord's day in Barnabas 15:9, discussed in Chapter 2.

Another important section of 2 Enoch is the story of Melchizedek, which has parallels both at Qumran and in the Letter to the Hebrews. More on this below.

As the Parables of 1 Enoch is the only major part of which not even a fragment has been identified in the Qumran library, several scholars have concluded that this part was probably composed after the fall of Jerusalem in AD 70. But the text itself does not offer any good clues about its dating; the majority of modern scholars favour a date in the first half of the first century AD, making Parables roughly contemporary with Paul.[11] We shall treat the Messianic ideas in Parables below.

If we accept a wide definition of the Essene movement, Enoch and Jubilees do at least qualify as proto-Essene. The main reason for not including them in the Essene core is that they do not say anything about the Teacher of Righteousness. (This may be said to parallel our characterisation of Essene-type texts as pre-Christian, if they do not speak of Jesus as the Messiah.) The absence of any mention of the Teacher is of course not surprising, if they were written before the Teacher joined the movement. (That he did so is stated explicitly in the Damascus Document, CD.) On the other hand, the many features which Jubilees and Enoch have in common with the central Qumran literature show to what extent Essene ideas were in the air among Jews in the second century BC.

Testaments of the XII Patriarchs

Fragments of different versions of this popular text have been found in Qumran, though in versions which are not the direct originals of the Greek versions, the ones we will consider here. As in the case of 1 Enoch, one of our difficulties with the Testaments is that the text, which probably originated in the second century BC, has almost certainly been revised by Christian scribes. Scholars have generally agreed that the original was pre-Christian Jewish.[12] This view naturally gets support from the Qumran finds. Several of the passages which have been suspected of being Christian additions are in fact such as are fairly typical of the Essene literature.[13]

The originals of the Testaments as we now have them were probably first written in Greek: Biblical quotations are from the Septuagint.[14] Some scholars propose that the country of origin may be Egypt. The importance of the Law is stressed. But it is the Law seen as an expression of Wisdom, as in Philo. For instance, circumcision and food laws are treated as metaphors of moral purity. The Sabbath laws are hardly even mentioned. There is no Jewish exclusiveness: the general impression is universalism. In fact, we recognise in the Testaments many of the characteristics of Philo's kind of Judaism. On the other hand, we should also remember that even the Qumran foundation texts, in spite of their extremely strong stand on the Law of Moses, do not very often specify any rules by means of actual examples. They also insist, when interpreting them, that the teaching of the leaders of the community should be scrupulously followed – above all, we may suppose, that of the Teacher of Righteousness. But it must be admitted that we have no precise evidence about what kind of interpretation the Teacher favoured for the Mosaic Law.

The somewhat paradoxical closeness of the liberal-minded Testaments to the Essene movement appears in many references from the Testaments to the Enoch literature. Indeed, Naphtali speaks of the 'writings of the holy Enoch'. Benjamin says 'Enoch the righteous'. Many references are to passages which are not found in the Enoch literature that has survived. As we noted Chapter 2, similar unidentified quotations occur, for instance, in Barnabas. Clearly much of the Enoch literature, obviously of great importance to the Essenes, has disappeared from our view. We may add that the Testaments of the XII, like Enoch, was very popular among Christians: Charles 1913 (2, pp. 282, 291–2) goes as far as saying 'Paul used it as a vademecum'.

A pervasive theme in the Testaments is the insistence on sexual purity (Reuben, Judah, Benjamin). As at Qumran, we find that the Two Ways, or the Two Spirits, also figure prominently (Judah, Asher). Like Qumran, the Testaments speak about Salvation coming to Israel from both Levi and Judah, and Judah admits that God has subjected the kingship to the priesthood. See below, in the section about Messiah concepts.

Universalism in the Testaments, in the sense of openness towards the Gentiles, comes out especially in Naphtali, where we read about the nations, i.e. the Gentiles: '[they] shall obtain a share in the twelve staffs of Israel'(5:8). It is also Naphtali who exhorts the Jews to live virtuously, since thus 'God will be glorified through you among the Gentiles', whereas in the contrary case 'God will be dishonoured among the Gentiles'. We need hardly doubt that the author had the Diaspora very much in mind.

Benjamin, likewise, has a universalistic concern for the Gentiles. At the Last Judgment 'the twelve tribes shall be gathered . . . and all the Gentiles' (9:2), and salvation is open to 'all the nations'. In Levi we read: 'from Judah a king shall arise, and he shall found a new priesthood in the world in accord with the gentile model, open for all nations'.[15]

The use of the words 'saints' and 'holy ones' about the people addressed is a clear link with the central Essene texts. Levi is made to say 'the Lord will raise up a new priest . . . he will grant the saints to eat of the tree of life/ the spirit of holiness shall be upon them . . . all the saints shall be clothed in righteousness' (18:23). And Dan: 'the Messiah . . . shall take from Beliar the captives (5:10) . . . the souls of the saints . . . all the saints shall refresh themselves in Eden, the righteous shall rejoice in the New Jerusalem' (5:12).

Messiah concepts

The word Messiah is not used at all in the Old Testament in the special sense that it has acquired in Christianity. In general it means simply 'anointed', and is used mostly about kings and priests in phrases like 'The Lord's anointed', 'His anointed'.[16] Its first occurrence in a sense approaching the Christian one is in the apocryphal Psalms of Solomon, dated to the middle of the first century BC. In the book of Daniel such a Messianic figure occurs, but is not called by the name of 'Messiah', but 'Son of Man', which we find also in the Parables part of 1 Enoch, dated to the first century AD. In general, Messianic figures regarded as Saviours do not occur frequently until after the establishment of Roman rule over Palestine. However, they are extremely diverse and variable. As is natural in a literature that deals with prophecies and revelations about the future, these Messiah figures are mostly connected with what was seen as the End-time, the time immediately preceding and sometimes including the Last Judgment.[17]

Qumran

As I said above, the word Messiah in the Qumran literature has in general the theologically neutral sense that it also has in the canonical Old Testament books. Like its Greek translation, *christos*, it means simply 'anointed', and is applied to kings (even foreign kings, like Cyrus of Persia), to High Priests and to prophets, including Moses. It should therefore cause no surprise that the Community Rule mentions two Messiahs, one from Aaron and one from Israel, and that these figures appear at the regular ritual community meal. Presumably they were just the acting priestly ruler of the Council and his non-priestly colleague. There is no indication that the End-time Messiahs would have a more exalted status, though the eschatological atmosphere of the End-time may have led to such speculations. The Teacher of Righteousness is never associated with the concept of an eschatological, superhuman Messiah.

The only fully superhuman Messiah figure among the Dead Sea Scrolls appears in a text fragment about the Old Testament figure of Melchizedek. It must be stressed, however, that neither the Old Testament Melchizedek, nor the Melchizedek of the Qumran fragment, is called 'the Messiah', or even 'a Messiah'.

Enoch, excluding the Parables

The figure of Enoch interested the Essenes because he was a descendant of Seth and the father of Methuselah, but above all because in Genesis 5:24 we read: 'Enoch walked with God: and he was not, for God took him.' This was commonly interpreted to mean that God took him direct to heaven.

In 1 Enoch, excluding the Parables, the Day of Judgment is barely mentioned, in a passage describing Enoch's prophecies about 'what will happen at the Day of Judgment'. In Jubilees, as is to be expected in a text which is in effect a rewritten version of Genesis, no Messianic figure at all appears.

In the older portions of 1 Enoch (excluding the Parables, which will be treated below), there are mentions of the Messiah, but nothing is said about his function, if any, at the End-time. On the heavenly throne we find, alone, 'the Holy Great One, the Lord of Glory, the Eternal King'. He it is who shall come 'to visit the earth with Goodness'[18] – a somewhat unexpected description of the visitation at the Last Judgment, though it agrees with the insistence on forgiveness in some Qumran texts (see Chapter 4).

The same picture of God, the Most High, as the only Judge, is found in 1 Enoch 99. Therefore a passage in 1 Enoch 105:2 is somewhat surprising: 'I and my Son will be united with [the righteous] for ever in the paths of righteousness.' R. H. Charles thinks that most of the older parts of 1 Enoch are from the first century BC. Modern scholars generally assign earlier dates to it. But this passage may be a late interpolation, introduced perhaps after the destruction of the Temple in AD 70.

2 Enoch contains, among other things, a detailed account of Enoch's journey through the heavens, up to the tenth heaven.[19] We are also told that God said to Adam: 'I will ... send thee whence I took thee/ Then I can again take thee at my second coming.' It is difficult to make much sense of this; the phrase 'second coming' is characteristic of much later Christian texts (see Chapters 1 and 2), and is therefore probably a late interpolation. In 2 Enoch 46:1 we get a different picture: 'When the Lord shall send a great Light ... then there will be judgment for the just and unjust.' The Light is an abstraction, but might be thought of as a personification of the kind Philo, for instance, often introduced. Accordingly it might be interpreted by some imaginative readers (for instance, Gnostics) as an impersonation of the Messiah.

But the most Messiah-like figure in 2 Enoch is Melchizedek. He is born to an old woman, obviously by divine intervention, and is wonderfully well developed. He becomes a priest, and eventually God takes him to Paradise, and preserves him as a 'High Priest for ever'.[20] Then we learn that 'in the last generation' there will be another Melchizedek, the first of twelve priests. And 'the last will be the head of all, a great archpriest, the Word and Power of God[21] . . . . He will be priest and king . . . in the centre of the earth,[22] where Adam was created . . . and there will be his final grave.' Thus, even if the writer thought of him as a Messiah, he did not consider him immortal. Somewhat incongruously, the text goes on to say that 'there will be another Melkisedek, the head of priests reigning over the people, and performing the liturgy for the Lord'.

The Melchizedek story has parallels with the story of Jesus in the Gospels. Whenever these strange passages were written – and they may certainly be later than the Gospels – they illustrate to what extent the Messiah concept occupied people's minds and fired their imagination. To add to the complexity, we should again note that the Samaritans did not expect a Davidic Messiah, but a new Moses.[23] (See the connection between the Teacher of Righteousness and Moses, Chapter 4.)

I shall not discuss 3 Enoch, which is probably as late as the third century AD. It mentions the Messiah son of Joseph, and the Messiah son of David,[24] finishing by saying that 'the kingdom of Israel, gathered from all the four quarters of the world, shall eat with the Messiah, and the Gentiles will eat with them'. The idea occurs also in the Testament of Levi, and elsewhere (see below). It sounds universalistic, as is to be expected in a strongly Gnostic text.

Enoch Parables

The most extensive text about an eschatological and supernatural Messianic figure outside the New Testament is the part of 1 Enoch called the Parables[25] (chiefly chapters 37–71). The text announces itself as a vision, where God appears to Enoch and tells him about the future and, in particular, about the End-time. As usual in apocalyptic literature, the picture is not very clear. There is no definite distinction between the universe before and after the Day of Judgment (called the 'Day of mine Elect'). Apparently the writer assumes that both Heaven and Earth would be transformed by God in such a way that all sinners would be destroyed. Only the righteous and elect would survive, living together with God and his angels.

In most respects, apparently, life on earth would continue as before, with the difference that no sinners would exist any more. For instance, angels would marry humans, and beget children (39:1), thus proving that the writer took quite seriously the meaning of the word *saints*, which was used both about the members of the Essene community, and (as among other Jews) about the angels of God. This particular aspect of what must be regarded as Paradise is remarkable, since in the story of the Watchers, developed out of Genesis 6:1–4, we read that angels who begot children with women gave rise to a race of Giants, generally regarded as enemies of God. But in the Enoch Parables, after the Judgment, no such dire consequences seem to be expected, obviously because in the purified world after the Judgment, the earthly population would be without sin. Thus 45:3 says: 'On that day Mine Elect One shall sit on the throne of glory/ and try their works. . . . Then I will cause Mine Elect one to dwell among them/ And I will transform the heaven and make it an eternal blessing and Light/ And I will transform the earth and make it a blessing/ And I will cause mine elect ones to dwell upon it/ But the sinners and evil-doers shall not set foot thereon . . . I shall destroy them from the face of the earth.'

Next, the writer goes on to another vision, clearly reminiscent of the book of Daniel, a vision in which 'the Ancient of Days' (presumably God) appears together with a 'Son of Man'. At that point God says to Enoch: 'Thou[26] art the Son of Man who hath righteousness/ the Lord of Spirits hath chosen you.' The subsequent lines, however, do not seem to be about Enoch, but 'the Elect One', a Messiah figure: 'His name was named before the Lord of Spirits. . . . He shall be a staff to the righteous/ the Light of the gentiles/ all the hope of those who are troubled of heart' (46–7).

This passage has a clearly universalistic ring – the Gentiles are admitted as well as the righteous Jews. But these ideas are not quite easy to reconcile with 45:4 and 46:1, where 'pagans' and 'sinners' are 'destroyed' and 'conquered'. To achieve a harmonisation, we must argue that the pagans can only be saved if they abandon their paganism. Universalism, in other words, does not mean tolerance.

The Messianic figure in the Parables, called the Son of Man or the Elect One, is never explicitly called the Messiah. It is true that at one place the writer says that the unrighteous have 'denied the Lord of Spirits and His Anointed' (48:7). Yet Anointed, here, does not necessarily mean more than Prophet, like Moses, or Isaiah, or Daniel, or, for that matter, the Essene Teacher of Righteousness.

It is his function at the Last Judgment that allows us to equate him with the Messiah of Christianity. In 61:1 we read, for instance, that 'the Lord of Spirits placed the Elect One on the throne of Judgment'. It is remarkable also that we find the idea that the Son of Man has been 'concealed from the beginning' (62:7), i.e. created before the Creation, like the Holy Ghost, Wisdom and Christ, in some of the Christian texts studied in Chapter 2. In the Enoch parables he is 'revealed to the holy and elect, the congregation of the holy ones' (62:7).

The last-quoted phrase could also be translated 'the congregation of Saints'. Undeniably such phrases form a perfect background to Paul's (and other apostles') visions of Christ in Heaven.

Testaments of the XII Patriarchs

In the Testaments (excluding clear Christian interpolations) the word Messiah does not occur, nor the corresponding Greek word, Christ. But a future great Jewish king or high priest is mentioned or hinted at in several places as the patriarchs prophesy about the future of their respective tribes.

In *Simeon* we read: 'the Lord will raise up from Levi someone as high priest, and from Judah someone as king' (7:1). In *Levi* a rather obscure passage, already quoted, which does not, however, seem to be a Christian addition, reads: 'from Judah a king will arise, and shall found a new priesthood in accord with the gentile model and for all nations. His presence is beloved as a prophet of the Most High' (8:11). In the context it seems clear that the new priesthood will be Levitical. The expression 'gentile model' (literally the model of the non-Jews, the Greeks and Romans) is, to say the least, somewhat bewildering. It is natural to associate the prophecies mentioned here with passages in the Essene *Community Rule* which talk about the two Messiahs from Aaron (Levi) and Israel.

At another place in Levi's testament the prophecy is different: 'the Lord will raise up a new priest. He shall effect judgment of truth over the earth for many days ... his star shall rise in heaven like a king (18:2). ... In his priesthood sin shall cease ... he will grant the saints to eat of the tree of life ... all the saints shall be clothed in righteousness' (18:9). All of this sounds quite eschatological. The priest who is 'like a king' seems to act as the judge at the End-time (though the reference may possibly be to God). The 'saints', presumably the members of the community, as often in the Qumran and Essene literature, are guaranteed immortality: 'eat of the tree of life'.

Again, this can hardly have been interpolated by a Christian, though the priest certainly fills functions attributed to Christ in the New Testament. But the word Messiah, or Christ, does not appear anywhere.

Judah is made to say: 'To me God has given the kingship, and to him [Levi] the priesthood, and he has subjected the kingship to the priesthood' (21:2). We have here the same idea as in the Levi text, and also in the Qumran Community Rule. Judah goes on to say that 'false prophets . . . shall harass the righteous' (21:9), after which 'there shall arise for you [Judah is speaking to his sons] a Star from Jacob in peace . . . this is the shoot of God the Most High' (24:1). The phrasing sounds eschatological: the Star from Jacob, based on Numbers 24:17, is a common enough symbol of the Messianic king. But in the Old Testament context there is no mention of the End-time, nor of the Messiah.

Dan also treats Levi and Judah together: 'From the tribe of Judah and Levi the Lord's salvation [will come]. . . . He shall take from Beliar the captives . . . the souls of the saints' (8:2). Thus here the Judgment is the Lord's, and he grants the members of the community eternal life: 'all the saints shall refresh themselves in Eden' (5:12).

Naphtali first admonishes his sons to 'be in unity with Levi and Judah' (8:2), but goes on: 'for through Judah will salvation arise for Israel' (8:3), which seems to assign a leading role to a king from Judah.

Joseph has what is probably a Christian interpolation, suggesting a connection with the Revelation of John in the New Testament. We read: 'a certain virgin . . . from her came forth a Lamb' (19:8). The lamb is later said to kill wild beasts. The lamb is again referred to in *Benjamin* 3:8 as 'the Lamb of God'. After this, Benjamin goes on to say that the twelve tribes of Israel will gather in Jerusalem(?), together with 'all the nations . . . until such time as the Most High shall send forth his Salvation through the ministration of the Unique Prophet' (9:2). Apparently this means that God himself acts as the Judge, with the Unique Prophet as a kind of Grand Vizier. This gets some confirmation in 10:9: 'for the Lord first judges Israel for the wrong she has committed, and then he shall do the same for all the nations. Then he shall judge Israel by the chosen gentiles.' The chosen Gentiles are presumably proselytes, or Gentiles who have lived virtuously without being instructed in the Law.

It is evident that the Messiah concept is in a fluctuating state in the Testaments of the XII. That is not surprising, if the original dates from the middle of the second century BC, with successive changes and additions down to Christian times.

2 Baruch

The apocalyptic 2 Baruch shows many parallels with 4 Ezra (see below), and was probably written at the same time, around the year AD 100. References to the fall of Jerusalem are quite obvious. Its revelations are attributed to Baruch, held to be the secretary of the prophet Jeremiah. God appears to Baruch and tells him about the coming Judgment: 'Behold, the days are coming and the books will be opened in which are written the sins of all those who have sinned and . . . the righteousness of all those who have proven themselves to be righteous . . . you shall see . . . the long-suffering of the Most High, which lasts from generation to generation' (24:1–2). There is no place here for a Christian suffering Messiah: it is God himself who suffers because of the sins of his people.

The Judgment is said to be preceded by twelve calamities (chapter 27). The Messiah is mentioned in several places, but in various roles. In 40:1 we read about 'the last ruler' (presumably the Roman emperor), and learn that 'my Anointed One will convict him of all his wicked deeds'. This is expanded in 72:2: 'when . . . my Anointed One comes, he will call all nations, and some of them he will spare, and others he will kill . . . those who have ruled over you will be delivered up to the sword'.

Accordingly, the writer is preoccupied with thoughts about revenge. But we note that some Gentiles will be saved, which may be connected with the fact that 2 Baruch is explicitly directed towards the Diaspora: Baruch is writing, he says, to his brothers in 'Babylon', in order to 'strengthen them' (77:12). When God is saying: 'I shall scatter this people among the nations that they may do good to the nations' (1:4), this almost sounds as a mandate to proselytise in the Diaspora. So it is perhaps not surprising that we read in 72:2 that some Gentiles will be saved on the day of Judgment. But the main emphasis is on saving the Jews from all over the world. They are assumed to be gathered in the Holy Land at the Last Judgment. The enemies of the

Jews are to be destroyed – the kind of vengefulness that is also found in 4 Ezra and in the Qumran War Scroll.

2 Baruch certainly takes a very nationalistic Jewish perspective. Obeying the Law is imperative: 'do not withdraw from the way of the Law' (44:2), and 'those who do not love your Law are justly perishing' (54:14). Further, the writer insists on 'the festivals and the sabbaths with their holy practices' (66:3, 84:8).

To obey the Mosaic Law is a sacred duty, though Baruch sees in his vision (41:3) that many of the Jews have abandoned it – a reference, perhaps, to some of the Christians of the writer's own times.

4 Ezra

The original of 4 Ezra is dated by most scholars to around AD 100. No fragments of the book have been found at Qumran. A later Christian editor has provided the originally Jewish work with a Christian framework, by adding introductory and concluding chapters. These will be left out of account here. 4 Ezra has parallels with the part of 1 Enoch called Parables. Extensive parallels are also found with 2 Baruch.

4 Ezra deals with the Last Judgment. God himself is the Judge. On that day there are no heavenly lights, 'only the splendour of the Most High'. To be saved on that day it is necessary to have followed 'the Ways of the Most High', and kept 'the Law of the Lawgiver perfectly'. 'The day of judgment will be the end of this age, and the beginning of the immortal age to come' (chapter 7).

The judgment is harsh: only he who 'will be able to escape on account of his works, or on account of the faith by which he has believed ... will see my salvation' (9:7). This is underlined by the grim statement that 'many have been created, but few will be saved' – a phrase which recalls Matthew 20:16 and 22:14.

Ezra has several visions. One is of a woman changed into a city, which is declared to be Zion. Another is of an eagle coming up from the sea, and is declared to be 'the fourth kingdom which appeared to your brother Daniel'. Ezra has a dream vision of 'something like the figure of a man come out of the sea ... that man flew with the clouds of heaven' (13:1). Finally God says (13:35) 'He will stand on the top of Mount Zion. . . . And he, my Son, will reprove the assembled nations ... and he will destroy them.' God also tells Ezra that he and his assistants, in heaven, will write books at the dictation of the Holy Spirit. About these books God says: 'make public 24, but keep secret

70'. By the 24, the twenty-four books of the Jewish Bible[27] are probably meant, while the 70 are probably the kind of 'secret' books exemplified by 4 Ezra itself.

There are two versions of the Messiah in 4 Ezra. In 7:27 we read that 'My Son the Messiah shall be revealed . . . and shall rejoice the survivors four hundred years.' Thereafter everybody, including the Messiah, will die, and the Day of Judgment arrives, apparently with God as the judge. In the later version, it is the man in Ezra's vision 'flying with the clouds of heaven', the Son of God, who acts as Judge. However, the word Messiah is not used about him. His divine status is underlined, not only by God acknowledging him as his Son, but also by his flying on the clouds, an expression presumably taken from the Biblical book of Daniel.

In 4 Ezra there is nothing of the universalism that we have found in the Testaments of the XII Patriarchs. Just as in the Qumran War Rule, the enemies of Israel, the Gentiles, or the Nations, are destroyed. Ezra's perspective, like that of 2 Baruch, is exclusively Jewish.

Our brief survey makes it clear that the Messiah concepts were extremely variable among the Jews in the centuries around the beginning of the common era. It is no wonder, therefore, that we found great variability among the Christians too, as appears from Chapters 1 and 2.

Chapter 6

The Letters of James, Peter and Jude

Before going on to a discussion of how the Church, in the end, managed to accommodate both the gnostically coloured theology that had pervaded first-century Christianity (see Chapters 1 and 2), and the rather concrete, historicised account that we find in the Synoptic Gospels and Acts, I shall devote the following two chapters to a number of New Testament books which can also be assigned to the first century. The way they have been treated illustrates further the difficulty that theological scholars have got into because of their assumption that the Gospel story is basically accurate as history. They also provide a background to my discussion (Chapter 10) of the crucial role of Ignatius, who was both a strong supporter – or rather, I would say, laid the foundation – of the historicised Jesus figure of the Gospels, and a guardian of the Gnostic heritage of Paul, further developed in the Gospel of John.

Though most of the Letters in the New Testament have traditionally been ascribed to Paul, modern scholars have put the genuineness of several of those in doubt. Some New Testament letters, however, right from the start, came with other signatures than Paul's. When the New Testament canon was being established, towards the end of the second century AD, some of these letters were included, if the Church regarded their authors as belonging to the first generation of Christian apostles. Letters which, in the view of the Church, belonged to a later generation, were excluded, such as those of Clemens Romanus, Barnabas, Ignatius and Polycarp. There was naturally no unanimity about which letters to include and which to exclude. But in the end seven letters were accepted, and came to be called the 'catholic' letters, or sometimes simply the 'canonical' ones.[1]

In this chapter I shall deal with three of these letters, leaving out the second letter of Peter, and all the three letters of John. 2 Peter is considered by practically all modern scholars to be a pseudepigraph dated to the second century AD, and 1–3 John are very closely connected with the Gospel of John, and probably written at roughly the same time, and perhaps even by the same author, in the second century. As I deal fairly extensively with the Gospel of John in Chapter 12, I do not take up the Letters of John here. Hardly any modern scholar connects them, or the Gospel, with the 'disciple' John of the Gospels and Acts.

The deeply rooted and probably mainly unconscious assumptions of theological scholars about Jesus and the early Christians are very conspicuous in their treatment of the letters of James, Peter and Jude. Before the advent of Biblical criticism in the eighteenth century, it was taken more or less for granted that these letters were in fact written by the men who are explicitly named as their senders, and who could fairly unambiguously be identified with the persons mentioned in the Gospels and in Acts.

In the critical eyes of modern scholars the excellent Greek style of all these letters seemed difficult to reconcile with the idea that they had been written by unlearned fishermen and artisans from Galilee. The same problem naturally arises in connection with Luke's presentation of the disciples as apostles and Church leaders in Acts (see Chapter 11). Luke's solution was to appeal to the descent of the Spirit, which gave the disciples the 'gift of tongues'.

But an even more serious problem was the fact that none of the letters have anything to say about the earthly Jesus. Paul's silence on that score might be explained as due to his late conversion: unlike the others, it was said, he had never been Jesus' companion. But Peter, according to the Gospels, had been Jesus' chief disciple, while James and Jude were seen as Jesus' natural brothers (see Chapter 11). Yet the catholic letters, supposedly written by Jesus' companions, who should really be the ones to know about his life and works, are completely silent on these matters. Instead, on these points they present the same picture as Paul and the six early texts analysed in Chapter 2.

Theologians confronted by these awkward facts have tended to maintain that the writers probably believed that their addressees were chiefly interested in the Jesus who was now in Heaven, in what he required from them, and in what he could do for them. Since all modern theologians agree that the Gospels were written at least a generation after Jesus' death, and no literary accounts about Jesus' life on earth exist, they assume that the Gospels must build their accounts on Jesus' words and deeds on 'oral traditions' about him. But, if the communities, according to the above argument, were not really interested in these matters, how can we credit them with preserving oral traditions about them?[2]

In fact, most theologians avoid the extreme form of the argument above. They simply hold that in the particular letters that have been preserved for us, the authors focused on other things. This way out, it seems to me, might perhaps serve for a single letter, or perhaps a few. But with a sequence of a dozen or so writings, all of them from the first century, and all yielding the same picture, while not a single one presents the contrary view, there is hardly any room for doubt: the earliest writers do not provide any information about the earthly Jesus, simply because they do not know much about him.

Now, if they do not know, they cannot have been Jesus' companions and contemporaries. Yet Jesus was clearly a well-established and revered figure in the Churches of God. The only natural explanation, it seems to me, is that Jesus' fame was of long standing – an argument which further strengthens the conclusions I have drawn above, especially from Chapters 1 and 2: Jesus was by no means a near contemporary of these early Christians, but a figure belonging to the late second century BC.

Modern Bible scholars, as we have seen, have no qualms about applying strict criticism to the books of the Bible. The canonicity of a writing does not exempt it from such criticism. But we have also seen that even the most critical theological scholars do not question one fundamental assumption, namely, that Christianity had its origin in Jesus, and that Jesus, as the Gospels say, was an early first-century Palestinian Jew from Galilee. That assumption, *which rests exclusively on the story of the Gospels*, is so firmly rooted in the conceptual framework of most theologians that it is generally not even made explicit: it is taken as an empirical fact.[3] The genuineness of the Gospel story could not be questioned.

Kümmel 1964, for instance, says about 1 Peter that it is 'without doubt a pseudonymous writing' (p. 309). He also refers to the 'careful Greek style' of the letter – hardly to be expected from a simple fisherman like Peter – and also that it contains 'no hint at any knowledge of the earthly Jesus' (pp. 308–9). Clearly his argument is based on the *assumption* that Jesus had lived in the first decades of the first century, and that the apostles had been his companions and disciples. In other words, Kümmel builds entirely on the Gospel story itself.

Accordingly, it was quite natural for these scholars to argue that the catholic letters must be pseudepigraphical. Unlearned Galilean fishermen *could* not be credited with a polished style of Greek, their theological ideas were difficult to fit into a period immediately following upon Jesus' death and, above all, the complete absence of any reminiscences about Jesus himself seemed completely incompatible with the writers having been his companions. Had they really not received any lasting impressions from such an extraordinary person?

All of this seemed a total mystery, and hence the suggestion that the letters must be pseudepigraphs seemed rational. After all, hardly any of these scholars believed that the Gospels themselves were written by Jesus' companions, though that was the impression created by the names that were traditionally given to their authors. What saved the Gospels, for their part, from the charge of pseudonymy was the fact that they did not themselves originally disclose who had written them. The names were added by later scribes.

Hence critical scholars suggested that James, Peter and Jude might all be pseudonyms, used by their authors to endow their writings with apostolic authority. This has also been the majority opinion among Protestant scholars for almost a century. Some Catholic scholars have followed suit.

However, the suggested explanation has problems of its own. The attestation of the letters is hardly weaker than that of many other canonical writings. Moreover, as the letters are all fairly short, and their theology neither very deep, nor very distinctive, it is tempting to see their inclusion in the canon as mainly due to their being so widely spread in the early communities: they had been around for a long time without being questioned. The objections that were raised against them later, towards the end of the second century and after, may be due to a greater theological awareness, as competition between Christians, mainstream Jews and Gnostics increased.

There are hardly any objective grounds for considering the letters as pseudonymous. The main reason for their rejection by modern critics is in fact the one spelled out above: it was almost impossible to believe that their authors had been Jesus' companions.[4] But, if we rid ourselves of the assumption that Jesus lived in the early first century, and that Peter and the others were his companions, that problem disappears.

We have in fact every reason to believe that at least the leading members of the Jerusalem Church of God, whose 'pillars' Paul had met, were able to write excellent Greek. After all, we have found that early Christianity was from the start mainly a movement of the Greco–Roman Jewish Diaspora, whose members had overwhelmingly Greek names, and spoke Greek as their mother tongue. And as, according to my hypothesis, Christianity developed out of Essene Diaspora communities, we have no reason whatever to expect our first-century AD writers to know very much about the life of their main founder and prophet, long since dead.

The letters, indeed, may well be pseudepigraphical, but the grounds most often given for considering them so are not valid. Instead, let us see what the writers, whoever they are, actually tell us about themselves and the communities they address. We may thus use them to round out our picture of first-century Christianity.

James

James calls himself 'the servant of God and of the Lord Jesus Christ', an entirely natural designation for a high-ranking spokesman for the Church of God. We note especially that he does *not* claim to be the 'brother of Jesus', something which yields further support to the arguments about this important question that I present in Chapter 11. If the writer of this epistle is really the James whom Paul calls both apostle and pillar, his self-designation is precisely what we should expect.[5]

The addressees are said to be 'the twelve tribes which are scattered abroad'. We have met with similar expressions for the Diaspora members of the Church of God in other early texts, such as Hermas, Didachē, Barnabas and Revelation (see Chapter 2). The wording, we have said, underscores the Jewish character of the early Christian communities, by employing the Jewish metaphor of the twelve tribes, and the concept of *diaspora*, dispersion.

The traditional theological explication of the phrase is that the Christians look upon themselves as the 'New Israel'. This is of course quite true. But so did the Essenes: they were the Elect, the Remnant, who stood by the covenant with Yahweh, which they thought the majority of the Jews had abandoned. The fact that the Essenes were elect did not make them any less Jewish: rather the contrary. Their inclusion of some Gentiles did not affect their fundamental Jewish-ness. That Jewishness permeates the whole of the letter of James: for instance, 2:21 refers to 'our father Abraham'. In fact, several recent scholars have suggested that the original of the epistle might have been purely Jewish, Christianised by simply adding 'Jesus Christ' in 1:1 and 2:1. As my hypothesis is that the earliest Christian communities may have grown out of Essene ones, they were of course Jewish. A clear Essene trait in James occurs in 1:17, where God is called 'the Father of lights' (*apo tou patros phōtōn*), an expression not found, as far as I can see, elsewhere in the Bible, but well in line with the symbolism of light employed by Essenes, Gnostics and Christians.

Peter

Peter also turns to addressees who seem to be Diaspora Jews: 'strangers scattered throughout Pontus, Galatia, Cappadocia, Asia and Bithynia'. The Greek is *eklektois parepidēmois diasporas*, literally 'the elect strangers scattered', where the word *parepidēmois* indicates that they are not native inhabitants of those regions. In other words, not Gentiles, but most likely Jews.

The Jewish identity of the addressees is further underlined in 2:12, where we read about them having their 'conversation honest among the Gentiles'. This reminds us of similar expressions in the early texts discussed in Chapters 2 and 5. Likewise, the letter stresses the advisability of orderly conduct and submission to the authorities, including the obedience of wives to husbands, and of servants to masters.

An interesting indication that the addressees might perhaps have a background as *lapsed* but repentant Jews, occurs in 4:3: 'the time past of our life may suffice us to have wrought the will of the Gentiles, when we walked in lasciviousness, lusts, excess of wine, revellings, banquetings, and abominable idolatries'. The expression 'wrought the will of the Gentiles' may be taken as a reference to the pressure that the Diaspora Jews naturally felt from the surrounding Gentiles, to conform to customs that their religion forbade them to partake in. As I have said (in Chapter 3), the allegorical law interpretation of the Essenes (and the Christians) freed them from the absolute demands, though of course *excesses* (mentioned twice, 4:3. and 4:4) were not permissible.

Unlike James, who says hardly anything about Jesus, Peter

repeatedly speaks about Jesus' sufferings, and even specifies 'on the tree', i.e. the cross. Yet though Jesus' suffering and its redemptive power are stressed, Peter never tells us what really happened at Jesus' death. Like the texts of Chapter 2, Peter never speaks about the crucifixion as an *event*, but only, and rather implicitly, as a *fact*.

This is not contradicted by 5:1: 'I, who am also an elder, and a witness of the sufferings of Christ, and also a partaker of the glory that shall be revealed.' The word 'witness' (*martus*) does not imply 'eyewitness', but simply conveys that Peter was convinced of, and ready to testify about the suffering. The way he speaks about Jesus' death throughout the epistle indicates that he has not actually *experienced* Jesus' death. Alternatively, of course, this particular passage might be a late insertion in the letter.

Such an interpretation is confirmed by 1:7–12. There Peter speaks about 'the appearing of Jesus Christ' [meaning, of course, at the impending End of time[6]], whom having not seen [*horōntes*], ye love; in whom, though now ye see him not, yet believing, ye rejoice'. Peter here does not imply that his correspondents differ from other persons who *have* seen Jesus in the flesh. Peter then goes on to speak about himself and his fellow apostles. In particular, he does not claim that he himself had indeed seen the living Jesus and his death. Instead, he tells about the prophecies of the Bible, 'which are now reported unto you by them that have preached the gospel unto you with the Holy Ghost sent down from heaven'. Thus his language is consistently theological, not realistic.

We should add that when Peter, in 5:4, speaks about Jesus' coming for the Last Judgment: 'when the chief Shepherd shall appear', he does not refer to it as a return, but simply as an appearance,[7] precisely as all other early texts do (see Chapter 2).

Jude

Jude's is the shortest of the three epistles. The author introduces himself as 'Jude, the servant of Jesus Christ, and brother of James'. Irrespective of whether the epistle is a pseudepigraph or not, it is reasonable to assume with most scholars that the author here refers to the James who is the leader of the Jerusalem community, the one whom a long theological tradition calls the brother of Jesus. Now if Jude is the brother of James, he would also, logically, be the brother of Jesus, according to all theologians since Eusebius, and also in the opinion of most modern scholars. Why, then, does he not call himself that, rather than the brother of James? It would have endowed him with even greater authority. We cannot but conclude that the author of the letter, whoever he was, did not consider either Jude or James as the brother of Jesus. Thus this epistle provides further support for our conclusion in Chapter 11: Jesus' brothers are constructions introduced, at the earliest, well into the second century.

The addressees are said to be 'sanctified by God', and in verse 3 we read about 'the faith which was once delivered unto the saints'. As we pointed out above, using 'saints' for Christians was common in the first century, but rare in the second. This is therefore an indication – admittedly not a very strong one – that Jude's letter belongs indeed to the first century.

Otherwise there is little to help us date the letter. Its main purpose is to condemn, in vehement language, infiltrators who have 'crept in unawares' into the communities, and whose chief characteristic seems to be loose sexual morals. Homosexuality is hinted at. Possibly a certain class of Gnostics are intended, who claimed freedom from ordinary moral restrictions. The saints are earnestly and repeatedly warned to keep away from them.

There is nothing at all about Jesus' life or death. The only reference to the imminence of the Last Judgment is that the communities are told (v. 18) to remember 'the words which were spoken before of the apostles of our Lord Jesus Christ . . . that . . . there should be mockers in the last time, who should walk after their own ungodly lusts', obviously another reference to the immoral infiltrators. The wording indicates that Jude thinks the activities of the apostles lay in the past. This, however, does not provide a dating: there were apostles before Paul (see Chapter 1). On the whole, a first-century date for the letter seems the most probable.

Concluding remarks

Thus there are no sufficient grounds for considering the three letters as pseudonymous. But of course we still do not know the identity of the authors. On the other hand, the fact that the letters were preserved, in spite of their slight size and fairly commonplace contents, shows that at least some communities thought them worth keeping. One reason may have been that they were always *believed* to come from these important members of the early Church.

We know from Paul that the Jerusalem community was important in the Christian movement of his time and also, that James was a pillar there (Gal 2:9), and that Peter was at least a well-known apostle (Gal 2:7) – leaving aside the question whether Paul's Cephas should be identified with Peter (see Chapter 11). These two, therefore, probably had the kind of reputation that made it interesting for other Christian communities to listen to them, even when their communications were not particularly weighty.

Jude is a more difficult case. As regards his suggested status as the brother of Jesus, we shall give reasons for doubting the substance of the whole of that story (Chapter 11). There is, however, another possible candidate. At various places in the Gospels and Acts, we find a Jude that might be our man. In Luke 6:16 we read about Jude the *son* of James. Further, John 14:22 has 'Judas ... not Iscariot'.[8] In Mark 3:18 the place of Luke's Jude seems to be taken by Thaddaeus, and in Matthew 10:3 he appears as Lebbaeus. (In all the Synoptics, the names only occur in the lists of the 'Twelve', which are probably taken from Acts 1:13. See Chapter 11.) A further possibility is that the reference is to Thomas, who in some texts, mainly Gnostic ones, is called Judas Thomas.

I shall be arguing in Chapter 11 that the names given to the disciples/apostles in the Gospels and Acts may be based on vague reminiscences about leading members of the Jerusalem church. So, even if we choose to consider 'Jude the brother of James' as a late addition, we have at least some evidence for identifying the Jude of the letter, together with James and Peter, with members of some standing in the early Christian movement.

The whole of this argument, of course, does no more than give some extra support to our conclusion that these catholic letters can be associated with the first-century Church. In other words, they may be treated as genuine expressions of the kind of Christianity to be found in that church, thus exemplifying the fairly wide diversity of opinions that existed within it, and which we have noted in other contexts as well.

Chapter 7

Colossians and Ephesians

We have said that the canonised New Testament books cannot be presumed to be more genuine and more reliable as historical documents than many other texts of the period we are concerned with. But they certainly have a special interest for us, simply by the fact that they have been accepted by many Christian churches of the time as important Christian witnesses. In this chapter I shall treat two New Testament writings which have not been included, for various reasons, in the previous discussions. Colossians and Ephesians are indeed canonical but, following the majority of present-day scholars, I exclude them from my corpus of genuine Paulines, mainly for stylistic reasons. However, though they are probably somewhat later than the genuine Paulines, they both appear to belong to the first century.

Colossians and Ephesians are closely connected. Many passages in Ephesians seem to be directly copied from the presumably somewhat earlier Colossians. Both letters were included in Marcion's collection of Paulines, and were accepted as genuine by most ancient writers. However, several early churchmen expressed doubts, both on stylistic and on theological grounds. Both employ a rather elaborate and ornate style. Their vocabulary also differs considerably from that of Paul. Theologically, the Gnostic colouring is unmistakable.

Hoffmann 1984, in a very interesting and detailed study of Marcion, thinks that a (lost) letter to the Laodiceans in Asia Minor formed the basis of Colossians and Ephesians, and concludes (p. 280) that 'the disciple of Paul responsible for the Laodiceans, no longer extant, but still visible beneath the surface of the redaction carried out in the Ephesian circle, was Marcion'. That is admittedly speculation, though it is in good agreement with Hoffmann's main thesis, viz that Marcion was active as early as *c.* AD 100, and in any case before the canonical Gospels had come into existence. (This also agrees with my own dating of the Gospels to the second century. See Chapter 9.) Hoffmann also holds that Marcion's teaching was a 'radicalisation' of Paul's theology, in which the Gnostic elements were emphasised. I think Hoffman's views make good sense. However, they have not been widely accepted among scholars, so the authorship of Colossians and Ephesians remains a riddle.[1]

Colossians

Colossians presents itself unambiguously as written by Paul. In the last verse, ostensibly written by Paul when he was a prisoner in Rome, we read 'the salutation by the hand of me Paul'. The letter has also been accepted as genuine from the earliest times onwards.

Theologically the letter contains much that we associate with Paul. The author lays great stress on the redeeming power of Jesus' death on the cross. Further, he emphasises that salvation comes through acceptance of the gospel (i.e. the preaching of Jesus; see Chapter 2, on Didachē), and trust in the Church, which represents the body of Christ. It is notable that the name Jesus is seldom used by itself in Colossians: commonly we read simply Christ, or – less often – Jesus Christ. The same holds for Ephesians.

The Mosaic law has no relevance for the church members. Like Paul, the author of Colossians lays stress on mutual love and respect, and on orderly and virtuous living.

However, on some points Colossians is definitely un-Pauline. It says hardly anything on the Last Judgment as the event when Jesus will come, in order to save the members of the church. Rather the contrary: the faithful seem *already* to have attained salvation by being baptised into the church. We read about 'the Father . . . who hath delivered us from the power of darkness, and hath translated us into the kingdom of his dear Son' (1:13). Accordingly, the 'translation' is assumed to have occurred already. The same idea is expressed in other places as well: 'Ye are risen with him through the faith of the operation of God, who hath raised him [Jesus] from the dead' (2:12), and 'If ye then be risen with Christ, seek those things which are above, where Christ sitteth on the right hand of God' (3:1). There is, however, one explicit reference to Jesus' appearance at the Last Judgment in 3:4: 'When Christ, which is our life, shall appear, there shall you also appear with him in glory.' But there is no elaboration of what will happen on that day. The writer does not show any concern at all about it, as is natural, since he assumes that the church members have *already* been accepted in the Kingdom of God during their lifetime. As always in the first century, Jesus' appearance is *not* spoken of as a return.

On the whole, I do not think that we should attach too much importance to the difference between Paul and Colossians on this particular point.[2] There is, after all, but a short step between Paul's strong faith that at the Last Judgment Jesus *will* save you from destruction, and the Colossian conviction that Jesus *has* already saved you by translating you into a new life. Given Paul's and his communities' preconceptions of the structure of the universe, with a multi-tiered heaven peopled by innumerable spirits of various kinds, some angelic and divine, others devil-like, ruled by Belial and other evil Powers, the distinction we have just outlined can hardly have been felt as irreducible.

Modern people live in a climate of opinion where there is a sharp dividing line between the material world and the supernatural one. In Antiquity there was no such sharp dividing line. The concept of 'law of nature' did not exist. The nearest approach to it was the concept of divine order. At most, therefore, people regarded the constitution of the world as created and supervised by God, who was often supposed to work by intermediaries: angels and Spirits. In a religion where God was assumed to be fundamentally good, the existence of evil had to be accounted for, basically, by the supposition that there were also evil spirits, perhaps directed by 'principalities and powers' (*archai*, *dunameis*), personified as Belial, or Satan.[3] We have encountered this kind of dualism in the Dead Sea Scrolls (Chapter 4). Obviously both the Paul of Romans and 1 Corinthians, and the 'Paul' of Colossians, moved in a conceptual world which was rather like that of many other literate and semi-literate people in Antiquity.[4]

Colossians often uses the same words and the same concepts as Paul. The members of the church are called 'saints', *hagioi* (e.g. 1:2,4,12) – a term which is hardly used at all in the Gospels. We also meet with the expression 'the Elect of God' (1:16), common also in the Qumran literature. The term 'principalities and powers' occurs in 1:16 and 2:10. We find references to 'the gospel', which clearly means, not a written text presenting the life and deeds of Jesus, but the interpretation of the Old Testament as prophecies about Jesus. In other words, the kind of message conveyed also by such texts as 1 Clement, Hebrews and Barnabas (see Chapter 2).

The redemptive power of Christ's suffering is symbolised by his blood (1:14, 20). Further, like the early Paulines, Colossians regards the Church as Christ's body. Colossians adds a subtle twist to this concept by calling Christ the head of the body, which must be regarded as a rather natural development. We also note that Colossians endorses Paul's insistence that, when raising Christ to heaven and seating him on the heavenly throne on his right side, God had freed the Christian communities from the requirements of the Mosaic law.

On the other hand, many commentators have remarked upon the considerable number of words and expressions in Colossians which do not appear at all in the generally recognised Pauline letters.[5] There are around thirty such words in this rather short letter, and I myself take this as fairly strong support for considering Colossians as pseudonymous.

Everybody agrees that Paul exhibits quite a few generally Gnostic traits. But the Gnostic character of Colossians (and Ephesians) is even more marked. The word mystery (*mustērion*) occurs four times (1:26,27; 2:2; 4:3). The word *gnōsis* itself occurs in Colossians 2:3: 'Christ in whom are hid all wisdom [*sophias*] and knowledge [*gnōseōs*]'. The transformation of man already in this world, through his faith in the risen Christ, is a Gnostic trait, as well as the idea that Christ has existed since before the creation. 'He is before all things, and by him all things consist . . . for it has pleased the Father that in him should all fulness [*plērōma*) dwell' (1:17–19). That idea was elaborated also in Philo, about the personified figure of Wisdom.[6] It also has affinities with the Stoic concept of *Logos* (word, order), and was developed as a symbol of Christ in the most Gnostic of the canonical Gospels, that of John (see Chapter 12). The dualism of light and darkness, God and Belial, is a feature common to the Dead Sea Scrolls and the Gnostics.

In spite of this strong Gnostic colouring, we should also observe that the author of Colossians criticises opponents whom he regards as intruders from the outside, and who seem to hold Gnostic ideas which he takes to be unacceptable. He is, for instance, eager to distance himself from those Gnostics who he thinks diminish the role of Jesus. He expresses this in somewhat veiled language in Colossians 2:3–4: 'the mystery of God, and of the Father, and of Christ; In whom are hid all the treasures of wisdom and knowledge. And this I say, lest any man should beguile you with enticing words.'

What the opponents say, however, is quite a natural Gnostic position, since in the Gnostic conceptual world the individual soul can

151

get in touch with God through various spiritual messengers. Surely the Gnostic Christians could accept Jesus as God's principal intermediary. On the other hand, if the collective judgment at the Day of Wrath, with Christ as judge, was not mentioned, Jesus might come to seem less essential. Hence Colossians insisted that Jesus was indeed the *supreme* mediator, ruling over both angels and principalities such as Belial.

One interesting feature in Colossians is a hymn-like passage in 1:12–21. Modern scholars[7] have found many points of resemblance with the Scroll of Hymns found in Cave 1 at Qumran (1QH), both as regards style and as regards theological ideas. Starting the hymn by giving thanks to God (Col 1:12) is a standard opening formula in the Qumran hymns, several of which are supposed by most scholars to have been written by the Teacher of Righteousness himself (see Chapter 4).

In the second verse of the hymn we read '[God] hath delivered us from the power of darkness, and hath translated us into the kingdom of his dear Son' (1:13). The opposition between darkness and light is very prominent in the central texts among the Dead Sea Scrolls, where the Two Ways' doctrine is expressed in terms of the two 'spirits' established by God among men, the spirit of righteousness, or Light, and that of unrighteousness, or Darkness. By God's grace, the members of the community have been granted shares in the portion of Light. Hence they are 'partakers of the inheritance of the saints in light' (1:12). The Essene character of this hymn is indeed very striking, and of course provides further support for the hypothesis of Essene roots for the early Christian communities that I have been exploring and testing throughout this book.

An interesting feature of Colossians is the exhortation in 2:14: 'Let no man . . . judge you in meat, or in drink, or in respect of an holyday, or of the new moon, or of the sabbath law.'[8] The writer presumably thinks of 'false' apostles who preach a more traditional Jewish doctrine, both as regards the Law, and as regards the calendar. The members of the Colossian church, we may presume, like other Pauline churches, followed a solar calendar which was by now in general use in the Empire, and which had long ago been adopted, though in a modified form, by the predecessors of the Christian Churches of God, among them the Essene ones.

Precisely as in other early texts, we hear nothing about Jesus' earthly life. His suffering and death on the cross are just mentioned as

152

theologically important facts: what actually happened is never considered. Even the heavenly Jesus is a very abstract figure: he has existed from the beginning of the world – 'by him were all things created' (Col 1:16), in him 'are hid all the treasures of wisdom and knowledge' (Col 2:3), a statement which implies that the church, which is the body of Christ, possesses such wisdom and knowledge.

The idea that the salvation has already come to the elect is emphasised repeatedly. 'We have redemption through his blood, even the forgiveness of sins' (Col 1:14). Further, the members of the church are said to be 'buried with him in baptism wherein also ye are risen with him' (Col 2:12), and 'If ye then be risen with Christ, seek those things which are above' (Col 3:1). These are vaguely Gnostic ideas (see Chapter 3).

Ephesians

In spite of its address, 'to the saints which are at Ephesus', which is probably a late addition,[9] Ephesians is an encyclical letter, not addressed to any particular church or group of churches. It can be regarded as an attempt to present Pauline Christianity systematically to those members, or prospective members, of the Christian churches who were not Jews, and did not wish to regard themselves as Jews. The existence of a substantial number of such people is clear, among other things, from the considerable success of Marcion's church after his excommunication from the Roman one in AD 144 (see Chapter 3). Marcion rejected the Old Testament altogether, basing his theology wholly on a single Gospel, and also, significantly, on a comprehensive collection of Pauline letters, including Colossians and Ephesians.

It is quite clear that Ephesians was aimed at a Gentile audience. The author, who (posing as Paul) was evidently himself a Jew, says 'ye in times past being Gentiles in the flesh' (2:11), and 'you Gentiles' (3:1), and 'I should preach among the Gentiles' (3:8). Obviously he implicitly refers to passages with the same import in Paul's genuine letters (1 Cor 12:2, Gal 3:7, 9). But in Ephesians the addressees are not a particular community, nor a particular group of communities, consisting of only Gentiles. I doubt whether any such communities existed at that time. Instead, the writing was most probably a general statement of Pauline Christian theology, aimed at Gentiles in general, irrespective of which community they belonged to. Indeed, the letter could be seen as a pamphlet meant for the general Greek-speaking reader, whether he was a member of the Christian church or not. (Note also Hoffman's views, referred to above.)

If so, we would have an explanation of the fact that Ephesians, in its oldest and best manuscripts, does not contain any address at all.[10] Moreover, the end of the letter does not contain any greetings to named addressees, which is otherwise normal.

Modern scholars are fairly unanimous that Ephesians was written at the very end of the first century, thus about a generation after Paul's death. At any rate, it is not likely to have been written later than the beginning of the second century, since Ignatius quoted it (see Chapter 10). The theology of Ephesians is clearly Pauline, but with several modifications, both in view of the later date, and in view of the audience envisaged: Gentiles in general, not specific Christian churches, which at this time presumably still had a predominantly Jewish membership.

The Pauline character of Ephesians appears from such features as the belief that salvation was attained through God's grace, not through works (1:5, 2:7, 2:9), the forgiveness of sins through Christ's suffering, his blood (1:7, 2:13), the strong insistence on belief and trust in Jesus, the suspension of the ordinances of the Mosaic law for the believers (2:15), and the concept of the church as the body of Christ (5:30, 2:20). The Pauline character is further enhanced by the numerous verbal similarities with passages in the genuine Paulines. Scholars have found echoes of practically all Paulines in Ephesians[11].

However, just like in Colossians, we also note features which are distinctly un-Pauline. For instance, the imminence of the Last Judgment does not figure at all, unless we count the veiled reference in 6:2: 'take unto you the whole armour of God, that ye may be able to withstand the evil day'. But this phrase may well be meant quite generally.

It is also noticeable that Ephesians says very little on the question of circumcision, which was a burning issue in the earlier Paulines. In Ephesians circumcision is barely referred to in passing. This is quite natural, in view of the largely Gentile audience. But even so, the indifference towards the issue may indicate a widespread attitude among the Christians towards the end of the first century. We may recall that circumcision was not a burning issue in most of the early texts analysed in Chapter 2, either.

The Gnostic colouring in Ephesians is very strong. Exactly as in Colossians, the eschatological expectation of the End of times was either rejected, or at least toned down very considerably. Instead, stress was laid on spiritual salvation. The faithful took part spiritually in Jesus' rising to Heaven. Baptism meant washing away sins, making the church members fit to enter the Kingdom of God. Spiritually, therefore, the Kingdom of God had already arrived for the believers. 'God . . . even when we were dead in sins, hath quickened us together with Christ . . . and hath raised us up together, and made us sit together in heavenly places in Christ Jesus' (2:5–6).

This spiritual transformation is sometimes expressed in terms of the concept of the 'old man' and the 'new man' (4:22, 4:25). It also serves to abolish the distinction between Jews and Gentiles: Jesus has 'abolished in his flesh the enmity, even the law of commandments contained in ordinances: for to make in himself of twain one new man' (2:15), the 'twain' being Jews and Gentiles. The writer concludes: 'Now therefore ye are no more strangers and foreigners, but fellow-citizens with the saints, and of the household of God' (2:19). The word saints in this instance is most naturally interpreted as God's angels. The idea was widespread both among the Gnostics and among the Essenes.

The author of Ephesians, like that of Colossians, otherwise uses the word 'saints' regularly about the members of the church. The word Christian does not occur at all. On this point Ephesians agrees with Colossians, and with Paul and other early writers. Other Pauline, and also Essene, terms in Ephesians are 'the elect' (1:4) and 'perfect' (4:13). Of the Gnostic vocabulary also used by Paul we note 'principalities and powers' (1:21, 2:2, 3:10), darkness and light (5:11, 5:13, 6:12), children of light (5:8), fullness (*plērōma*) (1:10, 1:23, 3:19, 4:13), mystery (*mustērion*) (1:2, 3:3, 3:9, 5:31, 6:19).

However, it is not principally the vocabulary that makes the text Gnostic, but the Gnostic trains of thought, such as 3:10: 'that now unto the principalities and powers in heavenly places might be known by the church the manifold wisdom of God, according to the eternal purpose which he purposed in Christ Jesus'. Another typical example of this rather turgid style is the following from 3:17–19: 'that Christ may dwell in your hearts by faith; that ye, being rooted and grounded in love, may be able to comprehend with all saints what is the breadth, and length, and depth, and height, and to know the love of Christ, which passeth knowledge, that ye might be filled with all the fullness of God'.

There are, however, also some indications that the writer of

Ephesians sensed the dangers of allowing full scope to the emotional subjectivity and mysticism of the Gnostics. Thus he reminds his readers that the revelation of the mystery of Christ did not come indiscriminately to everybody, but at first only to the apostles.[12] In 3:3–5, where he speaks with the voice of Paul, he says 'how that by revelation he [the Lord] made known unto me the mystery . . . which in other ages was not made known unto the sons of men, as it is now revealed unto his holy apostles and prophets by the Spirit'. In this way was safeguarded 'the unity of the faith . . . that we henceforth be no more children, tossed to and fro, and carried about with every wind of doctrine. . . . This I say . . . that ye henceforth walk not as other Gentiles walk, in the vanity of their mind, having the understanding darkened, being alienated from the life of God through the ignorance that is in them, because of the blindness of their heart' (4:13–18). On these passages follow exhortations to live virtuously and soberly, in mutual love and respect. The writer concludes: 'keep the unity of the Spirit in the bond of peace. There is one body, and one Spirit, even as ye are called in one hope of your calling, one Lord, one faith, one baptism, one God and Father of all, who is above all, and through all, and in you all' (4:3–6).

All this seems to me to show that the writer was quite aware of the centripetal tendencies of the Gnosticism whose basic theology he nevertheless followed, not only because in the main it was also Paul's, but probably also because he was aware that this mystically and emotionally loaded Gnosticism was widely spread among the Gentiles he saw as his audience. While Paul, whose hearers were probably to a large extent Jewish, could argue on the basis of the Old Testament, the author of Ephesians, addressing Gentiles at large, had to make use of this kind of popular philosophy. He did not argue for his theology on logical and rational grounds but, starting from the original and fundamental revelation of the gospel to the apostles, he chiefly appealed to his readers' sense of solidarity: love, mutual respect and orderly living.

These were worthy goals, but perhaps not inspiring enough to fire the readers' imagination. So the second century saw a development of the Gnostic movement in another direction, which threatened the unity of the church, as we shall see in Part II. One important sign of this was the excommunication of Marcion, and his establishment of a rival, Gnostically coloured, Christian church which cut loose almost completely from its Jewish roots. It was to flourish for several hundred years.

In the late first century Gnostic ideas were increasingly formulated in the form of docetic Gnosticism (see Chapter 3). It was the chief target of Ignatius' letters, and is, I think, to a large extent responsible for the radical change that took place in Christian theology during the second century. But apparently docetism had not yet come into being as an identifiable movement. However that may be, it is remarkable that neither Colossians, nor Ephesians, say a word about it (see my discussion below, Chapter 10).

In my analysis of the main letters of Paul (chapter 1) I came to the conclusion that Paul's virtually complete silence on the earthly Jesus had a very simple explanation: he was convinced that the figure that had appeared to him in his visions was a teacher and prophet who had lived and died long since. I subsequently found that not only Paul, but virtually all major Christian writings of the first century conveyed the same message about Jesus. Not one of the early writers gives any evidence of having seen Jesus in the flesh, or of having met anybody who had. I drew the conclusion that, like Paul, they had only experienced the *heavenly* Jesus, presumably in visions. Yet all spoke about him as a great and well-known teacher and prophet, who had (like many ancient prophets) been persecuted by the established powers of Israel.

It is interesting to note that Ephesians, at the very end of the first century, fully supports the conclusion that the Christians of Paul's time had experienced Jesus exclusively as a heavenly figure, appearing to them in visions. My quotation above from Ephesians 3:3–5 is quite revealing, since we read that 'the mystery of Christ' was revealed to 'his holy apostles and prophets by the Spirit'. This clearly points to visions, not experiences in the world of material reality. Moreover, we learn that the mystery 'in other ages was not made known unto the sons of men', which seems to me to imply that all the secrets of the 'gospel of Christ', including his divine nature, remained unknown until Paul and the other apostles received their revelations. This is also what my basic hypothesis about the origin of Christianity implies. It was the apostles' *visions*, aided by their bold interpretation of the Wisdom books of the Bible, that transformed Jesus into Christ. I return to these matter in Chapter 12.

All this, and my reading of the Dead Sea Scrolls, and above all the correspondences, even the overlap, between the first-century Essenes,

Gnostics and Christians, has led me to conclude that the Jesus of the first Christian visionaries was, at least to many of the first Christians, the revered Teacher of Righteousness of the early Essene movement. It is not at all surprising that religious seekers among the Diaspora Jews came to regard him as a prophet, and therefore joined the Essene and para-Essene movements throughout the Roman Empire. That does not mean that they were particularly well informed about him. The main thing, for them, was that he was indeed a prophetic figure. It was in that capacity that he could fill the role of the movement's heavenly leader.

The material presented here has provided further support for my hypothesis, to the extent that I think that the main question now is not whether the Teacher of Righteousness of the Essenes was in fact the figure – whether historical or not – behind the Jesus of Paul and his contemporaries. That may now be regarded as settled. The main question at this stage is why the second-century Christians substituted another, fictional Jesus, and how they managed to convince their communities on this point, and how they succeeded in obliterating virtually all evidence about the original, Essene Jesus. I shall address these questions in Part II.

With respect to Jesus as a historical person, Ephesians shows as little interest, and provides as little information as Paul and his contemporaries had done some fifty years earlier. There is nowhere any hint that the communities were beginning to locate him anywhere in space and time. On the contrary, in Ephesians, Jesus is even more decidedly than in Paul a heavenly figure, a spiritual being that reveals himself to the faithful exclusively through spiritual channels, where apparently mystical experiences play an important part. In this way Ephesians yields further support to the conclusion we will reach in Part II, namely, that large parts of first-century Christianity were largely Gnostic. Bishop Ignatius of Antioch sensed the dangers of this, and accordingly initiated a determined attack on the 'docetic' Gnostics, while at the same time making it possible for more mystically oriented, philosophical Gnostics to thrive in the Church.

Ephesians, I would say, marks the end of the first phase of the early Christian church both chronologically and theologically. Another batch of letters, those of Ignatius, as we shall see in Chapter 10, similarly mark the beginning of the second century, in which Christian theology was to take on a radically new appearance.

As I have been arguing throughout this book and especially in

Chapter 2, the canonical Gospels in reality had the Old Testament prophecies as their foundation. The Church, from the second century onwards, considered the Gospel stories as true history, which corroborated the prophetic value of the Old Testament passages. In addition they were seen as evidence of God's governance of the world in general, and of his special care for Jesus and the Church in particular.

To Paul and the other early Christian apostles, the 'gospel' (always used in the singular, and often with a defining attribute, 'gospel of God', 'of Christ', 'of salvation', etc.) meant the interpretation of the Old Testament as prophecies about Jesus, prophecies that promised salvation for the church members into the Kingdom of God. Collections of such prophecies seem to have been popular reading with both Essenes and Christians – see Chapter 2.

By contrast, the second-century Christians, to whom we shall turn in Part II, took the view that the Gospels (in the plural) were accounts of the earthly life of Jesus, his deeds and words. In this way they came to be seen as the foundation of both Church history and Christian theology.

Part II

Deconstructing the Gospels and Acts

Chapter 8

The Heavenly and the Earthly Jesus

In the preceding chapters I have been mainly concerned with ascertaining the nature of first-century AD Christianity and its background. I have adopted the perspective of the historian, trying to find out what the sources themselves tell us when interpreted on their own terms, i.e. in terms of their authors' own background knowledge.

It is evident that my approach is almost the opposite of the one employed by the majority of theological scholars through the ages. They have tended to interpret earliest Christianity in the light of the developed Christianity in the Gospels and Acts. They have read Paul's letters against the background of the considerably later Gospels and Acts. Support for this rather problematic procedure has been sought in two ways. First, by assigning unjustifiably early datings to the Gospels and, secondly, by positing an 'oral tradition' to bridge the remaining chronological gap between the supposed life of Jesus and the written accounts of his life.

For my part, I have consistently explored the hypothesis that first-century Christianity developed within a Jewish, Essene or para-Essene matrix, mainly in the Diaspora. I have pointed out that Paul and his contemporaries regarded Jesus as a prophet and teacher *long since dead*. My close study of 1 Clement, Hermas, Didachē, Barnabas, Hebrews and Revelation, which I have found reason to date around the sixties of the first century AD, supports the conclusions I have drawn from the Pauline corpus. I have also been able to suggest new avenues of research that have brought to light new data contained in the earliest Christian literature, and have discovered unsuspected connections between those data.

My hypotheses about the origin of Christianity in some branch of Essenism are not new. Alphonse Dupont-Sommer 1959 emphasised the Essene connection, and also the remarkable similarity of the

Teacher of Righteousness with Jesus, though in the end he decided that they should not be equated (see chapter 4). Further, G. A. Wells (1971, 1982, 1988) has made a carefully worked-out case for regarding Jesus as a prophet who had died long before the apostles started their evangelisation. Wells, unaccountably, has been passed over in silence by most theologians.

I do not claim that my hypotheses have been absolutely confirmed. Such certainty is not attainable in historical research. But they have been fruitful enough, and plausible enough, for me to use them now as a guideline for this second part of my study, where I try to explain how the Christianity of the Gospels developed, and why it differs so radically from that of the first century. In the process, new light will be thrown on old questions.

The present chapter is mainly an overview of the findings in the first part of the book, where Chapter 2, in particular, has illustrated how the earliest Christians formed their views about Jesus, by interpreting Old Testament passages as prophecies about the Messiah. Chapter 9 is concerned with questions of dating and about sources in general. Chapter 10 sets forth the importance of Ignatius, bishop of Antioch, for transforming the Jesus figure of the Church from the heavenly one of the first century AD to the human one of the second. Chapter 11 illustrates in greater detail some consequences of this reorientation for our interpretation of the New Testament. Chapter 12 discusses Gnostic–mystic elements in Christianity, and Chapter 13 is an overview of the whole investigation.

The Jews in the Roman Empire

My discussion in Part I focused on the first century AD. That was a time when Messianic ideas were rife among the Jews not only in Palestine, but throughout the Roman Empire, where the majority of the Jews were now living, forming what the Jews themselves called (in Greek) the *Diaspora*, the Dispersion. The *Pax Romana* under Augustus and his successors had created conditions favourable to economic progress throughout the Empire, and the prosperity of the Diaspora Jews was probably on the increase, as well as their numbers, especially in the Eastern cities and in Rome.[1]

At the same time, the Jews seem to have felt that they were not given their rightful place in the Empire. Palestine had been an independent, or semi-independent state for several centuries, during which it had been able to play two Greek powers, Ptolemaic Egypt and Seleucid Syria, against each other. For about a century, after a successful revolt against Antiochus Epiphanes of Syria in 164 BC, the Jews had made themselves practically independent under their own king. But in 63 BC Pompey conquered Jerusalem, and Palestine became part of the Eastern, Greek-speaking half of the Roman Empire. After the death of the Roman client king, Herod the Great, Palestine was reduced to a Roman province under a Roman governor. The Kingdom of David became just a dream of the very distant past, a thousand years earlier.

In the Diaspora, the Jewish minorities felt that they were discriminated against. In the Greek cities of the Eastern part of the empire, such as Alexandria, Antioch, Ephesus and Corinth, they were granted a considerable amount of self-government. But they did not possess the full citizen rights of the Greek section of the population, and only very few Jews were Roman citizens. Though the Jews had a definitely higher status than, for instance, the indigenous Egyptian population of Alexandria, what the Diaspora Jews aspired to was equality with the Greeks. After all, they could point to a rich cultural heritage, and a historical record that everybody agreed was of greater antiquity than that of the Greeks and Romans. Their monotheistic faith was generally respected as an unusually 'philosophical' religion. And they were numerous. Though exact figures are naturally unobtainable, most modern scholars think that five to ten per cent of the total population of the Roman Empire were Jews. There were also many Jews in the Parthian empire, the Eastern competitor of Rome.

Messianism

Under such circumstances it is not surprising that revanchist attitudes towards the Greeks and Romans, and dreams of the re-establishment of a powerful Jewish kingdom under a king like the legendary David caught the imagination of the Jews both in the home country and in the Diaspora – the two were continually in touch with each other.

The result was a militant messianism which modern scholars generally agree lay behind most of the Jewish revolts of the first century and the first third of the second.

Our chief interest here is the religious ideas and attitudes among the Jews of the first century AD. But religion and politics interact, probably

165

even more so in antiquity than at the present time. In any case, there is no doubt that people in general were then more than nowadays inclined to believe in the direct intervention of divine powers in human affairs. In the religious texts that we have been studying, such attitudes were a matter of course.

The connection between Messianic expectations among the Jews, and political developments in the world where they lived, is indisputable. The Book of Daniel, which contains the first definite expression among the Jews of a belief in life after death, and also a vision of a supernatural Messiah figure (although that word is not used), was written at a time (*c.* 165 BC) when the Jews were successfully asserting themselves, both in the political and in the religious sphere, against their Greek rulers, the Seleucid kings. And, when direct Roman rule was introduced in Palestine soon after the death of Herod the Great, in 4 BC, a number of popular leaders, with or without a religious programme, attracted followers in various parts of the country, according to the Jewish historian Josephus.

The Christian movement started around AD 30 among groups of religious visionaries, such as Paul. This was at a time when the Jews felt hard pressed by the Roman authorities in Palestine, and by the non-Jewish populace in the cities of the Diaspora, for instance, by serious pogroms in Alexandria in AD 38. That is part of the background for the outbreak of the disastrous Jewish War in Palestine in 66–74, culminating in the fall of Jerusalem and the destruction of the Temple in AD 70. The subsequent revolt in Cyprus, Cyrenaica and Egypt in 113–15, and the Bar Kochba rebellion in 132–5 had quite explicit messianic connotations.

We have seen in Chapter 5, however, that the Messiah was by no means a clear and unambiguous concept at the time. In the Old Testament *mashiah*, like its Greek translation, *christos*, meant no more than 'anointed', and was applied above all to priests. Gradually it was restricted to the High Priest and the King, and was extended also to prophets. But the word was chiefly descriptive, and did not, as it did later in Christianity and later Judaism, imply supernatural powers. Such connotations were only now, from the first century onwards, being elaborated in many different directions by various religious groups. What is common to most of these groups is that they developed their ideas on the basis of an intensive study and re-interpretation of the Old Testament.

The position of the Essenes

Ever since the discovery of the Dead Sea Scrolls in the 1940s and 1950s, the evidence has pointed to the Essenes as the most vital religious movement among the Jews of the time we are now concerned with. Before 1948 practically all we knew about the Essenes had to be gathered from accounts given by sympathetic outsiders, such as Philo, Pliny the elder and Josephus. The Dead Sea Scrolls have provided us with substantial parts of what appear to be the literary remains of the Essenes, hidden away and preserved in the Qumran caves for two thousand years.

It now appears that the Essenes were a wide-ranging and differentiated movement, with a monastic and priestly core in Judaea, and a somewhat looser lay organisation in the cities of Palestine. More importantly, I have found several indications that the Essenes were actively propagating their ideas in the Jewish diaspora and, also, that they were remarkably successful there.

The central Essene texts from the Qumran caves, such as the Community Rule, the Damascus Document and the War Scroll, make it clear that the Palestinian Essenes were very much preoccupied with thoughts about the End-time, and the hoped-for Kingdom of God, where Israel – i.e. the faithful 'remnant' of Israel, the followers of what the Essenes, and the Christians after them,[2] called the 'Way' – would play a leading part. These religious thoughts were anchored in new interpretations of the Bible, in which the Essenes claimed to possess special insights, thanks to the divine inspiration of their chief prophet and founder, the Teacher of Righteousness.

Needless to say, this claim to special insights, in which the literal meanings of the sayings of the prophets were superseded by the interpretation of the Teacher and his successors, opened the door to quite radical changes in the religious speculations of the Essenes. That process was certainly also helped by the new impulses that the Jews were being exposed to from the surrounding 'nations', especially in the Greek-speaking Diaspora.

After the discoveries at Qumran many scholars tended to regard the Essenes, and in particular those who stood behind the Community Rule, as extremely strict, observant and conservative Jews. Their consistent use of the Hebrew language rather than Greek strengthened that impression. So did the intense nationalism, or even chauvinism, of such a text as the War Scroll.

Such 'fundamentalism' caused surprise, in view of the pictures that Philo, Pliny and Josephus had drawn of the Essenes as serene philosophers, leading a peaceful and secluded life in complete devotion to God. However, the conservatism of the Dead Sea Scrolls is deceptive.

In the first place, the Essenes seem to have come into being as a splinter group from the *priestly* establishment in Jerusalem.

Secondly, their attitude to the Bible was in reality innovative rather than conservative, since they maintained that the holy writings were no longer to be read literally, in a straightforward manner, but allegorically, i.e. in ways which allowed religious imagination free rein. It is true that, at least formally, only a small Essene élite was allowed to use that freedom. But they used it to introduce far-reaching changes in the religious framework of the Bible. These were eventually to lead to the emergence of Christianity as a new religion.

Thirdly, these changes were often in a direction that meant an adjustment to the non-Jewish environment. An instance in point is the calendar, which implied rejection of the lunisolar calendar generally in use in the East and among 'mainstream' Jews, in favour of a purely solar one, in which the visible phases of the moon no longer had any relevance at all. The new calendar made them conform *in this respect* to the politically and culturally leading state of the Eastern Mediterranean, Ptolemaic Egypt, and therefore eventually to its cultural heir, Caesar's Rome.

Fourthly, their allegorical interpretation of the Bible was in line with similar developments in Greek culture, where ancient myths were being interpreted in new ways in which the rather crude myths of the Greek gods were allegorised to achieve a workable accommodation between adventurous Greek philosophy and the old traditional views. Thus the allegorical Biblical interpretation of the Essenes can be seen as part of a general liberation of the human enquiring spirit from the bonds of tradition. Philo's reading of the Bible is an instance in point.

Yet another aspect of the Essene movement has come to light as a result of intense research into the Dead Sea Scrolls. The information about the Essenes provided by Philo, Pliny and Josephus concerned explicitly only Essenes in Palestine. The Qumran discoveries, at first, seemed to confirm the picture of a purely Palestinian group: the extensive use of the Hebrew language in the Scrolls and the strict enforcement of the Mosaic Law.

We have seen, however, several indications of strong Essene

involvement with the Diaspora. For one thing, the innovative features of Essene theology and, in particular, the allegorical interpretation of the Bible, must have been very acceptable to Diaspora Jews in the Roman Empire, who were presumably particularly open to Greek ways of thinking: allegorical interpretation had for centuries been applied in the study of Homer, for instance. We have also noted that Philo, who was not himself an Essene, not only valued the Essenes highly but, also, that he himself advocated an allegorical reading of the Law. Thus the presumed underlying, 'inner' or 'spiritual' meaning of circumcision, namely, the 'circumcision of the heart', implying complete submission to God, was far more important to Philo than the actual operation, the removal of the foreskin of the penis. On the other hand, Philo insisted that both were required: the allegorical meaning corresponding to the spirit, the literal one to the body, as he put it.

Philo's veneration for the Essenes is in itself a good example of the favourable attitudes towards the Essenes that existed among educated people in the Jewish Diaspora. Moreover, as we have pointed out, what Philo says about the Therapeutae – that they were to be found in many parts of the Greco–Roman world – is a direct confirmation of how Essene ideas penetrated outside Palestine, and presumably above all among the Jews in the Diaspora.

There are further indications from Qumran itself. As we have noted in Chapter 4, the Damascus Document stipulated that the 'Guardian of the camps', clearly a leader of the Essene community, was supposed to master all the languages of the different member categories, implying an international membership for the movement. Moreover, many Scroll fragments refer to 'the Poor of the nations', and 'Thy people Israel in all the lands to which they were banished', clear references to the Diaspora.

In our discussion we have pointed to parallels between first-century Christians and Essenes, noted by scholars since the eighteenth century, and amply confirmed by the Dead Sea Scrolls. The fact that Eusebius, the church historian, actually took Philo's Therapeutae to be Christians, underscores the affinities of the Christians and the Essenes. We have also seen that the two groups used the same self-designation: above all the Saints or Holy ones, but also such expressions as the Elect, the Congregation of God, those of the Way. Further, the name used by Philo and Josephus, *Essēnoi* or *Essaioi*, is generally connected by modern scholars with an Aramaic version of Hebrew *hasidim*, meaning 'pious', 'holy'. Thus the name conveys more or less the same idea as the name which Paul gives his communities: the Saints, which was in use among all Christians in the first century AD.

In Chapter 1 we found that Paul and the communities which he addressed apparently regarded Jesus as a teacher and prophet long since dead. But *before Paul came and preached his gospel, Jesus was not seen as a Messiah*. That was also the situation in the communities addressed by Hermas, and in the early versions of Didachē, discussed in Chapter 2. It was Paul and the (unnamed) apostles who were contemporary with him that made them see Jesus in a new light. The apostles spread the news that Jesus had been raised from the dead and that they had seen him in visions, sitting on the right-hand side of God. On that basis the apostles felt justified in declaring that Jesus was the Messiah who would save the Elect, the members of the Church of God, from death and destruction on the Day of Judgment.

Further, many apostles, and above all Paul, believed that Jesus' appearance to them in visions was a clear sign that the Day of Judgment was to be expected very soon. On that day, they said, Jesus, as the Messiah, would arrive 'on the clouds of heaven'. As we have pointed out, several times, they never refer to Jesus' arrival as a *return*, which would surely have been the natural expression to use if Jesus' death had taken place just before, or only a few years before they experienced their visions. Instead, they generally use the word *parousia*, 'arrival', 'presence', or some equivalent expression. This can be seen as further support for the view that these writers, as well as the communities they addressed, regarded Jesus' earthly life as belonging to a distant past. They never indicate any sort of date.

I have adduced a fair amount of support for the hypothesis that the communities which welcomed Paul and several other Christian apostles were originally Essene, or para-Essene ones.

First of all, the extensive parallels between the Essenes and the earliest Christians. Both referred to themselves as 'the Saints', and their community as 'the church of God'. Both were Messianic. Both were strongly attached to such books as Daniel and Enoch.

Second, practically all of the apostles mentioned in the first-century Christian texts were Diaspora Jews. And, as we have seen, the Essenes were in fact very active in the Diaspora.

Third, the writers of our first-century texts, including Paul, generally adopt an 'allegorical' interpretation of the Bible, as the Essenes did also. In the Diaspora, this implied the possibility of interpreting the Mosaic Law's rules about food purity and circumcision in a way which must have been welcome to many Diaspora Jews.

Fourth, there are indications that the communities followed at least in some respects the Essene calendar. Pentecost always occurred on a Sunday, fifty days after Easter, and the Essenes introduced two additional Sunday feasts, fifty and a hundred days after Pentecost, which may be the background to the later Christian custom of regarding every Sunday as a feast day, eventually taking over functions from the Jewish Sabbath. Other features of the Essene calendar were new fasting days, and a month count that was quite independent of the phases of the moon. In this respect it resembled the reformed Roman one that Caesar imported from Alexandria.

Fifth, the extensive parallels between the Jesus of the first-century texts – *not* the gospel Jesus – and the Essene Teacher of Righteousness: a teacher and interpreter of the prophets, a founder of the communities, a man persecuted by the established powers, dead long since, but still remembered and venerated by his Church, the Church of God. Further, the religious ideas and sentiments expressed in many of the Essene hymns from Qumran show some striking similarities with those associated with Jesus and the Christians.

All this shows that there is reason to explore further the hypothesis that the first-century AD Christian communities were direct descendants of the wide-ranging Essene movement, which had been in existence certainly since the late first century BC, chiefly in the Diaspora, but also in Judaea, which contained at least one important Essene community in Jerusalem.

From inspired Teacher to divine Messiah

The decisive event for the Jewish communities which in the first century called themselves the Church of God were the visions received by Paul and other apostles in which Jesus appeared to them as raised to Heaven, sitting beside God. Paul, the only apostle from whom we have direct evidence, took his visions to be a sign that the End of Days was imminent. When it came, Jesus, as the Messiah, would save the members of the Church into a life of immortal bliss with God. At the same time, Jesus' own resurrection, evidenced by his appearance in Heaven, was taken as a guarantee that resurrection was possible for all believers. Jesus became, according to 1 Corinthians 15:20, the 'first-fruits of them that slept'. A similar conviction is expressed by Clemens Romanus in 1 Clement 24:1: 'our future resurrection, of which [God] has given us a foretaste in our Lord Jesus Christ, by resuscitating him from among the dead'.

Though Paul is our most important witness for all this, the picture he implies about the origin of Christianity is supported by many others, as discussed at some length in Chapter 2. Jesus' appearance in Heaven was evidently an electrifying, overwhelming experience for the Church of God. As its members were certainly at this time predominantly Jews or Judaisers, they naturally turned to the Bible (i.e. the Old Testament) for corroboration and confirmation of their visionary experiences. In particular, they searched the Biblical texts for prophecies that would confirm that their own Prophet and Teacher was indeed the Messiah.

Judging from our surviving first-century texts, the members of the Church of God had very little information about their Teacher, beyond the fact that he had been a great prophet, and their leader in the distant past. It is at least likely that they believed he had died as a martyr. In any case, among their 'proof texts' it was passages from Isaiah and from the Psalms about the sufferings of the faithful, that figured most prominently (see Chapter 2). Their conviction that Jesus was now in Heaven of course emphasised his spiritual, even divine, or at least supernatural nature. This was in fact a new idea. The Messiah figure among the Jews, as we have seen (Chapter 5), did not generally possess any supernatural features. And to orthodox Jews, a divine man was hard to accept. It conflicted with the uniqueness of God. But among those Jews who were open to Greek ways of thinking (perhaps above all in Alexandria) – and we may presume that many members of the Church of God were among their number – the divinity accorded to the Messiah was no doubt acceptable and even welcomed. The status and power of their Christ was raised to new heights.

Among the first-century Christians there were, as we have seen, sharp differences of opinion as regards the interpretation of the Mosaic law, and especially in the matter of circumcision. For a long time scholars have taken this question to have been the main dividing line between 'Christians' and 'Jewish Christians'. I have suggested that this distinction was hardly relevant in the first century, since, in the first place, most Christians then considered themselves as Jews (and in fact were Jews), and secondly because even non-Christian Jews could well accept an allegorical view of the Mosaic regulations: Philo is an instance in point. Certainly Paul himself considered the question of circumcision as very important. So did Barnabas in his letter. But Clement of Rome, writing not long after Paul's death, does not take up the question at all. Nor does Hebrews, which is, like 1 Clement, roughly contemporary with Paul.[3]

In the second century the Jewish Christians of Palestine–Syria, who called themselves Nazoreans and Ebionites,[4] considered Paul as an apostate mainly because he rejected the literal interpretation of the Mosaic law. Interestingly, the Nazoreans also seem to have rejected Paul's central message, namely, that Jesus was a supernatural figure, the Messiah. To the Nazoreans, Jesus was a purely human teacher and prophet, which is of course what the Teacher of Righteousness had been to the early Essenes, and to himself. Like most other Jews of the time, they looked upon the Messiah as someone who would arrive in the future.

A movement related to the Christian one, and in many ways its most important competitor, was that of the Gnostics. Apparently the Gnostic movement arose in the Jewish Diaspora. It was certainly very successful in Alexandria, that cultural melting-pot of the Roman Empire at the beginning of our era. Lack of evidence makes it impossible for us to say whether the Gnostics were from the start connected with the Essene movement. But there were certainly points of contact. Both had a dualistic world-view, with the good world of Spirit, Light and the Soul standing against the evil world of Matter, Darkness and the Body. In addition the movements shared a strong sense of the mystery of all existence. The mysteries rested with God, but could be revealed to humans through angels.

On one point the Gnostics seem to have differed sharply from the Essenes. Whereas the Essenes stressed the importance of the Church as mediator between the community members and God, and insisted on a strict hierarchical order in the communities, most Gnostics (though not one of their most successful Christian branches, the Marcionites) resisted all authority. Salvation came through inspiration from the spiritual sphere being directed to each individual soul. Accordingly they saw no reason to submit to the authority which the Essenes vested in the Church, including the Teacher of Righteousness. Nor could the Gnostics be expected to subscribe to the Christian idea of Jesus as a unique sacrifice atoning for the sins of men. To the Gnostics, salvation was an individual affair, depending on the enlightenment of the soul, mediated by angelic emissaries from God.

However, even on these theological issues it may have been

possible for the Gnostics to adjust themselves to Christian ideas. They might regard Jesus as an unusually powerful angelic emissary from God, an idea which fitted in with the Christian idea of Jesus as the Son of God.

The individualistic and inspirational ideology of the Gnostics certainly favoured the development of splinter groups among them, something which is documented both in the surviving literature and in the writings of their opponents, the Church fathers. Irenaeus names at least half a dozen different Gnostic groups.

One of the more important religious organisations in the mid-second century was the Church organised by Marcion, a rich ship-owner from Pontus, who attached himself to the Church of Rome, but who was excommunicated in AD 144, chiefly, it seems, on the question of the position of the Jewish Bible, the Old Testament, in Christianity. The Christians, like the Essenes before them, regarded the Old Testament as the foundation Scripture of their faith. Paul, Clement, Hebrews and Barnabas depend for their theology entirely on the Old Testament. It is the Word of God, the unique God who had in the beginning chosen Israel as his own people, and had now renewed his contract with the Essene Church of God, the people of the New Covenant.[5] The Teacher of Righteousness might interpret the Old Testament in new and radical ways. But for the Essenes there was no question about the ultimate authority of God's Word. In addition, of course, it was the Old Testament which provided the 'prophecies' that proved to them that Jesus was indeed the Messiah.

It is true that Paul declared that the arrival of Jesus as the Messiah had superseded the Mosaic law. Marcion eagerly adopted that idea, and drew the radical conclusion that the New Covenant that Jesus had secured for the Christians made the whole of the Old Testament obsolete. Further, Marcion argued that the God of the Old Testament could not really be the highest God. The highest God was entirely good, and therefore Jesus called him the Father. These ideas about the God of the Old Testament are also found among several other Gnostics, who distinguish the highest, real God from the Jewish God, whom they call the Demiurge, responsible for most of the evil that we observe in the world.

Marcion was quite successful. He established a church which persisted in the Eastern part of the Empire into the sixth century, in spite of persistent attempts by the main church to suppress it.[6] Eventually it seems to have merged with the Manichaean church.

Though many Church fathers regarded Marcion as an arch-Gnostic, he is not a typical one. His establishment of a viable Church organisation makes him stand out as exceptional among the Gnostics. Anyway, it is clear that a considerable number of Gnostics allied themselves with the Christians around the beginning of the second century. True to their basic view of the Saviour as a messenger from the spiritual world, they refused to regard Jesus as a human being. That was not difficult at a time when most Christians regarded Jesus as a figure of the distant past, and concentrated their thoughts on the heavenly Saviour who had appeared to several apostles. The Gnostics considered him as wholly divine, a kind of spiritual being who only 'seemingly' appeared to his followers as a man, exposed himself to persecution and eventually to death on the cross. The Church fathers called this Gnostic doctrine the 'docetic' heresy (from the Greek verb *dokeō*, to seem). They – first of all, it seems, Ignatius of Antioch – combated it violently. The canonical Gospels bear strong marks of this struggle. Indeed, one of the main reasons for propagating the Gospel story seems to have been the determination to combat Gnosticism, and in particular, docetic Gnosticism. Creating a flesh and blood Jesus, firmly anchored in history, proved to be an effective way of winning that struggle.[7]

One further important element in the cultural background of second-century Christianity remains to be discussed: mainstream Judaism. Though I have called Essenism one of the most vital movements among the Jews both in Israel and later in the Diaspora, in the centuries before the fall of Jerusalem and the destruction of the Temple in AD 70, the indications are that mainstream Judaism still commanded the loyalty of the majority of the Jewish people. Philo admired the Essenes, but he certainly was not an Essene himself, and does not give the impression that many Alexandrian Jews were Essenes. The same may be said about Josephus, who squarely places himself among the Pharisees. In the subsequent few centuries, when we can directly compare the Jewish synagogues with the Christian churches in the entire Greek-speaking part of the Roman Empire, we normally find the synagogue much larger and more richly endowed than the church.[8]

Thus the developing Christian church had to face competition not only with various splinter groups within its own ranks, but also with Gnostics and with ordinary, traditional Jews. These circumstances also exerted their influence on the shaping of the Christian self-image.

The history of Christianity as presented in Luke's book of Acts, and by Eusebius two hundred years later, creates the impression that Christianity was entirely the creation of Jesus, and broke away from Judaism and the Jews quite soon after the crucifixion of Jesus in the thirties of the first century AD. After Jesus' death, according to Luke, the apostles, following Jesus' command, turned to the pagans: the Jews had rejected Jesus by asking Pilate to release Barabbas, and demanding that Jesus should be crucified. Also, Luke leaves us with the impression that the work of the apostles in the Empire was henceforth directed more towards non-Jews than Jews. Christianity is thus presented by Luke as a new religion, separated right from the start both doctrinally and ethnically from traditional Judaism.

Our discussion in the preceding chapters has shown that Luke's and Eusebius' version of Christian history is a very slanted one. During the whole of the first century Christianity was in fact clearly one of several Jewish movements. The members of the Church of God were largely Jews, considered themselves as Jews and were looked upon as Jews by outsiders. The churches certainly welcomed proselytes. But it is quite clear that the early apostles directed their chief efforts to communities whose Jewish identity was firmly established, both ethnically and theologically. As the communities all regarded the Old Testament, the Septuagint Bible, as Holy Scripture, and were used to an allegorical interpretation of it, they were excellently equipped to lend a hearing to Paul and the other apostles.

As we have seen in the preceding chapters, the expansion of the Church during the first century AD had taken place almost entirely outside Palestine. However, the target of the mission was not primarily the pagan world, but the Jewish Diaspora within that world. Moreover, this was not, as Luke would have it, a new development which started after the Jews of Judaea had repudiated Jesus, an idea which Luke was anxious to spread as part of his effort to present Christianity as the genuine heir of Judaism, rightly understood.[9]

Internationalism via the Diaspora was something that had characterised the Essene movement, the original Church of God, even at Qumran. It continued to characterise the Christianised Church of God. Thus if, as I argue, Christianity developed among the Essene communities of the Church of God, the predominantly Diaspora character of Christianity seems entirely natural. What we have to get rid of is Luke's and Eusebius' assumption that Christianity originated in the works and deeds of a Jesus who lived in Galilee and Judaea in the first few decades of the first century AD.

The first-century Christian texts give no support at all to the Lukan story, and are indeed incompatible with it in several respects. So why did Luke, and the other Gospel writers too, present Jesus' life in the way they do? The answer has to be sought in the position of the Christian church at the time the Gospel writers compiled their works. As I shall argue in greater detail in the next chapter, the Gospels were all in the main composed outside Palestine in the second century, though individual parts may go back to earlier periods.

From Spirit to Body

The difference between the first-century texts and the Gospels and Acts is dramatic as regards the Jesus figure. Paul and most of the other early texts focus on Jesus' appearance as a divine figure sitting beside God in Heaven, which the writers interpret as an assurance of the possibility of resurrection for everybody, and also as an indication that the Last Judgment is imminent, implying salvation for the faithful. By contrast, none of our first-century authors has anything of much substance to say about Jesus' earthly life. They certainly assume that he has lived on earth, and was persecuted and killed there. *But those events are never presented as contemporary ones.* Nobody claims to have met any eyewitnesses of those occurrences. If, as the Gospels have it, Jesus had been active in Palestine only a few years before Paul started his evangelisation, this is hard to explain. On my hypothesis that Jesus, to them, was a revered, but long-since dead, prophet of the Churches of God, the problem disappears.

Paul was painfully aware that it was not easy to convince his audiences that Jesus, a crucified prophet, was the promised Messiah. It was, he says, 'a stumbling-block unto the Jews, and unto the Greeks foolishness' (1 Cor 1:23). The idea of a king accepting the sacrifice of himself in order to transfer his waning powers to a successor, and thus benefit his subjects, is not unheard of in the world, though the documentation is usually mythological rather than historical. But the Jewish Messiah had never been presented in that way before Paul. The 'suffering Servant of God' in Isaiah 53, and in several of the Psalms, it is true, offers some parallels. In fact, Isaiah himself meant the suffering servant to stand for the whole of Israel, suffering in the Babylonian exile. Further, there are indications that there circulated also a book about Isaac, in which Abraham really completed the sacrifice of his son, who was later resuscitated.[10] But certainly neither Isaac nor Isaiah were ever taken to be Messiahs. So it is understandable that Paul and his colleagues met with opposition.

None of the first-century texts we have analysed lays any weight at all on the person Jesus, the earthly Jesus, the Jesus who had once lived among men. Accordingly, the writers take it for granted that the identity of Jesus is wholly unproblematic to their readers. This is all the more remarkable, since all the texts we have been examining are directed to addressees in the Diaspora, and the indications are that most of them were actually written in the Diaspora. Hence it was virtually impossible for the readers of the texts to have any personal knowledge or experience of a nearly contemporary Palestinian Jesus. Since he was, in spite of this, a very well-known figure among the Diaspora Essenes, he must have been regarded by them as somebody whose fame had been established long ago. He must have made a deep impression for the memory of him to be still alive among them, as a one-time teacher and prophet. That the Teacher of Righteousness was indeed regarded as such a person among the Essenes is beyond doubt.[11]

What the Essene communities thought they knew about the Teacher of Righteousness was presumably that he had lived long ago, that he had been persecuted and maltreated, perhaps killed. Some of these ideas may have arisen through the liturgy of their church (see Chapter 1, about the Last Supper). But they had no reason to expect that the apostles would have anything of interest to report about such a person of the distant past. So, from their point of view, Paul's and the other apostles' silence about the life of their one-time teacher, Jesus, could cause no surprise at all. What interested them was that Jesus had recently appeared in visions to the apostles, and that the apostles – not only Paul – took this to mean that Jesus was now preparing to visit the earth for the Last Judgment, where he, as a divinely ordained Messiah, would save them and inaugurate the eternal Kingdom of God.

It is not surprising that most of the first-century writers spent much of their energy on convincing their audiences that Jesus really was the Messiah. On the whole, they did not try to achieve this by referring to Jesus' life. About that they presumably knew as little as their audience. What was important was to convince their hearers that the Jesus they already knew as a founder and great teacher of their organisation, the Church of God, was *in addition* the divinely ordained

Messiah. Their community would then become one of the Churches of God 'which are *also* in Christ' (my italics), to quote one of our texts.[12] Thus gradually the Essene Churches of God – or, rather, some of them – became *Christian* Churches of God.

So what they did was to search the Bible for passages which they could re-interpret as statements about the Messiah, and which could be plausibly taken as applying to Jesus. Paul seems generally to have kept aloof from such arguments. For him, the overwhelming impact of his vision of the risen Jesus appears to have been decisive. But in 1 Clement, Hebrews and above all in Barnabas, the technique of applying Old Testament passages to Jesus is employed quite frequently (see Chapter 2).

The members of the first-century Churches of God seem to have been quite happy with their very thin and abstract picture of the earthly Jesus. But the Church as an organisation felt threatened by the teaching of the 'docetic' branch of Gnostics. That teaching tended to weaken the humanity of Jesus, making it more difficult for ordinary people to see Jesus' resurrection as a foretaste of their own survival after death. As we shall see in Chapter 10, Ignatius of Antioch sensed the danger, starting an anti-docetic campaign where he forcefully insisted that Jesus was indeed a man, born of a woman. The Gospel writers enthusiastically and skilfully followed Ignatius' lead, creating a dramatic and moving story of Jesus' life and deeds.

Chapter 9

Beginnings of the Gospel Literature

Questions of dating

I have discussed questions of dating at various places in the preceding chapters. Necessarily so, since a historical investigation naturally hinges on establishing a correct chronological framework. In the history of ideas, of which history of religion and of theology form a part, it is the sequence of conceptual constructions and their interrelations that have to be sorted out.

In Chapter 2 I presented arguments for placing the six texts treated there firmly in the first century AD. In fact, all of them except Barnabas were even dated before the destruction of the Jerusalem Temple in AD 70. The most important consequence of my dating was that the six texts stood out as definitely older than the New Testament Gospels and Acts, while the traditional view, still prevalent among the majority of New Testament scholars, has been that the Gospels are the oldest Christian texts, with the exception of the Pauline epistles.

None of the Biblical manuscripts that has been preserved is an autograph, that is to say, actually hand-written by its author. In fact, except for some insignificant fragments containing passages from the Gospel of John, judged palaeographically to date from the first half of the second century, our oldest fairly complete manuscripts of the Gospels and Acts are from the third or fourth century AD. Accordingly, they have been exposed to changes, deliberate or accidental, by many different scribes.

Dating an ancient *manuscript* is a fairly straightforward matter. In rare cases the scribe himself may say when he completed his work (for instance, the H manuscript of Didachē, dated to AD 1056). Sometimes a date may be at least approximately inferred from the place and the circumstances in which it was found (cases in point are the Qumran

180

and Nag Hammadi finds). And in the last fifty years or so, various physical methods – e.g. Carbon 14 datings – have been developed, whereby the age of the paper or parchment used for the writing can be estimated (several Qumran Scrolls have been dated by such methods).

But the most common method, used since antiquity, has been the palaeographic one, in which the age of the manuscript is judged from the style of handwriting. Under favourable conditions palaeographic dating can result in datings within roughly half a century. The precision depends very much on the availability of comparative material, not to speak of the individual expertise of the judge. For instance, an early Egyptian fragment of John (see Chapter 12) was placed by one judge in the first half of the second century, whereas another expert placed it in the second half.

If we can date the oldest manuscript of a text, we can also say that the *text itself* must (except in the case of an autograph – see above) have been composed *before* that date. But we cannot specify how long before. For instance, in the case of the Didachē, we have to reckon with a period of about a thousand years between the available manuscript and the original text.

The chief difficulty in dating an ancient text is that we normally do not know to what extent the successive scribes have introduced modifications. Some of these may be due to sheer carelessness (for instance, omitting words or even lines). Others may be intentional: the scribe may replace an obsolete word by a modern one, or an unintelligible phrase by something which he thinks makes sense. But the most problematic cases are those where the scribe tries to 'improve' his original by changes and additions which are more in line with what he and his contemporaries think the text *ought* to say. In our material there is no doubt that such changes have been made in several places. Sometimes we can spot them by comparison with other manuscripts of the same text. (An instance in point is the oldest extant manuscript of Didachē, discussed in Chapter 2). Now manuscripts of Biblical texts down to the end of the Middle Ages can be counted in thousands. Hence the number of 'variant readings' is of course enormous. Still, the comparisons generally do not say much about any changes that may have been made before the oldest still extant manuscript was produced. We can make more or less informed guesses about the original text. But it is impossible to reach certainty. The discussions about Didachē and Hermas (in Chapter 2), are typical.

As regards the New Testament texts, Koester 1980–2 makes the important observation that the texts were probably even more variable *before* their canonisation, which in most cases occurred before the date of the oldest extant manuscripts. Accordingly, we have small chances of discovering changes that may have been made in the New Testament texts in the important period *c.* AD 50–180. In the case of the Gospels, moreover, we know for certain that passages and episodes have been transferred from one Gospel to another.[1]

One important way of dating a text is to search for clues that may connect it with historical events whose dates are known independently. An instance in point is the destruction of the Jerusalem temple. But the method is not without difficulties of its own. In the first place, the connection is more often hinted at than overtly stated. For instance, in Mark the destruction of the Temple is obliquely referred to as part of a prophecy. Those who insist that the prophecy is genuine, and not made after the event, naturally do not admit that it provides a way of dating the text. In Chapter 2 I have dated 1 Clement before the fall of Jerusalem because the present tense is used to describe the temple service, while Barnabas has been placed after the destruction, because he seems directly to refer to it.

An even more serious problem is the way in which the narratives in a text are put together, using episodes from different sources. (Such episodes are usually called pericopes, sections, in New Testament studies.) Strictly speaking, therefore, dating an episode may in fact only be valid for that particular pericope, not for the text as a whole. (For an argument of this kind see my discussion of Thiede at the end of this section.)

A text may also be dated by the style of its language. All languages undergo changes over time: late twentieth-century English differs at least statistically from early twentieth-century English, and there are also obvious dialectal differences between, for instance, British English and American English. The position is similar for ancient Greek and Latin, as well as for Hebrew and Aramaic. But the changes are often difficult to distinguish from purely personal peculiarities. Further, they proceed at different speeds in different kinds of literature. I have given examples of linguistic features that may serve as at least preliminary and approximate dating criteria: for instance, the use of *synagogue, apostle* and *saints* (see Chapter 2). More such statistical indications can undoubtedly be found, but would involve much tedious work, since large masses of text material have to be gone through in order to establish reliable criteria.[2] Yet even so certainty will never be attained.

Another way of arriving at a date for the text is to ascertain to what extent it has been used, or perhaps quoted, by other, datable writers. But parallels between texts are on the whole elusive, since ancient authors very seldom quote with exactness, and similarities are matters of degree. I give examples in my discussion of Ignatius's possible dependence on Matthew, in Chapter 10.

In light of all these pitfalls it is obvious that any datings of our kind of texts can only be tentative and approximate. Moreover, the dating has to be done with the help of criteria of the most diverse kinds, which have to be weighed against each other. A considerable element of subjectivity is inevitable. It is no wonder, therefore, that different scholars have arrived at different results. It is also understandable that their judgments of what is plausible and reasonable depends on what they know, or think they know, about other matters related to the problem at hand.

Our oldest fairly complete manuscripts of individual texts do not carry us further back than the fourth century AD. But, if we take into account possible mentions and quotations in other texts, we may reach older strata. We have, for instance, quotations from all the synoptic Gospels (but not John) in the writings of Justin Martyr, dating probably from the 150s. Further, Eusebius quotes one Papias, apparently writing about AD 140, who is said to mention both Mark and Matthew. All the New Testament Gospels are mentioned by Irenaeus in *c*. AD 180. He even gives us a reason for there being *exactly* four: like the four cardinal points of the compass.

Thus we have at least some tangible evidence that Mark and Matthew (in some form) were in existence before 140. For John, Luke and Acts the corresponding date is 150–60. As the destruction of the Jerusalem Temple in AD 70 seems to be implied in all the Gospels, we get a time-span between roughly AD 70 and AD 140 for these New Testament texts. In this time-span, most theological writers prefer the first thirty years, whereas a minority, and I myself, prefer the last thirty years.[3]

In addition to the arguments advanced by Koester and others (see note 3) I have, as we noted above, advanced linguistic criteria by which the Gospels and Acts can be classed, with some probability, as definitely later than the first-century texts analysed in Chapter 2. By criteria independent of each other, therefore, I can support a second-century date for *all* the Gospels and for Acts.

It seems obvious to me that the reluctance of almost all theologians to admit that the Gospels and Acts should be placed late rather than early in the interval between AD 70 and 140 is due to their common assumption that the Gospel stories depend on traditions based on memories of Jesus (whether oral or written) which go back to a Jesus presumed to have lived in Palestine in the first three decades of the first century. I should add that even Koester, whose critical acumen is evident, shares this assumption. It is quite certain, he says, that Jesus was crucified under Pilate. Furthermore, Koester accepts the common theological view that James is the physical brother of Jesus, which inevitably implies that he, like John, Cephas and of course Paul, were contemporaries of Jesus, who must therefore have lived in the first half of the first century. I discuss this in Chapter 11.

It is quite clear that scholars' firm adherence to the assumption of a first-century Jesus[4] has prevented them from exploring avenues of research which appear as obviously promising, if that constraint is removed. A very direct illustration is their treatment of the Letters of Peter, James and Jude (see Chapter 6). Most scholars refuse to accept them as genuinely written by the apostles who stand as their authors. But the reason given for rejecting them is in general simply that they contain no information about the earthly Jesus, which would of course be strange, if those apostles were really contemporaries and companions of Jesus.

But, if we accept instead the hypothesis I have been exploring here, we find that little, if anything, in these three letters prevents us from accepting them as genuine. On the contrary, they fit in very well in the first-century theological landscape, as I have outlined it in the present book. And their excellent Greek is not at all surprising, coming from the obviously learned members of the Jerusalem Church of God.

Evidently the assumption of a first-century Jesus, contemporary with Paul and the early apostles, is not supported by the first-century evidence, and is really incompatible with it. My own hypothesis of a much earlier, second-century BC Jesus, whose life the early apostles could know very little about, and who was only experienced *in visions* by Paul around AD 30, fits the facts much better. In the first century, the Diaspora Christians – of whom a majority were Jews – were mainly interested in confirming the Messiah status of their one-time founder and prophet. The desire to write what is really a Greek-style biography of Jesus – Gerald Downing has shown that there are close parallels between the Gospels and the Cynic Lives of philosophers, for instance, the frequent use of anecdotes (true or fictional) about the hero's sayings and doings: called *chreiai* in Greek[5] – is easy to understand in the second century, when the number of Gentiles in the Church certainly increased. And, above all, such a biography, presenting in concrete detail the life of a human being, could be used to good effect against the docetic Gnostics, a point I discuss in my chapter on Ignatius, Chapter 10, and in Chapter 12.

The material used for writing such a biography was most likely both traditions (including rites and liturgies) in the Church about its founder, and no doubt also the creative use of the imagination of the believers. There is no need to assume an independent oral tradition preserving memories of a Jesus supposed to have lived among the apostles in the beginning of the first century AD. Michael Fishbane,[6] who is critical of the reliance on undocumented oral traditions, writes 'there is evidence suggesting that prophetic groups and attitudes were involved in the shaping and composition of historiographical literature'. My own investigation, I think, provides evidence of precisely this kind of 'creative mythology'.

Before leaving this subject I should add that a German theologian, Carsten Thiede,[7] argues that some Greek fragments from Cave 7 at Qumran contain words or parts of words which can be construed as a passage from Mark. Accordingly, Thiede argues, Mark must have existed at least before 68, when Qumran was destroyed by the Romans. Using palaeographic criteria, Thiede goes on to argue that the fragments very probably should be dated as early as AD 50.

Thiede's arguments, widely acclaimed by the general press, have been welcomed by many conservative theologians, and also many ordinary Christians, but almost universally rejected by experts on New Testament manuscripts, for instance, Kurt Aland.[8] My own linguistic background includes a book on the use of linguistic statistics for determining authorship, and I agree fully with the sceptics (see note 2). The fragments are far too small (about a dozen not very clear letters only, distributed over four lines of text) to allow any firm conclusions.

Moreover, *even if Thiede's identification is accepted*, his conclusions are doubtful. First, Cave 7 is exceptional at Qumran. It is, together with Cave 4, alone in containing Greek manuscripts. More than that, *all* the identified fragments from the Cave 7 are Greek. Thus it is not unreasonable to argue that Cave 7 has a history that differs from that of the other caves. Hiding manuscripts in rock caves was by no means a unique phenomenon among the Jews.[9] Hence Cave 7 may well have been used by Christians as a hiding place for manuscripts, *after* the Roman occupation of the place ceased there, for instance, at the time of the Bar Kochba rebellion. This hypothesis receives a measure of support from the fact that Thiede has found in the cave a further three fragments, of which he classes two, though (wisely) with some hesitation, as belonging to New Testament texts (1 Tim and 2 Peter), which scholars have fairly unanimously dated well into the second century AD.

We may go further: even if we accept that the passage identified by Thiede may be Markan, it may well be part of a text which came from an early written source used subsequently by the compiler of Mark's Gospel. The passage contains no very distinctive words, and could in fact fit into a great number of different contexts, or be told about another hero than Jesus.

Under the circumstances I think the experts are right. Thiede has no good case for placing Mark's Gospel very early. In general, it is obviously unwise to rely too much on single passages in texts and, on the whole, to make very definite assertions on the basis of very few criteria.

Creating the Gospels: Jews, Christians, Essenes, Gnostics

In his closely argued book, *Ancient Gospels* (1990), Helmut Koester tries to sort out the complicated relationship between the earliest Gospel-like texts, including in particular some of the Nag Hammadi finds from 1945. Koester stresses the importance of examining canonical and non-canonical texts by the same criteria. This should really be uncontroversial. But, in the past, and indeed even today, many scholars have tended to give the canonical texts a privileged position, considering them as more reliable and more ancient than the non-canonical ones.

Koester brings out the composite nature of all the relevant texts, with interesting results. In very brief outline, Koester holds – like most twentieth-century scholars – that Matthew and Luke both have Mark as one of their sources, but in addition a source called Q (from German *Quelle*, 'source'), containing mainly 'sayings' of Jesus. The content of Q (also called the 'Synoptic Sayings Source') can to some extent be reconstructed on the basis of passages where Matthew and Luke agree, while having no correspondence in Mark. John is much more independent of the others, though several incidents in John, especially miracle stories, have correspondences in Mark, and therefore also in Matthew and Luke.

These ideas have been around for more than a hundred years, and have found wide acceptance. But Koester has gone further, by carefully searching the non-canonical texts for information on the sayings and deeds of Jesus. Formerly, scholars have tended to take it for granted that such information in the non-canonical texts ought to be seen as simply garbled versions of what is found in the canonical texts. Koester, however, finds that a good deal of it must be independent of the canonical Gospels, and may in fact be part of the rather wide-ranging material that Koester calls (1990, p. 200) the 'free tradition of sayings of Jesus'.

Thus some of the non-canonical texts – an instance in point being the mildly Gnostic Gospel of Thomas – are probably, at least in parts, older than the canonical ones. The canonical Gospels, Koester holds, were not the oldest *written* texts containing statements about what Jesus said and did, and about the oldest Christian communities. In view of the tiny proportion – a few per cent – of the classical literature that has been preserved, this is hardly surprising. Needless to say, the scanty documentation is a great problem for the historian

The view that the Gospels are based on oral traditions going back to Jesus' preaching was put forward as early as the second century CE by Papias (fl. *c*. AD 140) as quoted by Eusebius (fl. *c*. 330), by Irenaeus (fl. *c*. AD 180), and above all by Justin Martyr (fl *c*. AD 150). Justin seldom uses the word Gospel, but writes instead *apomnēmoneumata*, 'memories, memoirs' of the apostles, implying that they were written down from memory by 'apostles' who had themselves been eyewitnesses of the events. Justin's purpose in launching this term was no doubt to underline the authenticity and credibility of the Gospels. Eyewitness accounts carry more weight than hearsay. At the same time Justin's construction helped exclude Paul from the group of genuine apostles. Justin certainly did not mind that: it is significant that he never even mentions Paul in his writings, and never quotes any of his Epistles. He obviously realised what we have ourselves found in Chapters 1–2, namely, that Paul's theology, and also his account of early Christianity, was difficult to reconcile with that of the Gospels, and sometimes even contradicted them.[10] Accordingly the second-century Church may well have looked upon Paul as a dangerous writer: after all, the Gnostics regarded him as an ally. Hoffman 1984 suggests that the main Christian Church actively promoted the Gospels in order to combat the Marcionites, who held that Paul was the sole real apostle, and the sole receiver of a true revelation of God's gospel about Christ.

Justin's view of the Gospels as memories of the apostles has dominated the Church ever since, and is certainly even today the most commonly accepted one among Christian believers. But it does not stand up to critical inquiry. In the first place, the Gospels themselves do not name their authors. The names are not connected with the texts until after *c.* 140, more than a century after the events the texts tell us about.

Secondly, the connection of the names with Jesus' disciples is problematic, to say the least. Mark and Luke are not included in the list of 'the twelve' at all. Therefore later writers attempted to tie them to the apostolic circle by declaring that Mark was the interpreter and secretary of Peter,[11] and that Luke was a companion of Paul's. As for Mark, no evidence at all is produced. As for Luke, the name does indeed appear in some of Paul's letters. However, since Paul himself, according to the traditional Acts' history (in this case, supported by his own letters) did not join the Christian church until after Jesus' death, we are still left without any connection between Luke and a supposed eyewitness.

Matthew and John are names that occur in all lists of 'the twelve'. But their names are quite common ones, and thus do not carry much weight. Moreover, if we agree with the overwhelming majority of modern scholars, that Matthew, like Luke, depends on Mark (and Q), it is hard to see why he, as a presumed eyewitness, should prefer to rely on Mark, who is not even a disciple in the canonical Gospels. As for John of the Gospel of John, hardly any modern scholar considers him to be identical with the John of the Twelve.

Thus we can only conclude that ascribing the authorship of the Gospels to certain of Jesus' disciples was a step taken towards the mid-second century AD by members of the Church who, like Papias and Justin, were eager to find – or indeed fabricate – support for the view that the Gospels they chose to accept as canonical were the memories of Jesus' contemporaries.

Modern scholars do not in general regard the Gospels as eyewitness accounts, or based on the memories of eyewitnesses. However, the overwhelming majority still maintain that they are, in some way, based on the preaching of a man called Jesus, crucified in Jerusalem at the time when Pontius Pilate was prefect of the Roman province of Palestine.[12] Accordingly they hold that the Gospels at least reflect traditions, primarily oral ones, going back to whoever saw and heard this Jesus.

Some scholars have developed this view into a hypothesis that the early Christians developed a technique whereby Jesus' sayings were memorised by his followers with complete exactness, after the fashion of later Jewish rabbinic schools. This suggestion has found few adherents.[13]

The longer the time-span between the moment the sayings were heard, and the moment they were eventually put on paper, obviously the smaller is their reliability. It is therefore understandable that those who hold on to the hypothesis of an oral tradition have resisted a second-century date for the Gospels, which implies a time-span of about a century.

Koester (1990) has chosen a different solution to the problem. Briefly, he concludes that the canonical Gospels depend heavily on earlier *written* sources, which have disappeared, but may be at least partly reconstructed by means of a detailed comparison between various non-canonical texts. One such reconstructed text has of course been recognised for a long time, namely Q, the 'Synoptic Sayings Source'. Koester, following Kloppenborg 1989, assigns a date between AD 30 and 60 to Q, thus making it roughly contemporary with Paul's letters.[14]

Further, Q is related to the non-canonical Gospel of Thomas (see Chapter 12), where some of the sayings, Koester holds, appear to be more original than the corresponding sayings in Matthew and Luke.[15] Other non-canonical texts yield evidence that points in the same direction.

Koester's careful analysis also indicates that, though Matthew and Luke depend on Mark, their source is not the *canonical* Mark, but an earlier version which can be partly recovered through other comparisons. Thus the canonical Mark can be assigned a fairly late date, perhaps even later than Matthew and Luke. This construction solves another mystery, namely, that Mark, generally considered as the oldest text, is in fact the least well-attested of all the Gospels: fewer early manuscripts have been found, and we have fewer references to it in other texts. The above-mentioned Gospel of Thomas, together with other Gnostic texts, and the earliest version of Mark, probably provided material for the Gospel of John, whose earliest canonical version may be placed in the first half of the second century.

Thus, according to Koester, all the canonical Gospels, substantially in the form we know them, should be placed in the second century. This is also the position I have arrived at, on independent grounds. At the same time his meticulous investigation shows that they made use of various written sources which can probably be dated to the first century.

The most important of these sources was Q, the Synoptic Sayings Source, in which Kloppenborg 1989 thinks he has managed to trace several successive layers. Much of Q can be independently recovered through the Gnostic Gospel of Thomas, which probably also goes back to the first century.

A second early source is a collection of parables and miracle stories, preserved both in Mark and in the Gospel of John, where scholars refer to it as the 'Semeia Source'.[16]

Thirdly, there is material about the life of Jesus, to a large extent reconstructed on the basis of Old Testament passages, interpreted allegorically as prophecies about the Messiah. We presented and discussed much of this material in Chapter 2.

Though Koester, like practically all theological scholars, consistently refers to the source material as 'traditions' about Jesus, he is fully aware that these traditions are not necessarily either old or historically accurate. In fact, he writes (1990, p. 224) that 'the only historical information about Jesus' suffering, death and crucifixion was that he was condemned to death by Pontius Pilate and crucified'. On this point Koester presumably relies on Tacitus. That is unwise, since Tacitus published his Annals in *c.* AD 110, and thus could have got information, ultimately, from the Christians themselves, who were then in the middle of building up the Gospel story.[17]

Hence Koester's acceptance of the prevailing belief that Jesus was crucified under Pilate (prefect of the Roman province of Judaea, AD 26–36) is not as securely founded as he seems to think. He is also surprisingly uncritical towards the common theological view that James, the leading figure in the Jerusalem Church of God, was Jesus' physical brother: Koester writes in several places (e.g. pp. 51, 71) about 'Jesus' brother James', necessarily implying that Jesus and this James were near contemporaries.[18] As we have seen in Chapter 1, and develop further in Chapter 11, that conclusion does not stand up to scrutiny. Accordingly, I reject Koester's basic assumption about Jesus, namely, that his activities should be dated to the years around AD 30. I maintain that he was supposed by Paul and the apostles to have been dead for more than a century, when he appeared in Paul's *visions* in *c.* AD 30.

As regards the historical accuracy of the other 'traditions' about Jesus and early Christianity, Koester is evidently less certain, though he refrains from expressing his doubts explicitly.[19] But the way in which the Gospel story is built up, gradually accumulating more and more episodes, and combining completely different strands with each other, seems to me to make it clear that we have to do with the same kind of mechanism that is at work in most popular lore and folk tales. Once a figure has attained heroic stature, he or she tends to attract episodes which were originally associated with other persons, real or fictional. Instances in point are Alexander the Great, and King Arthur. Jesus obviously became such a figure in the Christian movement of the first few centuries AD.

Koester thinks the oldest retrievable version of Q primarily presents Jesus as a teacher and prophet.[20] He is not associated with any miracles: what is important are Jesus' words, not his person or his deeds. Thus there is nothing in Q about Jesus' sacrificial death, nor on the Messiah. The same holds for the Gnostic Gospel of Thomas, where Jesus' earthly deeds are never referred to. It is apparently the *risen* Jesus that speaks to his companions (see Chapter 12).

This inevitably reminds us of our findings about the six early texts treated in Chapter 2, of which Hermas has the Church, not Jesus, as the central symbol of holiness, and Didachē presents Jesus as a teacher and prophet, not a Messiah. Thus the position I have myself described in these early texts squares excellently with the one discovered by Kloppenborg and Koester as regards the early versions of Q, and the Gospel of Thomas.[21] We thus have further support for the view that *before* the campaigns by Paul and his colleagues, there were Churches of God that regarded Jesus simply as a teacher and prophet, not yet as the Messiah.

The fact that Q and Thomas put their sayings in Jesus' mouth naturally does not guarantee that they in fact go back to Jesus himself, though that would be a plausible hypothesis if Jesus had lived just a few decades before Q and Thomas were written. But if Jesus, as I maintain, had lived, or was supposed by the Essenes and the earliest Christians, to have lived in the second century BC, the plausibility disappears, and the hypothesis has to be scrutinised carefully.

It is certainly reasonable to suppose that the Essene Churches of God treasured reminiscences of their revered founder. However, in several cases the sayings ascribed to Jesus are demonstrably taken from other sources – which of course does not exclude the possibility that Jesus may have uttered them. For instance, Koester points out (1990, p. 63) that the saying, 'it is more blessed to give than to receive', declared to be 'the words of the Lord' in Acts 20:35, is in fact a common Greek aphorism. Another instance is the saying by Jesus in Matthew 11:25–6 and Luke 10:21, 'you have hidden these things from the wise and the clever, but have revealed them to the unlearned'. Koester 1990 (p. 57) says that the same words (*sophoi kai sunetoi*) are found in 1 Corinthians 1:19, where Paul declares that they are quotations from the Old Testament. Presumably they go back to Isaiah 29:14.

Such transfer of Old Testament passages to the story of Jesus is what we illustrated by means of a great many examples in our analysis of 1 Clement, Hebrews and in particular Barnabas, in Chapter 2. Koester discusses the phenomenon with reference to the incidents in the Gospel narrative of Jesus' death which, as he says, 'do not rest on historical memory, but were developed on the basis of allegorical interpretation of Scripture' (p. 224). He also quotes with approval Vielhauer's observation, '*The way in which the suffering of Jesus is described by the use of passages from the Old Testament, without quotation formulae is, in terms of the history of the tradition, older than the explicit scriptural proof; it represents the oldest form of the description of the passion of Jesus*'.[22]

All this agrees excellently with what I presented in Chapter 2. It is obvious that a narrative constructed in such a way can lay no claim to historical reliability. True, the fact that a saying is found in the Old Testament or, for that matter, in ancient Greek literature, does not prove that Jesus did not *also* use it. But clearly Matthew and John employ the same method of reconstructing the life and works of Jesus as I illustrated in Chapter 2 for Barnabas, who used it on a massive scale.

This supports the plausibility of the view that the Gospel story was based on a creative use of the Old Testament, not only for proving that Jesus was the Messiah, but also for the purpose of presenting a theologically valid Life of Jesus, which was what the Gospel writers were aiming at.[23] Since the audience, mainly Diaspora Jews, had not the slightest chance of verifying the facts of Jesus' life in Palestine, the Gospel writers chose instead to go in the opposite direction, using the known (the Old Testament) to prove the unknown (largely, the life of Jesus). And it worked.

I therefore find it somewhat misleading to call such stories 'traditions', a word which suggests a dependence on earlier accounts, going back, ultimately, to incidents that have really occurred, and were recorded by word of mouth, albeit perhaps in rudimentary fashion. The examples which Koester presents here, and the ones I brought forward in Chapter 2, make it fairly clear that we have to do simply with pious fiction, serving theological purposes.

I shall not go deeply into the other kinds of source material which were utilised in the various Gospels. Practically all the miracle stories have close parallels in other ancient popular literature, both Greek and Semitic.[24] Likewise, the childhood legends[25] about Jesus – nonexistent in Mark and John, widely different in Matthew and Luke – have near correspondences with contemporary biographies of kings and heroes.[26]

The correspondence, both in time and content, between the Gospel of Thomas and Q, again raises the question of the relation between Gnosticism and early Christianity (and Essenism). Half a century ago most scholars, following Irenaeus, believed that Gnosticism arose as a Christian heresy in the second century AD. As we noted in Chapter 3, there is nowadays fair agreement that Gnosticism's origin is pre-Christian, or perhaps contemporary with Christianity, and should be placed in the first century AD, or even earlier.

Though most of Gnosticism's mythology is Jewish, its metaphysics is mainly Neo-Platonic and neo-Stoic, though it includes a considerable share of elements from the Egyptian–Greek–Jewish 'Hermetic' sphere of ideas, which also influenced Christianity.[27] Another point of contact between Gnosticism and Christianity is the dualistic view of the world, expressed in Essenism and early Christianity as the contrast between Light and Darkness, Righteousness and Sin, God and Belial. A third point of contact is the idea of angels as messengers and mediators between the heavenly world of Spirit, and life in the flesh on earth. From the Gnostic point of view Jesus, a spiritual being himself, could be seen as an exceptionally powerful messenger from the spiritual world.

As we have seen from our analysis of Paul and the six first-century texts in Chapters 1 and 2, the Jesus figure presented there is also in all essentials a spiritual being, showing himself to the apostles in visions,

193

sometimes apparently in a heavenly setting. The Christians, represented by writers such as Paul, Clement of Rome, the author of Hebrews and Barnabas, saw Jesus as their long-since dead, purely human, but highly revered founder, who was raised from the dead as the Messiah, in fulfilment of what they saw as Old Testament prophecies. The Gnostics often put no weight at all on the Jewish Scriptures. If and when they took Jesus into account, they construed him as an exceptionally powerful angel sent by God.

In many respects, the difference between the earliest Gnostics and the earliest Christians was not very dramatic. Like the Essenes, the Christians interpreted the Bible in extremely arbitrary ways, exemplified in Chapter 2. But the interpretation was not originally left to the individual. It was controlled by the Church hierarchy. As its Jesus figure was firmly anchored in the Old Testament, the Christian Church preserved a strong Jewish identity. Many Gnostics, on the other hand, tended to break away from Jewry, so that they were eventually estranged from one of their main spiritual and social roots.

In the beginning, as long as the Jesus figure of the Christians was mainly a spiritual, heavenly one, who communicated with his adherents through visions and epiphanies, the Christians and the Gnostics could co-exist and cooperate quite harmoniously. As Koester (1990, p. 84) expresses it, 'Thomas's religious perspective, even if it is "Gnostic", may have been right at home in the first century'. But, in the end, the Christian elaboration of the Jewish Messiah concept, and the heavy reliance of their theology on the alleged Messianic prophecies of the Old Testament, made the two movements move further and further apart. The Christians created a Jesus who was seen as a human being of heroic dimensions, who was eventually raised from the dead and received divine status. Those Gnostics who had attached themselves to Christianity tended to have views which led to 'docetism', in which Jesus was seen as purely spiritual, and his human appearance as a kind of phantom. Some Christians, following Ignatius of Antioch, felt that this was a threat to their most cherished beliefs, and they consequently combated Gnosticism as a dangerous heresy.

Many Gnostics in the second century tried to adapt themselves to the ever more popular Jesus story of the Gospels, by accepting its attractive saga elements, but retaining the fundamental Gnostic view that Jesus was essentially a pure Spirit, who only 'seemingly' was a human being of flesh and blood. This did not help. The Christian Church continued to suspect and fear them as a threat to the authority of the hierarchy. Some Gnostic ideas, however, were allowed by the Church to be preserved in the Gospel of John, where they were neutralised by being placed in a strongly anti-docetic framework.[28]

Kloppenborg's *Formation of Q* supports in yet another way the hypothesis that first-century Christianity was predominantly a Diaspora phenomenon. Traditionally, scholars had taken it for granted that Jesus, as a Palestinian Jew, would himself speak Aramaic, presumably the language of the majority of the population there at the time. Now Kloppenborg argues (p. 64), and Koester agrees, that Q must have been written in Greek, like the Gospels where it is preserved. Moreover, Q shows an unmistakably positive attitude towards Gentiles. 'The . . . negative view of Israel . . . stands in sharp contrast to the rather positive and optimistic view of Gentiles.'[29]

Koester, for his part, in *Ancient Gospels* (p. 164), finds that the sayings employed in Q 'were known to Paul, were used in Corinth by his opponents, employed . . . for the composition of the Gospel of Thomas, and quoted by 1 Clement in Rome. . . . The document itself, in its final redacted form, was used for the composition of . . . Matthew and Luke, which both originated in the Greek-speaking Church outside of Palestine.' To this we might add that Koester (p. 289), like many other scholars, concludes that Mark did not live in Palestine, from his evident ignorance about Palestinian geography. Thus all the Synoptics, more or less, are products of the Diaspora.

I have drawn the same conclusion from the material presented in several previous chapters. Certainly the Essene movement *originated* in Palestine, even in Judaea. But that was in the second century BC. By the first century AD, the Essenes had propagated their ideas throughout the Roman Empire. It was chiefly in the Diaspora that the visionary, apocalyptic experiences of Paul and his colleagues succeeded in making the Church of God Christian, though its Jerusalem community continued to enjoy considerable prestige, as Paul's laborious collection of money for the 'poor saints of Jerusalem' makes clear. The Gospel story, according to which Christianity originated in Galilee and Jerusalem, is a second-century fiction. See further our discussion in Chapters 10–12.

The Gospels can obviously not be regarded as factual accounts of real events. Nevertheless, it is possible to extract at least some historical information from them, although in general only indirectly. It is indeed true that the Synoptics agree with each other on many points. But these correspondences cannot be used to confirm each other, since they mostly go back to a common source or sources, primarily Mark, the Synoptic Sayings Source and the letters of Ignatius. On all the points where the Synoptics do not follow their common sources, they differ widely, and thus do not provide any support for each other. In fact, on several points they contradict each other. For instance, in the childhood stories and genealogies of Matthew and Luke, and the death and resurrection stories in all the Gospels, not only the details, but the overall patterns as well, are largely irreconcilable. See Chapter 11.

Comparing the Gospels on one hand, and Acts and Paul's letters on the other, it is natural to conclude that at least the names of three disciples of Jesus, namely, Peter, James and John, can be traced to the leading members of the Church of God in Jerusalem, about whom Paul writes, especially in Galatians 1–2. His account is of course a subjective one. The connection is made explicitly in Acts, and we have no reason to doubt that the Jerusalem meeting took place around AD 50, and that the protagonists were in fact called James, Cephas and John, and that the Jerusalem Church also had other apostles. But we should note that Ignatius, though he strongly maintained that Jesus was crucified under Pilate, and thus must have considered him to be contemporary with Paul and all the other apostles, says nothing about 'the twelve', and names none besides Peter and Paul.

We can also be fairly confident about several matters which Paul does not indeed speak about explicitly, but which can be inferred from his letters, and sometimes supported by other early texts. Thus it appears that the Jerusalem Church of God had a central position in the Christian movement at the time, although most of the communities were certainly to be found in the Diaspora.

In this class of inferences I would also include the main finding of my investigation of the first-century AD Christian writings, namely, that the first-century Christians, before Ignatius, regarded Jesus as a man long since dead, not a contemporary belonging to the generation of the apostles. Further, that the Gospel story was wholly unknown to them (whereas most scholars, even today, believe they knew about it from some vague 'oral tradition'). In the main, the story was *created* in the second century. Ignatius' assertions were used as a point of departure.

It is essential to keep in mind that the Christians in the Church of God around AD 100 were not, and had never been, a homogeneous group. Some of them, like Paul, looked upon Jesus as the Messiah, and expected the Last Judgment to occur in the immediate future, where Jesus would be the Saviour of the faithful.

For others, the visions of the apostles primarily established the heavenly, divine character of Jesus, which in turn enhanced the power and significance of his teaching, preserved within the Church. Those people may have made up the readership of such collections of sayings as the Synoptic Sayings Source, and the Gospel of Thomas.

Yet others took the visions as signs that Jesus was a messenger from the spiritual world, sent by the Supreme God to save his children, the true believers, from the evil forces and powers of the material world. That group is exemplified by the various groups of Christian Gnostics.

Thus in all these Christian groups at the beginning of the first century AD, the heavenly nature of Jesus was an *inference from the visions of the early apostles*, strongly supported by an allegorical reading of the Old Testament. The contents of what the apostles taught, as well as the liturgy practised in the Churches of God throughout the Diaspora, did not necessarily change radically from what the liturgy had been before, and from what they had preached before, as members of the Essene Church of God, which was a Jewish, mainly Diaspora organisation with universalistic Essene opinions. Traditionally, scholars have probably made too much of Paul's rejection of circumcision for non-Jewish members of the Church. Paul was not so representative of first-century Christianity as scholars, especially Protestant ones, have tended to think.[30] Clemens Romanus, as we have seen, took a very relaxed attitude towards circumcision. So did the non-Christian Jew Philo.

Very possibly it was the middle group of Christians mentioned above, those whose main interest was the Church of God's way of interpreting the Bible allegorically, that represented 'mainstream' Christianity in the first century AD. Those people continued to listen attentively to the apostles, because the apostles showed them how to interpret the Bible in a way they found illuminating. The apostles' news about visions of the risen Jesus was certainly exciting, both by its implication of a blissful life after death, and by attributing divinity, or near-divinity, to their revered teacher and founding father. But the visions did not necessarily change their religious ideas and their religious practice very much. For such people, the Church of God remained basically what it had always been, a universalistic Jewish Diaspora movement, with a relaxed and markedly favourable attitude toward Gentiles.

197

As time went on, more and more of the Gentiles joined the Church of God, attracted by its openness to strangers, by its inner social cohesion, and also, presumably, by its religious message, which was now Christian, and included belief both in the divinity of their first teacher and founder, and in his power to provide salvation, eternal life, for the members of the Church.

It is understandable that the growing and increasingly Gentile membership of such a church was interested in learning more about the divine personality who was taken to be their founder. That kind of interest, we may argue, had not been so strong earlier in the century, for several reasons. First, the early Essene or para-Essene Church of God was certainly more Jewish than its Christian heir was at the end of the century. Secondly, the supposed divinity of Jesus naturally increased people's interest both in his preaching and in his life as a teacher on earth. This was probably true above all for people influenced by Greek ideas. Thirdly, the Church leaders were anxious to restrain the anarchistic tendencies which the Gnostic movement was threatening it with. They were naturally also wary of accepting doctrines which might endanger the strict monotheism of Judaism.

One of the ideas of the Gnostic apostles was their 'docetism', according to which Jesus had been only 'seemingly' a human being (Chapter 3). In reality, those Gnostics maintained, Jesus was pure Spirit, and the true Gnostic Christians communed with him as individual spirits, without the need for the Church as mediator. The emergence of Gnostic docetism was one of the main reasons for Ignatius' eagerness to insist that the apostles had lived as the companions of a tangible, physical, historical Jesus, who had been both man and God.

All of this contributed to the increasing demand both among ordinary members and among the Church leaders, for more biographical information about Jesus. Thus it is no coincidence that such literature began to be produced in the early second century, some two to three generations after the visionary experiences of the apostles. This development transformed the originally Essene Church of God, so that it became both less Jewish and more definitely Christian. It is only now that Christianity became a new religion.

There was one great obstacle against satisfying the new demand: the lack of information about their founder, Jesus. Even the Church leaders probably knew only about the contribution of the Teacher to the interpretation of the Jewish Bible and, possibly also, that he had been harassed and perhaps put to death by the politically powerful Jews of his time. They knew no more about the life of Jesus than about most Old Testament prophets.

However, the Church leaders presumably did know something of the history of its own apostles, whose visions and enthusiasm had contributed to raising the religious temperature in their communities, above all in the Diaspora, and to increasing their membership, and especially the Gentile part of it.

Paul and Peter – significantly, the only ones named by Ignatius – and perhaps a few more of the apostles, were apparently still remembered. Paul's letters seem to have been circulated among the churches of God all over the Diaspora, though we have to admit that we do not know how widely they were read.[31] Anyway, from these letters it could be inferred that the seminal visions of the risen Jesus had taken place in the thirties of the first century. It was natural (though of course not logically compelling) to suppose that Jesus' death had taken place not too long before he was raised to heaven. Thus one could conclude that Jesus had lived in the first decades of the first century.

This was enough to date Jesus' death, Roman style, in the time of the then Roman prefect of Judaea, Pontius Pilate. This is what Tacitus says in Annals 15:44, published, as we have seen, in the first decades of the second century, and no doubt based on information from Christians. Tacitus may in fact have got his information through his friend Pliny the Younger, who became prefect of Bithynia in Asia Minor in AD 111.[32]

In this manner one essential datum for a Life of Jesus, the answer to the question 'when?', could be established with considerable plausibility. The question 'where?' was not seen as problematic. Jesus was naturally assumed to be a Jew of Palestine. On this basis, it was for the biographers to construct a Life. There were clear models in ancient literature[33] for this kind of writing: biographies of kings, heroes, philosophers and prophets. Episodes in their lives which could be regarded as significant for their subsequent careers should be included and, if necessary, invented. To portray a philosopher (and a religious leader was seen as a philosopher), his teaching and memorable sayings were of course important. For a divine man and prophet, miracles, including predictions and healings, were essential.

One interesting feature of the Synoptic Gospels is their remarkable parallels with Lives of Cynical philosophers as published in the first and second centuries AD, e.g. Lucian of Samosata's *Life* of Demonax, and Diogenes Laertius' *Lives of Eminent Philosophers*, Book 6. This Cynical element has been brought out especially by F. Gerald Downing in several books (see Bibliography).

The originator of the Cynical school, Diogenes of Sinope, was a contemporary of Plato and Aristotle. Now, in the first and second centuries AD, Cynicism had become one of the most successful *popular* philosophies, having assimilated much of Stoicism. Its adherents advocated a simple way of life, where riches, reputation and conventional wisdom were scorned, and often ridiculed by means of pungent and pithy sayings. Those Cynics were popular preachers, wandering from town to town, often with a band of disciples.

It is no wonder, therefore, that the authors of Gospels, writing at the beginning of the second century about a hero whom they themselves assumed to have been active in the early first, provided their hero with a band of disciples (*mathētai*). The first-century Christians, as we know, never mention such followers. The Gospel writers, however, present their Jesus as a wandering preacher and wonder-worker – quite unlike the spiritual figure of the first-century Christians. And his style of preaching is presented in the way of Lucian and Diogenes Laertius, by means of anecdotes (*chreiai*) which include memorable sayings with a popular appeal. Here are two out of the numerous examples in Downing 1988, *Christ and the Cynics*:

Luke 6:27–9: 'Love your enemies, do good to them which hate you' – Diogenes from Sinope is quoted as saying, 'How shall I defend myself against my enemy? By being good and kind towards him.'

Luke 9:58: 'Foxes have holes, and birds of the air have nests, but the Son of Man hath not where to lay his head.' – Epictetus: 'the Cynic has to say, I have no property, no house, no wife nor children, not even a straw mattress, or a shirt.'

The Cynic colouring of the Gospel story of Jesus fits excellently with my findings in this book. The earliest Christians, from Paul to Ignatius, have no significant Cynic traits, as Downing recognises. But Downing, like the overwhelming majority of theologians through the ages, takes the Gospel Jesus to be the real, historical one. My own hypothesis, based on a close study of the first-century texts (especially in Chapter 2) provides an explanation of the contrast between the earliest texts and the Gospels.

The Cynic traits were introduced by the Gospel writers to fit their idea of a wandering preacher of their own time. It is certainly no coincidence that they represented their Jesus as a philosopher of the Cynic kind: that was the typical popular philosopher *at the time they were writing*. The scorn of the rich and the powerful, together with the pungency and wit of the sayings of such a man, when combined with the religious seriousness of the spiritual figure of the first-century Jesus, turned out as a very effective answer to the Church's main enemies, the docetic Gnostics. Ignatius could not have got better helpers.

The popularity of this kind of literature provided a further incentive for the Church leaders to encourage it. It is therefore not surprising that the second century saw a tremendous upsurge of highly fictionalised stories about Jesus and the early Christian heroes. The canonical Gospels and Acts are only the tip of the iceberg. The Church leaders' insistence that only the canonised texts were to be allowed in the Churches caused later authors to apply their talents instead to biographies of other heroes than Jesus. The enormously popular literature of the Lives of Saints is the spiritual offspring of the Gospel literature, from the third century onwards.

Chapter 10

Ignatius – Halfway Between Paul and the Gospels

Ignatius was bishop of Antioch, a metropolis second only to Alexandria in the Eastern part of the Roman Empire. He was taken prisoner by the Roman authorities, and was put on a ship to be taken to Rome, where he expected, and in fact eagerly desired, to die as a martyr. On its way, the ship stopped at Smyrna, where delegations from various churches in Asia Minor visited him. To those churches he wrote letters, where he deals with matters of Christian doctrine and Church policy. It is evident that he was a highly respected and important person among the Christians in this central part of their sphere of activity. The tone of his letters is friendly, but firm and authoritative. We get the impression of an intelligent and forceful person, and a natural leader.

Seven letters of Ignatius are considered as genuine: those to the Ephesians, Magnesians, Smyrnians, Trallians and the Philadelphians, as well as one addressed to the Roman church, and one to his younger friend and colleague, bishop Polycarp of Smyrna. Coming from an influential and highly valued Church leader, they give us precious insights into the state of the Church of God in the area.

Most scholars date the letters to the very beginning of the second century, which agrees with a statement by Eusebius that his martyrdom took place under Trajan (AD 99–117). In view of the general untrustworthiness of Eusebius, as regards what happened in the first two centuries AD, it is fortunate that the dating appears plausible on other grounds as well.

Ignatius takes an intermediate position between the first-century writers and the second-century ones, in terms of style and language (on this, see Chapters 2 and 9). Peter is never called a disciple: Jesus' disciples are never mentioned. Instead, Ignatius calls *himself* a disciple (*mathētēs*: e.g. IgnEph1:3, Tralles 5, Rom 5), and he also uses that term about the members of his own communities. Further, like Paul, and unlike the Gospels, Ignatius uses the term Church of God for the communities (e.g. Magn 10:1, IgnPhil address, Trall 12, Smyrn address), and sometimes calls the members holy, or saints (*hagioi*), e.g. Ephesians 8, Romans 1, Smyrnians 1:2. But, unlike Paul and other first-century writers, Ignatius sometimes also uses the words Christian and Christianity (e.g. Magn 4, IgnRom 3, Magn 10). Like Paul, and unlike the Gospels, Ignatius never uses the word synagogue for prayer-house.

The dates of the letters are interesting for the bearing they have on our dating, and indeed, our interpretation, of the Gospels. In the past, most theologians took it for granted that the Gospels, or at least the oral tradition supposed to predate the Gospels, came into being in the first century AD. Accordingly it seemed obvious to them that Ignatius must have had access to the Gospel story when he wrote the letters, the more so as he refers at several places to 'the gospel'. That has also remained the majority opinion of scholars until recently (see Chapter 8). Naturally, if the Gospels were written before Ignatius, and Ignatius wrote his letters around AD 100 – for which the evidence is unusually strong – my own thesis that Ignatius is the originator of the Gospel story cannot be upheld. The question of which came first, the Gospels or Ignatius, is therefore of prime importance.

As will appear, my own view is that Ignatius is earlier than the Gospels. It is significant that Ignatius never mentions any of the 'twelve', who play such an important part in the Gospel and Acts story. He mentions Peter: but he calls him an apostle, missionary, just as Paul does. Peter is not presented as a companion of Jesus, but he appears, with his own (unnamed) companions, when they experience the *risen* Christ. Ignatius, as is natural in view of his anti-docetic stand (see Chapter 3), emphasises that Jesus appears in the flesh on this occasion. It is interesting to note also that Ignatius makes no mention of Judas Iscariot, who was to occupy an essential place in the Gospel drama. On all these points Ignatius agrees with the first century texts, against the Gospels.

But there is more. Let us first consider the evidence which involves Matthew, comparing parallel passages:[1]

Smyrn 1:2: 'Jesus was baptised by John in order that all

righteousness should be fulfilled.' Mt 3:14–15 has a dialogue between John and Jesus where Jesus says to John: 'it becometh us to fulfil all righteousness'.

In Ign Polyc 2:2 Ignatius exhorts his correspondent, Polycarp, to 'be in all things wise like the serpent, and always harmless like the dove'. In Mt 10:16 this is recorded as a saying by Jesus to his disciples 'Be ye therefore wise as serpents and harmless as doves.'

Ign Eph 14:2: 'You know the tree from its fruits.' In Mt 12:33 Jesus says 'the tree is known by his fruit'.

Smyrn 7:1: 'The one who is able to understand, may he understand (*ho chōrōn chōreitō*)'. In Mt 19:12 Jesus says 'he that is able to receive it, let him receive it [*ho dunamenos chōrein chōreitō*).'

In all these instances the wording of the pairs is very similar, albeit not identical. There is no doubt that the passages are interrelated. The question is how. We note that Ignatius always presents the statements as his own, or perhaps as general truths. In Matthew, the pronouncement is explicitly laid in Jesus' mouth, as part of a dramatic interchange. The natural inference, therefore, is that it is Matthew who takes over the expressions from Ignatius, in order to fit them into his dramatised story of Jesus, of which we have no trace in Ignatius. If Ignatius had taken over the expressions from Matthew, and also regarded that Gospel as an eyewitness account, it is, to say the least, unlikely that he had suppressed their origin in Jesus himself. As sayings of Jesus their impact on his audience would of course have become even stronger.

Here are some of the correspondences between Ignatius and the Gospel of John:

Ign Phil 7:1: 'The Spirit . . . knows from where it comes and where it goes.' Jn 3:8 (Jesus says:) 'The wind bloweth where it listeth . . . but thou . . . cannot tell whence it cometh and where it goeth: so is every one that is born of the spirit.'

Ign Eph 5:2: 'if somebody is not within the sanctuary, he deprives himself of the bread of God'. Jn 6:33 (Jesus says:) 'my Father giveth you the true bread from heaven'.

Magn 7:1: 'The Lord has done nothing, neither by himself, nor through the apostles, without his Father.' Jn 5:19 (Jesus says:) 'I say . . . The Son can do nothing of himself, but what he seeth his Father do.' Jn 5:30 (Jesus:) 'I seek not my own will, but the will of the Father.' Jn 8:28 (Jesus:) 'I do nothing of myself, but as my Father hath taught me.'

Magn 8:2: 'there is only one God, manifested by Jesus Christ his Son who is the word issued from the silence [*autou logos apo sigēs proelthōn*], who in all things has made himself agreeable to the one who sent him'. Jn 5:19 (Jesus:) 'I say . . . the Son can do nothing of himself, but what he seeth his Father do.' Jn 8:29 (Jesus:) 'I do always those things that please him.'

Ign Phil 9:1: 'He is the door of the Father [*thura tou patros*]' Jn 10:7, 9 (Jesus:) 'I am the door of the sheep . . . I am the door, by me if any man enter in, he shall be saved.'

Ign Eph 6:1: 'the one whom the master of the house sends . . . we must receive him like the one who sent him . . . regard the bishop as the Lord himself.' Jn 13:20 (Jesus:) 'he that receiveth whomsoever I send receiveth me, and he that receiveth me receiveth him that sent me'.[2]

The pattern is the same for the correspondences between Ignatius and John, as between Ignatius and Matthew. In Ignatius we have no attribution of the phrase, or the idea, to Jesus; in John it is always put in Jesus' mouth, ordinarily as something he says to his disciples. The natural conclusion is that Ignatius did not rely on Matthew and John. It is much more likely that they rely on him, and that therefore the Ignatius letters are older than the two Gospels. And, as the date of Ignatius is fairly firm – the style as well as the contents point to the first century rather than the second – our dating of the Gospels in the second century must stand. As regards Ign Phil 9, it is possible that both Ignatius and John go back to Hermas, who employs a similar image of the door as the 'Son of God' (see Chapter 2).

Ignatius follows in the footsteps of practically all the first-century writers, by referring very sparingly, or not at all, to sayings which he attributes to the earthly Jesus. In the case of Paul, that is because both he and his audience looked upon Jesus as long since dead, so no direct quotations were to be expected. Ignatius' letters, on the other hand, make it quite clear that he assumed Jesus to have lived during the lifetime of the early apostles, less than a century before his own time. But building up a dramatic story of Jesus' life was a process that had only just begun. Ignatius started that process, making use both of his own authority as a bishop and would-be martyr, and also of previous writers' efforts to extract information from what they considered to be references to the Messiah in the Old Testament (see Chapter 2).

When Ignatius refers to 'the gospel', he seems to mean precisely such passages in the Old Testament.

Phil 5:2: 'Let us love the prophets, for they too have announced the gospel; they have placed their hope in him and have expected him; believing in him, they have been saved.'

Phil 8:2: 'I exhort you not to do anything in a spirit of controversy, but according to the teaching of Christ. I have heard some say: "If I do not find it in the ancients, I do not believe in the gospels [*euaggelioi*] ... the gospel is the completion of immortality [*apartisma estin aphtharsias*]." '

Smyrn 5:2: 'Some deny him [Jesus] out of ignorance ... those whom neither the prophecies nor the Law of Moses, nor even at present the gospel [*euaggelion*], nor the sufferings of each of us, have managed to convince.'

The quotations from IgnPhil indicate very clearly that 'gospel', in Ignatius, means the preaching of Paul and the other early apostles, based essentially on their allegorical interpretation of the Old Testament (see Chapters 1 and 2).[3]

To the contribution of his predecessors, notably Paul, Clement, Barnabas and the author of Hebrews, Ignatius added numerous details of his own. These were evidently designed to refute a docetic[4] interpretation of the earthly Jesus. Ignatius declares that Jesus was born as a human being, by a woman, whom he was perhaps the first to refer to by the name of Mary.[5] Her virginity is connected with the idea that Jesus, though declared to be of David's seed, has God for his father. Moreover, it is likely that the Church felt the need for a female cult figure: this was a time when the cult of the goddess Isis, husband of Osiris and mother of Horus in the Egyptian religious myth, was spreading all over the Empire. In later Christian iconography, Mary shared several features with Isis.[6]

Remarkably, however, Ignatius makes no attempt to offer any kind of evidence, whether in the form of written documents, or human witnesses. Apparently he relies completely on his own considerable authority as bishop, and also as a (future) martyr: after all, he wrote these letters as a prisoner on his way to Rome. Here are some examples:

> Ign Eph 18: 'Jesus, the Christ, was carried in Mary's womb in accordance with God's plan of salvation. He came from the seed of David, yet through the Holy Ghost. He was born and baptised in order to purify the water through his suffering.'
>
> Ign Eph 19: 'The prince of this world did not perceive the virginity of Mary, nor her childbirth, nor the death of the Lord ... Three tremendous mysteries were achieved in the silence of God [*en hēsuchiai theou*]. How, then, were they manifested to the ages? A star began to shine brighter than all other stars.'

Some commentators[7] believe the story of the star here is a development of Matthew 2. But it is sufficient to refer to the widely known Messianic prophecy of the 'Star out of Jacob' in Numbers 24:17. The idea of the 'prince of this world' being ignorant of the birth of Jesus is found already in Paul.[8] It is only Mary that is Ignatius' own contribution.

In the next quotation Ignatius introduces Pontius Pilate. We should note that he does not implicate Pilate in the actual events: Pilate is mentioned only to mark a point in time:

> Magn. 11: 'You must be completely convinced of the birth, the passion and the resurrection [*anastasei*], which happened under the governorship of Pontius Pilate.'

Incidentally, in the only letter among the Paulines to mention Pilate – the 'Pastoral' to Timothy, considered by most scholars to be written in the second century – Pilate does not play an active part.

Ignatius' anti-docetic tendency is very clearly expressed in his letter to the Trallians:

> Trall. 9–10: 'Jesus Christ, who came from David's seed, who was truly born from Mary, who ate and drank, and was truly persecuted under Pilate, truly crucified, and who died, seen by the inhabitants of the heavens, the earth, and the underworld, who has also been truly raised from the dead. . . . For if he has

only *seemingly* [my italics] suffered ... why am I in chains. ...
Is it for nothing that I deliver myself to death? In that case I am
lying against God.'

The emotional tone, echoing Paul in 1 Corinthians 15:13–15, is
unmistakable. At the same time it is clear that Ignatius does not even
try to present a rational argument. This is seen even more clearly in
the letter to the Philadelphians, the first and last part of which was
quoted above, in connection with our discussion of the meaning of
'gospel' in Ignatius:

Ign Phil 8–9: 'Some people say, 'If I do not find it in the ancient
records [*archaiois*], I do not believe in the gospel.' And when I
said, 'It is written', they said, 'that is just the question.' For me,
the ancient records are Jesus Christ, the inviolable ancient
records are his cross, his death, and his resurrection [*anastasis*]
and the faith which comes from him.... [9] For the most
beloved Prophets have announced him, but the gospel is the
completion of immortality.'

Clearly Ignatius cannot adduce any evidence over and above the
prophecies of the Old Testament and the preaching of the apostles.
What he relies on is his own subjective conviction.

A few more details are added in the letter to the Smyrnians:

Smyrn. 2: '... baptised by John ... nailed [to the cross] under
Pontius Pilate and the tetrarch Herod ... the resurrection made a
sign to his saints and his believers, Jews and Gentiles, in the body
of his church.'

Smyrn. 3: 'When he came to Peter and those who were with
him, he said to them ... touch me, and see that I am no lifeless
demon. And after his resurrection he ate and drank with them as
a human being of flesh and blood.'

In his letters Ignatius stands out as an eminently capable church
leader. He was certainly well aware that an effective way to strengthen
the faith of his community members was to express his own
convictions forcefully, and in concrete terms. Mary, John the Baptist,
Pilate and the group around Peter who touched Jesus and ate with him
after his resurrection were a piece of creative myth-making on

Ignatius' part.[9] Ignatius certainly knew how important myths are for strengthening the inner cohesion of a community. He refused to argue with dissenters, achieving success by the force of his personality. He simply did not need any evidence.

The fact that Ignatius has given us the first clearly datable mentions about the roles of Mary, John the Baptist, Pilate etc. does not exclude the possibility that those names had begun to circulate in the churches of God. But it was certainly Ignatius' authority that provided them with credibility among the faithful.

Ignatius, accordingly, was very important for structuring the Catholic Christian Church[10] which was gradually taking shape in the second century AD. He managed to make room in it both for the mystically oriented Pauline Christianity, with clear Gnostic affinities, appealing chiefly to 'religious intellectuals',[11] and for a much more concrete, earthly picture of Jesus with, in all probability, a more popular appeal. Ignatius continued the work of Paul. At the same time the passages I have quoted above show that his letters could serve as a groundwork both for the purportedly historical synoptic Gospels, and for the anti-docetic, but still basically Gnostic Gospel of John.[12]

The vaguely Gnostic features of Paul are found in Ignatius too. For instance, he refers to the members of his church as 'children of light', and often speaks about the 'mysteries' revealed to them. In Ephesians 9:1 he speaks about the community members as 'the stones of the Temple of the Father', strongly reminiscent of Hermas. In Trallians 5:2 he emphasises that, though he is in chains, he is 'capable of apprehending the heavenly things, and the hierarchies of angels, and the armies of the principalities, the visible and invisible things'. Like Paul (Rom 8:38) Ignatius often refers to the forces of darkness as 'principalities and powers' (e.g. Ign Eph 1:21, 3:10, 6:2).

But he also warns his flock about the dangers of listening too much to people who preach about these matters: his correspondents are not strong enough to digest them. This reminds us of Paul's words in 1 Corinthians 3:2: 'I have fed you with milk, and not with meat: for hitherto ye were not able to bear it', and also of Hebrews 5:12: 'Ye . . . have need of milk, and not of strong meat.' So Ignatius ends up by exhorting his correspondents to follow their bishop.

As we saw in Chapters 1 and 2, Paul and his contemporaries were convinced that they were living in the End-time. Ignatius does indeed speak about the end of days, for instance, in Ign Eph 11: 'These are the last days.' But he continues: 'Either we fear the wrath to come, or we love the present grace.' Ignatius clearly chooses the latter alternative: 'it is only when we are found in Christ that we enter the true life'. This is a Gnostic attitude, also found in Colossians and Ephesians, as we have seen. For the Gnostics, the spiritual realm had a present reality which was hardly dependent on a revolutionary change in the material world. Downing 1992, p. 94 speaks about 'the early acceptance of the social pyramid' in Clemens Romanus, Ignatius and Polycarp.

Ignatius' lack of an eschatological End-time perspective probably has to do with his view of the close interrelation of the spiritual and the material sphere, or, to use his own favoured terms, the flesh and the spirit. In Magnesiams 1 he writes that he wants the churches to unite 'with the flesh and spirit of Jesus Christ, our eternal life'. In the same way Ignatius insists that even after Jesus' resurrection he 'ate and drank as a human being of flesh and blood' (Smyrn 3). He also repeatedly stresses the parallelism between Jesus' blood and the love that created a bond between the members of the church (Rom 7:3, Trallians 8:1). The same desire for a perhaps mystical union with Jesus Christ is his concept of *imitatio Christi*. 'Be the imitators of Christ, as he is the imitator of his Father', he says in Philippians 7. He asks the Romans, in 6:3: 'Permit me to be an imitator of the passion of my God.' And in Smyrnians 1 he visualises the members of the church as 'nailed to the cross both in flesh and in spirit . . . established in charity by the blood of Christ'. All this naturally also served to strengthen the symbolism of the Eucharist meal, to which Ignatius attached great importance.[13]

While neither Paul, nor Colossians, nor Ephesians ever mention those Gnostics who regarded Jesus as a purely spiritual being, who only *seemed* to be human, Ignatius, as we have seen, attacked such 'docetics' vigorously and insistently. He does so by producing those pieces of purportedly historical information that would most directly refute the docetic views.

The fact that first-century writers hardly say anything about docetic Gnostics can be explained, if we suppose that docetic Gnosticism had not yet been fully developed in their time. On the other hand, if Hoffman 1984 is right, Marcion, as a young man, may have been propagating docetic views as early as around AD 100. The turn of the century was clearly a critical period for Christianity.

I have produced evidence that the first Christians all experienced Jesus as essentially a spiritual figure. He appeared to them in visions as somebody who had long ago lived as the unique teacher and founder of their Church, the (originally Essene) Church of God, and who had been persecuted and put to death by the rulers of those days. Now, thanks to their visions, they regarded him as a heavenly being, with whom they had direct visionary contact. If so, there was no great difference between the early apostles' Christ and the Gnostic Saviour, except that the apostles assumed that their Christ was their long since dead Teacher of Righteousness. Gnostics without a Christian background perhaps did not know about the Teacher at all. But even they probably did not find it difficult to believe that their heavenly Saviour had been able to assume whatever human form he wished.

In the early Churches of God, whether Christian or not, it was generally taken for granted that Jesus' earthly existence lay in the distant past (see Chapters 1 and 2). Very few concrete facts were known about it. But questions were bound to arise, as more and more episodes and concrete details were associated with the Jesus figure during the first century AD, mainly by reinterpreting Old Testament passages as prophecies about Jesus (see Chapter 2), and also, as his life got associated with real historical figures, such as Pontius Pilate, and early apostles, such as Peter, James and John, who were presumably still remembered in the churches of God.

As the first generation of apostles died away, there was no longer anybody left who could tell the new church members that the early apostles' experience of Jesus had been *exclusively* spiritual – as I maintain – and that Jesus' earthly life had lain in the distant past, even for them. As the earthly life of Jesus was gradually being reconstructed, chiefly out of Bible interpretations, that earthly existence also became more and more interesting. Thus it was natural to try to locate it firmly in history. That is what Ignatius did. A presumably living tradition in the late first-century churches placed, quite correctly, the beginnings of the Apostles' evangelisation around the year AD 30. With the ordinary way of dating events in Antiquity, i.e. referring to the reign of emperors, kings and governors, that meant, for Palestine, the prefecture of Pontius Pilate.

Thus the detailed 'life of Jesus', implicitly and somewhat vaguely outlined in the first century out of Old Testament sayings by such writers as Clemens Romanus, Barnabas and the author of Hebrews, could now, thanks to Ignatius, be explicitly pinned down historically, to the first three decades of the first century AD – the time of the 'evangelisation'. When that was done, seventy years after the start of the evangelisation, some two generations had come and gone, and a devastating war had ruined Palestine, and had also affected the Diaspora in various ways. Under such circumstances the time of the early apostles seemed very long ago. It must have seemed to belong to the distant past, just as the life and death of the Teacher of Righteousness must have appeared to the early apostles who saw him in heaven.

Moreover, we must remember that this kind of reconstructed story of Jesus was not meant for the Palestinian Jews, but for the Diaspora, and for the increasing number of Gentiles who had little or no contact with Palestine. Unlike Paul's communities, most of them could not be expected to know anything about the long-since dead Jewish prophet who Paul declared was the Messiah. Hence the late first-century church was likely to be receptive to the historicised Jesus figure which was now – and only now – taking shape. Gnostically oriented members of the communities were probably somewhat confused by the new ideas, since in their view Jesus continued to be essentially a spiritual being. The docetic theory can in fact be seen as a determined attempt to reconcile the Gnostic idea of a purely divine spiritual redeemer with that of the historicised earthly Jesus. Ignatius rejected such a half-way house.[14] He feared that it might compromise his firmly historicised and concrete Jesus figure of flesh and blood.

At the same time Ignatius, as a follower of Paul, was favourably disposed towards many ideas that can be classed as generally Gnostic. He also probably realised that Gnostic ideas were important to the 'intellectuals' within the church.[15] But as a practical church leader[16] he realised that the docetic doctrine was probably too esoteric to appeal to the rank and file of the Christian community, and also less effective in missionary work.[17] As a man of action, he decided to attack the docetic doctrine head-on, by firmly asserting that Jesus, though the Son of God, had walked on the earth as a human being of flesh and blood at the time of Pontius Pilate and John the Baptist.

Interestingly, Ignatius thus occupies a position half-way between Paul and the Gospels not only in his language, but also theologically. He is the first definitely to present Jesus as an early first-century figure. But he does not try to outline a biography of Jesus, complete with both sayings and deeds. Nor does he try to dramatise the Jesus story.

Another point where Ignatius may be seen as an innovator concerns the position of the bishop. Ignatius insisted very strongly that the bishop of each church should be the undisputed highest authority of his church. We have seen that this doctrine of a 'monarchical' bishop is not found in any of the first-century writings we have analysed, where, on the contrary, the bishop is looked upon as just one of many priests (*presbuteroi*), perhaps with special duties of acting as host to apostles and visitors from sister communities (see Chapter 2).

Ignatius emphasises the authority of the bishop in several ways:

Ign Eph 6:1: 'We ought to regard the bishop as the Lord himself.'

Magn 7: 'Just as the Lord did nothing without the Father, neither in his own Person, nor through the Apostles, in the same way you must not do anything without the bishop and the elders.'

Smyrn 8 exemplifies: 'it is not permitted to arrange the Eucharist meal without the bishop'.

Trall 2:1: 'When you submit to the bishop as to Jesus Christ, I do not regard you as living according to men, but according to Jesus Christ.'

Trall 8: 'he who acts without the bishop, the elders, and the deacons has no pure conscience'.

Trall 3 finds a theological foundation for the strict hierarchy of bishop, presbyterium, and deacons: everybody should show respect 'to the deacons as to Jesus Christ, to the bishop as representing the Father, and to the Elders as God's council and as the Apostles'.

It is of interest that Ignatius does not derive the authority of the bishop from the successive laying on of hands as a symbol of the Apostolic succession. That practice probably arose later: in the New Testament we find references to it only in late texts, such as Acts (18:18) and in the Pastorals (1 Tim 2:8, 4:14, 2 Tim 1:6). Its origin in the first apostles may therefore well be a Lucan myth.[18]

In his theology Ignatius evidently builds very much on Paul, whose emotional and mystical attitude he shares. In Ign Eph 1:3 he characterises Paul as 'the sanctified, the true witness, the praise-worthy'. Like Paul, Ignatius emphasises the redeeming power of Jesus' death on the cross, and on the significance of his resurrection. He frowns upon those members who regard the Mosaic law as binding upon Christians. Paul, we remember, made a distinction between Jewish and Gentile Christians on this point: ethnic Jews, he said, may continue to follow the traditional customs, whereas Gentile Christians must not adopt them. Ignatius, however, in Magnesians 8:1, makes no difference between Jews and non-Jews in his communities: 'If we now live according to the Jewish law, we admit that we have not received the grace.'

In Magnesians 9 Ignatius refers to the Sabbath law: 'those who lived according to the old order of things have come to the new hope, no longer observing the sabbath, but the day of the Lord, in which our life has been raised by him and by his death . . . some people deny this, but it is through this mystery that we have received the faith . . . to be found disciples of Jesus Christ, our sole teacher [*monou didaskalou*]'. On the face of it, Ignatius here seems to imply that Jesus' death took place on a Sunday. Perhaps he had the same view as Barnabas, namely, that Jesus' death and resurrection occurred on the same day, a Sunday. (See Chapter 2.)

The first sentence in the quotation from Magnesians 9 seems to imply that Ignatius here refers to members who previously followed Jewish customs. His constant references to the Messianic prophecies in the Old Testament – the foundation of the 'gospel' – indicate that the members of the churches he addressed had at least a fair knowledge of the Jewish Scriptures. On the other hand, he rejects the Jewish Law more radically than Paul does, and is more in line with Barnabas, which may be an indication that the Gentile membership is considerable. On the other hand, he says in Trallians 8: 'do not give a pretext to the Gentiles . . . so that the Church is not blamed', which suggests the traditional contrast between Jews and Gentiles, *we* and *they*. It may be of interest that Ignatius' younger colleague Polycarp, writing somewhat later as bishop of Smyrna to the Philippians, addresses them as *tēi ekklēsiai tou theou tēi paroikousēi Philippous,* where the word *paroikousēi*, 'sojourning', is the one ordinarily used by Paul and other Jewish writers for Diaspora Jews (see Chapters 1 and 2).[19] It is likely that the Christian communities, in Ignatius' time, were still to a large extent *ethnically* Jewish (see Chapter 3).

The main significance of Ignatius, I think, is that he managed to accommodate *both* Gnostic ideas *and* an anthropomorphic, human Jesus worship in the doctrine of the Catholic Church. That accommodation was not without its problems. They came into the open in the theological struggles of the following centuries, about the nature of the Trinity. But the tensions created by the struggles also introduced a new vitality into the theology of Christianity. We deal more fully with these questions in Chapter 12.

Chapter 11

The Jesus Story Takes Shape

Apostles and companions

The fact that Paul has practically nothing to say about Jesus' earthly life is widely recognised among scholars as an unsolved problem.[1] We have in 1 Corinthians 11:23–5 a reference to what in the Synoptic Gospels is the episode called the Last Supper. Paul there quotes some words of Jesus 'the same night in which he was betrayed'. But Paul does not give the names of any of those who were with Jesus on that momentous occasion. In fact Paul *never* mentions any disciples or companions of Jesus. However, in Paul's account of the *risen* Jesus we do encounter some names. A passage in 1 Corinthians 15:3–9 was analysed in some detail in Chapters 1 and 2, where I also hinted at the possibility that it might be a late insertion, and not written by Paul himself. But, even if we accept it as genuine, we get no further than evidence about a number of people who are said to have seen *Jesus as risen to heaven*. They are Cephas, 'the twelve', '500 brethren at once', James, 'all the apostles' and finally Paul himself. Note that none of those mentioned here are called disciples by Paul, but 'brethren' and 'apostles'.

Quite apart from the doubtful authenticity of the passage (see Chapter 1), the list raises problems of its own. We shall return to Cephas and James in due course. For now, it is necessary to point out that the phrase 'the twelve' is obscure in the context. Cephas is introduced in such a way that he appears to be distinct from Peter, and excluded from the group of twelve. James also seems not to belong to the twelve.

If we interpret this passage, not in terms of the Gospels and Acts, but in terms of Paul's own letters, we find that Cephas and James can be quite naturally identified with two of the three 'pillars' of the community of Saints in Jerusalem, whom Paul writes about, for instance, in Galatians 2:17–19, where at least James is called an apostle. Thus the phrase 'all the apostles', in Paul's usage, would mean missionaries like himself, more or less officially recognised as apostles by the Church. Paul in fact never says, nor implies, that the apostles were disciples or companions of Jesus. We have no clue as to who 'the twelve' are in this Pauline passage.

The obscurity of this passage cannot but increase our doubts about its genuineness. But, even if we accept it as it stands, it does not give us any information about any companions or disciples who are *contemporaries* of Jesus, and have met him in real life. This is not surprising, if Paul and those contemporary with him, such as James, Cephas and John, regarded Jesus as a man who had lived in the distant past. About such a man's life, and indeed death, they had no direct experience, since they had seen him only in visions (see especially Chapters 1 and 2). Peter, James and the others are therefore to be regarded as members of a Jerusalem community of Saints which treasured, presumably like all the other Churches of God, the memory of their great founder and teacher. But they were the contemporaries of *Paul*, not the contemporaries of *Jesus*.

If we turn to the six first-century texts discussed in Chapter 2, we find that they exhibit the same usage as Paul does. Not one of them ever uses the word *mathētēs*, disciple. Like Paul, they use *apostolos*, meaning 'missionary', or 'messenger', as in contemporary *koinē* Greek. But for Paul and his contemporaries the word seems to refer to a class of missionaries who are particularly authorised by the Church of God. This appears especially from Paul's usage. In 1 Corinthians 12:28 he writes 'God hath set some in the Church, first apostles, secondarily prophets, thirdly teachers, afterwards miracles ... diversities of tongues.' The first place given to the apostles is hardly a coincidence. Apostles and prophets are connected on several occasions. In Ephesians (which is probably not Paul's, but heavily dependent on him) we find them connected, in the same order, at three places: 2:20, 3:5, 4:11.

The usage in the six first-century texts of Chapter 2 is very similar to Paul's. *Mathētēs*, disciple, never occurs in any of them. *Apostolos* on the other hand, is not uncommon, and is often joined with words such as prophet or teacher. Hermas has five occurrences. In Vis 5:1 we read 'apostles, teachers, assistants'. Sim 9:15:4 has 'apostles, teachers of the proclamation of God's Son', in a passage implying that their number is forty, a figure which is also mentioned in Sim 9.16:5, 'the apostles and the teachers who proclaim the name of the son of God'.

In Hermas Sim 9.17:1 we first encounter the figure twelve in connection with the apostles. It is in a passage speaking about twelve mountains, symbolising the twelve tribes of Israel: 'These twelve mountains are the twelve tribes who divide among themselves the whole world; the Son of God was proclaimed to them by the apostles.' We should note that Hermas does not say that the number of the *apostles* was twelve. Instead, as we saw, he gives the number as forty.

In Didachē, the only occurrence of *apostolos* is 11:3 ff.: 'About the apostles and prophets, do according to the precepts in the gospel', which is followed by some fairly practical and worldly-wise recommendations on how to avoid being taken in by impostors. We note that, as in the other texts, *apostles* is joined to *prophets*.

1 Clement uses *apostle* in five places, two (5:3–5, 47:1) referring to Paul himself, one of which also includes Peter. Two instances stress the direct communication of the apostles with the heavenly world (42:1, 44:1): 'the apostles have received for us the good news through the Lord Jesus, Jesus has been sent by God'. The last instance in 1 Clement is 47:4, where he moderates his censure of the Corinthians by admitting that the behaviour that Paul had criticised them for was more forgivable than their present disorders, 'since your preferences went to apostles who were authorised [*memartyrēmenois*]'. Now, Clement insists, their support is given to unworthy men. This is, as far as I have been able to find out, the first (indeed, the only) explicit mention that apostles were 'authorised' (or perhaps rather 'tested', or 'certified'), presumably by the Church.

The high status of the concept of apostle is brought out in its single occurrence in Hebrews (3:1). 'Consider the apostle and high priest of our profession, Christ Jesus.' Revelation 2:2 also implies a high valuation: 'thou hast tried them which say they are apostles but are not'. In Revelation 21:14 we get, perhaps for the first time, a definite link between the apostles and the figure twelve. It is in a description of the writer's vision of the heavenly Jerusalem: 'the wall of the city had twelve foundations, and in them the names of the twelve apostles of the Lamb'.

One text of the group of six discussed in Chapter 2 remains to be considered, Barnabas. He uses the word *apostle* on one occasion (5:9), where he says about Jesus 'When he chose for apostles, future preachers of his gospel, men who were more than commonly sinful, it was in order to show that he had not come in order to call the righteous, but the sinners',[2] a conclusion which was perhaps natural for a writer who definitely has in mind the Diaspora, and the place of the Jews among the heathen. At one other place Barnabas clearly refers to the apostles, but without using the actual word. He is explaining the sacrifice of the red heifer (Numbers 19). 'The children . . . are those who have announced to us the gospel of the forgiveness of sins and the purification of the heart . . . those who are twelve to bear witness to the tribes, which are twelve in Israel' (Barn 8:3). The similarity to Hermas Sim 9.17:1 is remarkable.

To summarise: Paul and our other first-century texts never speak about Jesus' disciples: the word *mathētēs* never occurs, nor any equivalent. In other words, none of those texts employ words implying that the persons referred to were Jesus' companions. In all the six texts the word *apostolos* is used entirely in the Pauline sense of 'missionary, itinerant proclaimer of the gospel'. It is often combined with words such as prophet, or teacher, but clearly had somewhat higher status. The apostle is 'called' by Jesus, or by God. And he appears to have been authorised by the Church, though we are not told how this was done.[3] The high reputation of the apostle within the church naturally led to misuse. Paul speaks ironically about his opponents as 'these mighty apostles', and defends himself vigorously against those who do not think he, Paul, has the right credentials. Didachē gives advice about how to deal with false apostles, and Revelation condemns such people repeatedly.

The first-century texts yield a very meagre harvest of named apostles, though Hermas gives their number as forty, and the writer of Revelation implies that a (presumably prominent) group of twelve had their names inscribed on the foundation stones of the city wall of the heavenly Jerusalem. But no names are revealed. So the only first-century texts that contain any such names are the Pauline Letters and 1 Clement. Paul and Peter are mentioned in both. From 1 Corinthians 9:6 we can reasonably infer that Paul considered his companion Barnabas, who was probably not the same as the writer of the Barnabas Letter, as an apostle. Likewise, we may accept James on the strength of Galatians 1:19, 'But other of the apostles saw I none, save [*ei mē*] James the Lord's brother.' Perhaps we should include among the apostles all the three 'pillars' (Gal 2:9) James, Cephas and John, since Paul says that 'they [these three] gave to me and Barnabas the right hands of fellowship; that we should go unto the heathen and they unto the circumcision'.

This yields a first-century list of apostles consisting of Paul, Peter, Barnabas, James, Cephas and John (disregarding that Hebrews once includes Jesus). That is only half of the quota of twelve. And there are remaining problems. One is the identity of James, about which more later. The other is that Paul appears to take Peter and Cephas as two different persons – Peter as an itinerant apostle, Cephas as one of the three 'pillars'. In the Gospels, the name Cephas occurs only in John, and only once (1:42), where it is (correctly) said to be an alternative name for Peter.

In spite of the overwhelmingly Diaspora character of early Christianity, it is evident that Paul looks upon the Jerusalem community of the Church of God as the most important one, and that he recognised it as a centre. It was to them he went in order to 'see them which were apostles before me' (Gal 1:17). And though he says he met only two of them, Cephas and James, on his first visit (*c.* AD 35, see Chapter 1), he definitely implies that there were also 'other apostles' there.

The fact that Paul later (c. AD 50) went to Jerusalem in order to hand over the contributions which his communities in the Diaspora had made for the 'poor saints' in Jerusalem, and also in order to sort out his and Barnabas' position with the 'pillars', James, Cephas and John, is further indication that the Jerusalem leaders were influential. Indeed, it may have been those leaders who had the last word on 'authorising' and 'ordaining' the apostles of the Church.

Turning from these first-century texts to the Gospels and Acts we enter a very different landscape. First of all, the scene is no longer mainly the Diaspora communities, but Palestine, in particular Galilee and Jerusalem. Secondly, the number 12 is now applied to the group of disciples (*mathētēs*) of Jesus, a word never applied to the apostles in the first-century texts. In Acts, on the other hand, Luke consistently refers to these disciples as apostles. From Acts on, in fact, 'apostle' took on the new meaning of 'companion of Jesus', and in particular one of the Twelve.

This change is of course a consequence of the fact that the Gospel writers, unlike Paul and his contemporaries, did not regard Jesus as somebody whose death had occurred in the distant past. Instead, following Ignatius, they placed Jesus as a contemporary of the apostles, at the time of Pontius Pilate. Like Ignatius, the Gospel writers thought, reasonably enough, that Jesus' death had occurred just before Paul and the apostles saw him raised to heaven.

Nor is it surprising that Christians in the early second century AD adopted that scenario. They were writing almost a century after the visions that the apostles reported about. Moreover, certainly two of them, Mark and Luke, and probably all, were Diaspora Jews, who in the eyes of most modern scholars knew little about Palestine. Judging from their evident lack of knowledge about the Palestinian geography, they had apparently never been there.[4] They would have encountered difficulties if they had tried to get hold of reports, or even reports of reports, of eyewitnesses. In addition, a terrible and disastrous internal war had undoubtedly led to much destruction of both human memories and more tangible evidence.

Koester's reconstruction of such written sources indicates that they, like the first-century texts that are still available to us, contained very little information about the time and place of Jesus' life and death. The Gospel writers may of course have had access to writings which have subsequently disappeared without a trace. But, if we go by the remaining first-century AD texts, which exhibit no interest at all in Jesus' earthly existence, and by the reconstructions that are possible, it does not seem likely that the lost writings had anything to say about Jesus' life.

An important portion of the material used by the Gospel writers consisted of collections of sayings ascribed to Jesus, of which the Synoptic Sayings Source (Q), and the Gospel of Thomas are the chief examples. The ascription of the sayings to Jesus is naturally no proof that they really went back to Jesus; the sayings have many parallels in Jewish Wisdom literature and, for that matter, in other Oriental and Greek writings – for examples, see Chapter 9. It is a well-known phenomenon that popular heroes often attract to themselves both sayings, incidents and acts which originally were told about others.

The Gospel writers, eager to tell their readers about the Jesus they thought had died under Pontius Pilate, less than a century ago, were therefore not much hindered by their lack of genuine material about Jesus. And, since their readers – even those in Palestine, who were certainly a small minority – had no access to any better sources, the Gospel writers hardly ran the risk of being faulted by their contemporaries. Thus their main task was to compose a credible story which could form a suitable background to their religious message. Nor should we forget that the most important of their sources were the

Old Testament prophecies, so diligently researched and interpreted by their predecessors, particularly Clemens Romanus and the authors of the Letter to the Hebrews and of the Letter of Barnabas. I shall not bring forward this material again here, since it was treated rather fully in Chapter 2.

Now, since the Gospels aimed at reconstructing the life of what they were convinced was a preacher and prophet called Jesus, who according to the highly respected bishop Ignatius of Antioch had lived in Palestine less than a hundred years earlier, they naturally assumed that Jesus, like other religious teachers and philosophers in the Roman Empire of their time, had gathered disciples around him.[5] Now, as we have seen above, the first-century texts are completely silent about any companions and disciples of Jesus, for the simple reason that they did not know of any such companions of their long-since dead founder and teacher.

One possible source text, the Gnostic Gospel of Thomas, whose original may date from the first century, provides some clues as to the kind of source texts that the Gospel writers might have resorted to. It contains a collection of 114 sayings ascribed to Jesus, some of them answers to questions addressed to Jesus by some of his disciples (the Coptic loanword based on the Greek *mathētēs* is used). Four names are given: Thomas the Twin, Simon Peter, Mary and Salome. For most of the sayings no questioner is mentioned; the saying is just introduced by 'Jesus said'. In some cases the disciples put the question as a group.

Though it is possible, and indeed probable, that some of the names of the Nag Hammadi texts go back to sources earlier than the canonical Gospels – as Koester holds – we must keep in mind that the earliest preserved manuscripts of Nag Hammadi were produced between the second and fourth century AD. Also, we have every reason to believe that there was considerable give-and-take between the canonical and non-canonical texts during that period.

It is hardly possible to decide which names appeared first, or have the best credentials. Since the whole setting – early first-century Palestine – is fictional, it would also be rather futile. The names might be taken from anywhere. For some of them, however, a few clues are indicated below.

I shall here concentrate on the disciples mentioned in the canonical Gospels and Acts, keeping in mind that the canonicals, like all other texts at the time, were subject to revisions, additions and deletions, especially before their canonical status was generally recognised towards the end of the second century AD.[6]

The Twelve

Probably the earliest text to mention companions, or disciples – as distinct from apostles – of Jesus is the Gnostic, non-canonical Gospel of Thomas. It probably goes back to sources in the first century, and should therefore, at least for some parts, be dated before the canonical Gospels.

Of the four names of disciples mentioned in the gospel of Thomas, only Peter and Thomas occur in the list of the Twelve found in the Synoptics and Acts (there is no such list in John). Thus we get further confirmation that Peter is indeed considered as the chief apostle. Thomas will be dealt with below. Mary and Salome are not members of the Twelve in the canonical Gospels. But Mary Magdalene plays an important part towards the end of Jesus' career there, while Salome in the Gospels is only mentioned in connection with Jesus' burial.

The Gospel of John, to be discussed more fully in the next chapter, is largely independent of the Synoptics, though later revisions have been made, in which probably the whole of chapter 21 has been added. In John, the phrase 'the Twelve' occurs in four places (6:67, 70, 71, 20:24). But, if we disregard 'the sons of Zebedee', whose names are not given, in chapter 21, only about half as many are named: Peter, Thomas, Andrew, Philip, Nathanael and Judas Iscariot.

If we put together the names in John with those in the Synoptics, we note that (outside the bare lists, which are almost certainly late additions[7]) – I agree with Schmithals that the lists are most probably transferred from Luke's Acts – only Peter, Andrew and Judas Iscariot play an active part in all. Comparing all four canonical Gospels with the Gospel of Thomas, we see that only Peter is common to them all. He is by far the most frequently mentioned among the disciples. He is regularly mentioned first when they appear together, and often acts as spokesman for the rest. It is not surprising, therefore, that Ignatius, who never makes a reference to the twelve, nor indeed to any disciples, names Peter, the apostle, alone among those who experienced the risen Christ.

The picture of the disciples of Jesus that emerges can be summarised as follows. In the first century we hear nothing about *any* disciples. Instead we read about apostles, i.e. itinerant preachers like

Paul. And we have real evidence only for their preaching in the Diaspora. They preach the 'Gospel of God', or the 'Gospel of Christ'. But there is not a hint that they had been Jesus' companions. None of our first-century writers claims to have met anybody who had physically met Jesus. Instead, they rather imply that he had lived in the distant past. Therefore, the absence of any mention of disciples is quite natural.

The number of apostles is sometimes specified in the first-century texts in terms of Jewish 'round' figures, such as 40 (in Barnabas) and 12 (in Revelation). Twelve of course is normally associated with the twelve tribes of Israel, or the twelve sons of Jacob. Ultimately, the choice of the figure 12 may go back to astronomical and astrological speculations on the number of months in the year, well-known all over the world. Sometimes, as in Hermas and Barnabas, the Twelve are mentioned in connection with the twelve tribes of Israel sojourning in the Diaspora. Revelation maintains that the names of the twelve apostles were inscribed on the foundation stones of the walls of the heavenly Jerusalem. But no names are given. It is obvious that the number twelve, in all these instances, was introduced for doctrinal reasons. The Twelve were meant to indicate that the evangelisation aimed at the whole of Israel. The lack of any concrete details about them certainly indicates that kind of mechanism. The individuals, and their names, were filled in later.[8]

Let us now return to the question of the names. We shall soon discuss Cephas–Peter and James. As for John and James, the sons of Zebedee in the Gospels, we shall see that Acts is very confusing. But the fact that the three names, Peter, John and James, often occur together both in the Gospels and in Paul, supports the hypothesis that these three names were indeed taken up from traditions about early Christians in the Jerusalem Church of God. Naturally the leaders of that centrally placed church would be among those most likely to be remembered. We shall see that these three, whom Paul called 'the pillars', occupied a special position in the Church of God. The disasters caused by the Jewish War 66–74 would explain the evident vagueness and distortion of those memories in texts written in the second century AD.

The probability that the names of Peter, James and John stood for the Christian church leaders in Jerusalem does not guarantee that the other names of the twelve were taken from the same collective memory pool. It is impossible not to suspect that many of the other names were added at a fairly late stage, just to fill up the quota of twelve: the names may therefore be a rather haphazard collection, taken from many sources and from various places. Thomas and Philip presumably came from the Gospel of John, where they do play an active part.

I think it is obvious that Luke, at least when composing Acts, came to see that Peter, James and John, the leading disciples in his Gospel, were the same as the leaders of the Jerusalem Church of God in Acts. But I do not believe that the Gospel writers in general looked upon the disciples in this light, when they presented them as Galilean fishermen. Even Luke himself may not have known of any connection when he first composed his own version of Mark's story. After all, the step from an unlearned fisherman to a learned Church leader is tremendous.

In Acts, Luke shows that he is aware of that problem. In Acts 2 he tells us how the apostles were 'filled with the Holy Ghost', and thus received the power to speak 'with other tongues'. And in 4:13 we hear about 'the people around the High Priest', who are marvelling about the power of Peter and John: they were 'unlearned and ignorant men'. Their ability to preach abstruse interpretations of the Bible, and to convince the multitude, had to be considered a miracle. In the same manner we read in the Gospels how the Galileans, hearing Jesus preach, had marvelled that a carpenter's son could be so knowledge-able and so eloquent. In Acts Luke appeals to the same kind of miracle for the apostles.

While the *names* of the apostles may have some sort of partial and remote foundation in reality, we have no reason to regard the stories of how they were recruited by Jesus as anything but fictional. The same holds for such details as presenting Peter and Andrew, as well as James and John, as physical brothers. Here we have to do with a common feature in popular storytelling: the narrator tries to provide concrete details, and seeks to establish links of various kinds between the protagonists, in order to make it easier for the audience to remember them.

A superficial survey indicates that the Synoptic Gospels and Acts all contain, with slight variations, the same group of twelve names, whereas John has only about half a dozen, and partly different ones. But on closer inspection we find that most of the similarity is due to the complete[9] lists of twelve which are inserted in all of the Synoptics and Acts (Mk 1:14–19, Mt 10:2–4, Lk 6:13–16, Acts 1:13). There are, however, indications that the list has been largely taken from Acts. One such indication is that the placement of the list is quite natural in Acts, while it is very awkward in the Synoptics. And it is worth repeating that Ignatius never mentions the Twelve and names only Peter.

Therefore, if we disregard that list, we find that it is no longer true that John gives a smaller number of names of disciples than the Synoptics. They all mention around half a dozen 'active' disciples (the exact figure is problematic, for various reasons). Only three names occur in all the Gospels: Peter, Andrew and Judas Iscariot. To these we should perhaps add James and John, who appear, unnamed, as the 'sons of Zebedee' in John. Outside the lists, Thomas occurs only in John, and Matthew only in Matthew: in the other Gospels he appears, if at all, under the name of Levi.

Thomas

Thomas is a rather special case among the disciples, since he is mentioned (outside the bare lists) only in one canonical Gospel, that of John. There he appears on four different occasions (11:6, 14:5 and twice in 20:24–9).[10]

In the first of them, Thomas is presented as one of the more articulate disciples. When Jesus hears about the illness of Lazarus, he tells his disciples: 'Our friend Lazarus sleepeth, but I go that I may awake him out of sleep.' Apparently only Thomas understands Jesus to mean that Lazarus is dead. Thomas says to his fellow disciples 'Let us go, that we may die with him.' No other disciple opens his mouth.

On the second occasion Jesus tells his disciples to be of good cheer, 'because if I go and prepare a place for you, I will come again, and receive you unto myself'. Then Thomas is the first to speak 'We know not whither thou goest, and how can we know the way?' Jesus' answer is the well-known 'I am the way, the truth, and the life.' After this exchange come questions put by Philip and by Judas, 'not Iscariot', a somewhat mysterious figure (see below, the section about Jesus' brethren). The reference might be to 'Judas the brother of James', mentioned in Acts 1:13 and Luke 6:16, and possibly the author of the canonical Letter of Jude.

But the most important function of Thomas in John is in chapter 20, where Thomas, who was not present when Jesus, after his resurrection, appeared to the other disciples in a room 'when the doors were shut', tells them that he will not believe what they tell him 'except I see in his hands the prints of the nails, and put my hands into his side'. When that wish is later fulfilled, Thomas says to Jesus 'My Lord and my God', upon which Jesus says (20:29): 'blessed are they that have not seen and yet believed', a saying reminding the reader of 1 Peter 1:8, 'Jesus Christ, whom having not seen, ye love'. We may recall that Ignatius describes a similar scene featuring Peter and 'those who were with him'. In Ignatius the anti-docetic tendency is quite obvious.

In many ways Thomas here appears as more theologically informed than the other disciples. It is no coincidence that he is found only in the Fourth Gospel, which has a much more theological and less biographical character than the Synoptics – see the next chapter. Though John has many Gnostic traits, the Thomas passage about seeing Jesus and feeling his scars, has a clear anti-docetic and therefore at least superficially anti-Gnostic tendency: even the risen Jesus is not a phantom but a being of flesh and blood – but with superhuman powers, as he can walk through locked doors.

We have noted above that, beside Peter, Thomas is the only male disciple that is mentioned in the Gospel of Thomas. Here he appears as Judas Didymus Thomas, where the Greek Didymus, like the Aramaic Thomas, means Twin. In Gnostic texts, where his name is often mentioned, he is sometimes said to be the twin brother of Jesus – a construction which hardly increases the credibility of the story, since it just illustrates a common phenomenon in popular lore, where the characters in a story tend to be linked to each other in several different ways.

It is possible that John included Thomas in his story in order to appeal to those Gnostics who wished to make peace with the mainstream Christians. At the same time, his intention may have been to make room for at least some Gnostic ideas within his own church.[11]

Though Thomas appears in fairly early texts, his historical existence is of course doubtful. He is mentioned in the conventional lists of the Twelve, but not in the narrative portions of the Synoptic Gospels or Acts.

Judas Iscariot

Among the disciples, Judas Iscariot occupies a special position. Together with Peter and Andrew, he is the only one (the bare lists excluded) to be mentioned both in all the Synoptics and in John –

226

though we recall that he is not mentioned by Ignatius. But he differs from Peter and Andrew in that we are never told how he was recruited. Moreover, every time he is mentioned we are told that he was the one who betrayed Jesus. That is in fact his only function in the Gospel story. In all probability that episode is based on a passage in the Psalms, applied to Jesus in the manner we have commented on in Chapter 2. In John 13:21 Jesus says 'one of you shall betray me'. Those words are prefaced (Jn 13:8) by the following: 'that the scripture may be fulfilled, "He that eateth bread with me hath lifted up his heel against me"', which is a quotation from Psalm 41:9: 'mine own familiar friend, in whom I trusted, which did eat of my bread, hath lifted up his heel against me'. Interestingly, this passage is also applied to the Teacher of Righteousness in the Qumran Scroll of Hymns (1QH Vermes, p. 179). See Chapter 4.

Betrayal by a trusted friend is a not uncommon element in tragic dramas. It is not at all necessary to assume that the writers had any information about such an incident in Jesus' life. They might well have searched the Bible for this kind of quotation, in order to give support to a dramatic episode which they surely felt was effective. As all the Gospels mention Judas, he was probably a participant in the Gospel story at an early stage, perhaps at the end of the first century AD. But it is worth mentioning, also, that the communities may well have preserved vague memories about the betrayal of the Teacher of Righteousness.

Peter and Cephas

If we leave aside Judas Iscariot, it is fair to say that only three disciples are really active participants in the story told in the Gospels: Peter, James and John. Further, they appear both in the Synoptics and in John, though in that Gospel – and only in a probably late addition – James and John are not named, but simply identified as the sons of Zebedee. Naturally these three names remind us of the men whom Paul, in Galatians 2, calls the 'pillars' of the Jerusalem community of saints: James, Cephas and John. It is true that the obviously powerful, authoritative and learned men with whom Paul had to negotiate in Jerusalem, are difficult to identify as the simple Galilean fishermen that we encounter in the Gospels. But there is little room for doubt when we discover that James, and to some extent Peter, appear in Acts together with Paul, very much as Cephas and James do in Paul's letters.

As we have indicated above, the sources of the Gospel writers, on this point, were perhaps memories of leading members of the Jerusalem Church of God, at the time of the 'evangelisation' in the early first century AD. The writers of the Synoptic Gospels can hardly have taken them directly from Paul, since in that case, as we said, they would probably not have presented them in their Gospels as Galilean fishermen. It is only in Acts that we obtain tangible evidence that Paul's 'great apostles' are to be seen as the reality behind the Gospels' 'disciples'. The Gospel writers, whose sources may simply have been vague memories about the Jerusalem Church of God, invented their early history as fishermen,[12] and presented them as Jesus' companions and disciples. Then Luke, in Acts, presents them as important members of the Jerusalem community, which indeed they were, according to Paul's letter to the Galatians.

In John 1:42, Jesus says to Simon Peter, who has just been introduced to him by Andrew, Peter's brother: 'Thou art Simon the son of Jona: thou shalt be called Cephas, which is, by interpretation, A stone.' In spite of this pronouncement by Jesus, Peter is never called Cephas elsewhere in John. The name Cephas in fact never occurs in the Synoptics, nor in Acts. But the name which Jesus gives to Peter is not at all arbitrary; *kēphas* is indeed Aramaic for 'stone, rock', as is also Greek *petros*.

In Paul the position is the reverse: Cephas is the norm, and Peter is used only on one occasion, in Galatians 2:7–8 (it should be noted that the standard English translation sometimes says Peter when the standard Greek text has Cephas). In our other first-century texts Cephas never occurs, and Peter only once, in 1 Clement 5:3, where Clemens refers, somewhat obscurely, to Peter's death as a martyr.

The episode in Galatians 2 is about Paul's and Barnabas' negotiations in Jerusalem with the leaders there, James, Cephas and John, whom Paul looks upon as the 'pillars'. The question at issue is that of circumcision, where Paul insists that Gentile members of the Church should not be compelled to undergo the operation, whereas the Jerusalem people stand up for the established Jewish practice. Paul writes (Gal 2:7–9) 'when they saw that the gospel of the uncircumcision was committed unto me, as the gospel of the circumcision was unto Peter (for he that wrought effectually in Peter to the apostleship of the circumcision, the same was mighty in me towards the Gentiles:)

And when James, Cephas and John, who seemed to be pillars, perceived the grace that was given unto me, they gave to me and Barnabas the right hands of fellowship; that we should go unto the heathen, and they unto the circumcision'.

In this syntactically somewhat undisciplined Pauline passage the natural reading is surely that Peter is another person than Cephas. But this is not certain, since the pronoun *they* at the very end most naturally refers to James, Cephas and John. As these 'pillars' intend to pursue exactly the same policy on circumcision as Peter is said to do, that is, to consider it obligatory, it may well be that Peter is, after all, to be identified with Cephas. Peter is obviously an important apostle, since he is chosen as an example. Yet his name is never mentioned anywhere else by Paul. Cephas is obviously also an important person in Paul's letters. And he is an apostle, as appears clearly from 1 Corinthians 9:5. So, from the point of view of meaning, Peter and Cephas can step into each other's shoes.[13]

Scholars have failed to reach agreement on whether Luke had access to Paul's letters. Kümmel 1964 (p. 120 ff.) thinks that the differences between Paul and Luke, both as regards theology and as regards Paul's career, including the Jerusalem meeting, are so great that we must conclude that Luke did not know the Pauline texts. J.C. O'Neill 1961 (p. 18) agrees: 'I cannot believe that he [Luke] deliberately ignored Paul's letters.' G. Klein 1963 (p. 200), however, thinks it is probable that Luke did just that, and Koester 1980–2 seems to agree. I can myself well imagine that Luke (like Justin) deliberately ignored Paul's letters for doctrinal reasons.[14] But the lack of coordination between Luke's Gospel and his Acts, and the really muddled presentation of James in Acts 12 (see the next section), shows that Luke was a rather careless writer. But it is of course possible that the Pauline letters just were not available to him, and that he rested content with other sources, which have subsequently disappeared.

James, the brother of the Lord

With some hesitation, I have identified the disciple Peter of the Gospels and Acts with the apostle Cephas (and Peter) in Paul's letters. Our main reason was the general similarity of the character of Cephas in Paul, and that of Peter in Acts. The fact that Peter is once called Cephas in John, and conversely, that Cephas (apparently) is called

Peter once in the Pauline letters, and in addition only Peter occurs (once) in 1 Clement, provides some extra support.

There is, however, another kind of evidence as well, namely, the fact that Cephas–Peter is regularly mentioned together with James and John both in Paul and in Acts and, as we shall soon see, also in the synoptic Gospels. In Paul the three are mentioned by name together in Galatians 2:9, and at least James and Peter (Cephas) in 1 Corinthians 9:5 and Galatians 1:19.

One of our problems is that the name James, in the Gospels and Acts, occurs in a most confusing manner. In the first place the mentions are numerous. In the Gospels the most prominent, by far, is the James who is said to be the son of Zebedee, and the brother of John. Then we have, though only in the lists of disciples or apostles, James the son of Alphaeus. Further, there is James, mentioned in Mark 6:3 and Matthew 13:55, in a list of four brothers of Jesus, presumably physical brothers. He appears also, somewhat ambiguously, as one of the sons of Mary, in Mark 15:40, Matthew 27:56, and Luke 24:10. Finally, there is the James that appears as James the brother of Judas[15] towards of the end of the lists of the twelve, in Acts 1:13 and Luke 6:16. He is not one of the twelve, but his brother Judas is. This pair of brothers may also appear in the canonical Letter of Jude: 'Jude, the servant of Jesus Christ, and the brother of James', where most scholars think James is the brother of Jesus, which increases our bewilderment: if he was the brother of Jesus, why not say so? At the place corresponding to Acts 1:13, Mark and Matthew do not have Judas, but Thaddaeus (Mk 3:18) and 'Lebbaeus, whose surname was Thaddaeus' (Mt 10:3). Understandably, the number of variants for these lists in the preserved manuscripts is enormous.

The most bewildering passages about James are found in Acts 12. There we are first told that 'James the brother of John' was executed by Herod ('killed by the sword') in Acts 12:2. This is the James who is the most prominent disciple of Jesus in the Synoptics, together with John and his brother Peter. Accordingly it is reasonable to assume that these three are the same as the three 'Pillars' mentioned by Paul in Galatians 2:9. But in Acts 12 the name James suddenly reappears fifteen verses further down, in 12:17, where Peter asks some companions to take a message 'unto James, and the brethren'. As the author does not in any way warn the reader that the James of 12:17 should be taken as another person than the one mentioned a few lines earlier, in 12:2, the unprepared reader may be excused for assuming that the two mentions refer to the same person. But that is impossible, since the James of the first mention was killed in verse 2. When the confused reader realises this, he naturally wonders who the unannounced second James is.

Other early writers discovered the problem. Eusebius, quoting statements by Hegesippus (*c.* 180) and Clemens Alexandrinus (*c.* 200), solved it by asserting that there were two Jameses in Acts, 'one who was thrown from the pinnacle of the temple, and beaten to death with a fuller's club, and the other who was beheaded'. Eusebius and Acts 12 taken together allow us to infer that the James appearing in Acts 12:17, who was thrown from the pinnacle of the Temple, was the 'brother of the Lord', whereas the one who was beheaded is explicitly declared in Acts 12:2 to be the son of Zebedee, brother of John. Hegesippus adds that James 'the brother of the Lord' was called the Just since he was 'holy from the womb' (Eusebius 2.23:3), a phrase which harks back to Judges 13:7, about Nazirites.[16] The historicity of these stories, a century or two after the events, is of course doubtful: that two persons, both called James, were killed at about the same time, looks rather suspicious. The construction seems to be specially tailored to support Eusebius' decision to split Luke's James into two.

Even if we adopt the idea that Acts 12 refers to two different persons, we are in trouble, since *both* the James of Acts 12:2 and the James of 12:17 can be equated with Paul's 'pillar' in Galatians 2:9. 'James the brother of John' in Acts 12:2 is clearly one of the leading disciples in the Gospels, where he is usually mentioned together with John and Peter. Hence it is natural to equate the James of Acts 12:2 with the James who like Peter and John is a 'pillar' of the Jerusalem church in Paul's letter to the Galatians.

Unfortunately, the same also holds for the James who appears in Acts 12:17. He is evidently the leader of 'the brethren' in Jerusalem. He appears again in Acts 15:13, where he addresses the 'brethren' in an authoritative style, and also in 21:18, where the expression is 'James and all the elders'. The whole context of Acts 21:18 makes it clear that we have here to do with the Acts' version of Paul's meeting with the leaders of the Jerusalem church, described in Galatians 2. There can really be no doubt that the James appearing in Acts 12:17, 15:13 and 21:18 must be equated with the James whom Paul in Galatians 2:9 calls a 'pillar' in the Jerusalem church. After all, therefore, Acts 12:2 and Acts 12:17 do in fact refer to one and the same person, James the 'pillar'.

Accordingly, Eusebius' solution is of little help. My own solution of this problem is as follows. Luke, when writing Acts, believed all the time that the 'disciples' he has taken over from whatever sources he may have used for writing his Gospel were the same as the 'apostles' he later presents in Acts as the leaders of the Jerusalem church. Peter, James and John are clearly the most important disciples in the Synoptic Gospels (with John as something of a blind pipe). They continue to be so in Acts, where Peter and James are again the protagonists. Then, from some source, perhaps Josephus, Luke finds out that Herod caused James to be executed. He then inserts this piece of information in chapter 12:2. But he fails to see that this must be the wrong place, since James, the only James he is conscious of, James the son of Zebedee, continues very much alive, in 12:17, 15:3 and 21:18.

It was this mistake that compelled Hegesippus, Clemens Alexandrinus and Eusebius to split Luke's one James into two, James the brother of John, and James the brother of the Lord, taken to mean the physical brother of Jesus. That piece of creative reinterpretation of the story of Acts gave rise to nearly two thousand years of confusion among historians of the Christian Church.

The confusion has become even worse, as most theologians, through the centuries, insist that Paul's 'brother of the Lord' should be interpreted as 'brother of Jesus'. 'Brother of Jesus' is almost inevitably taken to mean 'physical brother', whereas 'brother of the Lord' might well be taken as 'one of the brethren in the Church of God'. But, remarkably enough, our prime witness, the author of Acts, who is also the author of the Gospel of Luke, says nothing at all about James being the brother of Jesus, anywhere in his two texts. To make matters worse, when the 'physical' brothers of Jesus make an appearance in the Gospels, they play very insignificant, even negative roles. How could any of them be transformed into an authoritative leader? It is to Luke's credit that he, for his part, never calls James either the Lord's brother, or Jesus' brother.

We should perhaps not forget that by making James, the 'pillar' whom Paul negotiated with in Jerusalem, into a 'physical brother of Jesus', Eusebius and later theological scholars in effect *made James into a contemporary of Jesus*. Thus their ingenious construction confirmed their belief that Jesus lived in the early decades of the first century. This surely must have made their construction seem all the more plausible to them.

232

I return to the question of the Brethren of the Lord in the section on Jesus' brethren in a later section of this chapter.

Mary and Joseph

Thanks to the partial overlap of Acts and the Pauline letters, the inner circle of Jesus' twelve disciples can be taken to have at least some historical basis – as contemporaries of Paul, not of Jesus: the stories told about Peter, James and John in the Gospels are highly fictionalised. But, since Luke's Acts represents these three as important members of the Jerusalem church of God, they must be equated with Paul's 'pillars' in Galatians 2:9. We may take it, as I said above, that the Gospel writers at least got the names of these disciples from vague memories or traditions about the most important leaders of that church.

When we turn to Jesus' own family, we get no such connection between the stories and history. None of our first-century texts have anything at all to say on the subject. This is quite natural on my hypothesis, which is that the historical background of the Jesus figure is to be found as far back as the late second century BC.

In John and Mark, which seem to be the earliest of the four canonical Gospels, and also largely independent of each other, the family of Jesus plays a very insignificant role. John and Mark also agree in having no story at all of Jesus' birth, childhood and adolescence. Further, there is no reference to Mary's virginity. That is hardly surprising, since neither Gospel contains any childhood story. In Mark Jesus' father is not mentioned at all. In John he is referred to cursorily: Jesus is simply identified in the ordinary Jewish manner of the time, as 'the son of Joseph'. The context is dismissive, and evidently meant to underline the plain, everyday character of Jesus' family. That is a popular saga motif: a prince growing up in a poor family, but destined to become a great hero, as befits his true royal origin.

For example, the people around him ask 'Is not this Jesus, the son of Joseph, whose father and mother we know? How is it then that he saith, "I came from heaven"?' (Jn 6:42). The context in the other passage where Jesus' father is mentioned in John (1:45) is equally dismissive. The disciple Philip tells his fellow disciple Nathanael, 'We have found Jesus of Nazareth, the son of Joseph', whereupon

Nathanael comments 'Can there any good thing come out of Nazareth?'

In Mark, where Jesus' father is not mentioned at all, and Mary plays a very minor part, Jesus' family appears to be as ordinary as in John. We read in Mark 3:32–3: 'The multitude . . . said to him, ''Behold, thy mother and thy brethren without seek for thee.'' And he answered them, saying ''Who is my mother, and my brethren?'' ' In Mark 6:13 the family is presented in the same manner as in John: 'Is not this the carpenter, the son of Mary, the brother of James, and Joses, and of Juda, and Simon? Are not his sisters here with us?'

Thus John and Mark have nothing substantial to say about Jesus' father and mother. John gives us the name Joseph, and Mark the name Mary. Their main function seems to be to emphasise the plain, ordinary character of the people among whom Jesus grew up, thus forming a foil against which his greatness would appear in bright colours.

In Matthew and Luke, both building on Mark's story, much more material is introduced. In the first place, we are presented with a complete genealogy of Jesus. It is designed to substantiate the claim that Jesus is the Messiah, who was (at the time: see Chapter 5) commonly believed to be a descendant of David. As the genealogies in the two Gospels differ on many points, they must be regarded as imaginary constructions.

Matthew and Luke also introduce stories of Jesus' childhood and adolescence. These two also differ widely from each other. For instance, the flight to Egypt is found only in Matthew, and the marvellous precocity of Jesus in the Temple is found only in Luke.

All of this serves the purpose of presenting Jesus as an extraordinary figure. It is all in conformity with the model of the heroic legend, adapted to the theological demands set by the Church's allegorical interpretation of the Bible.

The later Gospels, Matthew and Luke, flesh out the story of Mary and Joseph in various ways. Joseph remains a rather shadowy figure. His main function in Matthew is to receive angelic messages about Mary's childbirth, in dreams. Then he receives similar dream messages advising him to go to Egypt in order to escape Herod's cruel plans to murder all young children in Jerusalem. (Pharaoh's order to kill all Israelite boys in Egypt in Exodus 1:12 immediately comes to mind: Moses miraculously escaped, just as the child Jesus did. Moreover, as we have said above, the Samaritan Christians regarded

Jesus as the 'new Moses', and the parallel between the Essene Teacher of Righteousness and Moses seems to be implicit in the Damascus document. See Chapter 4.) Finally, the angelic advice is to leave Egypt and to settle in Nazareth (Mt 2:23: 'that it might be fulfilled which was spoken by the prophets, He shall be called a Nazarene'). As is common in Matthew, the main points in the story are said to fulfil Scripture passages. Thus the fictional nature of the story is made even more evident. Other instances in Matthew: 2:5, 2:15, 2:17, 2:23, 3:3, 13:35, 21:4, 26:5 etc.

In Luke, where Joseph is even more shadowy than in Matthew, we hear nothing about dreams. Instead, the angel himself, Gabriel, brings the message about the conception of Jesus directly to Mary. In both Gospels Joseph disappears from the story after the first few chapters, and is heard of no more.

We should remember that the first occurrence of the name of Jesus' mother outside the Gospels is in Ignatius' Letters, generally dated to the beginning of the second century AD. Ignatius (see Chapter 10) is very much concerned with combating the Gnostic heresy, and the view of the docetic Gnostics that Jesus was a phantom, not a man of flesh and blood. By insisting that Jesus was really born of a woman (though in this special case, a virgin), Ignatius emphasised the humanity of Jesus. The name Mary (Mariamne, Miriam) was very common at the time, and hardly raises any problems. But the number of women called Mary in the Gospels is truly astonishing: Mary Magdalene, Mary the mother of Jesus, Mary the mother of James, Mary the mother of Joses, Mary the mother of James the less and Joses, Mary the wife of Cleophas, the other Mary, all appear at the burial of Jesus in the various Gospels. The reader has a hard, or rather, impossible – and futile – job sorting them out.

Jesus' brethren

We have just seen that Jesus' brethren are sometimes mentioned in connection with his parents, Mary and Joseph. Four brothers are named in Mark 6:13: James, Joses, Juda and Simon. John, the other early canonical gospel, also mentions brothers of Jesus, but does not name any of them. Just as in Mark, their role is mainly to show how insignificant they are, and how little they appreciate Jesus, and he them.

Matthew 13:55 has the same story as Mark, with the same four names. In Luke 8:19–21, no names are given in the corresponding passage. Nor are there any *other* mentions of Jesus' brethren in either Matthew or Luke. However, in connection with the crucifixion of Jesus all the Synoptics mention sons of somebody called Mary: Matthew 27:56 Mary the mother of James and Joses; Mark 15:40 Mary the mother of James the less and of Joses; Luke 24:10 Mary the mother of James. We should note that of the many Marys mentioned in the Gospels at the crucifixion and burial of Jesus, not one is explicitly identified as the mother of Jesus. Thus it very much looks as if the full quota of four brothers of Jesus is arrived at by adding up the various sons of unspecified women named Mary in the crucifixion stories. It is evidently not advisable to take the list of Jesus' brethren at face value.

In John Jesus' mother is mentioned, but her name is never given explicitly. John 19:25 reads: 'there stood by the cross of Jesus his mother, and his mother's sister, Mary the wife of Cleophas, and Mary Magdalene'. On the possible reading that Mary the wife of Cleophas is the *sister* of Jesus' mother, the plausible conclusion is that John did not think that Jesus' (unnamed) *mother*, the sister of a Mary, was herself named Mary. But obviously these passages do not allow any firm conclusions.

It is remarkable that Luke, alone among the Synoptics, never names any of the brethren of Jesus, though he tells us, like John, that they existed. In Acts Jesus' brethren are mentioned just once (1:14), in connection with the list of the Twelve: 'These [the eleven] all continued with one accord in prayer and supplication, with the women, and Mary the mother of Jesus, and with his brethren.'

This is a mystifying statement. As neither Mary, nor Jesus' brethren ever appear again in Acts, it is very difficult to see why they should be shown the honour of joining the 'apostles' here. The more so, as they had seemed rather indifferent, even hostile, to Jesus and his preaching in all the Gospels. It is impossible to avoid the suspicion that we have to do with a late addition. The purpose may have been to support the claim that James was indeed the brother of Jesus (see above). Luke himself, as we have seen, keeps completely silent about the *names* of Jesus' physical brothers.

Thus we have a mention of four brothers of Jesus, but only in a bare enumeration in Mark and Matthew. James and Joses reappear in the lists of sons of 'Mary' (see above). Both Mark and Matthew mention Joses, Mark calls James 'James the less', presumably to distinguish him from James the son of Zebedee, whereas Luke says just Mary the mother of James. The identity of Simon is a mystery; we have no reason to think that either Simon Peter, or Simon the Zealot is intended. As for Jude, he is conceivably the one mentioned in Luke 6:16 and Acts 1:14 (but not in Mark and Matthew) as 'Judas the brother of James'.[17] Perhaps he can also be identified with the Jude who wrote the canonical Letter, and who describes himself as 'the servant of Christ and the brother of James'.

But all this is just guesswork. It seems to me our best course is to admit that we just do not know anything about Jesus' brothers. From the confusion of the texts quoted above, it seems their authors were equally ignorant. Their presentation is evidently no more than an inconsistent patchwork. This should not surprise us, since we must conclude that the whole story of a first-century Jesus, his family and his disciples, is wholly fictional.

Finally, let us consider again 'James the brother of the Lord' against the background of what has been presented in this section. The brothers of Jesus, as presented in the Gospels and Acts, are too insignificant for any of them to be easily identified with the clearly competent and respected leader of the Jerusalem Church, often referred to in later Christian literature as James the Just. Moreover, the confusion and inconsistency of the presentation in the various Gospels shows that their account, on this point, is not to be trusted.

The whole idea of identifying James with a physical brother of Jesus, as I have argued, is due to Eusebius' attempts to make sense of Luke's confused presentation in Acts 12. Owing to Luke's mistake in having James, the apostle, killed in the beginning of that chapter, Eusebius thought, logically enough, that all subsequent mentions of James in Acts must mean somebody else. He concluded that this person was the Jerusalem church leader whom Paul, in 1 Galatians 19, called 'James, the brother of the Lord'.

It was naturally tempting to take this expression to mean the physical brother of Jesus. Did it not nicely explain why he so suddenly, from Acts 12:17 onwards, plays such a leading role among the Twelve? As against this it must be said the Gospels never included Jesus' physical brothers among the disciples, and that their mentions of them are rather dismissive. It is, as we said, hard to understand that theological scholars have accepted the construction whereby a physical brother of Jesus was presented as the leader of the Jerusalem church.

'Brother' is used in the New Testament in the sense of 'member of the community' much more often than in the sense of 'physical brother'. Of course this does not prove anything in the individual case. But, in the present instance, the fact that Luke himself never says anything about James being Jesus' brother (or, for that matter, the Lord's brother) is a telling indication that he, at least, never thought he was. As we said above, Luke certainly looked upon the James that he writes about both in his Gospel and in Acts, as one of the disciples of Jesus, whom both he and Jesus called brethren. So, if Luke ever read Paul's letter to the Galatians in the form we have it, he would certainly have interpreted (Gal 1:19) 'James, the brother of the Lord' as 'James, the leading brother of the Jerusalem Church of God'. So should we, in spite of Eusebius.

Nazareth

All the Canonical Gospels mention Nazareth as a town connected with Jesus' early life. John has Philip say (1:46) 'We have found him, of whom Moses in the law,[18] and the prophets did write, Jesus of Nazareth' whereupon Nathanael retorts 'Can there any good thing come out of Nazareth?' Mark simply says (1:9) that Jesus came 'from Nazareth of Galilee, and was baptised of John in Jordan'. Luke explains how Mary conceived Jesus (1:26): 'the angel Gabriel was sent from God unto the city of Galilee, named Nazareth'. In Chapter 2, Luke explains how Jesus was born in Bethlehem after his family had gone there for the 'taxing' decreed by Augustus. Matthew, for his part, does not mention Nazareth until after the flight to Egypt (2:23): Joseph 'came and dwelt in a city called Nazareth, that it might be fulfilled which was spoken by the prophets, ''He shall be called a Nazarene'' (the Greek text has *nazōraios*). Thus the two oldest Gospels, Mark and John, simply mention that Jesus 'came from Nazareth' at the start of his career as a preacher, whereas the two later ones have quite different, more detailed accounts, as is to be expected in the creation of a legendary story.

Matthew's Scripture quotation is in line with his policy of constructing his story of Jesus with the help of Old Testament passages which he takes to be prophecies about Jesus (see Chapter 2). Interestingly, the Old Testament passage here does not mention Nazareth, but uses the adjective *nazōraios*, which is often rendered 'from Nazareth' in the English translation. That adjective, however, has quite a different meaning in the Old Testament. In fact, it is quite possible that Matthew, and the other Gospel writers, got the idea of connecting Jesus with Nazareth on the strength of a 'folk etymology' among Greek-speaking Jews of the word *nazōraios*.[19]

There is an interesting possibility that the adjective *nazōraios* may also form a link between Essenes and Christians. We do not know what words the Aramaic-speaking communities of the Church of God used for 'perfect', 'holy', 'separate'. According to Schoeps 1949, the Jewish Christians of Syria called themselves *nazōraioi,* a term (in the form of *nozrim*) used later by Muslims about Christians in general. The fourth-century Church father Epiphanius[20] states, according to Schoeps 1949, that the Christians (he does not speak specifically about Jewish Christians) first called themselves *nazōraioi.*

This word in fact occurs in many places in Acts, e.g. 24:5, in which the Jerusalem priests speak about Paul as 'a mover of sedition among all the Jews throughout the world, and a ringleader of the sect of the Nazarenes [*nazōraioi*]'. It is thus here their opponents, not they themselves, that refer to the Christian church as the 'sect' of Nazoreans. Later, according to Epiphanius, the Christians called themselves *Iessaioi*, which looks suspiciously like a garbled form of *Essaioi*. If so, there is an intriguing possibility that the Essenes – and the Aramaic-speaking Jewish Christians – used a term including the stem *nzr*, meaning 'keep oneself separate', which is ordinarily given as *naziraios, nazeiraios*, 'nazirite, nazir', but in some manuscripts of the Septuagint translated as *hagios*, 'holy' (e.g. Judges 13:7; 16:17).

An episode in Acts 21:23–4 throws an interesting sidelight on all this. Paul has gone to Jerusalem, where he is asked by James and the elders to explain why he says the Gentile Christians do not have to follow the Mosaic law on circumcision and table purity. The elders wish to have an assurance that, whatever the Gentiles are permitted to do, Paul himself abides by Moses. Therefore they say (21:23) 'We have four men which have a vow on them. [24] Them take, and purify thyself with them, and be at charges with them that they may shave their heads, and all may know that those things, whereof they were informed about thee, are nothing, but that thou thyself also walkest orderly, and keepest the law. . . . [26] Then Paul took the men, and the next day purifying himself with them, entered into the temple, to signify the accomplishment of the days of purification.'

What is interesting about this episode is that the 'vow' upon the men, and the purification required, conform remarkably to the regulations for 'Nazirites' in Numbers 6:2 'When either a man or a woman shall separate themselves to vow a vow of a Nazarite, to separate themselves unto the Lord . . . all the days of the vow of his separation there shall no razor come upon his head. . . . [8] All the days of his separation he is holy to the Lord.'

Accordingly the men of the Jerusalem community that were to accompany Paul in his purification considered themselves as Nazirites (*naziraioi*) according to Numbers 6. This implied that they were 'holy'. Even in the New Testament itself, therefore, we find Christians (Paul and the men from the Jerusalem community) looking upon themselves as Nazirites, though the word itself is not used in this connection. But the word *nazōraios* is, like *nazeiraios*, a loanword from Hebrew. For a Greek speaker – and almost all Christians at the time spoke Greek as their mother tongue – the words were likely to be confused with each other. Nazōraios occurs frequently in the New Testament, though in most modern translations it is translated 'from Nazareth', obviously on the authority of Matthew 2:23.[21]

If, as seems likely, Matthew follows the practice of Barnabas and others, 'spoken by the prophets' in Matthew 2:23 refers to a definite passage in the Old Testament. It is almost certainly Judges 13:5: *naziraion estai Theou*, or 13:7: *naziraion Theou estin*. This does not exclude the possibility that Matthew, and the other Gospel writers, had other reasons as well for choosing Nazareth as Jesus' home town. The Essene foundation text called the Damascus Document (CD) speaks about 'Damascus' as the place where the community was established. Damascus could well stand for Syria in general, including even Galilee. Some support for this speculation is provided by the existence of Jewish Christians in this region in the second century AD and later.

In the context of Judges 13:7 the reference is to Samson, a 'Nasirite', as the English translation has it. Seeing that *nazōraios* is not a linguistically satisfactory derivation from Nazareth, it seems far more acceptable to take it to be a rendering of the word meaning holy, which was used, as we know, by both Christians and Essenes about themselves. None of this, of course, is wholly conclusive.

We might add that if the New Testament word *nazōraios* was taken to mean 'the holy one', 'the separate one', and thus was in effect the self-designation first of the Essenes, and later of the Christians, we have a solution of one of the mysteries of the New Testament, namely, the complete absence of any reference to one of the main religious movements in the Judaism of the times, the Essenes. If our reasoning is correct, they were not left out, but appeared under the name *nazōraioi*, a word which has been mistakenly assumed to refer to the little town of Nazareth in Galilee (and never mentioned in the Old Testament).

It is interesting also to note that Paul, in Romans 1:1, describes himself as 'separated unto the gospel of God'. The Greek word is *aphōrismenos*, which corresponds quite well with Hebrew *nzr*, meaning separate.

Accordingly, 'Jesus of Nazareth' would be a mistranslation of 'Jesus the Nazorean', or grecicised, Jesus the Essene.

Chapter 12

John, Paul and Gnosticism

In the previous chapter I tried to show, in some detail, how the authors of the Synoptic Gospels exerted themselves to build up their largely fictional story of the 'physical' Jesus, his 'disciples' and his family, on the foundation of the Old Testament Messianic prophecies as interpreted by first-century theologians, and Ignatius' bare assertions about Jesus' birth and his death. In the present chapter attention will be centred on the efforts of those Christians who continued to adhere to Paul's primarily 'spiritual' view of Jesus. We therefore bring together matters that have been treated separately, though less fully, in other chapters. Some repetition is inevitable, but hopefully this will be of some value.

The position of John's Gospel

Before the onset of modern scholarly criticism of the Bible, in the eighteenth and nineteenth centuries, the author of the Gospel of John was self-evidently taken to be Jesus' disciple John, the son of Zebedee, and the brother of James. He was also thought to be identical with the author of Revelation.

However, even during the early centuries of Christianity several Churchmen were sceptical about according canonical status to the Gospel of John.[1] That is hardly surprising. Though there are, to be sure, contradictions between Matthew, Mark and Luke, the Synoptics do at least present the story of Jesus in a similar manner, and also exhibit numerous textual parallels. John presents the story very differently, and his Jesus expresses himself in quite another style.

Moreover, many second-century churchmen found the theology of John hard to accept. Some of them went so far as to condemn it as the work of a well-known Gnostic heretic, Cerinthus.[2] But Irenaeus

242

included John's Gospel in the canon, and sought to secure its place there by declaring that the canon should contain exactly four gospels, corresponding to the four cardinal points on the map of the world. Still, in spite of Irenaeus' support for John, several Christian churches continued their resistance, largely on theological grounds. In the end agreement was reached by declaring that the Synoptics told the 'bodily' story of Jesus' life on earth (*sōmatikē*), while John told the story from a 'spiritual' point of view (*pneumatikē*) – a not unreasonable characterisation.

When the nineteenth-century Bible scholars resumed the discussion, there could of course be no question of excluding John from the New Testament canon. But John always tended to be put on a somewhat lower level than the Synoptics in terms of historical value. One way of supporting this view was to maintain that, since the Synoptics told the story in a much more straightforward and realistic manner, they must be nearer to the events they were describing, and thus older. Even when the critical scholars reached fair agreement that the Synoptics, too, were written after AD 70, John continued to be placed last. However, the question was reopened in the 1930s, when an Egyptian papyrus fragment, containing a few lines of John 18:31–8, was dated palaeographically to *c*. AD 125. That is older than any other canonical Gospel text fragment.[3] This obviously makes it difficult to date John later than the Synoptics. Koester 1990, p. 267 summarises his position as follows: 'while an early draft of the Gospel may have come into existence soon after the middle of the first century, it was probably not composed in its present form until the very end of the century, and later redactional comments were added even during the second century'.

Though it is dangerous to base an argument on a very brief fragment, which might after all be part of an early source text rather than the Gospel as such,[4] it must be admitted that the late dating of John, very common a century ago, had no firm foundation. However, theologically and stylistically it cannot be denied that John is in a class of its own. When the early Church characterised John as 'spiritual', and some of the churchmen ascribed it to the Gnostic Cerinthus, they could certainly find support in the text. As the struggle against Gnosticism was apparently at its height in the second century, the wariness of the churchmen is understandable.

I agree with the German scholar, Udo Schnelle, that it was only

because the undoubtedly Gnostic colouring of the text was accompanied by a very strong *anti-docetic* line of argument that John was
eventually canonised.[5] In the opening chapter of John, Jesus is indeed
represented, Gnostic fashion, as a spiritual being who had existed even
before the world began.[6] Yet the author repeatedly asserts the physical
humanity of the earthly Jesus. Even after his resurrection Jesus does
not simply appear visually to the disciples (as he does in Matthew and
Mark – Luke is similar to John at this point), but he invites them to
feel his wounds, and sits at table with them, eating and drinking.
Everybody assumed, of course, that spirits had no material bodies
which could be touched and felt, and that they did not eat and drink,
since they had no real bodies. In other words, just as in the Synoptics,
Jesus in John is a real human being who could suffer, feel pain and
fear death just as ordinary men.

This was precisely the kind of message that Ignatius tried to convey
in his own rather high-handed fashion, as we saw in Chapter 10. As
the anti-Gnostic stand of the church was – at least at first – primarily a
matter of combating the idea of the *docetic* Gnostics, to the effect that
Jesus had only seemingly suffered, and only seemingly died and
indeed only seemingly lived with his disciples, John's very energetic
anti-docetic stand on these points was welcomed, and given more
weight than its Gnostic tendencies in other matters.

For others, on the other hand, the theological foundation of the
Gospel was undoubtedly important. If the arguments I have brought
forward in this book are acceptable, early Christianity was highly
diversified even from the start.[7] The earliest pre-Christian Essenes in
the Judaean desert had been élitistic religious extremists. In the
Diaspora, their nationalistic zeal had been considerably reduced, while
their radical, allegorical interpretation of the Bible won them
adherents among liberal-minded, universalistic Jews, and probably
also among non-Jews influenced by current popular versions of
Hellenistic philosophy of a vaguely Platonic type. At the same time
apocalyptic movements among the Jews led to an increased interest in
eschatology, involving expectations about the Last Judgment and the
End of Days. All these movements and ideologies certainly affected
both Jews and non-Jews in the melting-pot of peoples which was the
burgeoning Roman Empire.

Visions and revelations in early Christian texts

The pre-Christian Essene Churches of God, which, to judge by Philo, struck roots among liberal-minded Diaspora Jews, were apocalyptic in the etymological sense of that word:[8] believing in revelations from God, or from his messengers. Among other things, these Diaspora Essenes were convinced that God had revealed deep truths to their revered Teacher of Righteousness. But we have no particular reason to think that they were primarily concerned about eschatology: the End of the world. In this section I shall study the early Christian literature in general, in order to bring out the importance of revelation and visionary experience in that literature.

As far as we can tell, it was Paul and some of his contemporaries among the apostles that mainly contributed the eschatological element to the Churches of God, by interpreting their vision of the risen Jesus – apparently their name for the Teacher of Righteousness[9] – as a message from Heaven that Jesus, as the Messiah, would soon appear on the earth for the Last Judgment. On that day Jesus would save those who believed in him from damnation on the Day of Wrath.

My analysis of Paul's letters (Chapter 1) has led me to conclude that the chief content of his *euaggelion*, his 'good news' to the Churches of God, was that the appearance of Jesus to the apostles proved that Jesus had been raised to Heaven as the Messiah. Paul, as a member of a universalistic church of God, naturally saw the Messiah as the Saviour of all believers, irrespective of their ethnical origin. The salvation, in turn, meant eternal life in the Kingdom of God. Paul is not very explicit on what the entry into the Kingdom of God implied, though he makes at least an attempt in 1 Corinthians 15:39–51: the resurrection involves, he says, a complete change of the physical body into something non-physical: 'It is sown a natural body: it is raised a spiritual body.'

It was because Paul and his contemporaries among the apostles had received their revelations and visions of the risen Jesus that they started their 'evangelisation'. But I argue (Chapters 1 and 2) that they and their audience assumed that Jesus' life belonged to the distant past. That was a natural assumption, if he was considered as the founder of their church. Neither Paul nor the others seem to know much about the earthly Jesus, beyond that he had been a teacher and prophet, who had been persecuted by the mighty men of his time, and had in the end been captured and put to death. All of this was presumably preserved as traditions within the Essene and para-Essene Churches of God. As Paul interpreted Jesus' death on the cross as a sacrifice for the sins of his people, Jesus' passion and death assumed supreme importance in his theology, and subsequently throughout Christianity. But Paul was not the only apostle of the Church. We have clear evidence that other apostles held different theological views.

We have seen that the Jesus of the early versions of Didachē was in fact presented as simply a revered teacher. Nothing at all is said on his sacrificial death. Hebrews comments on the theological import of Jesus' death on the cross. But otherwise Hebrews hardly concerns itself with Jesus' passion, and is equally reticent about the Last Judgment. Further, while Paul maintains that non-Jewish members of the Church must not be forced (indeed, should not allow themselves) to be circumcised, many others who reckon themselves as Church members do not attach any weight to this issue at all.

Everybody admits that Paul's experiences of Jesus took place after Jesus' resurrection 'from the dead'. As he declares in 1 Corinthians 15:15 that the resurrected body is spiritual, we may take it that he regards his experience as a spiritual one, or more simply, a vision of the spiritual Jesus. In 1 Corinthians 9:1 Paul asks, rhetorically, 'Have I not seen [*heōraka*] Jesus?', implying that his revelation has some sort of visual character.

Since the traditional – and as I maintain, mistaken[10] – view is that Paul was the only one of the early apostles that had not experienced Jesus 'in the flesh', it is important to point out that Paul himself never suggests that there was a difference between his own and his contemporaries' experiences of Jesus.[11] In the famous catalogue about how he had acquired his knowledge of Jesus' death, in 1 Corinthians 15:1–8, Paul emphasises, first, that Jesus died for our sins *according to the scriptures*, and also, that he was buried, and rose again on the third day, *according to the scriptures*. Accordingly, as I argue in Chapter 2, he does not refer to eyewitness reports, but to scriptural evidence. He does not specify that evidence: it is quite likely that he, like 1 Clement, Barnabas and Hebrews, is referring to allegorical interpretations of Bible passages.[12]

Proceeding in Paul's text to the events after Jesus' death and his resurrection, we still do not discover any difference between Paul and the others, except that Paul definitely comes last. First, he says, Jesus was seen (*ōphthē*) by Cephas, then by 'the twelve', then by 'above 500 brethren at once', then by James, then 'all the apostles', and last of all by Paul himself. There is no hint that anybody 'saw' the risen Jesus in any other way than Paul did, and it is surely a natural conclusion that Paul thinks all of them experienced a spiritual vision of the risen Jesus. We get an idea of what kind of vision Paul has in mind, since he discusses these matters in some detail in 1 Corinthians 15:35–55, parts of which we quoted in Chapter 1.

It is of interest that in his catalogue of people who have 'seen' Jesus, Paul names only two, Peter (or rather Cephas: see Chapter 11), and James. Peter's primacy here is supported by Luke 24:34, but not by Matthew and Mark, nor by John. In fact, the discrepancies between the canonical Gospels seriously weaken their credibility on this point, irrespective of the difficulty of ascertaining whether such a private experience as a vision has occurred at all.[13] As for Paul's specification of the sequence of witnesses (whether the passage is genuine or not,[14]) its lack of conformity with the canonical Gospels indicates that the passage can hardly be based on them.

A possible instance of Paul experiencing a revelation from the *earthly* Jesus is his famous account of the Last Supper in 1 Corinthians 11:23–6. 'I have received of the Lord that which also I delivered unto you, That the Lord Jesus in the same night in which he was betrayed took bread: And when he had given thanks, he brake it, and said, Take, eat: this is my body, which is broken for you: this do in remembrance of me. For as often as ye eat this bread, and drink this cup, ye do shew the Lord's death till he come. [*achris hou an elthē*].' Several scholars hold that Paul here makes use of his knowledge of cultic practices connected with the communal meal in the churches of God, which I think is very plausible. I discussed the above passage, and also another one, 1 Corinthians 10:16, in Chapter 1. Paul may have had a vision of Jesus himself appearing in such a cultic context.

More details about Paul's visionary experiences are to be found in 2 Corinthians 12:2–4: 'I knew a man in Christ above fourteen years ago (whether in the body, I cannot tell; God knoweth;) such an one caught up to the third heaven. And I knew such a man, (whether in the body, or out of the body, I cannot tell: God knoweth;) how that he was caught up into paradise, and heard unspeakable words, which it is not lawful for a man to utter.' We should here note especially the emphasis on the secret character of the information received through revelation. We return to this point below.

Visions or revelations of this kind seem to have been frequent experiences with Paul, who writes in 2 Corinthians 12:7 about the 'abundance of the revelations' that he has received. Sometimes these revelations concerned rather mundane things, for instance, his decision to go up to Jerusalem with Barnabas to see 'them which were of reputation', meaning James, Cephas and John. 'I went up by revelation', he says (Gal 2:2). Paul also stresses (Gal 1:11–12) that he received the gospel 'not after man . . . neither was I taught it but by revelation of Jesus Christ'.

Of the six early texts treated in Chapter 2, revelations and visions have a prominent place in two: Hermas' *Pastor*, and the Revelation of John. In Revelation, a brief passage (Rev 1:10–12) says: 'I was in the Spirit on the Lord's day, and heard behind me a great voice . . . I am Alpha and Omega, the first and the last. . . . What thou seest, write in a book.' The author then describes a vision of a heavenly figure which may be taken as Jesus. This vision forms the framework for the whole book, which in turn consists of further visions, leading up, eventually, to the Last Judgment.

Hermas' *Pastor* also consists of a whole series of visions, in which various angelic figures convey messages of a religious nature to the author. But Jesus does not appear, at least not explicitly, among the figures, though the visions exhibit religious ideas with vaguely Essene or Christian traits.

In the other texts discussed in Chapter 2, visions and revelations are seldom referred to explicitly. 1 Clement, for instance, does not mention visions and revelations at all. But, as I argue in Chapter 2, his way of referring to Jesus' resurrection as a fact, rather than as an event, is an indication that he had no independent evidence of it, and that accordingly not only Paul, but also the other apostles, *inferred* the resurrection from their own and their colleagues' visions of the risen Christ.[15]

James W. Charlesworth, a highly respected American theologian, writes: 'After the Exile . . . God is thoroughly majestic and transcendent . . . knowledge of him is obtained almost always only through sacred books, the descent of angels, the gift of vision, or the journey of a seer through the various heavens'.[16] This is entirely in line with my interpretation of Paul's and the apostles' visions of Jesus. As a divine figure, Jesus could really only be seen in visions.

In the Gnostic literature revelations abound. That is not surprising, since the Gnostic religion is based on the duality of matter and spirit, the spirit being the part of the individual that alone can receive revelations from the Highest Spirit, God (see Chapter 3). Hence the

Christian Gnostic writings, where Jesus figures as the essential link between God and men, give much prominence to the phenomenon of revelation.[17]

We noted above that in Paul's catalogue (in 1 Cor 15) of people who had seen the risen Jesus, he includes only two names, Peter and James, though he mentions 'the twelve' and even '500 brethren'. No real support for Paul's singling out of Peter and James can be found in the canonical Gospels. But James is clearly given a prominent position in many Gnostic writings. In the so-called *Gospel of the Hebrews*[18] the first appearance of the risen Christ is to James, who is also said to be present at the Last Supper.[19] In another Gnostic text, the *Kerygmata Petrou*, there is a letter from Peter to 'James, the lord and bishop of the holy Church', which again underlines the prominent position given to James.[20]

Unfortunately the dates of these Gnostic texts are extremely difficult to ascertain. The extant manuscripts are late, and early mentions are scarce, since the Church frowned upon them. Much of the Gnostic literature is contained in the Nag Hammadi collection, which was buried in its cave in the fourth century. Palaeographic datings cover the period *c*. AD 100–300. Except possibly for the Gospel of Thomas, the originals of most of the writings mentioned here are thought to be from the second century AD, contemporary with or later than the canonical Gospels: they presuppose the existence of the Gospel story of Jesus.

A passage in *Kerygmata Petrou*[21] throws an interesting sidelight on the well-known episode in the Synoptics,[22] where Jesus asks Peter, John and James, 'Whom think ye that I am?' Peter answers, 'Thou art the Christ', upon which Jesus asks the disciples not to tell anybody, something which again underlines the secret nature of revelations, and is well in line with the frequent references in the New Testament to the 'mystery' of Christ. In *Kerygmata Petrou*,[23] Peter is made to say: 'The eyes of mortals cannot see the incorporeal being of the Father or of the Son . . . to a pious, natural and pure mind the truth reveals itself: it is not acquired through a dream, but is granted to the good through discernment. For in this way was the Son revealed to me also by the Father. . . . Wherefore I know the power of revelation . . . it rose in my heart to say, and I know not how I said it, "Thou art the Son of the living God".' It seems we have to do with a vision by means of the mind's eye, a kind of intuition. Psychologically this certainly makes sense: strong beliefs are probably more often created by an intuitive process than by the use of explicit evidence or rational argument. In the conceptual landscape in which Peter and James, and their contemporaries lived, it was natural to call this process revelation, and to assume that it came from God, or Jesus.[24]

It is indeed particularly in the Gnostic literature that we find references to revelation in relation to episodes in Jesus' life.[25] In *Eugnostos* and *Sophia of Jesus Christ*, two closely related Nag Hammadi texts, the risen Jesus speaks to his twelve disciples in Galilee. But of the twelve only four are named: Philip, Matthew, Thomas and Mariamne (presumably Mary Magdalene).[26] The text specifically points out that 'the Saviour appeared not in his first form, but in the invisible Spirit', which makes it clear that we have to do with a spiritual vision or revelation. Further, in the *Apocryphon of James*[27] the twelve disciples – of whom only Peter and James are named – are sitting together trying to remember what Jesus had said to each of them. Then suddenly the risen Jesus appears among them, helping them to remember his words. When Jesus is about to leave them he says, 'Blessed are they who have proclaimed the Son before his descent[28] that, when I have come, I might ascend [again]'[29]. Finally he tells the twelve 'Leave James and Peter to me that I may fill them', presumably meaning that he intends to reveal secret truths to them.[30] Their favoured position among the disciples is obvious. Therefore it is perhaps not surprising that Paul singles them out in 1 Corinthians 15. We should add that at the beginning of the text James tells a correspondent that he is sending him 'a secret book' which apparently contains precisely this revelation of Jesus to him and Peter.

The scene with the disciples in the *Apocryphon of James* may contain clues to the interpretation of the most famous of the Gnostic Gospels, the *Gospel of Thomas*.[31] Here the opening sentence says 'These are the hidden sayings that the living Jesus spoke and Judas Thomas the Twin recorded.' Then follows a series of 114 pronouncements by Jesus, sometimes, but not very often, introduced by a question by one or more of Jesus' followers, of whom only Thomas, Peter, Mary (Magdalene) and Salome are named. Jesus' pronouncements are isolated sayings. They are not placed in a narrative framework. About a quarter of them are to be found among the Synoptics' sayings, e.g. in the Sermon on the Mount. Others are not recorded at all in the canonical Gospels. Here are a few examples:

(1) Whoever finds the interpretation of these sayings will not experience death
(3) The Kingdom is inside you
(51) What you look forward to has already come, but you do not recognise it
(114) Simon Peter said to them, 'Let Mary leave us, for women are not worthy of Life. Jesus said, I myself shall lead her in order to make her male'

The Gospel of Thomas appears very much as a collection of revelatory communications by Jesus to his followers. Though the pronouncements are attributed to 'the living Jesus', the complete lack of any situational details point to the same kind of background as that in the *Apocryphon of James*, namely, disciples experiencing spiritual revelations of the risen Jesus.[32] After all, Jesus was of course 'living' after his resurrection though, as we learn from the quotations given above, he could be experienced only in visions, and even those only to the select few, and in a spiritual mode. The fact that they are often said to be 'hidden' or 'mysteries' agrees with their revelatory character.[33] Among Gnostics, moreover, the word 'living' is an attribute particularly applied to spiritual beings.

Considering the strong Gnostic colouring of the Gospel of John, it is not surprising that Jesus' appearances in it also have a revelatory character. As Koester puts it (1990, p. 256) 'the Johannine discourses ... resemble more closely the revelation discourses of Gnostic writings'. Koester's detailed analyses[34] leave little doubt that the Gospel of John, both in its theology and in its representation of Jesus' sayings and deeds, is rather heavily dependent on the Gnostic literature.

At the same time, John's Gospel, though certainly Gnostic, is, as he said, strongly anti-docetic, since it seizes every opportunity to stress the physical characteristics of the earthly Jesus. In fact, the author goes quite far in his anti-docetic zeal, by representing even the risen Christ as possessing a human body: Thomas is allowed to feel Jesus' scars with his hands, and the resurrected Jesus eats and drinks together with his disciples.[35]

Though John and many other texts referred to in this chapter are Gnostic, their authors certainly look upon themselves as Christians, belonging to the Church of God. This leads on to the question of how widespread Gnostic ideas were within early Christianity. I said in the chapter on Ignatius (Chapter 10) that his polemics were definitely aimed against docetism, not against Gnosticism *per se*. After all, Ignatius was a great admirer of Paul, and in Ignatius' letters we find reminiscences even of the most Gnostically oriented of the Paulines: Ephesians. And that Pauline Christianity contained a considerable number of Gnostic traits is undeniable. Scholars have often remarked upon the parallels between Paul and Philo: those parallels mainly concern the complex of ideas which we also find in Gnosticism.

Hence we have to admit that a conspicuous and successful branch of the Christian movement in the first century, the Pauline one, was strongly influenced by Gnostic ideas, such as the dualism between the spiritual world of light and the physical world of darkness, the possibility for the spiritually enlightened to obtain, by individual revelations, secret information and guidance from the spiritual world, and the prospect of an eternal spiritual life for the elect of God.

The physical and the spiritual

As I explained in Chapter 8, there was no real cause for conflict between Christians and Gnostics, as long as both groups believed themselves to be in touch with the *risen* Christ, who was evidently a heavenly figure. I have shown that this was exactly the situation in the first century AD, according to *all* the texts of that time. But at the beginning of the second century AD, perhaps stirred by the success of Marcion's preaching,[36] bishop Ignatius of Antioch, and presumably other churchmen as well, insisted very strongly on locating Jesus in the historical context of the early first century, thus, by implication, making Jesus roughly contemporary with Peter, James and the other early apostles. By the same token, the earthly existence of Jesus came to attract more and more attention. The Jesus figure thus emerging proved immensely successful: it was concretely and poignantly human and, at the same time, thanks to its close links with the Old Testament prophecies, spiritual, exalted and divine.

The Gnostics, for their part, continuing to concentrate on the spiritual and essentially divine Jesus who had revealed himself to the first-century apostles, tried to safeguard their own picture of him by means of the docetic doctrine, in which the newly constructed historical Jesus was indeed accepted, but declared to be only a kind of phantom, the outer appearance of the really and essentially divine one.

Ignatius, as I have argued, was the first to articulate the Church's refusal to accept the construction of the docetic Gnostics. Above all the Church insisted that belief in Jesus must necessarily include belief in the historical Jesus figure which was gradually being built up around AD 100. This build-up continued throughout the second century, and was eventually consolidated by an immense number of legends about martyrs and saints. In the end, the Gnostics lost out to the Church. The hiding of the Nag Hammadi collection of Gnostic manuscripts around the year AD 400 probably marks the end of Gnosticism within the Church.

That the process took such a long time is an indication of the deep roots of Gnosticism within Christianity. At the same time, Gnosticism, with its individualism and subjectivism, undoubtedly involved grave dangers for the Church. Irenaeus classed Marcion as a Gnostic. But the main reason for Marcion's expulsion from the Roman Church in AD 144 was perhaps not so much docetism, as his rejection of the Old Testament, something which threatened the very foundation of the divine status of Jesus. The threat to the Church was serious: Marcion's organisation survived for many centuries, especially in the East.

The fact that John was eventually canonised, admittedly in the face of strong opposition, shows that the compromise position which John advocated – Gnosticism without docetism – was successful in persuading many Gnostically oriented members to stay within the Church. It probably also helped to attract outsiders, and above all Gentiles. After all, even Paul's influence worked for the preservation of Gnostic attitudes. Marcion's radical, Gnostic interpretation of Paul met many willing hearers. Moreover, Gnostic ideas were not so very far from the popular philosophies of the time, such as Neo-Platonism and neo-Stoicism. Augustine, Christianity's first important philosopher, who was brought up in his childhood as a Christian, became a Neo-Platonist after starting philosophical studies. He then turned to Manichaeism, which exhibits many Gnostic features, before returning to the Church at the age of 43, in AD 387. Several of his opponents accused him, not without reason, of retaining traces of his Manichaean, Gnostic, ideas. (It is worth noting that Koester, in Robinson & Koester 1971, p. 128, asserts (referring to Puech) that the Gospel of Thomas is identical with a Manichaean writing with the same name. It may be worth noting also that the Marcionite church eventually, in the fifth century, seems to have merged with the Manichaean one.)

Anyhow, whatever the reasons, John got accepted as part of the Christian canon.[37]

It is reasonable to presume that John's Gospel was deliberately designed both to appeal to the Gnostics, and at the same time to avoid conflicts with the Church. The solution adopted, judging from the final product, was to incorporate the main outline of the Synoptic story, while giving prominence to Gnostic elements and Gnostic theological tenets which did not clash with the preconceptions of the main church. Obviously the author also tried to avoid polemics.

As the author or authors of John clearly knew the Synoptic story quite well, we may presume that the final version of the Gospel was in the main written later than the Synoptics.[38] Also, there was naturally no need for a compromise until after both parts in the conflict had come into being. Obviously the canonical John builds on earlier Gnostic writings, as Koester has shown. The much-discussed papyrus fragment dated to *c.* AD 125 might itself be part of such an early Gnostic source.

A clear difference between John and the Synoptics concerns the disciples. Let us disregard the bare lists of the twelve in the Synoptics and Acts. Then we shall find that John, which contains no such list, has in fact as many names of apostles as the others. But the names are remarkably different. It is true that Peter (most often called Simon Peter) is indeed a prominent figure in John. But James and John are not named at all, though the 'sons of Zebedee' are mentioned once. Otherwise the most active apostles in John are Philip and Thomas. In addition John names Andrew, 'Judas, not Iscariot'[39] and Nathanael. None of these, except Andrew, occur in the Synoptics. The names of the individual apostles are not unimportant, since, as Koester points out, the apostles, especially in Gnostic writings, are often associated with revelations that they experienced and communicated individually. In this context it is surprising that James, mentioned often in Gnostic writings as the recipient of revelations, is not named at all in the Gospel of John.

I have suggested that the anti-docetic Gnosticism of John was meant as a compromise position between the mainly 'physical' Jesus figure of the Gospels and of the main church in the second century, and the 'spiritual' one of the Gnostics, and also, we must add, of Paul and most of the first-century Christians. But John's compromise does not by any means make him anxiously keep a strict middle way. The opening chapter of the Gospel presents a triumphant spiritual message, with its poetic picture of the Logos, which represents at the same time God, God's Wisdom and the Holy Ghost, all of them apparently united in Jesus.

Later on in the text the stories of Jesus' miracles are presented in such a way that Jesus' divine status is brought out clearly and emphatically. For instance, Nicodemus (3:2) says 'no man can do these miracles ... except God be with him'. The Samaritans, likewise: 'This is indeed the Christ' (4:42). Both Peter (6:69) and Martha (11:27) declare that Jesus is 'Christ, the Son of Man'.

Jesus' statements about himself in John are also much more direct and outspoken than in the Synoptics. When the Samaritan woman speaks about the Messiah that will come, Jesus says (4:26) 'I that speak unto thee am he.'[40] Further, Jesus expounds Old Testament prophecies about himself: 'Moses ... wrote of me' (5:46). He also repeatedly talks about his predestined fate: 'my time is not yet come' (7:8; and also 7:30, 8:20) until we read in 13:1 'His hour was come', and 16:32, where Jesus says 'The hour cometh', and 17:1, 'the hour is come'.

A typically Gnostic idea is that of the Spirit coming from above, and then ascending again, which is expressed in 3:13, 'No man can ascend to heaven except he that came down from heaven', and also 6:62, 'What and if ye shall see the Son of Man ascend up where he was before?' In 16:28 Jesus declares this about himself: 'I came forth from the Father.' The Gnostic idea that all the 'saints', the members of the church of God, belonged to the heavenly region of Light is found in 17:14: 'they are not of the world, even as I am not of the world'. Accordingly, we are not surprised to hear Jesus say (18:30): 'My kingdom is not of this world.'

I think the analysis and interpretation of John that I have offered in this chapter solve many of the problems that previous scholars have had to struggle with. Their difficulties have to a large extent arisen because of their inability to rid themselves of the universally prevalent presupposition of the general correctness of the Synoptics story of Jesus as a first-century Palestinian preacher. Once the possibility is admitted that the Jesus of the earliest, first-century Christians was not such a person, but was a heavenly figure whose earthly appearance had belonged to a much earlier period of time, the Gnostic nature of the Christianity of Paul's letters and other first-century texts appears altogether natural. In this light, Irenaeus' admission of John's Gospel into the canon appears as a very wise measure.

My solution in the main supports a second-century date for John. As I said above: there was no need for John until docetic Gnosticism had come into existence. The evidence is that this did not happen much before Ignatius, around AD 100. In general, I doubt whether John's

Gospel was fully conceived before Luke had finished his two-volume work.

Chapter 13

Overview

For nearly two thousand years, almost everybody has assumed that the history of Christianity, as set forth in the Gospels and the Acts of the Apostles, has been at least in its main outlines reliable and correct. In modern times, to be sure, legendary and miraculous elements in them have been played down, or disregarded, both by theologians and by the general public. But the basic story of Jesus as the founder of Christianity, living in Palestine in the first half of the first century, and crucified under Pontius Pilate, has never been seriously questioned in the scholarly theological literature.

In this book I maintain that precisely the basic story of Jesus in the Gospels has to be completely abandoned as an account of 'what really happened'. The Gospels and Acts were composed roughly a century after the time in which they themselves place Jesus and the Apostles. They are certainly not eyewitness accounts. Nor are they secondary reports of such accounts. Bluntly: their story is fiction.

A thorough study of all the available source material makes it evident that the Jesus figure of the Gospels and Acts differs radically from the Jesus figure of literally all the first-century Christian writings. The earliest Christians – Paul and his fellow apostles: Peter, James and the rest – never saw or met the earthly Jesus, Jesus 'in the flesh'. They encountered him only in visions and revelations: as a 'spiritual' being. Jesus of Nazareth, born of Mary at the end of Augustus' reign, is a fiction created in the second century by the Gospel writers.

But, though the earliest Christians had never experienced Jesus in the flesh, he was by no means unknown to them. They knew Jesus because he was the great prophet and founder of the religious movement that they belonged to, namely, a branch of the Essenes, a reform movement of Judaism originating in Judaea in the second century BC. Now, after some two hundred years, the movement had branched out in various directions, and grown quite strong among the Jews of the Diaspora, especially in the Hellenised Greek-speaking parts of the Roman Empire.

The Essenes continued to regard their founder, whom they called the Teacher of Righteousness, as their great prophet, and also as a martyr. They knew, or thought they knew, that he had been harassed and eventually put to death by the Jewish priestly hierarchy. To Paul and the earliest apostles, Jesus, as they called him, dead for more than a hundred years, remained the great interpreter of the 'mysteries' of the Bible. Their visions of Jesus as raised to heaven and sitting beside God, convinced them that he had risen from the dead. His resurrection proved what their Church already believed: that immortality was possible for humans. Further, the apostles took their visions of Jesus sitting beside God as a sign that the Last Judgment was near, at which Jesus, as the Messiah, would save those who belonged to the Church he had founded, the Church of God.

All Christian writings which can be plausibly dated to the first century AD present this 'spiritual' picture of Jesus, Jesus raised to Heaven. The earthly Jesus is clearly of little interest to the earliest apostles and their audience. But a dramatic change occurs after *c.* AD 100. For in the second century AD Christians, while still naturally insisting on the divinity of Christ, focus their attention on the Jesus who had once lived among men. It is the earthly Jesus who is the main actor in the Gospel story.

But this earthly Jesus is in the main a largely fictional creation of the Gospel writers. The change of focus from a heavenly to an earthly Jesus seems to have been initiated by the highly respected Ignatius, bishop of Antioch, Ignatius, who is thought to have been martyred in Rome under the emperor Trajan (98–117). Ignatius asserted, authoritatively, but without providing any evidence, that the earthly Jesus had died when Pontius Pilate was governor of Judaea (AD 26–36). His choice of Pilate as a reference point in time may well be due to his knowledge that Paul had experienced his decisive vision of the risen Christ at that time. Thus at one stroke Ignatius made Jesus a contemporary of Paul and his colleagues among the apostles. Starting from there, the Gospel writers created the poignant and moving story of Jesus and his disciples, which has held the field ever since. My book is an attempt to show how and why this decisive change in the Christians' view of Jesus came about.

The Essenes exhibit several similarities with Christianity. The most palpable one is their use of the same names for the members of their movement: the Church of God, the Saints, the Elect, the Poor, those of the Way. There are also striking correspondences in their interpretation of the Bible: for instance, their Messianism, their belief in immortality and their way of interpreting Old Testament sayings as prophecies about the Messiah.

But there are also striking differences. One is the strict hierarchical organisation of the Essene communities, where members were ranked according to their knowledge of the Scriptures, and by the religious purity of their life. Another is their extremely strict adherence to the Mosaic law. On these points at least some of these communities were miles apart from the Christian communities, and especially the Diaspora ones, which welcomed Gentile members, and whose organisation appears rather loose, at least before Ignatius of Antioch.

In view of the differences between the early Palestinian Essenes of the Dead Sea Scrolls, on one hand, and Paul's communities on the other, we must assume that the Essene movement in the Diaspora had undergone considerable changes in the 150–200 years intervening between the first appearance of the Essene Teacher of Righteousness and the evangelisation started by Paul. Fortunately such changes can be documented in various ways. The descriptions of the Essenes given by Philo of Alexandria *c.* AD 20, and by the Jewish historian Josephus in *c.* AD 80, portray a much more open community than that of the Qumran documents. Philo's Therapeutae, a branch of the Essenes, had a philosophical, universalistic outlook. Their most notable Essene feature, besides their self-designation as the 'saints', is their emphasis on an 'allegorical' interpretation of the Bible, including, we may presume, a non-literal, 'spiritual' reading of the Mosaic law. In these respects many Essenes seem to have moved a long way towards the positions where we later find the Christians in the first century AD.

I have also found some evidence in the Dead Sea Scrolls that the Palestinian Essenes directed their attention more and more to the Diaspora, which in itself would be likely to soften their originally hostile attitudes towards strangers and increase their understanding of non-Jewish, Gentile customs and ways of thinking. Indeed, even the early Essenes of the Qumran documents can be looked upon as reformers in relation to earlier Jewish religious views.

The later Essenes' interpretations of Bible texts as prophecies about the fate of the Teacher of Righteousness were eagerly taken up by the

Christians, who later used a similar technique for creating a history of the life and teaching of Jesus.

There exists some evidence that the Essenes deliberately strove to attract the Jewish Diaspora in the Roman Empire, and that their efforts bore fruit. First of all, we have Philo's statement about the Essene branch he calls Therapeutae, namely, that they were found 'in many places in the inhabited world'. I have also drawn attention to a passage in the Latin poet Horace, indicating that Roman Jews in the late first century BC numbered their Sabbaths consecutively through the year, Essene fashion. Further, the first letter of Clemens Romanus, which I have found several reasons to date to Nero's time, rather than, as most previous scholars, the nineties of the first century AD, indicates that the Roman Church of God had been in existence at least as early as the first few decades of the first century AD, and hence *before* what Paul calls 'the beginning of the evangelisation', *c.* AD 30. This would imply that the Roman church before Paul was Essene rather than specifically Christian. That is to say, they regarded Jesus as a great teacher and prophet, not as the Messiah, the Christ. The early date suggested by a passage in Clement's text would agree well with the Horatian passage, but not at all with the traditional view of the origin of Christianity.

The 'evangelisation' by Paul and the other apostles presumably started in the thirties of the first century AD. It was strongly Messianic, but of a spiritual rather than political kind. It thus coincided with a period, both in Palestine and in the Jewish Diaspora, which culminated in the disastrous revolt of the Palestinian Jews against the Romans in 66–74, and had repercussions in Cyrenaica and Egypt in 115–17, and in the Bar Kochba rebellion in 133–5.

The evangelisation initiated by the apostles was directed chiefly to liberal Essene communities, calling themselves 'the Church of God', and dispersed in the Eastern part of the Roman Empire and, in addition, Rome itself. There was also an early Essene community in Jerusalem, which has been documented archaeologically. Paul clearly looked upon it as especially important. The Jerusalem Church of God also came to recognise Jesus as the Messiah. But it differed from Paul in the matter of the Mosaic law. Its leaders did not accept Paul's theological argument to the effect that Jesus, the Messiah, had 'ended the law'. Paul encountered opposition in regard to his view of the law in other churches as well. But he never yielded on this point, which he naturally looked upon as important for attracting Gentiles – and certainly also many Diaspora Jews.

It would be a mistake to assume that all the Diaspora Essenes were generally observant Jews before Paul appeared with his message. The allegorical interpretation of Scripture, which all Essenes practised, allowed them great freedom, at least in principle. Therefore the questions of circumcision and food purity, for instance, do not seem to have been very live issues in most Diaspora communities. Clemens Romanus and the author of the Letter to the Hebrews, both approximately contemporary with Paul, do not even mention them. And as more and more Gentiles were attracted to the various communities of the Church of God, laxness in these matters naturally became more common.

Pliny the Younger's letter to Trajan, written probably *c*. AD 112, concerns his inquiries about Christians in the Roman province of Bithynia in Asia Minor, where he was governor. Pliny's impression is that they were pious, peaceful and rather harmless people, who met for prayers and communal meals. That description would fit both early Christians and Essenes of the Therapeutae kind.

The name Essene, which is probably a Greek form of an Aramaic word meaning 'pious', does not occur in the New Testament and is in fact practically non-existent outside Philo, Josephus and Pliny. Under the circumstances it is not easy to trace the group. It seems likely that a fair number of Essene churches became Christian as a result of the early first-century evangelisation. Essenes who did not turn Christian may have joined other Jewish synagogues.

In the New Testament, the relations between Jews and Christians are generally represented as strained, or even hostile. But this is probably a biased picture. Archaeological and literary evidence shows that Jews and Christians lived amicably and peacefully together for centuries. Many visited both Christian churches and Jewish synagogues.

Though I have suggested that a substantial number of Diaspora Jews joined the Essene movement and later turned Christian, they were probably never a majority even among the Diaspora Jews. Comparing Christian churches and synagogues during the first three or four centuries of our era, we almost always find that the synagogue in a particular city is bigger and more richly endowed than the Christian church.

We do not know much about other first-century AD Christian churches than those Paul's letters inform us about. But other first-century Christian documents make it clear that Paul's views on certain particular issues were by no means shared by all Christians. Obviously the Christian movement which was started by Paul and those 'who were apostles before him' was far from uniform – just as neither Essenism nor Judaism as a whole were uniform.

Concurrently with the rise of Christianity in the first-century Greek-speaking Jewish Diaspora, there developed another, more 'philosophical' movement, called Gnosticism, chiefly among Diaspora Jews, apparently above all in Alexandria, the intellectual centre of the Roman Empire at the time. Gnosticism can be characterised as a religious and mystically coloured variant of middle Platonism with marked Jewish elements. Its members regarded the supreme God as the essence of Light and human souls as sparks of that Light which had been imprisoned in dark Matter. Their only chance of escaping from that prison was by the help of angels of Light, emanating from God.

It is easy to see that some of these Gnostics could be attracted by the Christian message and that, conversely, the Christians could welcome the Gnostic elaboration of their spiritual world. I think this is precisely what happened in the first century AD. Though Christians and Gnostics certainly differed on many theological points, they could also give each other support. Christianity did not originate in Gnosticism, nor did Gnosticism, contrary to the early Church Father Irenaeus' assertions, arise as a perversion of Christianity. The two movements developed in parallel, and partly coalesced.

However, such a union was not without its dangers. First of all, Gnosticism was essentially a religion centring on the individual. It was strongly subjective, and therefore tended to rebel against authority. The Christian Church hierarchy, which was taking shape at the time of Ignatius, was naturally suspicious of such anarchic tendencies. Moreover, some Gnostics found it hard to accept that Jesus, a spirit from God, could really suffer as a human being. It could not be Jesus, they said, that suffered and died, but an ordinary human being, possessed, in some sense, by Jesus. Jesus himself only 'seemingly' suffered and died. This theory was called 'docetism' (from the Greek verb *dokein*, 'seem'). But, if Jesus Christ was only *seemingly* a man, and only seemingly suffered and died, how were ordinary men to identify with him, and how could Jesus' resurrection count as a promise of immortality for such ordinary men? Theologians might perhaps find solutions for such problems. But the Church felt, probably with reason, that ordinary people were likely to be disturbed.

And what would become of the many Old Testament prophecies which pious Christians (and before them the Essenes) had applied to Jesus and the Teacher of Righteousness? Towards the end of the first century these prophecies, ferreted out by diligent and learned Christian theologians, such as Clemens Romanus, Barnabas and the author of the Letter to the Hebrews, were beginning to add up to an outline of a Life of Jesus Christ, the man who was also the Son of God. The docetic ideas, appearing around AD 100, about a Christ who was a spirit, not a man, were all the more disturbing, since in the late first century the apostles who had received visions of Jesus some seventy years ago were no longer among the living. There was now nobody to contradict the quite natural interpretation that those visions were encounters with the real, living Jesus. Paul and his audience had regarded Jesus as a martyr long since dead, and there is nothing to show that the other apostles differed from Paul in this respect. But now, at the beginning of the second century AD, it seemed entirely natural to believe that Jesus had died shortly before the apostles had received their revelations, namely, around AD 30. To the Gospel writers, that was almost a century ago. It was also a sufficiently long time to render futile any search for real evidence about the gospel story, particularly in view of the chaotic state of Palestine after the revolt against the Romans in 66–74.

Thus we have at this juncture, around AD 100, two diverging tendencies in the Christian movement. One was 'physical', giving more and more weight to the earthly Jesus, and the other was 'spiritual', attracted chiefly to the heavenly Jesus, Jesus of the *Spirit*.

It was at this moment that the Christians began to create for themselves a new perception of their own history. It seems the change was initiated by Ignatius of Antioch, an able, forceful and centrally placed Christian leader, in letters which he wrote to various Churches of God in Asia Minor, at a time when he was going to Rome in order to die as a martyr – an end which he greatly desired. Ignatius was bishop of Antioch, the third largest city in the Roman Empire at the time, after Rome and Alexandria. He decided that Gnosticism, and particularly the docetic Gnostics, had to be firmly resisted. The spiritual Jesus should not be allowed to overshadow the human one. Instead, the two should be united. Ignatius reached his goal by using his considerable authority as a bishop and a would-be martyr, asserting, in no uncertain terms, that Jesus was indeed born of a woman, the virgin Mary, that he had been baptised by the well-known

John the Baptist, had been crucified under Pontius Pilate and resurrected and raised to Heaven by God. All this placed Jesus unambiguously in the first decades of the first century AD. That was the time when the apostles had received their revelations of Jesus as raised to Heaven, revelations which had started off the 'evangelisation', as Paul called it.

It is to a large extent in accordance with Ignatius' assertions about Jesus' birth by Mary, his baptism by John the Baptist and his execution under Pilate, that all the second-century Gospel writers – Matthew, Mark, Luke and John – built their story of the life of Jesus. In their accounts Jesus was a man who was at the same time divine, the Son of God, and also human, an early first-century Palestinian wonder-worker, preacher and prophet. To flesh out Ignatius' bare historical data, the Gospel writers added the considerable number of Old Testament prophecies that first-century Christian writers had brought to light in order to show that God had preordained Jesus' life on earth and that Jesus was indeed the Messiah. None of the first-century Christian writers, however, had tried to weave these episodes into a dramatic life story. Nor had Ignatius. The Gospel writers were the first to do so.

The Old Testament passages, which Paul, Clemens Romanus, Barnabas and the author of Hebrews interpreted as prophecies about Jesus, dealt above all with the passion story. Psalm 22 contributed Jesus' poignant cry on the cross: 'My God, My God, why hast thou forsaken me?' Jesus' passion and its redemptive power were brought forward by means of Isaiah 53:5: 'He was wounded for our transgressions, he was buried for our iniquities: the chastisement of our peace was laid on him; and with his stripes we are healed.' Even the episode with the soldiers at the foot of the cross was rendered in the words of Psalm 22: 'the assembly of the wicked have inclosed me: they pierced my hands and my feet . . . They part my garments among them, and cast lots on my vesture.'

The preaching of Jesus, and especially the sayings collected by Matthew in the Sermon on the Mount, are partly taken from the rich Jewish 'wisdom' literature in the Bible, to which were added similar 'sayings of the wise' from other sources, including Greek ones, as we have seen. In addition we naturally have to reckon with teaching traditions and liturgical practices preserved in the Essene Churches of God. The Gospel writers seem to have taken much of their material from collections of such sayings, and presented them as sayings by the

264

earthly Jesus. But in several Gnostically coloured collections they are presented, interestingly, as sayings or revelations of the *risen* Jesus, communicating with his followers after his death.

The three Synoptic Gospels, setting forth the words and deeds of Jesus after the manner of Greek Lives of philosophers (in particular, Cynic philosophers) proved very popular and came to determine completely subsequent Christians' view of themselves and their history. Dozens of similar such stories were produced by various writers in the second century, followed in later centuries by equally imaginative and popular Lives of Saints. The Church could not but recognise their success as propaganda for Christianity among the masses.

At the same time, the spiritual aspects of the Jesus figure had to be preserved. The Church naturally wished to retain the allegiance of the theologically more informed and philosophically minded intellectuals within its fold. Ignatius achieved this by stoutly defending Paul and his spiritualised world-view, while at the same time rejecting the docetic heresy by insisting on the humanity of Jesus, and locating him definitely in first-century Palestine. In the late second century the Church father Irenaeus secured the same goal by establishing a New Testament canon which did not only contain the popular Synoptic Gospels, but also the gnosticising, but firmly anti-docetic, Gospel of John. To these were added the Letters of Paul. Owing to their undeniable Gnosticising tendencies, Paul's letters had in fact been eclipsed in the Church for several decades in the second century: Luke, for instance, and Justin Martyr never mention them. Perhaps they did not even know about them.

The Gospel writers' use of Old Testament passages for building up a full Life of Jesus was not wholly uncontroversial. First of all, we have Marcion, a rich shipowner from Asia Minor, who was a radical interpreter of Paul's teaching. He successfully established his own, independent Church organisation in Asia Minor, whose most distinctive trait was a complete rejection of the Old Testament, the Jewish Bible. This was a view which Marcion shared with many non-Christian Gnostics. Marcion, rejecting the Old Testament, naturally did not like the emphasis that the Gospel writers put on the Old Testament prophecies. Judging from the very meagre textual material from Marcion that has been preserved in writings of his opponents, he tried to weaken the position of the Old Testament by pointing out the *discrepancies* between the Gospel story and the prophecies. He assumed that the Gospel story was historically true and concluded that the prophecies were not correct: the Old Testament was wrong.

Interestingly, Justin Martyr, a stout defender of the Gospel story, argued in the opposite direction. To him, the perfect *agreement* between the Old Testament prophecies and the Gospels proved that the prophecies were indeed divine ones, proving also the divinity of Jesus Christ. Remarkably, therefore, both Justin and Marcion had already at this early date, in the middle of the second century, come to accept the Gospels as unquestionable historical accounts – a clear indication of the persuasive power of the drama presented in them.

Though we find hardly anything about the earthly Jesus in non-Christian Jewish writings from before the third century, it is remarkable that later rabbinic sources also seem to assume the basic historicity of the Gospel Jesus. But they naturally do not admit that Jesus was the Messiah, or God's son, and freely add further fictional stories to denigrate the character of the presumed earthly Jesus. In fact, the only person to question explicitly the historicity of the Gospel Jesus figure appears in Justin Martyr's *Dialogue with the Jew Trypho*, written *c.* AD 150. There Trypho is made to say '*Christ, if he has indeed been born, and exists anywhere, is unknown. . . . You . . . invent a Christ for yourselves.*'

Trypho's scepticism did not prevail. The Gospels, with their moving story of Jesus, were a complete success. Within a further two hundred years, Christianity had become a recognised State religion in the Roman Empire. Its largely fictional history, created by the second-century Gospels and the Acts of the Apostles, and elaborated further by the fourth-century Church historian Eusebius, was to remain practically unchallenged for almost two millennia. It is true that the Church exposed itself to inner tensions by following Ignatius' lead, recognising *both* the 'physical' Jesus of the Synoptic Gospels, and the 'spiritual' Jesus of Paul, John and the Gnostics. But, thanks to the wide span of ideas thus incorporated in its doctrines, the Church managed to survive and prosper.

Epilogue

If we have to accept that the Jesus of the Gospels is fiction, where does that leave Christianity? Does everything fall apart?

I do not think so. I cannot see that it makes much difference whether Jesus lived on earth in the late second century BC, or in the first century AD, or indeed was a theological construction built upon an interpretation of a supposed pronouncement by God. Nor does it matter, essentially, whether Paul and the apostles experienced him in visions and revelations, rather than in real life. If we believe that God exists, surely the way in which he makes himself known to us is irrelevant. Even Moses was not allowed to see God face to face on Mount Sinai. And Paul, no mean theologian, emphasises that divine beings have to be experienced 'spiritually', not 'physically'. The Teacher of Righteousness was certainly regarded as a human being by the Essenes. But both he and his followers were believed to stand in a special relation to God. There is no reason why we should regard him otherwise. Nor, for that matter, reject the Gnostic idea that every human being can treasure within him or her a spark of the divine Light. As for immortality and salvation, which certainly were very important to Paul and the earliest Christians, they are not affected at all by the *historical* reorientation that I have set forth here.

All religions originate in man's deep desire to find answers to the great questions of life. Whence have we come? Where are we going? What is the meaning of existence, of life – my life, anybody's life? What is right and just, what is wrong and unjust? Some of us try to find the answers to those questions by conscious reflection and hard thinking. Others try instead to achieve a state in which they can apprehend an answer which may at least strike them intuitively as immediately and self-evidently true.

These two alternative ways to reach insight – that of the philosopher

267

or scientist, and that of the visionary prophet – do not exclude each other. On the contrary, many seek to combine them. As seen through the lenses of modern science, it is clear that both philosophical thinking and prophetic inspiration and intuition have their foundation in the interplay of man's genetic constitution and his experience in life. Since we all belong to the same human species, we should not be surprised to find common traits in a philosophical religion like Chinese Confucianism, a religious, but fundamentally atheistic philosophy like Buddhism, and a clearly monotheistic religion like Judaism and its daughters, Christianity and Islam.

When Paul and other apostles were overwhelmed by their vision of Jesus as the Messiah, and when the Old Testament prophets and Paul, as well as Muhammad, were overwhelmed by God himself, and heard him speak to them, or when Gautama Buddha felt he had reached the ultimate state of insight, we have in each case to do with a strong, subjective experience which has been formed and coloured by each individual's earlier experience and his or her social and intellectual background.

Each of these founders of religions has of course been convinced that his own insight has reached the utmost and absolute Truth. But this is a subjective conviction, not an objective fact. We simply cannot avoid the conclusion that it is impossible for us to arrive at the ultimate truth. That is a conclusion that scientists have learned to live with: science is a tool for understanding the universe we live in, including ourselves. That understanding can grow indefinitely. But it will never be complete. It is time for us to realise that the same holds for religious insights.

But we have a long way to go. Religious people, whatever faith they confess, have been extremely reluctant to admit what modern scientifically informed people now usually take as self-evident, namely, that none of the sacred books, nor any of our scientific theories, can be said to contain the ultimate Truth, God's Word. They contain the attempts of human beings to express what they have taken to be God's Word. To put it in less religious terms: they contain the attempts of men and women to understand the world in which we live. All these attempts are at best only so many steps on the road to better understanding. And we do not reach even this unless we keep questioning the results we have reached, constantly exerting ourselves to find better ways to organise our constantly expanding experience.

There need not be conflict between religion and science – whether natural science or historical scholarship. Belief should not be opposed to knowledge. In scientific work, *both* are essential. Newton would not have been able to formulate his theory of gravity, unless he had *believed* that it would be possible to express mathematically the knowledge about the movements of planets which Kepler had reached on the basis of Tycho Brahe's observations. The same holds for Einstein, who had to construct a mathematical theory in order to accommodate the mass of new data that nineteenth- and twentieth-century astronomy and physics had brought to light.

But, if this interplay of belief and knowledge is to succeed, we must realise that neither belief nor knowledge is something absolute, something that we have finally and definitely got hold of. Both are *provisional* means of reaching insights that are hopefully deeper. Though there is no ultimate truth, we must try to reach higher and higher on the way towards it. As Goethe expressed it: *Ewig strebend sich erhebend* – 'Constantly striving, rising higher'.

Bibliography

Abbreviations

Aufstieg: *Aufstieg und Niedergang der Römischen Welt*. Herausgegeben von Hildegard Temporini und Wolfgang Haase. Walter de Gruyter, Berlin, New York.

FRLANT: Forschungen zur Religion und Litteratur des Alten und Neuen Testaments. Göttingen.

RQ: *Revue de Qumran. (Qumran Review.)* Paris.

Editions of ancient authors, with translations

Apocrypha and Pseudepigrapha: *see* Charles 1913, Charlesworth 1983, Hennecke 1963

Barnabas: *see* Prigent, 1971

Clemens Romanus: *see* Jaubert, 1971

Didachē: *see* Audet, 1958

Eusebius: *see* Lake, 1926, 1942

Hermas: *see* Brox, 1991

Ignatius: *see* Paulsen, 1985

Iosephus: *see* Thackeray, H et al

Justin Martyr: *see* Marcovich, 1994

Irenaeus: *see* Sagnard, 1952

Minucius: *see* Rendall, Gerald H. 1931

Philo: *see* Colson, 1949

Qumran (Dead Sea Scrolls): *see* Vermes, 1987

Polycarpus: *see* Paulsen, 1985

Tertullianus: *see* Glover, T.R. 1931

The Nag Hammadi Library in English (NHL): *see* Meyer 1977

Adler, William. *Primordial History in Christian Chronography,* Washington, 1989

Aland, Barbara, & Delobel, Joel (eds). *New Testament Textual Criticism.* Contributions to Biblical Exegesis & Theology 7, Kok Pharos, Kampen, 1994

Aland, Kurt. *Studien zur Ueberlieferung des Neuen Testaments,* Gruyter, Berlin, 1967

Albani, Matthias. *Astronomie und Schöpfungsglaube . . . Henochsbuch,* Neukirchener, Verlag, 1994

Allegro, John M. *The Dead Sea Scrolls,* Pelican Books, Harmondsworth, 1958

Althaus, Paul. 'Der gegenwärtige Stand der Frage nach dem historischen Jesus', Bayr, Akademie der Wissenschaften, Sitzungsberichte, Phil. Hist Klass, 1960–6.

Angus, S. *The Mystery Religions and Christianity,* New York, 1925

Attridge, Harold W. & Hata, Gohei (eds). *Eusebius, Christianity, and Judaism,* Brill, Leiden, 1992

Attridge, Harold W. Review of Herbert Braun: *An die Hebräer,* Journal of Biblical Literature 106, 348–350, 1987

Audet, Jean Paul. *La Didaché.* Paris 1958

Augustinus. *Confessiones,* (ed.) Pierre de Labriolle. Collections des Universités de France, Paris, 1947

Aune, David E. 'Charismatic Exegesis in Early Judaism and Early Christianity', in Charlesworth & Evans, Journal for the study of the Pseudepigrapha, Suppl. Series 14, Sheffield, 1993

Bammel, Ernst. 'Christian Origins in Jewish Tradition', New Testament Studies 13, 317–335

Barr, James. *The Hebrew/Aramaic Background of hypocrisy in the Gospels,* Journal for the Study of the Old Testament, Supplies Ser. 100, Sheffield, 1990

Bauckhan, Richard. 'Pseudo-Apostolic Letters', Journal of Biblical Literature 107, 469–494, 1988

Bauer, Bruno. *Kritik der evangelischen Geschichte der Synoptiker* 1–3, Leipzig, 1846

Bauer, Bruno. *Christus und die Caesaren,* Der Ursprung des Christenthums aus den römischen Griechentum, Berlin, 1879

Bauer, Walter. *Das Leben Jesu im Zeitalter der neutestamentlichen Apokryphen,* Tübingen, 1909

Bauer, Walter. *Rechtgläubigkeit und Ketzerei im ältesten Christentum,* Tübingen, 1934

Baumgarten, Joseph M. 'The Counting of the Sabbath', Vetus Testamentum 16, 277–286, 1966

Baumgarten, Joseph M. 'Some problems of the Jubilees Calendar', VT 32 1982

Baumgarten, Joseph M. '4Q 503 (Daily Prayers) and the Lunar Calendar', RQ 12, 399–407, 1985–7

Baumgarten, Joseph M. 'The Calendars of the Book of Jubilees and the Temple Scroll', Vetus Testamentum 37, 71–72, 1987

Beckwith, Roger T. 'The Earliest Enoch Literature and its Calendar', RQ 10, 365–403, 1979–81

Beckwith, Roger T. 'The Significance of the Calendar for interpreting Essene Chronology and eschatology', RQ 10, 167–202, 1979–81

Beckwith, Roger T. 'St Luke, the Date of Christmas and the Priestly Courses at Qumran', RQ 11, 73, 1982–4

Beckwith, Roger T. 'The Pre-history and relationships of the Pharisees, Sadducees and Essenes', RQ 11, 3–46, 1982–84

Bell, H. Idris. *Cults and Creeds in Graeco-Roman Egypt*, Liverpool University Press, 1953

Best, Ernest. *Ephesians,* Journal for the study of the Old Testament: New Testament Guides, Sheffield, 1993

Betz, Hans Dieter. 'Zum Problem des religionsgeschichtlichen Verständnis der Apokalyptik', Zeitschrift für Theologie und Kirche 63, 391–409, 1966

Betz, Otto. *Probleme des Prozesses Jesu.* Aufstieg 25:1, 565–647, 1982

Betz, Otto & Riesner, Rainer. *Jesus, Qumran und der Vatikan.* Brunner, Giessen 1993

Beyschlag, Karlmann. 'Zur Simon Magus Frage', Zeitschrift für Theologie und Kirche 68, 395–426, 1971

Bickerman, Elias J. *The Jews in the Greek Age,* Harvard UP, Cambridge Mass. 1988

Bilde, Per. 'Josefus beretning om Jesus , Dansk Theologisk Tidsskrift, 99, 99–135, 1981

Birkeland, Harris. 'Das Problem der Entstehung Islams', Die Welt als Geschichte, 18, 213–221, 1958

Boardman, J. et al (eds). *Oxford History of the Classical World,* Oxford University Press, 1986

Böhlig, Alexander, & Wise, Frederik. *Zum Hellenismus in den Schriften von Nag Hammadi*, Harrasowitz, Wiesbaden, 1975.

Boll, Franz. 'Hebdomas', in Pauly & Wissowa, Realencyklopädie der classischen Altertumswissenschaft, 1894

Borgen, Peder. *Philo, John and Paul*, Scholars Press, Atlanta, 1989

Bousset, Wilhelm. *Die Religion des Judentums im späthellenistischen Zeitalter*, Handbuch zum Neuen Testament 21, Mohr, Tübingen, 1926

Bovon, Francois. 'The Synoptic Gospels and the Noncanonical Acts of the Apostles', Harvard Theological Review, 81, 19–36, 1988

Boyarin, Daniel. *A Radical Jew: Paul and the Politics of Identity*, University of California Press, 1994

Braithwaite, R. B. *An Empiricist's view of Religious Belief,* Cambridge University Press, 1959

Brandes, Georg. *Sagnet om Jesus*, Gyldendal, Copenhagen, 1925

Brandon, S. G. F. *The Fall of Jerusalem and the Christian Church*, London, 1951

Brettler, Mark Zvi. *The Creation of History in Ancient Israel*, Routledge, London, New York, 1995

Brock, Sebastian. 'The Two Ways and the Palestinian Targum.' Journal for the Study of the Old Testament, Suppl Series 100, Sheffield, 1990

Brown, Schuyler. *The Origins of Christianity*, (rev. ed.), Oxford, University Press, 1993

Brox, Norbert. *Der Hirt des Hermas*, Komm. zu den apostolischen Vätern 7, Göttingen, 1991

Bruce, Frederick Fyvie. 'The Acts of the Apostles', Aufstieg 25:3, 2569–2603, 1985

Bruce, Frederick Fyvie. 'To the Hebrews', Aufstieg 25:4, 3496–3521, 1987

Buchanan, George Wesley. *To the Hebrews*, The Anchor Bible, Doubleday, Garden City, N.Y., 1972

Buchanan, George Wesley. *New Testament Eschatology*, Mellon Biblical Press, Lewiston N.Y., 1993

Bultmann, Rudolph. *Das Verhältnis der urchristl Christusbotschaft zum histor. Jesus*, Heidelberg, Akademie der Wissenschaften, Phil. Hist Klasse, 1960:3

Burgmann, Hans. 'Ein Schaltungsmonat nach 24,5 Jahren in Chassidischen Sonnenkalender?', RQ 8, 65–73, 1972–5

Burgmann, Hans. 'Die Interkalation in den sieben Jahrwochen des Sonnenkalenders' RQ 10, 67–81, 1979–81

Burkert, Walter. *Ancient Mystery Cults,* Harvard University Press, Cambridge Mass, 1987

Burtchaell, James Tunstead. *From Synagogue to Church,* Cambridge University Press, 1992

Callaway, P.R. 'Qumran origins: from the Doresh to the Moreh', RQ 14, 637–650, 1989–90

Callaway, Phillip R. 'The History of the Qumran Community', Journal for the Study of the Pseudepigrapha, Suppl. Series 3, Sheffield, 1988

Cambridge History of Judaism 2, Cambridge, 1989

Camelot, P. Th. Clemens Alexandrinus: Les Stromates. Paris, 1954

Carmignac, Jean. 'Qui était le Docteur de Justice?', RQ 10, 235–246, 1979–81

Challaye, Félicien. *Le christianisme et nous,* Christianisme 42, Paris, 1932

Charles, R. A. *Apocryhpha and Pseudepigrapha of the Old Testament,* 1913

Charlesworth, James H. 'In the Crucible', See Charlesworth & Evans, Journal for the Study of the Pseudepigrapha, Suppl. Series 14, Sheffield, 1993

Charlesworth, James H. *The Pseudepigrapha and Modern Research,* Scholars Press, Atlanta, 1981

Charlesworth, James H. The Old Testament Pseudepigrapha, Doubleday, Garden City, New York, 1985

Charlesworth, James H. 'The historical Jesus', Aufstieg 25:1, 451–476, 1982

Charlesworth, James H. *The Old Testament Pseudepigrapha and the New Testament,* Doubleday, New York, 1983, 1985

Charlesworth, James H. & Evans, Craig A. *The Pseudepigrapha and Early Biblical Interpretation,* Journal for the Study of the Pseudepigrapha, Suppl Series 14, Sheffield, 1993

Charlesworth, James H. (ed). *The Messiah,* Fortress, Augsburg, 1992

Charlesworth, James H. (ed). *The Old Testament Pseudepigrapha,* London, 1983

Charlesworth, James H. (ed). *Jesus and the Dead Sea Scrolls,* Doubleday, New York, 1992

Chilton, Bruce. 'God As Father', in Charlesworth & Evans, 1993

Chilton, Bruce, & Evans, Craig A. (eds). *Studying the Historical Jesus,* Brill, Leiden, 1994

Collins, John J. & Charlesworth, James H. *Mysteries and Revelations,* 1991

Collins, John J. *The Apocalyptic Imagination,* Crossroad, New York, 1984

Collins, Raymond F. *Introduction to the New Testament,* SCM Press, London, 1992

Colpe, Carsten. *Die Religionsgeschichtliche Schule,* 1961

Colson, F. H. et al. *Philo.* Loeb Classical Library, London, 1949-

Conzemius, Victor. *Kirchengeschichte als nichttheologische Disciplin,* Römische Quartalsschrift 80, 31–37, 1985

Couchoud, P.-L. *Le Mystère de Jésus,* Christianisme 3, Paris, 1926

Crick, Francis. *The Astonishing Hypothesis.* Scribner, New York, 1993

Cumont, Franz. *Les religions orientales dans le paganisme Romain,* Paris, 1929

Cumont, Franz. *l'Egypte des astrologues,* Bruxelles, 1937

Daalen, D. H. van. 'The emunah/pistis of Habakkuk 2.4 and Romans 1.17', Studia Evangelica 7, 523–27, 1962

Dahl, N. A. *Jesus the Christ,* Fortress, Minneapolis, 1991

Dahl, Nils Alstrup. *Eschatologie und Geschichte im Lichte der Qumrantexte,* Festschr. Bultmann, Zeit u Geschichte, ed. Erich Dunkler, 1964

Daniélou, Jean. *Théologie du Judéo-Christianisme,* Paris, 1957

Daube, David. *The New Testament and Rabbinic Judaism,* London, 1956

Davids, Peter H. 'The Pseudepigrapha in the catholic epistles'. See Charlesworth & Evans, 1993

Davies, P. R., & White, R. T (eds). *A Tribute to Geza Vermes,* Journal for the Study of the Old Testament, Sheffield, 1990

Davies, Philip. *Khirbet Qumran Revisited,* Coogan et al., 1994

Davis, P. R. 'The Teacher Righteousness and the End of Days', RQ 13, 313–317, 1988

Davis, P. R. 'Where is Damascus?' RQ 14, 503–520, 1989–90

Davis, P. R. 'Qumran and Apocalyptic or Obscurum per Obscurius', Journal of Near Eastern Studies 49, 1237–134, 1990

Dearman, J. Andrew. *Religion and Culture in Ancient Israel,* Hendrickson, Peabody Mass., 1992

Dehandschutter, B. 'The Gospel of Thomas and the Synoptics', Studia Evangelica 7, 157–160, 1962

Dennett, Daniel. *Consciousness Explained.* Allen Lane, London, Boston, 1991

Derrett, Duncan M. 'Social history . . .' Aufstieg 25:1, 549, 1982

Deutsch, Nathaniel. *The Gnostic Imagination,* Brill, Leiden, 1995

Dibelius, Martin, & Greeven, Heinrich. *James*, Revised by Heinrich Greeven, Fortress, 1975

Dimant, Devorah. 'The Biography of Enoch and the Books of Enoch', Vetus Testamentum 33, 14–29, 1983

Downing, F. Gerald. *Cynics and Christian Origins*, T&T Clark, Edinburgh, 1992

Downing, F. Gerald. *Cynics, Paul and the Christian Churches*, Routledge, London and New York, 1988

Downing, F. Gerald. *Christ and the Cynics*, Journal for the Study of the Old Testament, Manuals 4, Sheffield, 1988.

Drews, Arthur *Die Christusmythe*, 1–2, Jena, 1910–11

Driver, G. R. *The Judaean Scrolls*, Oxford, 1965

Droge, Arthur J. 'The Apologetic Dimensions of the Ecclesiastical History', in Attridge & Hata (eds), 492–509, 1992

Drury, John (ed). *Critics of the Bible, 1724–1873,* Cambridge University Press, 1989

Duncan, M. & Derrett, J. 'New Creation: Qumran, Paul, the Church, and Jesus' RQ 13,597–608, 1988

Dupont-Sommer, Alphonse. *Les Écrits esséniens decouverts près de la Mer Morte,* Paris, 1959

Ehrman, Bart D. *The Orthodox Corruption of Scripture,* Oxford University Press, 1993

Eisenman, Robert H. *Maccabees, Zadokites, Christians and Qumran* A New Hypothesis, Brill, Leiden, 1983

Eisenman, Robert H. *James the Just in the Habakkuk Pesher,* Brill, Leiden, 1986

Eisenman, Robert H. & Wise, Michael. *The Dead Sea Scrolls Uncovered,* Ellement, Shaftesbury, 1992

Ellegård, Alvar. 'Jesus, Paul, and Early Christianity', Lychnos, Lärdomshistoriska Samfundets Årsbok 1990

Ellegård, Alvar. *Myten om Jesus,* Bonniers, Stockholm, 1992

Ellegård, Alvar. 'Den esséiska kalendern', in Kronholm, 1996

Encyclopedia Britannica, 15th ed. 'Biblical Literature', Chicago, 1986

Encyclopedia of Religion, Mircea Eliade. (ed.) 'Biblical Literature', Macmillan, New York, 1993

Englund, Gertie (ed). *The Religion of the Ancient Egyptians*, Almqvist & Wiksell, Uppsala, 1989

Ettisch, Ernst. Eschatologisch-Astrologische Vorstellungen in der Gemeinderegel', RQ 21, 3–19, 1959–60

Evans, Craig A. 'Luke and the Re-written Bible', in Charlesworth & Evans, 1993

Evans, Craig A. *Nag Hammadi Texts and the Bible*, Brill, Leiden, 1993

Feld, Helmut. 'Der Hebräerbrief', Aufstieg 25:4, 3522–3601, 1987

Feldman, Louis H. *Jew and Gentile in the Ancient World*, Princeton U.P., 1993

Finan, Thomas, & Twomey, Vincent (eds). *The Relationship between Neoplatonism and Christianity*, Four Courts, Dublin, 1992

Finney, Paul Corby. *The Invisible God: The Earliest Christians on Art*, Oxford UP, New York, 1994

Fishbane, Michael. *Biblical interpretatione in Ancient Israel*, Oxford UP, 1988

Fitzmyer, J. A. 'The Dead Sea Scrolls and the New Testament after Forty Years', RQ 13, 609–620, 1988

Flusser, David. *The Dead Sea Sect and Pre-Pauline Christianity*, Scripta Hierosol. 4, Jerusalem, 1958

Flusser, David. 'Jesus and Judaism, Jewish perspectives', in Attridge & Hata, pp. 80–109, 1992

Foakes, F. J. & Lake, Kirsopp (eds). *The Acts of the Apostles*, London, 1920

Ford, J. Massyngberde. *Revelation*, Anchor Bible, Doubleday, Garden City NY, 1975

Fornberg, Tord, & Hellholm, David. *Biblical texts in their ... contexts*, Festschrift Lars Hartman, Scandinavian UP Oslo, 1995

Fox, Robin Lane. *Pagans and Christians*, Viking, London, 1987

Franzmann, Majella. *Jesus in the Nag Hammadi Writings*, Clark, Edinburgh, 1996

Frend, W. H. C. *Martyrdom and persecution in the early Church*, Oxford, 1965

Frey, Jean-Baptiste (ed). *Rome, 1936–1952*; KTAV, New York 1975

Froidevaux, L. M. *Irénée de Lyon*, Sources Chretiennes, 62, Paris, 1959

Frölich, J. 'The symbolical language of the annual apocalypse of Enoch', RQ 14, 629–636, 1989–90

Gerleman, Gillis. *Der Heidenapostel*. Almqvist & Wiksell, Stockholm, 1989

Ginzel, F. K. *Handbuch der mathematischen und technikschen Chronologie*, I-III, 1906–14

Giordano, Carlo, & Kahn, Isidoro. *The Jews in Pompeii,* Procaccini, Naples, 1979

Glover, T. R. *Tertullian: Apologia,* Loeb Classical Library, 1931

Goguel, Maurice. *La Vie de Jésus,* Payot, Paris, 1952

Golb, Norman. 'The Problem of Origin and Identification of the Dead Sea Scrolls', Proc. Am. Philos. Soc. 124, 1–24, 1980

Golb, Norman. *The Dead Sea Scrolls,* American Scholar 58, 177–207, 1989

Golb, Norman. 'Khirbet Qumran and the Manuscripts of the Judaean Wilderness: Observations of the Logic of their Investigation', Journal of Near Eastern Studies 49, 103–114, 1990

Golb, Norman. *Who Wrote the Dead Sea Scrolls?* Simon & Schuster, New York, 1995

Goldstein, Bernard R., & Cooper, Alan. 'The festivals of Israel and Judah . . .', Journal of the American Oriental Society, 110, 1990

Goldstein, Jonathan A. *Semites, Iranian, Greeks, and Romans,* Brown Judaic Studies, 217, Atlanta, 1990

Goodenough, Erwin R. *Goodenough on the History of Religion and on Judaism,* Scholars Press, Atlanta Ga., 1986

Goodenough, Erwin R. *Jewish symbols in the Greco-Roman period,* 1–12, Pantheon Books, Kingsport, Tenn., 1953–1966

Goodman, Martin. *The Ruling Class of Judaea,* Cambridge UP, 1987

Goodman, Martin. *Mission and conversion,* Oxford UP, 1994

Grabbe, Lester L. 'The End of the World in Early Jewish and Christian Calculations', RQ 11, 107–108, 1982–4

Grant, Robert M. *Gnosticism and Early Christianity,* Clarendon, Oxford, 1966

Grant, Robert M. *Eusebius as Church Historian,* Clarendon, Oxford, 1980

Greenfield. J. C. & Stone, Michael E. 'The Enochic Pentateuch and the Date of the Similitudes', Harvard Theological Review, 70, 51–65, 1977

Grelot, Pierre. 'Jean 8.56 et Jubilés 16.16–29', RQ 13, 621–628, 1988

Gressman, Hugo. *Der Messias,* Göttingen, 1929

Griggs, C. Wilfred. *Early Egyptian Christianity*, Brill, Leiden, 1990

Grässer, Erich 'Der Historische Jesus im Hebräerbrief', Zeitschrift für die Neutestamentliche Wissenschaft, 63–91, 1957

Grözinger, K. E. (ed). *Qumran,* Darmstadt, 1981

Guerra, Anthony J. 'Romans: Paul's Purpose and Audience', Revue Biblique 93, 219–237, 1990

Guerra, Anthony J. *Romans and the apologetic tradition,* Cambridge. UP, 1995

Gärtner, Bertil. *Die rätselhaften Termini Nazoräer und Iskariot,* Horae Soederblomianae 4 Lund 1957

Gärtner, Bertil. *The Temple and the Community in Qumran and the New Testament,* Cambridge UP, 1965

Hadas-Lebel, Mireille. 'Évolution de l'image de Rome auprès des Juifs.' Aufstieg 20:1, 715–856, 1987

Haenchen, Ernst. *Die Apostelgeschichte,* Göttingen, 1956

Haenchen, Ernst. A Commentary on the Gospel of John, ed. R. W. Funk with Ulrich Busse, 1980

Haenchen, Ernst. *John* 1–2, Fortress, Philadelphia, 1984

Hahneman, Geoffrey. *The Muratorian Fragment and the Development of the Canon,* Clarendon, Oxford, 1992

Harnack, Adolph von. *Geschichte der altchristlichen Literatur bis Eusebius,* Leipzig, 1893-

Harnack, Adolph von. *Die Mission und Ausbreitung des Christentums in den ersten drei Jahrhunderten,* Wiesbaden, 1924

Hartin, P. J. & Petzer, H. (eds). *Text and Interpretation,* Brill, Leiden, 1991

Hazlett, Ian (ed). *Early Christianity,* SPCK, 1991

Hedrick, Ch. W. & Hodgson, Rob. (eds). *Nag Hammadi, Gnosticism, and Early Christianity,* Hendrickson, Peabody Mass., 1986

Hellholm, David (ed). *International Colloquium on Apocalypticism.* Mohr, Tübingen, 1983

Hemer, Colin J. *The Book of Acts in the Setting of Hellenistic History,* Mohr, Tübingen, 1989

Henaut, Barry W. *Oral Tradition and the Gospels.* Journal for the Study of the Pseudepigrapha, Suppl. Series 3, Sheffield, 1993

Hengel, Martin. *Judaism and Hellenism,* Philadelphia, 1974

Henne, Philippe. *L'Unité du Pasteur d'Hermas,* Cahiers de la Revue Biblique 31, Paris, 1992

Henne, Philippe. 'La Datation du Canon de Muratori', Revue Biblique 100, 54–75, Paris, 1993

Hennecke, Edgar. *New Testament Apocrypha,.* Translated by R. Mc L. Wilson, 1–2, Lutterworth, London, 1963

Henten, J. W. van (ed). *Die Entstehung der jüdischen Martyrologie,* Brill, Leiden, 1989

Hoffmann, Paul (ed). *Zur neutest. Überlieferung von der Auferstehung Jesu,* Wege d Forschung, 522, 1988

Hoffman, R. Joseph (ed). *The Origins of Christianity,* Prometheus, Buffalo, 1985

Hoffman, R. Joseph. *Marcion: On the Restitution of Christianity*, American Academy of Religion, Series 46, Scholars Press, Atlanta, 1984

Hollenbach, Paul W. 'The conversion of Jesus', Aufstieg 25:1, 196–219, 1982

Hopkins, Denise Damkowski. 'Hodayot, a reassessment', RQ 10, 323–364, 1979–81

Hübner, Hans, 'Paulusforschung seit 1945', Aufstieg 25:4, 2649–2840, 1987

Iacubovici-Boldisor, Constantin. *Die urchristlichen Mysterienkulte . . .* Uni Press, Hochschulschriften 91, Lit, Münster, 1997

Irmschen, Johannes. 'Die Geschichte des frühen Christentums als Bestandteil der Altertumswissenschaft', Klio 7, 408–409, 1989

James, William. *Varieties of Religious Experience.* London, 1903

Jaubert, Annie. *Epitre aux Corinthiens.* Sources Chrétiennes, 167, Paris, 1971

Jaubert, Annie. 'Le calendrier des Jubilées et la Secte de Qumran', Vetus Testamentum 3, 250–64, 1953

Jaubert, Annie. 'Le calendrier des Jubilées et les jours liturgiques de la semaine' Vetus Testamentum 7, 35–61, 1957

Jeremias, J. & Michel, Otto (eds). *Wissenschaftliche Untersuchungen zum NT*, 12, Mohr, Tübingen, 1988

Joly, Robert. *Hermas, Le Pasteur.* Sources Chrétiennes 53, Paris, 1958

Jonas, Hans. *The Gnostic Religion,* Boston, 1958

Jonge, M. de, & Woude, A. S. van der. '11 Q Melchizedek and the New Testament', New Testament Studies, 12, 301–326, 1966

Josipovici, Gabriel. *The Book of God*, Yale University Press, 1988.

Juster, Jean. *Les Juifs dans L'Empire Romain,* Paris, 1914

Kant, Laurence H. 'Jewish inscriptions in Greek and Latin', Aufstieg 20:2, 671–713, 1987

Kasher, Aryeh. *The Jews in Hellenistic and Roman Egypt,* Mohr, Tübingen. 1985

Kee, Howard Clark, *The New Testament in Context,* Prentice-Hall, Englewood Cliffs. 1984

Kee, Howard Clark. 'Defining the 1st c. CE Synagogue', New Testament Studies 4, 1995, 481–500, 1995

Klausner, Joseph. *The Messianic Idea in Israel,* Allen & Unwin, London, 1956

Klein, Günther. *Die Zwölf Apostel*, FRLANT (NF) 59, Göttingen, 1961

Klijn, A. F. J. *Jewish-Christian Gospel Tradition*, Brill, Leiden, 1992

Kloppenborg, John S. *The Formation of Q.*, Fortress, Philadelphia, 1989

Kloppenborg, John S. et al. *Q-Thomas Reader*, Polebridge Press, Sonoma, Cal., 1990

Knibb, Michael A. 'The Teacher of Righteousness – a Messianic Title?', in Davies P. R., & White, R.T., Sheffield, 1990

Koester, Helmut. 'Überlieferung und Geschichte der frühchristlichen Evangelienliteratur', Aufstieg 25.2, 1463–1542

Koester, Helmut. 'Häretiker im Urchristentum als Theologisches Problem', Festschrift Bultmann, 1964

Koester, Helmut. '*Gnomai diaphoroi*, Zeitschrift für Theologie und Kirche 65/2, 60–203, 1968

Koester, Helmut. *Introduction to the New Testament* 1–2, Gruyter, New York, 1980, 1982

Koester, Helmut. *Ancient Christian Gospels*, SCM Press, London, 1990

Koskenniemi, Erkki. *Apollonius von Tyana*, University of Åbo, Finland, 1992

Kosmala, Hans. *Hebräer, Essener, Christen*, Studia Post-Biblica, Leiden, 1959

Kraabel, A. T. 'The Disappearance of the God-fearers', Numen 28 113–126, 1981

Kraabel, A. T. *Goodenough on the beginnings of Christianity*, Brown Judaic Studies 212, Atlanta, 1990

Kraft, R. A. & Nickelsburg, G. W. E. (eds). *Early Judaism and its modern Interpreters*, Scholars Press, Atlanta, 1986

Krause, Martin (ed). *Gnosis and Gnosticism*, Brill, Leiden, 1981

Kronholm, Tryggve (ed). *Qumranlitteraturen*, Almqvist & Wiksell International, Stockholm, 1996

Kuhn, Heinz Wolfgang. 'Der irdische Jesus bei Paulus als traditionsgeschichtliches und theologisches Problem', Zeitschrift für Theologie und Kirche, 67, 295–320, 1970

Kümmel, Werner G. *Einleitung in das Neue Testament*, by Feine, Behm & Kümmel, Heidelberg, 1964

Kümmel, Werner G. *Das Neue Testament im 20 Jahrhundert*, Stuttgart, 1970

Kümmel, Werner G. 'Jesus der Menschensohn?' Sitzungsberichte der . . ., Goethe-Universität Frankfurt, 20:3, 1984

Kümmel, Werner G. 'Dreissig Jahre Jesusforschung', Bonner Beiträge, 60, 1985

Kysar, Robert. 'The Fourth Gospel', Aufstieg 25:3, 2389–2480, 1985

Köhler, Wolf Dietrich. *Die Reception des Matthäusevangeliums in der Zeit vor Irenaeus*, Mohr, Tübingen, 1987

Laato, Timo. *Paulus und das Judentum*. Åbo Akademi, Finland, 1991

Lake, Kirsopp, & Lake, Silva. *An Introduction to the New Testament*, Christopher's, London, 1938

Lake, Kirsopp & Oulton, J. E. L. *Eusebius, The Ecclesiastical History*, Loeb Classical Library, London, 1926, 1942

Lampe, Peter. *Die Stadtrömischen Christen in den ersten beiden Jahrhunderten*, Mohr, Tübingen, 1989

Laperrousaz, E. M. *Qoumran*, Paris, 1976

Laperrousaz, E. M. *Les Manuscrits de la Mer Morte*, Paris, 1978

Lease, Gary. 'Jewish Mystery Cults since Goodenough', Aufstieg 20: 858–880, 1987

Lehmann, Martin. *Synoptische Quellenanalyse*, Berlin, 1970

Lehmann, M. R. 'Ben Sira and the Qumran literature', RQ 3, 103–116, 1961–2

Leipoldt, Johannes (ed). *Umwelt des Urchristentums*, Berlin, 1975

Lignée, Hubert. 'La Place du Livre des Jubilés et du Rouleau du Temple', RQ 13, 331–345, 1988

Lilla, Salvatore R. C. *Clement of Alexandria*. A study in Christian Platonism and Gnosticism, Oxford Theological Monographs, Oxford, 1971

Logan, A. H. B & Wedderburn, A. J. M. (eds). *The New Testament and Gnosis*, Festschr Robert Mc L. Wilson, Edinburgh, 1983

Lohse, D. E. 'Wie Christlich ist die Offenbarung des Johannes?' New Testament Studies 34, 321–338, 1988

Lüdemann, Gerd. *Untersuchungen zur simonianischen Gnosis*, Göttingen, 1975

Lüdemann, Gerd. *Paulus, der Heidenapostel*, Göttingen, 1980

Lüdemann, Gerd. *Das frühe Christentum nach der Traditionen der Apostelgeschichte*, Göttingen, 1987

Mack, Burton L. *Mark and Christian Origins*, Fortress, Philadelphia, 1988

Mack, Burton L. *A Myth of Origin*, Fortress, Philadelphia, 1991

MacKay, Heather A. *Sabbath and Synagogue*, Brill, Leiden, 1994

MacMullen, Ramsay. *Paganism in the Roman Empire*, Princeton UP, 1981

Magne, Jean. *From Christianity to Gnosis and from Gnosis to Christianity*, Brown Judaic Studies 286, Scholars Press, Atlanta, 1993

Maraoka, Takamitsu. 'Essene in the Septuagint', RQ 8, 267–268, 1972–5

Marcovich, Miroslav. *Iustini Martyris Apologiae*, Patristische Texte und Studien, Gruyter, Berlin, 1994

Marshall, Howard. 'Palestinian and Hellenistic Christianity', NTS 19, 271–287, 1973

Marshall, J. L. 'Melchizedek in Hebrews, Philo, and Justin Martyr', Studia Evangelica 7, 339–342, 1962

Martin, Jochen & Quint, Barbara (eds). *Christentum und Antike Gesellschaft,* Wissenschaftliche Buchgesellschaft, Darmstadt, 1990

Martinez, Florentino Garcia (ed). *The Dead Sea Scrolls Translated*, Brill, Leiden, 1994

Martinez, Garcia & Woude, A. S. van der. 'A Groningen Hypothesis of Qumran Origins', RQ 14, 521–541, 1989–90

Meinhold, Johannes. *Sabbat und Woche*, FRLANT: 5, Göttingen, 1905

Ménard, Jacques-É. *L'Évangile selon Thomas*, Leiden, 1975

Metzger, Bruce M. *The Canon of the NT*, Oxford UP, 1989

Meyer, Marvin (ed). *The Nag Hammadi Library in English*, San Francisco, 1977

Meyers, Eric M. 'The Cultural Setting of Galilee', Aufstieg 19:1, 686–702, 1979

Miller, J. Maxwell & Hayes, John H. *A History of Ancient Israel and Judaea*, Westminster Press, Philadelphia, 1986

Miller, John W. *The Origins of the Bible*, Paulist Press, New York, 1994

Moessner, David P. 'Suffering, Intercession, Eschatological Atonement', in Charlesworth & Evans, 1993

Momigliano, Arnaldo. *Pagans, Jews, and Christians*, Wesleyan UP, distr. Harper & Row, 1986

Morgan, Robert. *Biblical Interpretation*, Oxford UP, 1989

Morgenstern, Julian. 'The Calendar of the Book of Jubilees', Vetus Testamentum 5, 34–76, 1955

Murphy-O'Connor, Jerome (ed). *Paul and Qumran*, Chapman, London, 1990

Neugebauer, Otto. 'The origin of the Egyptian Calendar', Journal of Near Eastern Studies, 396–403, 1942

Neusner, Jacob. *Development of a Legend*, Brill, Leiden, 1970

Neusner, Jacob. 'The Formation of Rabbinic Judaism' Aufstieg 19:1, 3–42, 1979

Neusner, Jacob. *Wrong Ways and Right Ways in the Study of Ancient Judaism*, Scholars Press, Atlanta, 1988

Neusner, Jacob. *Foundations of Judaism*, Fortress, Philadelphia, 1989

Neusner, Jacob. *Jews and Christians*, SCM, London, 1991

Neusner, Jacob (ed.). *Religions in Antiquity*, Festschrift Goodenough, Leiden, 1968

Neusner, Jacob (ed). *Christianity, Judaism, and other Greco-Roman Cults*, 1–4, Brill, Leiden, 1975

Neusner, Jacob (ed). *The Christian and Judaic Invention of History*, Scholars Press, Atlanta, 1990

Neusner, Jacob, et al. *New Perspectives on Ancient Judaism*, Vol. 1, Brown Judaic Studies 206, Scholars Press, Atlanta, 1990

Newman, Carol A. 'Apocalyptic and the discourse of the Qumran Community', Journal of Near Eastern Studies, 49, 135–144, 1990

Newton, Michael. *The Concept of Purity at Qumran and in the Letters of Paul*, Cambridge UP, 1985

Nickelsburg, George W. E. *Jewish Literature between the Bible and the Mishnah*, Fortress, Philadelphia, 1981

Niederwimmer, Kurt. 'Die Frage nach dem Verfasser des zweiten Evangeliums', Zeitschrift für die Neutestamentliche Wissenschaft, 58, 172–188, 1967

Niederwimmer, Kurt. *Die Didache*, Komm. zu den apost. Vätern 1, Göttingen, 1989

Nijendijk, Lambartus W. *Die Christologie des Hirten des Hermas*, Utrecht, 1986

O'Neill, J. C. *The Theology of Acts in its Historical Setting*, SPCK, London, 1961

O'Neill, J. C. 'Glosses and interpolations in the Letters of St Paul', Studia Evangelica 7, 379–380, 1962

Pagels, Elaine. *The Gnostic Gospels*, Random House, New York, 1979

Pareti, Luigi et al. *History of Mankind*, 1–3, London, 1965

Parker, Richard A. *The Calendars of Ancient Egypt*, Oriental Inst. Univ. of Chicago, Studies . . . 26, 1959

Parker, Richard A. & Dubberstein, Waldo H. *Babylonian Chronology*, Brown Univ. Studies 19, 1956

Paulsen, H. *Die Briefe des Ignatius und der Polykarpbrief*, Handbuch zum Neuen Testament 18, Tübingen, 1985.

Pearson, Birger A. *Gnosticism, Judaism and Egyptian Christianity*, Fortress, Minneapolis, 1990

Pearson, Birger A. (ed). 'The Future of Early Christianity', Festschr. Koester Fortress, Minneapolis, 1991

Petersen, William L. 'What text can NT Textual Criticism ultimately reach?' in Aland and Delobel, 1994

Petrement, Simone. *A Separate God. The Christian Origins of Gnosticism*, Harper & Row, San Francisco, 1990

Philonenko, Marc. *Les interpolations chrétiennes des Testaments des Douze Patriarches et les Manuscrits de Qoumran*, Paris, 1960

Philonenko, Marc. *Joseph et Asenath*, Brill, Leiden, 1968

Pokorny, Petr. 'Das Markusevangelium', Aufstieg 25:3, 1969–2035, 1985

Pomykala, Kenneth E. *The Davidic Dynasty*. Tradition in Early Judaism, Early Judaism and its Literature, no. 7, Scholars Press, Atlanta, 1995

Pratscher, Wilhelm. *Der Herrenbruder Jakobus*, FRLANT 139, Göttingen, 1987

Prigent, Pierre. & R. A. Kraft. *Epitre de Barnabé*, Sources Chrétiennes, 172, 1971

Reitzenstein, R. *Die Hellenistischen Mysterienreligionen*, Leipzig, Berlin, 1927

Rese, Martin. 'Das Lukas-evangelium', Aufstieg 25:3, 2258–2328, 1985

Riaud, Jean. 'Les Thérapeutes d'Alexandrie', Aufstieg 20:2, 1189–1295, 1987

Riddle, Donald W. 'The Cephas-Peter problem', Journal of Biblical Literature 59, 169–180, 1940

Riesenfeld, Harald. 'Sabbat et Jour du Seigneur', Festschrift R. W. Manson, 1959

Robinson, James M. *Logoi Sophon*. Zur Gattung der Spruchquelle Q, Festschr, Bultmann, 1964

Robinson, James M. & Koester, Helmut. *Trajectories through Early Christianity*, Fortress, Philadelphia, 1971

Robinson, James M. & Koester, Helmut. Trajectories through Early Christianity, Fortress, Philadelphia, 1971

Rordorf, W. A. *Der Sonntag*, Zürich, 1962

Rordorf, W & Tullier, A. *La Didachè*. Sources Chrétiennes, 248, Paris 1978

Rudolph, Kurt. *Die Gnosis*, Göttingen, 1979

Rudolph, Kurt (ed). *Gnosis und Gnosticismus,* Wissenschaftl. Buchgesellschaft, Darmstadt, 1975

Räisänen, Heikki. *Beyond NT Theology*, SCM, London, 1990

Sacchi, P. 'Messianisme à la lumière de 11 Q Melch', Zeitschrift für die Alttestamentliche Wissenschaft, 100, Suppl., 205–213, 1988

Sagnard, F. *Irénée de Lyon, Contre Les Hérésies*, Sources Chrétiennes 34, Paris, 1952

Sanders, E. P. *Jesus and Judaism,* SCM 1980

Sanders, E. P. (ed). *Paulus und der Historische Jesus,* Philadelphia, 1980

Sanders, J. P. 'Why the Pseudepigrapha?' in Charlesworth & Evans, 1993

Sanders, E. P. (ed). *Jewish and Christian Self-determination*, Philadelphia, 1980

Sandmel, Samuel. *Philo of Alexandria*, Oxford UP, 1979

Schaefer, Konrad R. 'Zechariah 14 and the Book of Zechariah', Revue Biblique, 100, 368–398, 1993

Schiffman, Laurence H. *Reclaiming the Dead Sea Scrolls*, Jerusalem, 1994

Schmithals, Walter. *Das Kirchliche Apostolat*, FRLANT 61, Göttingen, 1961

Schmithals, Walter. *Paulus und Jakobus,* FRLANT 85, Göttiongen, 1963

Schmithals, Walter. 'Paulus und der Historische Jesus', Zeitschrift für die Neutestamentliche Wissenschaft 53, 145–160, 1968

Schnelle, Udo. *Antidoketische Christologie im Johannesevangelium.* FRLANT 144, Göttingen, 1987

Schoeps, H. J. *Theologie und Geschichte des Judenchristentums*, Mohr, Tübingen, 1948

Schoeps, Hans Joachim. *Paulus*, Mohr, Tübingen, 1959

Schwarz, Daniel H. 'On Quirinus, John the Baptist, The Benedictions, Melchizedek, Qumran and Ephesus', RQ 13, 635–646, 1988

Schürer, Emil. *Geschichte des jüdischen Volkes im Zeitalter Jesu Christi*, 1901

Schürer, Emil 'Die siebentägige Woche', Zeitschrift für die Neutestamentliche Wissenschaft 6, 1–66, 1905

Schürer, Emil. *The History of the Jewish People in the Age of Jesus*

Christ, A new English ed, revised and edited by Geza Vermes, Fergus Millar, and Martin Goodman, III:1, Clark, Edinburgh, 1986

Schäfer, Peter. *Hadrian's Policy in Judaea and the Bar Kochba Revolt*, Journal for the Study of the Old Testament, Suppl. Series 100, Sheffield, 1990

Schönfeld, Hans Gottfried. 'Zum Begriff Therapeutai bei Philo', RQ 3, 219–240, 1961–2

Scott, Alan. *Origen and the Life of the Stars,* Oxford UP, 1991

Segal, Alan F. *Paul the Convert*, Yale UP, 1990

Segal, Alan F. *Two Powers in Heaven*, Brill, Leiden, 1977

Segal, Alan F. *Rebecca's Children*, Harvard UP, Cambridge Mass, 1986

Segal, Alan F. *The Other Judaisms,* Brown Judaic Studies 127, Scholars Press, Atlanta, 1987

Segal, J. B. 'Intercalation and the Hebrew Calendar', Vetus Testamentum 7, 250–307, 1957

Sharpe, Eric John. *Comparative Religion: A History,* Duckworth, London, 1986

Shuler, Philip L. 'Philo's Moses and Matthew's Jesus', Studia Philonica Annual 2, 86–103, Atlanta 1990

Siegel, Jonathan P. 'Two further Medieval References to the TR', RQ 9, 437–440, 1977–8

Silberman, Lou H. 'The Two Messiahs of the Manual of Discipline', Vetus Testamentum 5, 77–82. 1955

Silberman, Neil Asher. *The Hidden Scrolls*, Putnam, New York, 1994

Simon, Marcel. *Les Premiers Chrétiens,* Paris, 1952

Simon, Marcel. *Les Sectes juives au temps de Jésus,* Presses Universitaires Francaises, Paris, 1960

Simon, Marcel. *La Civilisation de l'Antiquité et le Christianisme*, Paris, 1972

Sjöberg, Erik. *Der Menschensohn im Äthiopischen Henochbuch*, Acta reg. Soc Hum. Lit 41, Lund, 1946

Smallwood, E. Mary. *The Jews under Roman Rule,* Brill, Leiden, 1976

Smith, Jonathan Z. *Map is not Territory,* Chicago UP, 1993

Smith, Morton. *Clement of Alexandria,* Harvard UP, 1973

Snyder, Walter F. 'When was the Alexandrian calendar established?' American Journal of Philology 64, 385–398, 1943

Sordi, Marta. *The Christians and the Roman Empire*, Croom Helm, London, Sydney, 1983

Spicq, C. (rev. B. W. Buchanan, To the Hebrews) RQ 8, 651–654, 1972–5

Spicq, C. 'Hebrews' Aufstieg 25:4, 3602–3618, 1989

Spicq, C. 'L'Épitre aux Hebreux et Philon', Aufstieg, 25:4, 3602–3618, 1987

Stambaugh, John E. & Balch, David L. *The New Testament in its Social Environment*, Westminster Press, Philadelphia, 1986

Stanton, Graham. 'Origin and Purpose of Matthew's Gospel', Aufstieg, 25:3, 1889–1951, 1985

Stauffer, Ethelbert. 'Jesus, Geschichte und Verkundigung', Aufstieg, 25:1, 3–130, 1982

Stegemann, Wolfgang. 'War der Apostel Paulus ein römischer Bürger?' Zeitschrift für die Neutestamentliche Wissenschaft 78, 200–229, 1987

Stendahl, Krister (ed). *The Scrolls and the New Testament*, Harper, New York, 1957

Stendel, Annette. *Der Midrasch zur Eschatologie* (4Q Midr Eschat), Brill, Leiden, 1994

Strauss, David Friedrich. *Das Leben Jesu kritisch bearbeitet*, Tübingen, 1835

Stroumsa, Gedaliahu A. G. *Another Seed: Studies in Gnostic Mythology*, Brill, Leiden 1984

Swanson, Dwight D. *The Temple Scroll and the Bible*, Brill, Leiden, 1995

Teeple, Howard M. 'The Origin of the Son of Man Christology', Journal of Biblical Literature 84, 213–250, 1965

Teeple, Howard M. 'The Oral Tradition that never existed', Journal of Biblical Literature 89, 56–67, 1970

Thackeray, H. St John. *Josephus*, vol. 1–9, Loeb Classical Library, 1926–

Theissen, Gerd. *The Gospels in Context*, Clark, Edinburgh, 1982

Thiede, Carsten P. *The earliest gospel manuscript?* Paternoster Press, 1992

Toynbee, Arnold (ed). *The Crucible of Christianity*, London, 1969

Turner, John D. (rev. Henry A. Green, *The Economic and Social Origins of Gnosticism*), Journal of Biblical Literature 107, 156–158, 1988

Tyloch, Withold. 'Quelques Remarques sur la provenance essénienne du Livre des Jubilées', RQ 13, 347–352, 1988

Ulrich, Eugene, & Vanderkam, James (eds). *The Community of the Renewed Covenant (Qumran)*, Notre Dame, Indiana, 1994

Urman, Dan & Flesher, Paul V. M. (eds). *Ancient Synagogues*, Brill, Leiden, 1995

Vanderkam, James C. 'Bible Interpretation in 1 Enoch and Jubilees', in Charlesworth & Evans, 1993

Vanderkam, James C. *The Dead Sea Scrolls Today,* SPCK, Eerdmans, Grand Rapids, Michigan, 1994

Vanderkam, James C. *The Book of Jubilees*, Peeters, Loewen, 1989

Vermes, Geza. *The Dead Sea Scrolls: Qumran in Perspective*, Fortress, Philadelphia, 1981

Vermes, Geza. *Jesus the Jew*, SCM, London, 1983

Vermes, Geza. *The Dead Sea Scrolls in English*, Sheffield, 1987

Vielhauer, Philipp. 'Erwägungen zur Christologie des Markusevangeliums', Festschr. Bultmann, 1964

Vielhauer, Philipp. *Geschichte der urchristl. Literatur*, Gruyter, Berlin, 1975

Voelz, James W. 'The Language of the New Testament', Aufstieg, 25:2, 893–977, 1983

Wacher, John (ed). *The Roman World II*, Routledge & Kegan Paul, London, 1987

Wacholder, Ben Zion. 'Does Qumran record the Death of the Moreh?', RQ 13, 323–330, 1988

Waerden, B. L. van der. 'History of the Zodiac', Archiv für Orientforschung 16, 216–30, 1952–3

Walker, William O. Jr. *The Relationships among the Gospels*, Trinity UP, San Antonio, 1978

Wallis, Richard T. (ed.). *Neoplatonism and Gnosticism*, New York State UP, 1975, 1986

Weder, Hans. *Das Kreuz Jesu bei Paulus*, FRLANT (NF) 125, Göttingen, 1981

Wells, George A. *The Jesus of the Early Christians*, Pemberton, London, 1971

Wells, George A. *The Historical Evidence for Jesus*, Prometheus, Buffalo, 1982

Wells, George A. *Did Jesus Exist?* Pemberton, London, 1988

Wells, George A. *The Jesus Legend*. Chicago. 1996

Wendland, Paul. *Die Hellenistisch-Römische Kultur*, Handbuch zum Neuen Testament 2, Tübingen, 1972

Werblowsky, R.J. Zwi. 'Messianism in Jewish History', Journal of World History, 30–45, 1968

Whiteley, D. E. H. 'Was John written by a Sadducee?' Aufstieg 25:3, 2481–2505, 1985

Wieluch, D. 'Zwei Neue antike Zeugen über Essener', Vetus Testamentum 7, 418–419, 1957

Wilcox, Max. 'Jesus in the Light of his Jewish environment', Aufstieg 25:1, 131–195, 1982

Wilken, Robert L. *The Christians as the Romans Saw Them*, Yale UP, 1984

Will, Édouard & Orrieux, Claude. *Ioudaismos–Hellenismos,* Presses Univ. de Nancy, 1986

Wilson, R. M. L. *Philo and Gnosticism,* Studia Philonica Annual 5, 84–92, Atlanta, 1993

Winston, David. 'Judaism and Hellenism: Hidden Tensions in Philo's Thought', Studia Philonica Annual 2, 1–19, Atlanta, 1990

Wise, M. O. 'The Teacher of Righteousness and the High Priest', RQ 14, 587–613, 1989–90

Wise, Michael Owen. *Thunder in Gemini*. Journal for the Study of the Pseudepigrapha, Suppl. Series 15, Sheffield, 1994

Wolter, Michael. *Die Pastoralbriefe als Paulustradition*, FRLANT, Göttingen, 1988

Wolters, Al. 'The last treasure of the Copper Scroll', Journal of Biblical Literature, 107, 419–429, 1988

Zerbe, Gordon. 'Pacifism and Passive Resistance in Apocalyptic Writings', in Charlesworth & Evans, 1993

Zimmermann, Alfred F. *Die urchristlichen Lehrer*, see Jeremias & Michel, 1988

Zur, Yiphtah. 'Parallels between Acts of Thomas 6–7 and 4Q 184', RQ 16, 105–107, 1993

Notes

Page numbers are given before each note number.

Chapter 1 *(pp. 13-30)*

13   1. See Chapter. 9, on dating.

14   2. Besides Koester, e.g. W. Stegemann 1987, p. 228.

14   3. On this, see Lüdemann 1980, 1, p. 41, Schmithals 1961, p. 237, Schmithals 1963, p. 40. Schenken in Pearson (ed) 1991, p. 319 says Koester was the first to doubt that Paul was from Tarsus, and that he was a Roman citizen. Stegemann 1987, p. 228 says it is 'not likely' that Paul was a Roman citizen.

15   4. That date is based on the following argument. Most of our texts, including both Paul, the six texts treated in Chapter 2, and the Gospels, are consistent with the first 'apostles' having experienced visions of the risen Christ around AD 30–35. As I shall argue below, this does not mean that Jesus' crucifixion occurred then. But the visions were taken as evidence of his resurrection. Bultmann (quoted by Kloppenborg 1989, p. 20) also stresses that no Christianity existed before the resurrection.

15   5. Gal 1:12.

       6. Meaning Mark, Matthew and Luke. The word synoptic refers to the fact that these Gospels, as distinct from John, present Jesus' deeds in roughly the same sequence. In this way they can be presented together in parallel columns, offering a simultaneous, synoptic view.

16   7. Charlesworth 1993, p. 125 suggests it may be a quotation from a Jerusalem catechism. See also Brown 1984, p. 34: 'the phrases "on the third day" and "the Twelve" do not occur elsewhere in the Pauline corpus, and the Greek verb forms rendered "he was raised" and "he appeared" are not found outside this chapter.'

16   8. See Hoffmann (ed) 1988, pp. 92–103.

17   9. See Chapter 2, last section. A. Harnack, in Hoffmann 1988, p. 92–103, and MacArthur, ibid., p. 196 express similar opinions.

17   10. Wisdom literature is a cover term for such Biblical books as Proverbs, Job, the Songs of Solomon, Ecclesiastes, and apocryphal books like Ben Sira (Ecclesiasticus) and the Wisdom of Solomon. Many of the Psalms also have the character of Wisdom literature.

18   11. The importance of the Wisdom traditions for early Christians is well

291

brought out in Wells 1996.

18   12. I discuss these matters in Chapter 12. Hoffman 1984, p. 131, and several other scholars, thinks 1 Cor 15:5–8 may be an interpolation.

19   13. We might add that Wolter 1988, p. 104 quotes Hieronymus as saying that, according to the Gospel of the Hebrews (note: not the *Letter to the Hebrews*), it was James who saw the risen Jesus first. See also Chapter 12.

19   14. Kuhn 1970, pp. 295–320 is one of the highly respected contemporary theological scholars who recognises that Paul's silence on the earthly Jesus is a real problem for the theologian. Similarly Kümmel 1985 in Merklein (ed), p. 31 ff.

20   15. In Rom 16:16 we read 'Churches of Christ'. But this chapter in Romans may be post-Pauline.

20   16. e.g. 1 Cor 10:32; 15:9; Gal 1:13.

20   17. See especially 1 Cor 9.

20   18. For a rather speculative account of Paul and the Jerusalem community, see Eisenman 1997.

21   19. Feldman 1993, p. 322, maintains that synagogue sermons were generally directed to Gentiles present, for the purpose of proselytising. See also Z. Safrai in Urman and Flesher (eds) 1995, p. 203, on the openness of the synagogues: 'community centres'. They also served as hotels for visitors.

21   20. Apostates are considered an important problem in Hermas and Hebrews (ch. 2), in Philo (ch. 3), and also in 2 Baruch (ch. 5). Note also that the word sinners may refer to Jews who interpreted the law allegorically. See below.

21   21. See Chapter 3, especially on Hermas. See also Guerra 1995, p. 26. Note also that in Gal 2:2 we read 'the gospel which I preach among the Gentiles (*en tois ethnesin*).

23   22. On Christians and Essenes, see Chapter 4.

24   23. Such a usage is found in Rom 16:16, 1 Cor 15:9, 16:19 and Gal 1:13.

24   24. On *sunagōgē*, see Chapter 2.

24   25. The holiness idea is probably partly due to Isa 62:12, where the holiness of the elect is connected with the End of Time.

24   26. See Chapters 9 and 11. The word used for 'be separate' is Greek *aphorizō*, harking back to Lev 15:31 and 22:2 Hebrew *nazar*. See also Isa 52:11.

24   27. Hoffman 1984, pp. 243, 268 stresses the strong overall Jewish presence in such cities of Asia Minor as Laodicea, Colossae and Ephesus.

25   28. In 1 Thess 2:16 Paul speaks of the 'Jews ... forbidding us to speak to the Gentiles that they might be saved'.

25   29. On the changes in the communities' conceptions of Jesus, see Chapter 2.

25   30. Charlesworth 1985, p. 123 says: 'None of the OT passages [on the Last Judgment] describes a general forensic judgment following a resurrection.... The Old Testament Day of the Lord originally involved punishment of God's enemies.'

25   31. Charles 1913, II, p. 164 ff. has a long list of textual parallels.

25 32. Schoeps 1959, p. 32 points out that eschatological high tension apparently lasted in Palestine throughout the period from Daniel to Bar Kochba, nearly three centuries. On the imminence of the Judgment, see also Rom 13:2 'the day is at hand', Rom 16:22 'Maranatha' (Lord, come!), 2 Cor 5:10 'the judgment seat of Christ', Philipp 2:16: 'that I may rejoice in the day of Christ', 1 Thess 1:10: 'Jesus which delivered us from the wrath to come', 1 Thess 5:2: 'The day of the Lord so cometh as a thief in the night.'

26 33. See Chapter 3, in connection with Philo.

26 34. 1 Cor 11:26 'ye do show the Lord's death till he come' (*achris hou an elthē*), and 1 Thess 1:10 'to wait for his Son from heaven' (*anamenein ton huion autou ek tōn ouranōn*) (note: not the *return* of his Son). Otherwise, the most common Greek expression is simply *parousia*, 'arrival'. See also Chapter 2, end. It is worth noting that, in Jn 14:3, Jesus says, 'If I go and prepare a place for you, I will *come again* and receive you unto myself.' This was a natural way to express oneself in a context where Jesus lives among his disciples. At the same time it shows that the avoidance of the word *return* in the first-century texts is a significant indication that their authors did *not* regard the earthly Jesus as a contemporary.

26 35. Hoffman 1984, p. 110. Note also Irenaeus' polemics against those (among them, primarily Marcion) who thought 'Paul alone knew the truth' (*Against Heresies*, 3:13).

Chapter 2 (pp. 37–77)

31 1. An excellent discussion of the problems involved, with reference to the New Testament, is to be found in Bart D. Ehrman 1993.

32 2. See Griggs 1990, p. 175, quoting Bart Ehrman.

32 3. On synagogues, see also Chapter 11.

32 4. There are two instances in Revelation, but only in the sense of 'community', not 'building'. On this, see Urman & Flesher 1995.

33 5. See Urman & Flesher, summarised pp. xx–xxv.

33 6. Several writers have indeed drawn attention to the absence of the word synagogue in Paul, and its frequent use in the Gospels (Kraabel 1981, p. 118; MacKay 1994, p. 155). But they have not put these facts in connection with the dating of the Gospels. And I have not seen any mention of the absence of the word in the first-century texts I discuss in Chapter 2 – which were so dated by me before I had discovered their usage as regards *sunagōgē*.

33 7. Ignatius, writing probably in the first decade of the second century AD, has two instances of *saints*: Phil 12:3, and Smyrna 1:2.

33 8. See this chapter, below.

34 9. First suggested by Baumgarten 1982, p. 285.

35 10. *Saints* occurs in all the documents, *Church of God* in Hermas, Didachē and 1 Clement, *elect* in Hermas and Clement.

35 11. The word synagogue here should be taken in the original sense of

'community', not 'building'.

35   12. Hengel 1974, p. 140 says the first occurrence of the idea of Two Ways is in Ben Sira (Ecclesiasticus). Charlesworth 1992, p. 187 thinks the Two Ways' concept is influenced by Essenism.

38   13. Present-day scholars regard the Letters to Timothy as second-century productions, which of course further reduces the strength of Eusebius' argument on this point.

38   14. Harnack 1893, 2, p. 190 mentions that Tertullian had Clement as the *first* bishop of Rome.

38   15. See Chapter 3.

39   16. Jaubert 1971, pp. 167–8, note 6.

39   17. Several Qumran documents, for instance, give 60 as the maximum age for community leaders. See 11QT, fol 57, CD, fol 10.

40   18. Jaubert 1971, pp. 19–20.

40   19. Feldman 1993, p. 54–75.

42   20. See above, this chapter, the notice about Horace and the Sabbaths, Chapters 3 and 4.

42   21. That is the picture of Jesus that emerges from Didachē and Hermas, below.

44   22. See Koester 1990, pp. 1–48 for a full discussion of the meaning of *euaggelion* in the early texts.

44   23. On the importance of Luke's Acts of the Apostles, and Eusebius's Church History in cementing this consensus, see below Chapters 8–11.

45   24. I use the edition of Robert Joly, *Sources Chrétiennes* 53, 1958.

45   25. Note that Clemens Alexandrinus, who leaned towards Gnosticism, and suffered for it, appreciated Hermas, and considered it as 'inspired'and thus worthy of being included in the 'canon'.

45   26. Joly 1958, pp. 11–16. Nijendijk 1986, p. 192, suggests *c.* AD 100 'in the present form'. Brox 1991 sides with the majority for AD 140.

45   27. Koester 1990, p. 243 suggests the fourth century for the Muratori fragment. Against this, see Brox 1991, p. 15, n. 3. Koester 1980:2, p. 258 dates Hermas 60–160, while Hahneman 1992 argues strongly for a date 'before AD 100'.

46   28. Joly 1958, p. 58 ff.

46   29. The Romans at this time naturally regarded the Christians as Jews, and naturally could not distinguish between Christians (in the modern sense), and other Messianic Jews. The expulsion of Jews, 'who were stirred up by one Chrestus', is mentioned by Suetonius (writing in the early second century, in *Vita Claudii* 25:3–4).

47   30. See Chapter 3.

47   31. In 4 Ezra 10:27 and 10:47 we read about a vision of a woman changing into Mount Zion.

47   32. E.g. 1 Cor 3:9; 6:15; 12:27; 2 Cor 6:16; Rom 12:5.

48   33. See Kloppenborg et al., 1990, p. 102, who hold that the Gospel versions can hardly be connected with Isa 5. Instead, they seem to be influenced by Cynic ideas. On Cynicism and Christianity, see Downing 1992.

48   34. It is worth mentioning, in this connection, that Minucius Felix's novel

Octavius, usually dated to the beginning of the third century, never names Jesus, or Christ, though the hero is called a Christian. Obviously, Minucius regarded the Christians as a branch of the Jewish community.

48   35. p. 16 in his edition.

49   36. See my discussion on 'return' in Chapter 1.

49   37. See Grant 1966, p. 122: 'thoroughly Jewish', 'Essene'.

49   38. 'Sinners' presumably here referring to lapsed Jews.

49   39. It is useful to keep in mind that the '12 tribes' are, in the period we are concerned with, largely fictional. See Kraabel 1990, p. 104, Miller et al. 1986, pp. 78, 92, 108.

50   40. Koester 1980:2 p. 258 calls Hermas 'basically Jewish', and Grant 1966, p. 123 agrees that it is 'very Jewish'. The fact that it was not included in the later Christian canon may be simply that it was clearly not written by one of the apostles or a follower of an apostle (Kümmel 1964, p. 36).

50   41. Hengel 1974, p. 140 points out that the notion of Two Ways is first found in Ben Sira. Flusser, in Charlesworth 1992, p. 187, looks upon the Didachē version as 'composed in a group that was strongly influenced by Essenism'.

50   42. Martin Hengel 1974, p. 140 points out that the concept of Two Ways is found in *Ecclesiasticus* (Ben Sira), dated in the second century BC.

50   43. The word *ethnos*, plural *ethnē*, which in classical Greek simply means 'nation, people', usually means 'Gentiles, pagans' in a Jewish text, a usage later adopted by the Christians. However, in this context it probably includes also those Jews who live among the Gentiles. See Guerra 1995.

51   44. I use the editions of W. Rordorf and A. Tuilier, *Sources Chrétiennes* 248, 1978, and of J. P. Audet, 1958.

51   45. Koester, in his *Introduction* 2, 1980, p. 158, says 'end of I AD'. Streeter, in Kloppenborg 1989, p. 18, calls it 'a first-century manual of Christian instruction'. Niederwimmer 1989 places it tentatively at the beginning of the second century, with the Jewish portions older than that.

51   46. On the significance of Sunday, see the section on Barnabas, in this chapter.

52   47. Daube 1956, p. 111 declares that Christian baptism originated in Jewish proselyte baptism. On p. 109 he says that some Pharisaic teachers maintained that baptism alone was sufficient to make a male proselyte Jewish. Some argued that as baptism was the decisive rite in the case of a woman, so it should be in that of a man. Later, such universalism came to be regarded as dangerous. Ronny Reich, in Urman and Flesher 1995, pp. 289–97, concludes, admittedly on rather slight archaeological evidence, that first-century synagogues in northern Palestine normally had an immersion bath, a *miqweh*.

53   48. Koester 1991, p. 169: 'The last section of the Sermon on the Mount consistently follows the "Two Ways".'

53   49. See D. Flusser in Attridge & Hata, eds, p. 85, who calls the prayer 'utterly Jewish', and J. Charlesworth in *Aufstieg* 25, p. 464, who refers to parallels in the OT Pseudepigrapha.

53   50. The Qumran expression is, more literally, 'seekers of smooth things'.

53   51. Jaubert 1957, pp. 35–61. It should be noted, however, that the position is not quite clear.

53   52. See Koester 1990, p.1–48, for a thorough discussion of the semantic development of the word.

54   53. See Guerra 1995, p. 26.

55   54. For instance, Mt 2:15, 2:17–18, 2:23, and Jn 12:37, 15:25, 19:36.

55   55. Koester 1980–2, 2, p. 278 confirms that 'the material presented by Barnabas represents the initial stages of the process that is continued in the Gospel of Peter, later in Matthew, and is completed in Justin Martyr'.

55   56. I use the edition of P. Prigent and R. A. Kraft, *Sources Chrétiennes* 172, 1971. They discuss the dating pp. 25–7.

55   57. Koester 1980, II, p. 158 places it around 100.

55   58. Metzger 1989, p. 56 mentions that Clemens Alexandrinus and Origen both regarded the author of the letter as Paul's companion Barnabas.

56   59. For a thorough and critically acute investigation of Davidic messianism see Pomykala 1995.

56   60. On the celebration of Sunday, see also below, and Chapter 5.

56   61. See Koester 1980:1, p. 261.

57   62. In the Greek alphabet the letter н is ēta, pronounced with a long e.

58   63. See Dubarle in Grözinger 1981, p. 216

58   64. The editors do not translate this *kai*, without giving any reasons for the omission. On the significance of the Sunday, see also the discussion of 2 Enoch, ch. 5.

58   65. I discuss the Essene calendar in Chapter 4, and in an article in Swedish (see Kronholm, T. (ed) 1996).

59   66. For Biblical texts I use the British revised authorised version.

60   67. See my discussion on a similar passage in 1 Clement, above.

60   68. See for instance E. J. Bickerman 1988, p. 260, F. F. Bruce in *ANRW* 25, 3514, H. Feld in *ANRW* 25, 3591, E. Isaac in Charlesworth (ed) 1985, II, p. 84, H. W. Attridge 1989, p. 9 says AD 60–100.

61   69. Kosmala 1959 also notes that the Jesus *logia* in Hebrews are in the main quotations from the Old Testament.

62   70. On the Messiah as the Son of David, see Pomykala 1995.

62   71. Philo, *De specialibus legibus* I:55

62   72. Kosmala 1959 argues that Hebrews was directed to a Jewish audience.

63   73. Hoffman 1984 suggests that the letters address Marcionite churches.

63   74. Koester 1982 II, p. 250 opts for the end of the first century, and so does D. H. Lohse 1988, p. 334.

64   75. See Momigliano 1986, p. 114. There seem to have been contemporary legends about Nero returning. He was a popular hero in some circles.

64   76. Sib. Oracles 7, 135. In Charlesworth, James (ed) I, 1983: 'The Hellenistic–Jewish or Christian character of the bulk of the Sibylline Oracles is generally admitted.'

64   77. Charlesworth 1985, p. 125 remarks that the 12 tribes connect Revelation with the Letter of James, 1 Peter, Q, and Mark's Judaean sources.

65   78. See Isa 1:10 and Ezek 23:27.

65   79. Wells 1971 mentions that a medieval form of a Jewish thanksgiving prayer ends: 'Come thou, gracious one.'

66   80. It is worth pointing out that the 'heavenly Jerusalem' is found in 1 Enoch 90, and the Messiah represented as a lamb in 1 Enoch 81:90.

66   81. See Koester 1990, p. 86: the Gospel of Thomas, like Q, has nothing on Jesus' death. Also p. 165: his theology does not include the cross or the resurrection.

67   82. Schoeps 1959, p. 45 points out that the savage attacks on Paul in the Pseudo-Clementines centred on the fact that Paul had to rely on visions.

67   83. We must bear in mind that the common popular astronomical world-view of the time regarded the Heaven, quite concretely, as a sphere or vault above the earth.

67   84. See Harnack 1922 in Hoffman (ed) 1988, p. 92–103.

67   85. Harnack 1924, p. 334 suggests that the passage in 1 Cor 15 is 'a formula of the Jerusalem community', which I think makes sense.

67   86. The 'scripture' referred to may be Hos 6:2.

68   87. Koester 1990, p. 165 points to 'evidence for the continuation of a theology of followers of Jesus that had no relationship to the *kerygma* of the cross and resurrection', and names the Gospel of Thomas, the Dialogue of the Saviour, and the Gospel of John as examples.

68   88. In Toynbee (ed) 1969, p. 269 it is pointed out that the sign of the cross did not 'signify only the Passion. As the last letter of the Hebrew alphabet it was the name of Yahveh, or Christ, and traced as a "seal" (*sphragis*) on the forehead it signified that the believer belonged to him.' Further, H. I. Bell 1953, p. 90 asserts that 'the Egyptian *ankh*, the symbol of life, passed gradually into that form of the Christian cross known as the *crux ansata*'. See also J. M. Robinson in Hoffman 1985, p. 295 on the pre-Christian use of the cross as a symbol of immortality.

69   89. J. Klausner 1956, p. 293 notes that in the Jewish literature, too, the Judge is sometimes the Messiah, sometimes God himself.

70   90. See Koester 1990, pp. 42, 43 and 218, 223, 224, 379, with further references.

70   91. See G. W. Buchanan 1972, p xxii: 'the rabbis frequently took statements of the Old Testament, changed them . . . and . . . applied them to the Messiah.'

70   92. Metzger 1989, p. 42 points out that 1 Clement invokes 'Jesus' words' twice, but the Old Testament a hundred times. For the two instances, see above, the section on 1 Clement.

71   93. Rom 16, however, is of doubtful authenticity.

72   94. Kloppenborg 1989, p. 248 finds that the temptation story 'has every appearance of a later interpolation'.

73   95. Kloppenborg 1989, p. 247 suggests that the story of the temptation was taken from the apocryphal Assumption of Moses. For other parallels see Heb 1:5 ref. Ps 2:7, Heb 2:12, 5:5 and 7:17 ref Ps 110:1, Heb 2:12 ref Ps 22:2, Heb 11:5 ref Ps 40:6–8.

74   96. On the use of apocryphal Scripture, see Chapter 5, especially on Enoch.

74   97. See discussion in Prigent 1971, p. 104, note 5.

74   98. See, e. g., Did 10:5, Herm Vis 3.5.3, Clem 26:1, 49:5. We also find it in other early texts, e.g. Hebr 10:1, 10:14, 13:21, Barn 4:11, 6:19.

75   99. See Hengel 1974, p. 153.

76   100. On the last days as the last epoch, see above.

77   101. On the passage in 1 Cor 15, see Chapter 1.

77   102. It is remarkable that Mt 27:53 has it that 'many of the bodies of the saints which slept arose' when Jesus died.

77   103. The nearest we come is Heb 9:28: 'So Christ was once offered to bear the sins of many: and unto them that look for him shall he appear the second time without sin unto salvation.' The Greek (*ek deuterou*) says 'a second time', or 'once again' rather than 'the second time'.

Chapter 3 (pp. 79–95)

79   1. Alexandria is mentioned in Acts 6:9, about Stephen's difficulties with the synagogues of Cyrene, and 18:24, where the apostle Apollos is said to have been born in Alexandria.

79   2. Remarked upon by Bauer 1934, p. 49.

79   3. Koester 1980–2:1, p. 274 estimates the Jewish population of the city at 100,000 in the first century AD. Hegermann, in Leipoldt 1975, p. 306 thinks Alexandria had a larger Jewish population than Jerusalem. Simon 1952, p. 19 calls Alexandria 'the Jewish metropolis'. Rudolph 1979, p. 304 finds that the Gnostic movement reached its height there.

80   4. Kasher 1985, p. 25 points out that the Jewish uprising in Palestine caused difficulties for the Egyptian Jews too. During the war thousands of Jewish rebels fled to Alexandria, where many ordinary Jews welcomed them, while the Jewish leaders tried to get rid of them.

80   5. Goodman 1994, p. 48 states that the decrease in Egypt after 115 is accompanied by an increase elsewhere in the Empire.

81   6. Among the Jewish writings suggested to have originated in Egypt are the Psalms of Solomon and the Sibylline oracles no. 3,5,11 (Hellholm ed. 1983, pp. 648, 656), Test. Abraham, Test. Job (Nickelsburg 1981, p. 162). Koester 1990, pp. 245, 253 states that the Gospel of John was widely known in Egypt; Schnelle 1987 quotes Marlyn: 'probably originated in Egypt'; Henne 1992, p. 46 points out that Hermas was 'exceptionally popular in Egypt'.

81   7. In particular, the Pentateuch, also called the Torah, the Law.

81   8. It is remarkable that Philo never refers, at least explicitly, to any Jewish writings outside the generally accepted canon – an indication of his 'orthodoxy'.

81   9. *The embassy to Gaius.*

81   10. There is hardly any evidence, however, that he was read outside Jewish or Christian circles. See Sandmel 1979, p. 14.

81   11. He preferred the Stoic term *logos*, 'word', 'order' to the Platonic term *nous*, 'reason' for the divine principle governing the universe. See Segal

1977, p. 162, About another leading philosophical school at the time, the Cynics, see Downing 1988, 1992.

81   12. There was a revival of Neo-Pythagoreanism in the first century BC, says Armstrong in Toynbee (ed) 1969, p. 211.

82   13. On the widespread idea of the divinity of stars, see Scott 1991.

82   14. On the very close dependence of Clemens Alexandrinus on Philo, see Lilla 1971. Like most Christian writers, Lilla seems to assume that Clement was a pagan Athenian before he became a Christian. However, I cannot find that Clement's Athenian origin has any real foundation. It seems to me far more likely that he was a liberal Jew like Philo. To such a man, in second- to third-century Egypt, Egyptian Christianity must have appeared quite attractive.

82   15. Wilken 1984, p. 126.

82   16. BJ 2.8.10.

82   17. BJ 1–3, p. 383.

83   18. BJ 1–3, p. 383.

83   19. BJ 2.8.6–10.

83   20. On the etymology of *essene*, see Schonfeld 1961–2, p. 219, Meyers 1979, p. 730. See also Chapters 4 and 8. Allegro 1979 (1992) pp. 12, 64, thinks it derives from Aramaic *asa*, 'healer'. We should note that Philo translates *therapeutae* as 'healers'.

83   21. Many modern scholars refer to the Therapeutae as an Egyptian branch of the Essenes: e.g. Hengel 1974, p. 247, Kuhn in Stendahl 1957, p. 75. It is true that Philo describes only the Alexandrian Therapeutae, whom he apparently knows from his own experience. But he makes it quite clear that they were an Empire-wide movement. Unaccountably, most modern scholars have it that Philo locates the Therapeutae *exclusively* in Alexandria.

83   22. Vita contemplativa II:21.

83   23. See Chapter 4.

84   24. The Hebrew term for Wisdom, *hokmah*, is grammatically masculine, while Greek *sophia* is feminine. Hence some writers preferred the Greek masculine words, *nous* (reason) and *logos* (word, order). See the beginning of John's Gospel.

87   25. Koschorke in Krause (ed) 1981, p. 192, holds that Egypt was a stronghold of Gnosticism. Lilla 1971, p. 143, even maintains that 'most probably Christianity came to Egypt under the form of Gnosticism'. Similarly Koester 1980–2:2, p. 222, Bell 1953, p. 96.

87   26. See Meyer 1977. A much more elaborate edition is under way, edited by Birger Pearson. Sixteen volumes are planned, which began in 1975.

87   27. See Pearson 1990.

87   28. On the Gnostics, see Rudolph 1979, Krause (ed) 1981, Stroumsa 1984 and, above all, Jonas 1958, a German philosopher strongly influenced by Heidegger and Jung. For an empathetic account, see Pagels 1979. See also Sandmel 1979, and Kraabel 1990, editing an article by Goodenough.

89   29. This is well brought out by Lilla 1971, especially pp. 148–9, on the concept of 'mystery'.

89   30. See Segal 1977, pp. 208–19.

91   31. *Archon* is also used by Paul, e.g. in 1 Cor 2:6. It is also found in the Gospels.

91   32. Known in the West in the Arabicised form *Almagest,* where *al* is the Arabic definite article, and *magest* renders the Greek *mēgistē.*

91   33. See Lilla 1971, on the close links between Gnosticism and Middle Platonism.

92   34. See Goodenough 1953 and Kraabel 1990.

93   35. Some of the legends of Simon were incorporated in the story of Dr Faustus.

95   36. We should keep in mind that the Gnostics also used the designation *Saints* about themselves. Many of the later Gnostics certainly considered themselves as Christians, though the Catholic Church, e.g. Irenaeus, considered them as arch-heretics. The relationship between the early Gnostics and Christianity is an interesting subject, well worth an investigation of its own.

Chapter 4 (pp. 96–124)

96   1. See Charles 1913, Charlesworth 1992, Nickelsburg 1981.

96   2. See Vermes 1981, Martínez (ed) 1994.

96   3. Philonenko 1960 on Test. XII Patr.

97   4. Vanderkam 1994, especially pp. 23–4 and 95–7, rejects Golb's conclusions, but had at that time no access to Golb 1995.

97   5. That the library mirrors a wide range of religious opinion is nowadays accepted by many researchers. See Swanson, p. 241, Talmon in Ulrich and Vanderkam (eds) 1994, p. 8.

97   6. Devorah Dimant in Ulrich et al. (ed) 1994, p. 178. Dimant does not say Essenes, but 'Qumran community'.

98   7. See for instance Stendel 1994, p. 2, Talmon in Ulrich and Vanderkam (eds) 1994, p. 8.

98   8. See, for instance, Nickelsburg 1981, p. 122. Allegro 1992, p. 12 suggests instead Aramaic *asa* meaning 'physician', which might be connected with Philo's therapeutae, which also can have this meaning.

99   9. This view is expressed by Vermes 1981, p. 106, and also S. Talmon in Ulrich et al, (ed) 1994, p. 8: 'This [Qumran] commune, however, only constituted the spearhead of the much wider community of the Renewed Covenant' (Talmon seeks to avoid the term *Essene*).

100   10. See Vanderkam 1994, pp. 29–70, for an informative overview.

100   11. War 2.8.1–10, Ant. 15.10.5.

101   12. Meaning, belonging to both Levi and Judah? On a strict interpretation of the Jewish laws, that would not be possible, since descent is exclusively on the male's side. On the other hand, it does not seem that ordinary Jews kept track of which tribe they belonged to. Paul's mention that he belonged to Benjamin is exceptional. See Goodman 1987, p. 69, who says that a person's tribe is rarely mentioned in the first century AD.

Miller 1986, p. 78 admits that the idea of a twelve-tribe Israel must be considered as 'doubtful'.

101   13. J. A. Goldstein in *Cambridge History of Judaism*, 2, p. 350 says: 'the faith in a Davidic Messiah is conspicuous by its absence from the literature earlier than the Psalms of Solomon.... Only at ... 1 Enoch 90:37 [by spiritual ancestors of the Essenes] is there a Davidic Messiah figure in a text of this age.' See also Pomykala 1995.

101   14. Gen 14:18–20. See also Psalm 110:4: 'Thou art a priest for ever after the order of Melchizedek', which is presumably the basis for the importance attached to Melchizedek in Hebrews 5 and 7.

101   15. 1QS, Vermes, pp. 75, 77.

101   16. 1QM, fol 16, Vermes, p. 121.

101   17. fol 19, Vermes, p. 124.

101   18. Golb 1995 writes 'may well be written by the Teacher of Righteousness'.

101   19. CD fol 12, Vermes, p. 97.

101   20. CD fol 13, Vermes, p. 98.

101   21. CD fol 13, Vermes, p. 99.

101   22. CD, B fol 2, Vermes, p. 91. Note the reference to Salvation, which might suggest 'Jesus' (meaning roughly Salvation) to a Christian reader. For a somewhat reticent discussion of this, see Eisenman & Wise 1992, p. 244.

102   23. CD 2, p. 84 in Vermes. This rather harsh maxim is expressed at several places. On the other hand, we also have compensating pronouncements, e.g 1QS 10 (Vermes, p. 76) 'I shall pursue [my enemy] with goodness', quoted below in this chapter, in the section about the Teacher of Righteousness.

103   24. See Boll, under Hebdomas in Pauly-Wissowa's *Dictionary*.

103   25. Philo devotes much space to the week and the holy number 7, e.g in *De Specialibus Legibus*.

104   26. Note the intriguing correspondence between these figures and the cards in an ordinary pack: 52 cards, 4 suits with 13 cards in each. The origin of this system is an enigma.

104   27. Lignée 1988 thinks it was the main reason for the separation of the Essenes from the mainstream Jews. This may be overstating the case.

104   28. Beckwith 1979–81, p. 386.

105   29. As pointed out at the beginning of Chapter 2, another peculiarity of the Essene calendar was the consecutive numbering of sabbaths through the year, apparently documented also in Horace's *Satires*.

105   30. CD, 1QpHab. Also Josephus, 'perform their rites by themselves'.

105   31. See, e.g., CD 3 (Vermes, p. 85) 'He unfolded before them His holy Sabbaths and his glorious feasts' and CD 2 (Vermes, p. 87) 'They shall keep the Sabbath day according to its exact interpretation, and the feasts and the Day of Fasting according to the finding of the members of the New Covenant in the Land of Damascus.'

105   32. See also our discussion of *nazeiraios, nazōraios* in Chapter 11.

105   33. However, Will & Orrieux, p. 203 characterise Essenism as 'a form of

Hellenistic Judaism', and M. Delcor in *Cambridge History of Judaism*, 2, pp. 416–20 points out that 'the book of Ben Sira, clearly influenced by Stoicism, commended itself especially to the... Essenes'. But Delcor adds that it may have been due to Ben Sira's mention of Zadokite priests.

106 34. 4Q 504, 1, Vermes, pp. 217–19.

106 35. *Quod omnis probus liber sit*, 81.

106 36. On synagogues, see Urman et al., 1995.

106 37. On proselytes and missionary work, see Goodman 1994. He recognises that Diaspora communities were more open to proselytes (Goodman 1987, p. 98), and that many converted, but doubts that the Jews were missionaries (1994, p. 61). Feldman 1993 thinks that conversion was 'considerable', though he finds it difficult to document missionary activities. He adduces Matt 23:15, where it is said that the Pharisees 'compass sea and land to make one proselyte'. Perhaps it is fair to say, with Goodman 1994, p. 175, that the Jewish mission was due to 'strife among Jews'. I think my reading of the early Christian texts supports the view that the Christians not only took over their missionary zeal from the Essenes, but that they built very much on an Essene foundation in the Diaspora. Goodenough 1986, in an article from 1933, cites Philo as evidence for the existence of Jewish proselytism in the Diaspora.

106 38. E.g. *Vita contemplativa* 29.

107 39. 1QS 9, Vermes, p. 75.

107 40. 1QS 9, Vermes, p. 75. 'Israel' obviously means Jews other than the Essenes themselves, who look upon themselves as the 'remnant', the only true Jews, those of the New Covenant. This usage was carried over into the New Testament, where 'the Jews' often corresponds to the Essene 'Israel'.

107 41. CD 4, Vermes, p. 85.

107 42. CD 6, Vermes, p. 87.

107 43. CD 6, Vermes, p. 87.

108 44. 1Q 22.2, Vermes, p. 265.

108 45. They were included, however, in Ethiopia and some other Eastern churches.

108 46. It must be admitted, though that, by modern scholarly standards, the eventual attributions of the canonical books of the Bible cannot be called very reliable either.

108 47. Dupont-Sommer 1959.

108 48. W. Grundmann quoting Jeremias in Murphy O'Connor et al. (ed) 1990, p. 86. See also Betz & Riesner 1993, p. 118, and references to medieval mentions in Siegel 1977–8, pp. 437–40 and, further, Wieluch 1957, pp. 418–19.

109 49. According to Bickerman 1988, p. 61, Hebrew *pesher* is derived from an Akkadian word meaning 'solving dreams'.

110 50. 4Q 175.

110 51. Stendel 1994, p. 169 dates the Habakkuk *pesharim* to the middle of the first century BC, other *pesharim* to 75–0.

111   52. Vermes, p. 30.

111   53. Vermes p. 31.

111   54. One reason for presenting what in reality are prophecies as interpreta-
      tions of older sayings by Old Testament prophets may be the
      widespread belief that prophecy had ceased with Daniel. This would
      explain the widespread use of Pseudepigraphy in the centuries after
      Daniel. Another way of accommodating new religious ideas is
      exemplified by the book of Isaiah, where modifications were simply
      added as parts of the original text. Modern scholars have distinguished
      at least three different writers behind the name of Isaiah.

113   55. Damascus may stand for Syria as a whole, including the northern part of
      Palestine, Galilee. This may explain the persistent connection of
      Christianity with Galilee.

113   56. See Lignée 1988, p. 333.

114   57. For instance, Nickelsburg 1981, p. 137: 'at least seven' of the hymns,
      and Kraft in Murphy O'Connor et al. (eds) 1990, p. 131. Charlesworth
      1983, p. 728 finds 'striking and frequent parallels between the Odes of
      Solomon and the Dead Sea Scrolls, especially the Hodayoth'.

114   58. Golb 1990, p. 113 holds that the Hodayot hymns are hardly sectarian,
      but generally Jewish. He develops this thesis further in Golb 1995, pp.
      362, 366.

117   59. He can hardly be wholly imaginary, for surely the organisation needed a
      leader.

120   60. The Test. Benjamin speaks about the 'Unique Prophet'. Laperrousaz
      1978 translates '*maître unique*' where Vermes (p. 90) has simply
      Teacher of Righteousness. See also Vermes, p. 186.

121   61. Interestingly, Siegel 1977–8, p. 438 mentions Karaite texts and some
      medieval references to the Teacher of Righteousness as a kind of
      Messiah figure. Wieluch 1957 refers to similar mentions by Isidorus and
      Philastrius.

Chapter 5 (pp. 125–138)

126   1. M. Delcor, in *Cambridge History of Judaism* 2, p. 424, points out that in
      the Greek version of Enoch, Biblical quotations are always in the
      Hebrew form of the text, indicating a Hebrew original. Charlesworth
      1985, p. 31 emphasises that Enoch is a composite text, the result of four
      centuries of writing, beginning in the third century BC.

126   2. M. Delcor, in *Cambridge History of Judaism* 2, pp. 431–4, says
      'everything points to the Essenes'.

126   3. See Ulrich et al. (eds) 1993.

126   4. Goldstein 1990, p. 166 says: 'the author of Jubilees 2:8–10 rewrote Gen
      1:16–18 to exclude the possibility of a lunar calendar'.

126   5. Flusser 1958, p. 240. Vermes 1981, pp. 1, 107 calls it 'an annual
      spiritual survey'. Harrelson in Neusner (ed) 1968, p. 93 says the
      Renewal of the Covenant is celebrated in the North of Palestine at the

Festival of Weeks, i. e. Pentecost. See also Jaubert 1953, p. 250, and my discussion of Jesus' resurrection in Barnabas, ch. 2.

127   6. See B. Isaac in Charlesworth 1983, 1, p. 5 ff. and Sjöberg 1946.

127   7. See Vanderkam in Charlesworth (ed) 1983, 1985, p. 99.

127   8. 2 Enoch (MS J) 28:5.

127   9. 2 Enoch (MS J) 32:2.

127   10. 2 Enoch (MS J) 33:1.

127   11. Teeple 1965, p. 229 finds it likely that Parables was pre-Christian. Segal 1977, p. 204 says 'perhaps post-Christian', Collins 1984, p. 143: first half first century AD; Klausner 1956: AD 68.

128   12. See Nickelsburg 1989, p. 226.

128   13. See Philonenko 1960.

128   14. G. C. Kee in Charlesworth 1983, 2, p. 777.

129   15. This may well be the source of Josephus' famous prophecy about Vespasian.

130   16. Bickerman 1988, p. 178.

130   17. For an overview, see Klausner 1956, *The Messianic Idea in Israel.* See also *Cambridge History of Judaism* 2, p. 350, and Charlesworth, 1992 b, pp. 19, 25.

131   18. 1 Enoch 25:3.

131   19. The number of 'heavens' is variable in our texts. In the oldest ones there is just one heaven, in later texts (including Paul) we have three. Under the influence of astronomy we then have seven, sometimes (as here) extended further.

132   20. A phrase used about Jesus in Hebrews.

132   21. The Greek word *Logos* is of course used in John's gospel about Jesus. See below.

132   22. 'Centre of the earth' in this text certainly refers to a flat earth. Perhaps simply Palestine is intended.

132   23. Segal 1987, p. 198. On the development of Jewish views on the Davidic dynasty, see Pomykala 1995.

132   24. On these, see Klausner 1956, p. 361, where he refers to 'later *midrashim*'.

132   25. The text is nowadays mostly dated to the first part of the first century AD. See Nickelsburg 1981, pp. 215–23, Charlesworth 1985, p. 91.

133   26. i.e. thou, Enoch. This is Charlesworth's translation. Charles, in his 1913 ed., does not identify the Son of Man with Enoch, leaving the possibility that Jesus is intended.

138   27. According to a count which accepts only the Law and the prophets before Daniel, but excludes Daniel and other texts classed as 'Scriptures' in the Jewish canon.

Chapter 6 *(pp. 139–147)*

139   1. See Kümmel 1964, p. 292 for an explanation of the terms.

141   2. See my discussion about the 'oral tradition' in Chapter 11.

141   3. See, for instance, Charlesworth 1992 a, p. 7, about the 'impossibility' of

explaining the appearance of the Gospels without assuming the existence of an oral tradition going back to Jesus.

142   4. See Kümmel 1964, pp. 292–313 for an overview.

143   5. Charlesworth 1985, p. 86 dates the James letter before 70.

145   6. See 4:7, 'the end of all things is at hand'.

145   7. The word used here is *phanerōthentos*, not the usual *parousia*.

147   8. The reference here may be Thomas, as in Jn 14:22. See Chapter 12, footnote 39.

Chapter 7 *(pp. 148–159)*

149   1. See Koester 1980–2, 2. pp. 261–71. Kümmel 1964, pp. 241–64 argues that Col is genuinely by Paul, whereas Eph is pseudonymous.

150   2. In fact, Paul says in 1 Cor 1:18: 'The preaching of the cross is to them that perish foolishness, but unto us which are saved it is the power of God.'

150   3. Charlesworth 1985, p. 66 finds that the writer's universe is 'cluttered with demons and angels'.

150   4. H. D. Betz 1966, p. 397 calls it 'the common view of late Hellenism'.

151   5. See Kümmel 1964, Koester 1980–2.

151   6. We also find it especially in the Book of Proverbs and in Ben Sira. See also Chapter 2, section on pre-existence.

152   7. See Eduard Lohse 1971.

152   8. See Chapter 2.

153   9. Best 1993, p. 12. See also Vielhauer 1975, pp. 205–6.

154   10. See Koester 1980–2.

154   11. See Koester 1980–2, Kümmel 1964.

156   12. On the significance of revelations, see Chapter 12.

Chapter 8 *(pp. 163–179)*

164   1. Bickerman 1988, p. 247 also speaks about 'mass conversion to Judaism' in the first century BC. But the evidence is thin.

167   2. Practically all Christian texts, including Paul, the six texts of Chapter 2, and the Gospels and Acts, contain several instances of 'the Way' (Greek *hodos*). See also Chapters 4 and 5.

173   3. Schoeps 1948, p. 48.

173   4. See Klijn 1992.

174   5. See Ulrich and Vanderkam 1994.

174   6. Koester 1990, p. 36 and, above all, Hoffman 1984.

175   7. Metzger 1989 holds that the Church fought the Gnostics by referring to the Synoptic Gospels. Harnack, cited in Rudolph 1979, p. 174 declares that Christians did not object to Gnosticism in the first century AD, at which time Christians and Gnostics stood quite near each other. Schnelle 1987 maintains that Jn was used (probably after emendations) as a way of neutralising docetic Gnosticism, which I think makes sense. Logan & Wedderburn 1983, p. 143 implicitly criticise this view. Hoffman 1984, against the prevalent views of modern theologians,

holds that Marcion propagated his 'radicalised' version of Paul before *c.* AD 100, and thus before the canonical Gospels, which may have been written as a reaction to Marcion. That evidently agrees well with my hypothesis. See also Chapters 10 and 12.

175   8. See Kraabel 1981, p. 117.

176   9. This view of Luke's aim is fairly uncontroversial. See, e.g., Lüdemann 1980:1, p. 41, Schmithals 1961, p. 237 and Schmithals 1963, p. 48, where he adds that we have no good explanation for Luke's decision to propagate the idea. I for my part find it quite natural: mainstream Judaism, after all, was officially recognised by the Roman authorities, and was a strong competitor of Christianity. The Church had much to gain, both from weakening the mainstream organisation, and from laying claim to its privileges.

178   10. Koester 1990.

178   11. See Chapter 4.

179   12. Koester 1980–2, II, p. 268, quoting an early manuscript of Ephesians. See also 1 Thess 1:1 'the church of the Thessalonians which is in God the Father *and* [my italics] in the Lord Jesus Christ'.

Chapter 9 (pp. 180–201)

182   1. For a well-documented discussion of these matters see Bart D. Ehrman 1993.

182   2. I have some experience in the field, documented in Ellegård 1962, *A Statistical Method for Determining Authorship*, and Ellegård 1962, *Who was Junius?* See also Morton & McLeman 1966.

183   3. For convenience, I here give references to various contemporary scholars' datings of New Testament texts (somewhat simplified: many writers avoid giving dates.)

Acts	Goodman 1994	certainly before 100
	Koester 1980–2: 2, p. 310	before 135
	Kraabel: Goodenough, p.122	early 60s
	Klein, quoted by Kümmel	115–30
	O'Neill 1961, p. 21	115–30
	Kümmel	80–100
	Johnson in Neusner 1975:II, p. 126	140 (answer to Marcion)
	Schmithals 1961, p. 243	120–30 (quot. Klein)
Hebrews	Attridge 1989, p. 9	60–100
	Bruce in *ANRW* 25, p. 3514	before 70
	Hofius in *ANRW* 25, p. 3591	60
	Bickerman 1988, p. 260	before 70
	Charlesworth 1993, p. 84	before 70
	Feld in *ANRW* 25, p. 3586	60
	Spicq in *RQ* 1972–5	before 70
Cath. Ep.	Bauckhan, p. 490	'authentic'
	Dibelius 1975, p. 45	80–130
	Koester 1980–2, p. 56	end 1st c, or after
	Kümmel 1964, p. 309	end 1st c.
	Lüdemann Paulus II, p. 192	early 2nd c.

	Schoeps 1949, p. 343	early 2nd c.
Jn	Stauffer in *ANRW* 25, p.5	90
	Kysar in *ANRW* 25, p. 2436	90–100
	Segal 1977, p. 216	end 1st c.
Lk	Stauffer in *ANRW* 25, p. 5	80
	Bruce in *ANRW* 25, p. 2576	late 60s
	Kümmel 1964, p. 94	70–90
Mk	Stauffer in *ANRW* 25, p. 5	60–65
	Bruce in *ANRW* 25, p. 2591	64–65
	Dunn in Charlesworth 1992, p. 260	before 70
	Kümmel 1964, p. 55	70
	Pokorny *ANRW* 25, p. 2021	60–70
Mt	Stauffer in *ANRW* 25 p. 5	68
	Stanton in *ANRW* 25, p. 1942	before 115
	Kümmel 1964, p. 70	80–100
	Köhler 1985, p. 95	before 115
	Stanton in *ANRW*, p. 1242	70–115
Rev	Buchanan 1993, p. 189	70
	Charlesworth (ed) 1983–5, p. 87	90
	Ford 1975	before the gospels (70)
	Collins in Hellholm (ed), p. 739	95
	Kümmel 1964, p. 341	81–96
	Lohse 1980	90

184   4. Lehman 1970, p. 13 calls this 'a basic assumption', *Grundvorausset-zung*. Schmithals 1962, p. 154 argues against the existence of the oral tradition, in the same manner as I do above: if the early communities were not interested in Jesus' life, as the texts indicate, how could they preserve an oral tradition about it?

184   5. See Downing 1992, and also Koester 1980–2, II, p. 47, 63.

185   6. Fishbane 1988, p. 78.

185   7. Carsten Thiede 1992. Thiede 1996, in a popular book written together with a journalist, maintains his views against opponents, without, in my view, any substantial arguments.

185   8. See Aland 1967. Stanton 1996 is also very critical of Thiede's argument.

185   9. Convincingly demonstrated by Golb 1995.

187   10. Koester 1990, pp. 37, 43.

188   11. The source of this statement may be the Muratori fragment, whose authority is doubtful, to say the least. See Chapter 2.

188   12. See Koester 1990, p. 224.

188   13. Kloppenborg 1989, p. 49 says 'the thesis of Gerhardsson and Riesenfeld of a rabbinic-type transmission of tradition in early Christianity has been rejected decisively', and refers to scholars like W. Davies, H. Teeple, G. Widengren and J. Neusner. The last emphasises that we have little evidence of the rabbis before the end of the second century AD, and, moreover, that the traditions within rabbinic Judaism are, like most oral traditions, changed according to the views of the tradent. Brown 1984, p. 43 is also critical.

189	14. Koester 1990, p. 159–71 for a detailed discussion.
189	15. Koester 1990, p. 85.
190	16. Koester 1990, p. 204, 286.
190	17. He may also, as we said above, have got the information from his friend Pliny the Younger, who was Governor of Bithynia around 110.
190	18. See Chapter 11.
191	19. See Mack, in his Introduction.
191	20. Koester 1990, p. 160, with reference to Kloppenborg 1989.
191	21. See Koester 1990, p. 84, and my discussion of Gnosticism.
192	22. Koester 1990, p. 218, quoting Philipp Vielhauer, *Geschichte . . .* , p. 646. Koester notes that the idea was first suggested by Martin Dibelius.
192	23. Bultmann also thought so. See R. Collins 1992, p. 63.
193	24. Koester 1980–2, II, p. 63.
193	25. Koester 1990, p. 303 uses this word himself.
193	26. See Koester 1990, p. 303 on the popularity of such legends.
193	27. The 'Hermetic' literature, collected in medieval times in the collection Corpus Hermeticum, is named for the Greek god Hermes, held to be the equivalent of the Egyptian god Thoth. In the Greek–Alexandrian mythology he is referred to as Hermes Trismegistos, 'Thrice-greatest Hermes', to underline his exceptional powers. This complex of ideas combines mysticism, astrology, alchemy, religion of a Gnostic type and philosophy.
194	28. See Koester 1990, p. 263, and also Udo Schnelle 1987. The anti-docetic tendency of Jn is discussed in Chapters 8 and 12.
195	29. See also Kloppenborg 1989, pp. 231, 241.
197	30. Including myself in *Lychnos* 1990.
199	31. On Luke's knowledge, or lack of knowledge, of Paul, see Chapter 12.
199	32. Pliny had inquired about Christians in Bithynia, according to a letter he wrote to Trajan. That Pliny did not have his information from 'official' Roman archives is clear from the fact that he calls Pilate *procurator*, not the correct *praefectus*.
199	33. See Kloppenborg 1989, pp. 263, 294.

Chapter 10 (pp. 202–214)

203	1. Metzger 1989, p. 48 finds that Ignatius stands closer to Matthew than to the other Gospels.
205	2. We might perhaps include Trall 11:2: 'Those are not the plantation of the Father.' Jn 15:1 (Jesus:) 'I am the true vine, and my Father is the husbandman.'
206	3. On the meaning development of *gospel*, see Koester 1990.
206	4. See Chapter 3.
206	5. As will be seen in Chapter 11, there is much confusion in the Gospels about the Marys mentioned there. In the Gnostic writings, especially, it is Mary Magdalene that plays the most prominent part.
206	6. Toynbee 1969, p. 236, in editorial text, with picture of Isis and Horus

(Harpocrates): 'The parallel with the Madonna and Child of Christian iconography is too obvious to need comment.'

207　　7. E.g. P. Th. Camelot 1951.

207　　8. 1 Cor 2:8, on Jesus' death: 'which none of the princes [*oudeis tōn archontōn*] of this world knew, for had they known it, they would not have crucified the Lord of Glory'.

208　　9. See above, quotations from Trall 9–10 and Smyrn 3.

209　　10. It is in Smyrn 8.2 that the words *katholikē ekklēsia* occur for the first time.

209　　11. See Bauer 1934, p. 227: 'several Gnostics, like Valentinus, Marcion, Basilides valued Paul highly'.

209　　12. See Udo Schnelle 1987.

210　　13. On the possibility that the story of the Last Supper was influenced by early Christian (or indeed Essene) liturgy, see p. 29.

212　　14. If Hoffman 1984 is right, Marcion may have propagated docetic views as early as the end of the first century. Thus it is possible that Ignatius may have had Marcion in mind when he attacked docetism.

212　　15. On these, see Angus 1925, p. 268. Wendland 1972, p. 169 talks about the importance of finding a place for Gnosticism within the Church: *Verkirchlichung der Gnosis*. Deutsch 1995, p. 19, referring to Scholem, speaks about Gnosticism as 'the cultivation of revelatory, esoteric and soteric (*sic*) knowledge by a social élite'. According to Wilken 1984, p. 151, Porphyry, the biographer of Plotinus, argued that third-century Christians had abandoned the cult of the transcendent Jewish God in favour of the cult of Jesus. Ignatius' achievement was to accommodate both.

212　　16. At least, that is the impression his letters make. We might also point to his 'ready acceptance of the social pyramid', which Downing 1992, p. 94 attributes to him.

212　　17. Bell 1953, p. 103 thinks it was the historical, human Jesus which gave Christianity the advantage over other syncretistic religions of Antiquity.

213　　18. In this connection we should note Ign Eph 17: 'The Lord received oil on his head, in order to breathe onto the Church an odour of incorruptibility [*aphtharsian*].' Some commentators refer to the well-known episode in the Gospels about the woman who poured oil on Jesus' head (Mt 26:7, Mk 14:3, Lk 7:37 and Jn 11:2, where the woman is identified as Mary from Magdala). But the significance of anointing an important person with oil is mentioned quite often in the Old Testament, so there is no ground for assuming dependence on the Gospels (see, e.g., Lev 8:12, 14:18, 21:10, Sam 10:1, Ps 23:5). Again, therefore, the dependence may in fact be the other way round.

214　　19. In later times, the word *paroikia* came to be used generally about Christian communities. (The English *parish* is derived from it.) It is ordinarily explained that the Christians saw themselves as just 'sojourners' in this world, whereas their real home was in Heaven. It is not likely that such a meaning had yet developed in the first few centuries AD.

Chapter 11 *(pp. 215–241)*

215   1. See, e.g., Kümmel 1985, p. 31 (*auffällig*), Kuhn 1970, p. 299.

218   2. Cf Peter's confession that he is a 'sinner' in Lk 5:8.

218   3. See Chapter 1, section on 1 Clement.

220   4. See, e.g., Kümmel 1964, p. 54, Koester 1980–2:2, p. 164, Goodman 1957, p. 22.

221   5. On the Cynics and Christianity, see Downing 1992.

222   6. See Koester 1980–2:2, p. 20.

222   7. Schmithals 1961, p. 62 thinks Matthew and Mark have their 12 apostles from Luke's Acts.

223   8. Cullmann in Stendahl 1957 suggests that 'the twelve' might be specifically the Jerusalem apostles. One possibility is that the enigmatic expression 'the brethren of the Lord' (1 Cor 9:5) might indicate specifically members of the Jerusalem community. See below, on James, the 'brother of the Lord'. It is of interest to note that 1 Cor 9:5, 'Have we not power to lead about a sister, a wife, as well as other apostles, and as the brethren of the Lord, and Cephas' raises problems similar to those raised by 'the twelve', since the syntax seems to exclude both Cephas and the brethren of the Lord from the apostles.

        It is interesting to note that in Mt and Mk, *apostle* is used in the Lucan sense only in the lists (Mt 10:2), which I suggested were taken over from Acts in a late revision. Luke, who uses *apostle* in a few other places as well has it in the list (Lk 6:13), where the corresponding Markan passage (3:14) reads 'And he ordained twelve, that they should be with him, and that he might send them forth to preach.' Then follows the full list of names, the same as in Acts. This supports my conclusion that the lists in the Synoptics were taken over from Acts.

224   9. The lists are found in Mk 1:14–19, Mt 10:2–4, Lk 6:13–16, Acts 1:13. The lists do not altogether agree with each other. Acts points out that Judas Iscariot is left out, for obvious reasons. In the others, there are differences in the order. And, whereas Acts and Lk include 'Judas the brother of James', Mk has Thaddaeus, and Mt has 'Lebbaeus, whose surname was Thaddaeus'. Note that we are not told which 'James' Judas is the brother of.

225   10. The whole of chapter 21 seems to be a late addition.

226   11. On Jn as an attempt to accommodate Gnostic ideas within canonical Christianity, see my discussion in Chapters 8 and 12, and Schnelle 1987.

228   12. Indeed, they may have preserved memories of a Qumran hymn (1QH5 Vermes, p. 178): 'Thou hast caused me to dwell with the many fishers/ who spread a net upon the face of the waters,' possibly written by the Teacher of Righteousness.

229   13. It should be noted that Clemens Alexandrinus took Peter and Cephas to be different persons. See Bauer 1934, p. 119. Other witnesses for the two being distinct: Koester 1980–2:2, p.22, Riddle 1940, p. 175. If Peter and Cephas are different persons, it does not affect my chief argument,

which is that the protagonists in Acts, and accordingly also in the Gospels, are based on the protagonists in the Jerusalem church, as portrayed in Paul.

229 14. Hoffman's (1984) findings about the struggle of the mainstream Christian church to destroy Marcion, who was a strong champion of Paul, may be adduced in support of this view.

230 15. The Greek text really says *Ioudas Iacōbou*, 'Judas, son of Jacob'. The English translation 'brother' may be an attempt to bring this mention into harmony with the mentions of Judas and James as Jesus' brethren, in Mk 6:3 and Mt 13:55. See below in the section about Jesus' brethren.

231 16. See the section on Nazareth, below.

237 17. The Greek text has *Ioudas Iakōbou*, normally meaning 'the son of James', The English translator has evidently tried to 'improve' the text. See above, note 15.

238 18. 'The law' must here be read as the Torah, the books in the Old Testament ascribed to Moses. In fact, there is no mention of Nazareth anywhere in the Old Testament as we now have it.

239 19. Klaus Berger 1996 also argues for taking *nazōraios* as referring to *nazirite*, though he does not enter into a discussion of the connection with Nazareth.

239 20. See Schoeps 1949, p. 10.

240 21. Franzmann 1996, p. 35 says that the Gospel of Philip contains reflexions on the three names of Jesus: Jesus, the Nazarene (Nazorean) and Christ.

Chapter 12 (pp. 242–255)

242 1. See e.g. Kümmel 1963, Koester 1980.

242 2. See Koester 1980–2, 1990.

243 3. News about earlier papyrus fragments are continually turning up in the press, but are in general turned down by competent scholars. On Thiede's widely published arguments for an early fragment of Mark, see Chapter 9.

243 4. On this, see Chapter 9.

244 5. This is argued by Schnelle 1987.

244 6. See Chapter 3. The Gnostic affinities of the Wisdom writings is emphasised in Robinson & Koester 1971, p. 71.

244 7. See also Mack 1991.

245 8. Etymologically, the word *apocalypse* means simply 'revelation'. In present-day English, *apocalyptic* has come to mean 'having to do with the catastrophic end of the world', a meaning due of course to the name that is often given to the Revelation of John: the *Apocalypse*. In the context of its time of origin, it is a revelation of the End-time.

245 9. I discuss the question of the name Jesus in Chapter 4.

246 10. See Chapter 2.

246 11. Kraabel 1990, p. 29 thinks John's Jesus was the same as Paul's.

246 12. The reference to the third day may be a re-interpretation of Ps 16:10, on a corpse starting to rot after three days.

247   13. In the Nag Hammadi text the Apocryphon of James, James and Peter do occur as the first witnesses of the risen Jesus.

247   14. See also my discussion in Chapter 1.

248   15. I cannot refrain here from referring to the eminently sensible views of the father of American psychology, William James, whose *Varieties of Religious Experience* (1902) is still well worth reading.

248   16. Charlesworth 1983–5, p. xxxi.

249   17. On this see Koester 1990, p. 90. See also Koester 1990, p. 120, on Jesus as a 'hidden mystery'.

249   18. In Hennecke 1963, pp. 158–87.

249   19. In these Gnostic texts, James is never called the 'brother of Jesus'. This obviously supports my argument about these matters in Chapter 11.

249   20. We note that nothing is said in this text about James being the brother of Jesus. See Chapter 11.

249   21. I quote from Hennecke 1963.

249   22. Mk 8:27–9, Mt 16:13–16, Lk 9:18–20.

249   23. Hennecke 1963, p. 122.

250   24. On the importance of unconscious cognitive processes in modern cognitive science, see Dennett 1991 and Crick 1994.

250   25. Koester 1990, p. 61 remarks on Paul's 'recourse to the authority of certain persons' for certain sayings. This practice may well have to do with the sayings being based on a revelation, which is often an individual experience. Many examples are given below.

250   26. Mary (Magdalene) is a prominent 'disciple' in many Gnostic texts.

250   27. Nag Hammadi Library (NHL) 1977, pp. 29–36.

250   28. As we have noted repeatedly, there is no mention of Jesus' *return*. Descent here implicates the Gnostic view that Jesus was a Spirit from Heaven.

250   29. The somewhat problematic syntax is found in NHL p. 36.

250   30. The class of words meaning full is a characteristic feature of Gnostic language.

250   31. As Koester 1990, p. 200 indicates.

251   32. Koester, in Robinson & Koester 1971, p. 167, does not think the Gospel of Thomas is meant as a post-ascension revelatory discourse – Jesus appearing to the twelve apostles is also a feature of the *Epistula Apostolorum*. See Koester 1990, p. 47–8. Here all the apostles are named: remarkably, both Peter and Cephas occur.

251   33. On this see Koester 1990, p. 90.

251   34. Koester 1990, pp. 173–267.

251   35. See particularly Schnelle 1987. But the role of Ignatius in this matter must be taken into account.

252   36. See Chapter 7, with reference to Hoffmann 1984.

253   37. J. M. Robinson, in his Introduction to Robinson & Koester 1971, expresses somewhat similar views.

254   38. Robinson, in Robinson & Koester 1971, dates Jn to AD 90, but provides little concrete evidence. It is in any case certain that the Gospel was revised later in the second century.

254   39. This may well indicate Thomas: one MS in fact reads Judas Thomas, and another simply Thomas. See Koester in Robinson & Koester 1971, p. 128.

255   40. Other such 'I am' pronouncements are found in 6:35, 10:7, 11:25.

Index

The letter i in front of page number indicates 'important', ii 'very important'. Examples: 'Alexandria, i61' means 'see p. 61, important reference', and 'Egypt, i81n6' means 'see note 6, p. 81, important'. References to concepts in chapter headings and section headings are consistently marked ii or i.

In the notes section at the end of the book, pp. 291–312, the page on which the note is found in the text is indicated in front of the note number.

References are often to concepts (meanings) rather than to words. Complete coverage is attempted only for names of authors referred to.

Individual books have to be looked up in the Notes or in the Bibliography, pp. 270–290.